D1244626

# Italian Communism
# in Transition

# Italian Communism in Transition

*The Rise and Fall of
the Historic Compromise in Turin,
1975–1980*

Stephen Hellman

*New York   Oxford*
OXFORD UNIVERSITY PRESS
*1988*

Oxford University Press

Oxford   New York   Toronto
Delhi   Bombay   Calcutta   Madras   Karachi
Petaling Jaya   Singapore   Hong Kong   Tokyo
Nairobi   Dar es Salaam   Cape Town
Melbourne   Auckland
and associated companies in
Berlin   Ibadan

Copyright © 1988 by Oxford University Press, Inc.

Published by Oxford University Press, Inc.,
200 Madison Avenue, New York, New York 10016

Oxford is a registered trademark of Oxford University Press

Library of Congress Cataloging-in-Publication Data
Hellman, Stephen.
Italian Communism in transition: the rise and fall of the
historic compromise in Turin, 1975–1980 / by Stephen Hellman.
p.     cm.
Bibliography: p. Includes index.
ISBN 0-19-505335-4
1. Communism—Italy—Turin. 2. Turin (Italy)—Politics and
government. 3. Partito comunista italiano. Turinese Federation.
I. Title.
HX295.T87H44 1988
335.43'0945'12—dc19                               87–31287   CIP

2 4 6 8 9 7 5 3 1

Printed in the United States of America
on acid-free paper

*To my mother, Anne Hellman,*
*and in memory of*
*my father, Louis Hellman*

# Preface

Most studies based on fieldwork owe something to luck, and this is no exception. A series of coincidences put me in Turin, provided me with an initial subject, and then helped my final project take shape. In 1973, I had spent a few months in Turin while researching the Italian Communist Party (PCI) in two neighboring Piedmontese provinces. My work often brought me to the party's regional headquarters for Piedmont, which took up one floor of a building otherwise filled with the offices of the Turinese Federation of the PCI. There was, then, no crystal ball at work for me: I originally gathered a considerable amount of material on the party organization in Turin simply because I happened to be there.

The summer of 1973, even in retrospect, was tense but rather dull. It was a time of political stalemate and apparent stagnation. There were hints that the PCI's line was changing, but nothing suggested the impending, momentous results of the referendum on divorce. If I jumped at the chance to do some additional research, it was strictly because this, after all, was *Turin*, a place that could not fail to stir a student and supporter of the Italian workers' movement. The window of my office at the Einaudi Foundation looked out on a building in which Antonio Gramsci had once lived. The route between my apartment and office still contained many factories that had been occupied by the workers in 1920. And the dust of the "hot autumn"—the militant cycle of struggles between 1968 and 1972 in which Turin, true to form, had played a prominent role— had barely settled.

Anyone who has tried to carry out field research at this level in Italy knows that appointments often cannot be kept, providing far more unplanned free time than even the most relaxed researcher could want. Happily for me, if things did not go well on the floor where regional headquarters was located, I could stroll downstairs and see who was available. I thus ended up spending a good deal of time talking with Turinese functionaries and militants, and I collected whatever data and documents they were willing to provide. I got to know some younger functionaries quite well, because I was able to take a relaxed attitude toward them and their federation. Everything I learned about Turin was an unscheduled bonus.

Then, in 1975, the PCI swept the local elections and took over the government of almost every major city in the country, including Turin. On the eve of the heyday of "Eurocommunism," Turin temporarily became, in the phrasing of one news magazine, "the largest city with a Communist government between Prague and Havana." Because I knew how weak the PCI's organization had been prior to this success, and because I also knew what a purely oppositional party the Turinese Communists had been until 1975, I decided to study the transition between opposition and government in the Piedmontese capital. The news that some of my best contacts in the party—and some of my closest friends in Turin—were now running the PCI federation and occupying high offices in the city or province made me especially confident that the study was feasible. When I mooted the possibility during a short field trip in 1976, my contacts seemed pleased, and even flattered, at my interest.

I was especially intrigued by the thought of former organizational cadres, many of them products of one of the most volatile and militant labor movements in Italy, having to adjust to the awesome responsibilities of public office in a large urban industrial center. The local party's plight was complicated by a national strategy that was the very soul of moderation: the PCI was bidding for admission to the government and doing everything possible to reassure people that it was highly responsible. Until 1975, the PCI was in power *only* in "red" areas, which excluded major metropolitan centers and were favored by extremely powerful left subcultures and organizational networks. For the first time, at least in Italy, it appeared possible to clarify how the demands of government affect a classical workers' party—not from historical documents and brilliant speculation, but as the events actually unfolded. Stretching out before me was a host of little-explored but highly significant research questions. And my own earlier work on party organization provided me with a unique vantage point for assessing this transition.

Or so I thought. From the time I arrived in Turin in 1977, the PCI's fortunes began to turn—a coincidence my Communist friends often, and sarcastically, recalled. (During the 1979 elections, they jokingly offered to subsidize my vacation—as long as I promised to travel outside Italy and stay away until the votes were counted.) As the party's difficulties multiplied, it became obvious to me that the PCI was undergoing a genuine crisis. I found my original research plan impossible to carry out because of the increasing paralysis of the party both as a local political force and as a mass organization. By 1977–78, to study any aspect of the PCI was to study the party's strategic and political crisis.

At the same time, I had obtained exceptional access to the inner workings of the organization. A decade earlier, when I began to study the PCI, it would have been unthinkable for an outsider to attend a meeting of the party apparatus, and hence it did not occur to me to ask. (I think I might have been more brazen had I had no friends at all in the upper ranks of the party. I did not want my own potential blunders to reflect back on people who had nothing to do with them.) But one day, when some functionaries were discussing one of the party's most serious problems and I expressed interest in the topic, they noted that the next meeting of the apparatus was going to address that very subject, and I should therefore attend. After that, I went to every meeting of the apparatus that I could, though I consciously absented myself when matters such as budget or personal salaries were on the agenda (which was always posted next to the elevator).

It was this access, in fact, that convinced me that I had to focus my research primarily on the crisis and its impact on the PCI as a mass party. For one thing, the apparatus's own confusion and inability to act left no doubt in my mind about how serious the crisis was. For another, I was increasingly struck by the inadequacies of the entire range of responses the Turinese PCI had at its disposal, and I was equally struck by the way the party leadership nevertheless kept falling back on these responses, for they had no others. It occurred to me more than once that I might be witnessing firsthand the radical decline, if not the eclipse, of the mass party as an effective instrument of the workers' movement. And if that was the case, I would have not only an interesting but also a historically important story to tell.

Thus, although I set out to analyze one sort of transition in the PCI, I ended up witnessing a rather less triumphant and much different transition—one that, in fact, is not yet complete. It is striking that the PCI's basic dilemma has remained so similar to what it was more than seven years ago. This is perhaps the most convincing testimony to just how critical a juncture the late 1970s were in the history of Italian communism. It also indicates the depth of the transitional crisis in which the party is caught up.

This book has been many years in the making, and I owe many people a debt I can never repay for the help they provided at various stages of my research and writing. Above all, I wish to thank the leaders, militants, and secretarial staff of the Turinese Federation of the PCI for contributing so generously of their time and for being so patient with me.

Many friends and colleagues have been helpful in their comments on parts of my work, provocative and stimulating in discussions, or both. They include Giuseppe Berta, Miriam Golden, Jane Jenson, Richard Locke, Leo Panitch, Gianfranco Pasquino, Ted Perlmutter, Gianfranco Poggi, George Ross, and Donald Wallace. I am especially grateful to Donald Blackmer, Joel Krieger, and Raymond Seidelman, who read complete drafts of whatever I had produced at the time, provided me with very helpful suggestions, and raised my spirits more than they know.

In Italy, my research trips were inevitably enriched by conversations with and encouragement from Aris Accornero, Marzio Barbagli, Giuseppe Berta, Renato Mannheimer and Chiara Sebastiani. Gianfranco Pasquino deserves special mention for his generosity and helpfulness.

As he has always done, Sidney Tarrow read and commented on everything I gave him—and chastised me for not producing more, and more rapidly. As I have always done, I continued at my own pace but benefited enormously from his criticism while enjoying his friendship.

The research reported here was launched with the help of a sabbatical research grant from the Social Sciences and Humanities Research Council of Canada. I also received vital support from York University, in the form of a travel grant, and especially from a Faculty of Arts Fellowship that permitted me to use the academic year 1983–84 free from teaching and administrative responsibilities.

My visits to Turin would have been far less productive, and infinitely less enjoyable, without the encouragement and support of Professor Mario Einaudi and the Fondazione Luigi Einaudi in Turin. On all my field trips, the Fondazione graciously provided me with a base, including an all-important telephone and the unheard-of luxury of knowing that phone messages would be accurately passed on to me. Mrs. E. Giordano and the entire staff of the Fondazione were inevitably courteous, friendly, and helpful.

Much of the first draft of this book was written during a six-month stay at the Institute for Advanced Study of the Hebrew University of Jerusalem. I would like to thank the director of the Institute, Dr. Aryeh Dvoretsky, as well as the efficient and helpful staff. I am most grateful to Shlomo Avineri for inviting me to participate in the seminar he cochaired at the Institute in 1980–81. This is only one of the many occasions when his friendship and support have been extremely helpful to me over the past two decades, and I am pleased to acknowledge my debt to him.

The Social Studies Faculty Centre at Oxford University was kind enough to furnish me with an office and access to its word processor during a one-term visit. I owe special thanks to Zbigniew Pelczynski of Pembroke College and the Centre, who was responsible for my presence there and whose friendship and generosity made our stay in Oxford so enjoyable.

A separate and special mention goes to the following people, first encountered in Turin, in deep appreciation of their encouragement, hospitality, and simple friendship over many years: Giuseppe Berta, Marisa Ceppi, Oscar Chiantore, Anna Chiorino, Bice Fubini, Edoardo Garrone, Renzo Gianotti, Emi Lanfranconi, Tonia Maione, and Giovanni Salvestrini.

Finally, I wish to thank my wife, Judith Adler Hellman, for the kind of support I hope I remain wise enough never to take for granted. Teaching in the same department, doing research in the same country, and completing books at the same time suggest an overdetermined relationship and possible disaster. That we have survived all this, and much else, in good humor I attribute almost entirely to her strength, kindness, and good sense. Her intelligence and editorial judgment have also been of immeasurable value in this book, as in all my other work.

*Toronto*                                                                                  S.H.
*October 1987*

# Contents

# Italian Communism
## in Transition

# Introduction: Communist Parties in the Crisis of Advanced Capitalism

## Communist Parties and Parties of the Left

With a few notable exceptions, recent developments in the advanced capitalist world have not been kind to parties of the left, whether in power or not. Most of the more important historic leftist parties have had an extremely difficult time adjusting to the changed political and socioeconomic dynamic of the Western democratic regimes since the 1970s. Among those that have benefited from what some have called "postcapitalist developments," moreover, there has been a tendency to jettison many of the policies and/or organizational qualities that marked them as distinctively leftist in the first place. The apparent exhaustion of their programs and activities has been particularly notable where, as across Latin and Mediterranean Europe, they have come to power within the last decade.

Although not all observers would paint so bleak a portrait,[1] the consensus appears to be that the left, on balance, has lost strength or identity (and often both). And whatever one says about the left in general, the fate of the stronger communist parties has been even more unequivocally negative. A scant decade ago, these parties in Latin Europe spearheaded the "Eurocommunist" phenomenon and seemed on the verge of a breakthrough. Yet by the end of the 1970s, they slipped into a stagnation and decline which still show few signs of a turnaround. After their brief moments of glory, they are politically isolated and mired in crises that, on the whole, appear far more severe than those faced by most socialist and social-democratic formations.

If the Communists' crisis is more serious, this is undoubtedly the result of a variety of historical considerations that have clearly affected their flexibility and adaptability and made them especially vulnerable to some of the challenges of the current situation. They have been much less conditioned by the compromises of government than have Socialists of varying persuasions. Most important of all, of course, is the fact that communist parties were consciously constructed to avoid the ideological and organizational weaknesses of the traditional socialist parties. This did indeed insulate them against some of the historic weaknesses of the socialist movement. But it also powerfully conditioned the way they would act in, and interact with, the complex societies and institutions of advanced capitalist democracy. These factors would not be so deeply imprinted in the collective history and consciousness of communist parties were it not for the further, and decisive, fact that they usually spent no less than a quarter-century under the even more rigorous and oppressive constraints of Stalinism, which reinforced dogmatic and sectarian behavior and belief patterns.

Each communist party has experienced these elements differently, but all have been marked by them. It would be surprising if their own identities—and the image they project to significant proportions of the public—did not reflect these often turbulent, and relatively recent, histories. This is not to argue that communist parties are so unique that they can only be understood by means of exceptional criteria. Rather, it is to point out that in addition to facing the problems that other parties on the left have had to face in recent years, their plight has been made more complicated because of their specific legacy.

This might seem to be a strange way to introduce a study of the Italian Communist Party (PCI), which is easily the most powerful and successful of the Western communist parties. To be sure, its fortunes have waned notably since the mid-1970s, when it ruled most of Italy's most important cities and appeared to have a chance to become the largest political party in the country. Still, compared to the fate of the other major parties that shared the Eurocommunist label, the PCI has much more to celebrate than to lament.

The Spanish Communist Party (PCE), in spite of being the most audacious and unorthodox of the lot, has been reduced to a badly divided rump with roughly 5 percent of the vote and significant strength in only two areas of the country. The French Communist Party (PCF), after a brief period in government in a totally subaltern position, appears to be close to a similar, if not quite as disastrous, reduction in strength and importance. The PCF's most recent electoral forays have given it a bare 10 percent of the vote, after nearly two decades marked by an apparently unshakable claim to a fifth of the electorate.

The Italians, in contrast, still claim more than a quarter of the vote since touching their historic high of 34.4 percent in 1976.[2] Party membership is roughly 1.5 million, which may be considerably less than the high point in recent years (1.8 million, also in 1976), but, as with the vote, this is a level no other communist party in the West even approaches. Like their counterparts, Italian Communists have faced isolation and stagnation since the end of the 1970s. Unlike them, they do so from a position of relative strength on the left in their own country. Comparatively, the first question that comes to mind is to explain not the PCI's difficulties but its relative success.

One of the most common responses to this question has been the assertion that the PCI is no longer really a communist party at all, in any traditional understanding of that term. Such arguments used to be heard only from those to the left of the PCI who wanted to expose the party's policies as "reformist," thereby denying it serious Marxist credentials.[3] (Conversely, most right-wing critics have insisted—ignoring mountains of evidence—that the PCI's evolution has been grossly exaggerated or else largely cosmetic.)[4] Observers from a variety of perspectives have increasingly noted that the PCI resembles some of the more resourceful, innovative, and successful *socialist* parties of northern and western Europe. Some eschew historical labels altogether and speak of "'new types' of Left parties."[5]

There is much that is suggestive in this observation, particularly for the student of Italian politics who knows how the PCI has grown since World War II, displacing the Socialists as the main party of the left and appealing in the 1970s to many of the younger, white-collar, and secularized strata that the more successful socialist parties have attracted in their countries. We should not, however, accept this interpretation too hastily. To do so could lead us to ignore the extent to which so many of the PCI's most critical characteristics remain distinctively communist. It is certainly the case that this is no longer a "traditional" communist party, but without the proper context, neither its relative success nor many of its most intractable problems are fully comprehensible.

Take, for example, a major concern of this study, party organization. Compared to other parties of the left, organization continues to play a much more central role in all communist parties, including the PCI. This centrality is far more deeply and extensively rooted in Communists' collective identities. At the same time, the political marginalization of Communists has made them heavily reliant on their own independent organizational resources in order to survive and operate successfully in the surrounding society. The strong socialist parties' own earlier histories include similar phases of dependency. But they have generally evolved, especially since World War II, in contexts where they enjoy privileged relations with unified and powerful unions, and where they have had access to—and frequently were able to shape, thanks to long periods in government—postwar state and social structures. Under these circumstances, quite logically, strictly internal organizational considerations have been displaced.

For the strong communist parties, in contrast, none of these conditions holds. They have not been parties of government, and the labor movements in their respective countries are historically divided and weak in terms of access to social services and channels of resources.[6] Denied these more institutional sources of sustenance, communist parties have had to rely heavily on their own structures to provide everything from funding to communications to mobilization to various means of satisfying their rank and file. It is therefore not at all surprising that this machinery would undergo immense stress when the conditions under which it must operate are dramatically altered, for example, when the party strategy changes from one of opposition to one that aspires to (or actually does) govern, or when society undergoes profound changes that call original organizational schemes into question.

These considerations bring forward another example of the characteristically "communist" problems that vexed the PCI in the 1970s. All parties may want to govern, but few have to go to extraordinary lengths to prove they are worthy of governing in Western democracies. For the PCI, this became the dominant question of the decade. It dictated most of the party's doctrinal revisions, the evolution of its strategy, its reading of events, and, of course, its political behavior. The top leadership of the party enunciated and was profoundly committed to a strategy of "historic compromise." This called for the collaboration of *all* major parties in order to ensure the broadest possible unity around Italy's democratic institutions. There were many reasons for the strategy to take this broad and moderate form, as we will see in the next chapter and subsequently. But the major motive was to demonstrate the PCI's democratic legitimacy. It is surely not a coincidence that only Communists (the PCE made a similar proposal) came up with such strategic responses to the crises of the 1970s.

## Transitional Crises and Western Communism

Why, then, did the PCI fare so much better in the 1970s than its fraternal parties across the Alps and Pyrenees? The concept of "transitional crisis" can help us understand the longer-term, as well as the more recent, experiences of Western communist parties. The framework that follows is primarily derived from the PCI's experience and should thus be viewed as quite tentative, subject to all the caveats that generalizing in this fashion requires. Still, if the PCI is the most successful example of a type of party, there could be some benefit in treating it, cautiously, as a paradigmatic case.

In the broadest sense, a transitional crisis is a watershed which challenges at least several, and perhaps all, of the major dimensions of party activity: doctrinal, strategic, organizational, and behavioral. A crisis occurs because the limits of the status quo have been reached. New conditions are such as to *require* adjustments; old outlooks, codes, and actions turn out to be inadequate to the tasks the party sets for itself. Many things which enabled it to operate in the past not only do not help but may even hinder its identity and operations in the present. A compelling working hypothesis would be that such crises tend to arise at the same time across national boundaries, but this by no means need always be the case.

While a framework of this sort would represent a hopelessly confining straitjacket— or imply an overly deterministic sense of party development—if it were suggested for *all* parties of the left, it is useful for communist parties because so many of their decisive historic moments (beginning with their origins) were responses to external stimuli. What I propose to do here, however, is not to provide a list of all possible historical watersheds for the communist parties of western Europe since their beginnings but to restrict myself to the postwar period. Readers familiar with the history of the communist movement of modern Europe know that all three of the parties mentioned underwent crucial formative experiences in the interwar period,[7] and these events would have to be—and, indeed, in the case of the PCI will be—mentioned in any extended discussion of the party's history and evolution.

Western—especially Latin—European communism since World War II has had to confront three similar transitional crises. (The individual parties have had to face a number of their own, more specific, crises as well, but that need only eventually concern us in the Italian case.) All of these, by their natures, are multidimensional processes that the parties face in a given conjuncture. But how a party responds—or fails to respond— will have a profound effect on its later development and evolution.

First, in all countries that were under Nazi occupation during the war, or under right-wing dictatorships up to or beyond the postwar period, these parties had to emerge from clandestinity, where they usually survived as small sects. The circumstances of this surfacing varied enormously, but the need to adapt (or readapt) to conditions of mass democratic politics always involved extensive disruptions.

Second, all communist parties, including those that were still underground at the time, underwent a profound trauma in 1956 with Khrushchev's first revelations of the horrors of Stalinism. Subsequently, all these parties undertook at least a limited degree of "de-Stalinization." This sweeping concept embraces practically every aspect of party life and behavior and can serve as shorthand here for the democratization of the party organization, including the replacement of the most sectarian leaders and cadres; the development of more autonomous national strategies; elimination of the most sectarian aspects of party doctrine; a more than tactical acceptance of representative democratic institutions; and the demonstration of more critical independence from the USSR. *How much* de-Stalinization took place, and the period over which the most intensive part of the process stretched, also varied greatly. But in all cases, leaders and members were badly disoriented, and the parties suffered considerable losses of membership and public support.

Third, in the middle to late 1970s, several communist parties, including the PCI, PCE, and PCF, appeared to be experiencing "Eurocommunization." This is a problematic and often imprecise concept. Its notoriety was directly related to these parties' claims to be legitimate political actors worthy of a governing role in their respective countries. Their claims derived from exceptional political developments: the broader structural crisis of the 1970s led to especially severe tests of these countries' regimes (Spain's post-Franco evolution is, of course, a very special case); at the same time, detente between the United States and the Soviet Union lessened international tensions to a notable degree.

Because of the dimensions of the crisis of the 1970s, which undermined many long-established political assumptions and patterns throughout the advanced capitalist world, but especially because of the claim to a governing role, this period put exceptional demands on the Communists. Their wider democratic and their programmatic credibility were simultaneously challenged. In a certain sense, this transition demanded the pushing of de-Stalinization to its outer limits. Exactly what these limits might be, and how far each party would or could push, determined the extent of crisis and change in each.

## The Eurocommunist Parties' Transitional Crises: A Synthetic Review

The overview that follows will briefly refer to the major aspects of each party's crises, how these were conditioned by specific events, and, in the very broadest sense, how each party was affected by the way it experienced the crisis. The most important aspects of the PCI's earlier crises will be discussed at the relevant points in several of the chapters that follow (especially in Chapters 1 and 3 through 5).

Reemergence or "surfacing" worked out best for the PCI in view of conditions prevailing in the immediate postwar period. It enjoyed fairly broad legitimacy in the heady aftermath of the Liberation struggle against the Nazis and their by then totally discredited Italian fascist allies. Perhaps most importantly, the PCI leadership was deeply committed to a strong *mass*-party structure. A tight "bolshevik" heritage remained in place with regard to internal discipline and the demands put on truly militant cadres, but the party also welcomed into its ranks almost anyone willing to join—and more than two million people were. The Italian Communists thus emerged at the end of the war with a curious hybrid party that combined cadre and mass characteristics and turned out to be exceptionally well suited to the requirements of the period it faced. (Ironically, the fact that the PCI was quickly to become an isolated *opposition* party was *not* in the leadership's original plans.) The Spanish party had similar aspirations when it came out of thirty-five years of clandestinity, but almost none of the conditions at the time was as favorable as in Italy.

In France, there were many more direct parallels to Italy, and the PCF emerged immediately as the largest party on the left (and, for a time, in the Republic). But the PCF's leadership was not nearly so committed to a model of a more open, mass-party structure. Having been spared a fascist interlude of twenty or more years, the party was much less disrupted by postwar developments than was its Italian counterpart. In other words, while the PCI can be said to have reconstituted itself almost entirely in the more open and expansive postwar period, the PCF's behavioral patterns in a mass-democratic context were really formed in the 1920s and 1930s, when obedience to the twists and turns in Moscow's line were at their peak.[8] Thus, in spite of superficial similarities, the immediate postwar period had a radically different meaning for the PCI and the PCF. It was profoundly transitional for the PCI, whereas it was more of a disruptive interlude prior to a "return to form" in the cold war for the key leadership of the PCF at all levels.

De-Stalinization was experienced very differently in the three parties. The PCF ignored most doctrinal and organizational issues for as long as it could, and tended as well to shy away from overt criticism of the USSR. In the late 1960s, and increasingly in the 1970s, its criticism of the USSR's policies, often tinged with the hues of Gallic nationalism, became more frequent. But sustained critical analysis of the Soviet system has been notable for its near absence in the French party. The PCE, a clandestine organization with most of its leaders in Moscow, faced a particularly daunting challenge. There were intense factional struggles at the very top of the party in the post-1956 period, however, with a clear if cautious de-Stalinized line emerging victorious.

A much more decisive victory over the most sectarian elements was achieved when the PCE officially condemned the Soviet-led invasion of Czechoslovakia in 1968. This condemnation caused a split in the PCE leadership and generated heavy-handed Soviet interference in support of the losing faction. One could thus say that de-Stalinization along many key dimensions was not truly carried out until the early 1970s in the Spanish party, but the circumstances ensured that criticism of the USSR would henceforth be especially strong. It is probably most accurate of all, however, to see the post-1968 battle as a *separate* transitional crisis for the PCE. This would again underscore that these crises can only be understood in specific contexts and are not rigid steps or stages that all parties must ascend to reach an (idealized) point of arrival.

The PCI experienced both an earlier and a more thoroughgoing de-Stalinization than either of its two counterparts, although the PCE's harsher criticism of the Soviet Union and readier recourse to open internal debate have often been cited to show the Italian party's limits. The PCI's situation was undoubtedly eased by the top leadership's commitment to the mass-party concept. Changes were also forced at a more rapid pace than the leaders alone might have undertaken by the existence of a *socialist* party that maintained a close relationship with the PCI until 1956 and did not engage in open hostilities—as was the case in so much of western Europe in the 1940s and 1950s— even when the two drew farther apart. Other critical events, especially concerning the organized labor movement, also precipitated a number of moves away from the more manipulative behavior patterns of a "traditional" communist party vis-à-vis allied mass organizations such as unions.

But the PCI was not simply reacting blindly to external stimuli in the mid-1950s. If it felt the need to act, this is largely because party leaders and cadres possessed and were eager to implement a model of party organization and behavior that was a far cry from the traditional one. Decisive evidence of this commitment can be found in the replacement of the leading cadres who were entrenched in the party's vitally important provincial structures. This was accompanied by painful and disruptive conflicts, but it was a process the top leadership felt had to be undertaken. It by no means eliminated all prior traces of the Stalinist tradition, but it was a very important step.

Still, events broke very much in the PCI's favor in this period. For one thing, the crucial years (1956–1959) did not coincide with a political crisis in Italy. The French case, which witnessed the fall of the Fourth Republic, provides a telling contrast as well as an additional explanation for PCF foot-dragging in the matter of de-Stalinization. It was fortunate for the PCI as well that there were no major elections held in that period.[9] Moreover, although the party lost a significant proportion of its membership (and a number of prominent leaders as well), it was able to stall wholesale changes in the lower and middle ranks of the organization until after the worst initial shocks had been weathered by the rank and file.

This brings us to the crisis of the 1970s, which I have labeled "Eurocommunization" for lack of a better term, but which has obvious limits. The most notable is that the wider crisis of Western capitalism that contributed so much to Eurocommunization shows no signs of abating in the late 1980s. There are many valid ways to assess the broader phenomenon, depending on the focus of one's analysis. It can be viewed as the end of the long postwar boom cycle, and hence the crisis of the Keynesian welfare system that assumed constant economic growth to fuel it. Alternatively, one can speak with equal confidence of the profound societal changes, particularly in relation to this economic restructuring, that have accompanied what some call postcapitalist development. Traditional structures and values began to erode rapidly in the late 1960s, which undermined, among many other things, traditional Catholic subcultures (a development of no small moment in countries such as Spain and Italy). The class structure, never rigid, changed much more rapidly, with service-sector and white-collar employment, often in the state sector, growing enormously, generally at the expense of traditional blue-collar sectors. The diffusion of education and the mass media among large segments of the lower strata undermined the educational function that the historic organizations of the left have traditionally exercised. For the purposes of this study, it is less important to analyze the precise parameters of these broader changes than to remember, at all times, that they form the backdrop to the phenomenon that came to be known, however briefly, as Eurocommunism.

Although the political situation varied dramatically in the three countries, the broader crisis created an opportunity in each for the left, which included relatively large and important communist parties, to assume at least a share of national power. As noted already, this opportunity carried with it a double challenge. As potential governing parties, the Communists had to reassure broad sectors of society of their democratic bona fides, but they also had to propose a convincing alternative to the tired, discredited center-right governments that had ruled their respective countries for a very long time. (The Spanish case is an obvious exception with some interesting similarities.) As we know, the outcomes differed, but the Communists fared poorly in all cases. In France they have been marginalized, in Spain all but obliterated, by dynamic socialist parties. In all cases, their organizations have been weakened, and their strategies are at best uncertain.

This brief review has provided several ways to illuminate the PCI's more successful transit of the current crisis. A purely descriptive, country-by-country comparison would underscore the importance of the recent transition to democracy in Spain and the ability, in France and Spain, of "new" socialist parties to win the competition on the left by being more responsive to the conditions created by the crisis of the 1970s. As noted earlier, such a comparison would also emphasize the PCI's ability to occupy much of the political "space" of a modern socialist party thanks to its more advanced evolution. As this study will do, it would then turn to more specifically Italian developments to analyze and assess the factors that blocked the PCI just short of its primary objectives in the period.

The concept of transitional crisis helps, however, when we turn to some of the reasons for the PCI's differential evolution and success. The French and Spanish parties, for example, confronted two crises simultaneously in the 1970s. The Italians may be the last remaining Eurocommunist party because they had faced the two earlier crises and weathered them fairly successfully. As I have noted several times, this was due to both fortuitous timing and favorable conjunctures but also to firm, committed action on the part of the top leadership. In contrast, the lack of will of the leadership of the PCF to confront de-Stalinization eventually took its toll—and also helped dictate the sectarian turn the party took when it was outmaneuvered by the Socialists at the end of the 1970s. The Spaniards, for all they had done regarding de-Stalinization, were helpless when confronted by an extremely unfavorable conjuncture: their emergence and consolidation coincided with the period in which they also had to adapt to the conditions that put Eurocommunization on the agenda. Either crisis, in more favorable conditions, has pushed much stronger parties to their limits. The two combined proved overwhelming to the PCE.

## Transitional Crisis and the PCI

A transitional crisis is defined by both the multiplicity and the profundity of the disruptions suffered by a party. Even the best or most "normal" of times for a complex organization like the PCI will be filled with challenges, but these are not necessarily disruptive. And only when there is a widespread or particularly intense disruption of normal activity along one dimension of the party's life is it proper to speak of a "crisis," at which point it is appropriate to speak of an ideological, strategic, political, or organizational crisis. A *transitional* crisis occurs under even more restrictive circumstances: (1) the party is wracked by several crises either simultaneously or in very close order; (2) this multiple phenomenon is compressed in time; (3) the disruption of the status quo is extensive. It is obvious, even without hindsight, that the party cannot continue to operate exactly as it has done in the past, and, if the crisis is severe enough, the party's future could even be called into question.

From the preceding survey, there should be no doubt that for the PCI the two crises prior to the one that is the subject of our study were transitional crises. It is less easy to know exactly how to label another period of great difficulty, the middle third of the 1960s. The Communists were threatened with domestic isolation as the Socialists broke with them and joined the Christian Democrats (DC), Italy's dominant and ruling party since 1946, in Center-Left governments on both the national and the local levels. This period also witnessed some of the most extensive and lively debates in the party's history. But, although the debates were concerned with organizational themes, one cannot point to a true organizational crisis. Membership declined, but quite gradually. The Stalinist old guard had already been replaced at the middle levels of the party, and little turnover took place among low-level leaders. It was a vitally important period for the PCI, and in some ways it even presaged what was to occur a decade later, but, on balance, I would not call it a true transitional crisis. The party was deeply discomfited but not profoundly disrupted. (See Chapter 1.)

In the last analysis, the years 1962 to 1966 are notable in PCI history because while most of the "big issues" were raised, events allowed the party to avoid having to act on them. Ideological and strategic debate was extensive but quite limited in terms of the issues that were genuinely redefined or reexamined. Ritualistic assertions of "the correctness of the party line" and "the power of Marxism-Leninism" were widespread. On the political front, the challenge of the Center-Left faded as the government's most ambitious reform proposals failed, and the Communists were soon the clearest beneficiaries of these failures. They gained a million votes (roughly 3 percent) in the 1968 elections, while the Socialists and Social Democrats, who had reunited in 1966, lost 5 percent.

The most recent period is both similar to and different from the other transitional crises. It is similar by definition in the piling up of several crises, including, for the very first time, a loss of popular support in a general election. But it differs in the less intense, more drawn-out form these crises have taken. In a certain sense, the crisis continues today, even though the critical disruptive period ended in 1979. While this has unquestionably provided the PCI with breathing space and time to adjust to its new situation, the fact remains that the situation is a new one. Many bridges to the past have been burned, and the shortcomings of many analyses and internal organizational practices have been openly conceded. Unceremoniously relegated back to the opposition, the PCI does not have any painless fallback positions. Indeed, to its great credit, it did not turn in on itself or, for instance, revert to a more hard-line, pro-Soviet stance in the wake of defeat—as did, to a significant extent, the PCF at about the same time. [10]

Stopped just short of at least an important share of power, the PCI has moved back into the opposition but refuses to be a permanent opposition party. It has obviously been baffled since 1980, in an uncertain political conjuncture, about what its next steps ought to be.

I noted at the beginning of this introduction that it would be premature to speculate too much about where the PCI might be heading, since its crisis is very much still in progress. At this point, however, we can certainly say where it has been, and that is taking the concepts that originated in the postwar period as far as they can go. It will provide some sense of the kind of discussion that has been taking place in the PCI since the 1970s to note that many prominent party intellectuals have suggested that the whole idea of a mass-membership party of the traditional type, and that includes the PCI's hybrid variant, must be rethought. [11] In this view, neither the class structure nor the forms that politics now take in advanced capitalist systems conform any longer to the configuration that informed Marx or the founders of the mass parties of the European left. Others, bringing to mind comments made at the beginning of this introduction, have seriously suggested that the party change its name—and with it, of course, a great number of established practices.

This discussion suggests some of the problems we can expect to find in the PCI in crisis. Some of them—such as the tension between governmental and oppositional roles or between electoral and cadre organizational requirements—have always been present but will undoubtedly be aggravated by the transitional situation. Other problems, such as the impact that new social strata and new political generations have on the party's ability to function, are *potentially* highly disruptive, but their very existence inside the party and the degree to which they actually interfere with its established activities need to be empirically determined. How much a party's structures mediate or filter an external environment in flux and how much—and in what ways—they are altered or obstructed by an environment that corresponds less and less to the original organizational principles around which the party was constructed, are among the main questions this study attempts to address. Until this initial task is accomplished, we can only continue to assert that a transitional crisis has occurred; we must eventually demonstrate its existence.

It would therefore be out of place to attempt here to spell out all the possible—or even most likely—variations that can be expected in the PCI's operations as it has to confront a new situation. From all that has been said, we can anticipate a large number of serious difficulties to face the party simultaneously. We can also expect, if there is any accuracy at all in the observations about the new and fluid nature of so many of the phenomena of the 1970s, abundant evidence of the party's inability not merely to manage but also to comprehend many of the challenges it has to confront. To address any of these issues convincingly, however, requires a level of analysis much different from that employed to this point.

## Transitional Crisis Closely Observed:
## The PCI in Turin, 1975–1980

If the defining characteristics of a transitional crisis are the multiple, paralyzing disruptions suffered by the party, we must find a way to demonstrate and assess these disruptions. We must, in other words, focus on the party's specific policies, behavior, and organizational activities. And we need to do so in a way that clarifies the origins and extent of the tensions and problems it faces.

If this were a study of strategy alone, we could restrict the focus to the national level, and documentary evidence would suffice. Indeed, since strategy is a crucial and, I will argue, a central driving component of the present crisis, it will receive considerable attention. Hence the bulk of Chapter 1, which establishes the context of the PCI's crisis in the 1970s, will address the political options consciously chosen by party leaders. I argue explicitly that the "historic compromise" guided many of these choices and in fact must be seen as a major cause of the party's problems. If we recall that in this period the PCI faced a dual challenge, my argument is that party strategy and actions represented an extreme response to only one exigency (legitimation of the PCI) at the expense of the other (to provide a persuasive answer to the crisis in the country). There may well be no ready answers to the crisis of the late capitalist social formation, in Italy or elsewhere. But this particular response was doomed from the start because it misread—at times willfully—many of the most critical trends under way in the country.

The first chapter will also introduce and begin to discuss the PCI's hybrid character as a cadre party with mass qualities. The political dimension of the crisis will establish the national context for the party's activities in the 1975–1980 period. The objective difficulties that greatly limited the PCI's options will be analyzed, but so will the fact that the party took numerous actions—and failed to take others—because of its strategic choices. Finally, we will close the discussion with a very brief recapitulation of the organizational aspects of the party's crisis. Organizational questions will receive less attention in the first chapter only because they are so important that they take up the entire second half of the study.

With the wider context established in Chapter 1, we will then proceed to the heart of the study, which is an examination of the strategic, political, and organizational difficulties in the Turinese federation of the PCI between 1975 and 1980. Nearly two years in Turin during this period provided abundant firsthand information, supplemented by access to the party's archives.[12] Especially from 1977 to 1979, fieldwork was extensive. I attended party meetings at every level, from the grass roots up to the apparatus of the federation. I also took part in or observed a myriad of party activities. Finally, I carried out systematic interviews with the members of the apparatus of the Turinese PCI, discussing their jobs, personal backgrounds, and general attitudes, as well as their views on questions of party policy and strategy. The material collected in Turin sheds considerable light on the PCI's operations and provides an inside perspective on the way the party lived through the peak period of crisis.

Chapter 2 will discuss the PCI's turbulent history in Turin and show why we find here a neat distillation of the party's dilemma since the mid-1970s. Turin's larger historical significance, to Italy and to the PCI, is well known. It was an epicenter of the mass mobilizations of the 1960s and 1970s and thus has been one of the centers of the broader social changes that have challenged both party and society. But it is most of all Turin's genuinely transitional nature in this period that makes it such an interesting window on the PCI's crisis.

On the surface, the party here achieved precisely what it was supposed to: it rode the waves of popular protest and disgust with the ruling DC, becoming the largest party in the area by the end of the 1960s and the governing party by the mid-1970s. It did this at a time when the party's national strategy, the "historic compromise," emphasized the PCI's qualifications and right to govern the entire country. Yet the Turinese PCI had been, since the 1950s, an extremely militant *opposition* party. Its organization, built and conditioned around the mobilization of dissent, now had to undertake a radical change of gears, at a time when the party machine was under intense pressure from several different quarters. It thus represents an extreme illustration of the tension between the party's contemporary strategy and its historical identity. The party's difficulties are, in this sense, exaggerated in Turin, but that also makes the underlying problems and contradictions easier to read.[13]

Chapters 3 and 4 address, respectively, the political and strategic dimensions of the crisis as it was experienced in Turin. To provide a broad perspective on the party's political problems, I examine three cases in the third chapter. Each focuses on a different aspect of party theory and strategy, and each illustrates the impact of the party's national choices on its local actions.

In the fourth chapter, we turn to the period (1978–1980) when the party's problems became so severe as to require it to change the line, first modifying and then abandoning the "historic compromise." This chapter moves back and forth between the national and the local levels of the party, focusing in particular on the various tensions that rose to the surface in the federation as problems multiplied and the national leadership grudgingly and ambiguously altered the party line. Since this period embraced several serious setbacks for the PCI—including the 1979 general elections, in which the Communists lost votes nationally for the first time since the war—the internal debates often became quite intense. This chapter thus provides an inside perspective on how the PCI actually experienced a change in its strategy; along with Chapter 3, it also clearly illuminates the major fault lines that were progressively exposed during the crisis.

So many of the most serious problems of the 1970s directly or indirectly raised organizational questions that, starting with Chapter 5, the focus of this study moves to the party organization. The fifth chapter establishes the wider context of the crisis of the party as a structure that evolved from a number of postwar precepts. I begin with the specific Marxist and Leninist legacies and how these have been applied by Italian Communists to give their own hybrid formation its distinctive qualities. I then review the way these qualities have been put into practice over the postwar period. This general discussion of the party's structural evolution is illustrated with specific examples from the Turinese federation. This chapter also discusses at some length the way some of the classical debates in mass parties of the left—such as the nature and class character of cadres—have been addressed in the PCI and how the terms of debate developed, nationally and in Turin, in the present period.

Chapter 6 addresses the organizational dimension of the transitional crisis in Turin, developing the themes raised in Chapter 5 but focusing primarily on the major structural problems that have been revealed throughout the study. Here, as elsewhere, the thrust of the analysis is not simply to describe the strains and conflicts that exist but to get at their sources. In many instances, for example, the crisis aggravated tensions built into any mass organization, such as generational or center-periphery conflicts. But in other cases, such as the dominant work style and "model of militancy" that reigns in the PCI, the relationship between territorial and factory organizations, the proper relationship between local communist governments and local party structures, and others as well, the underlying tensions can be traced to the PCI's *specific* organizational arrangements. This chapter includes detailed analyses of the membership, cadres, and top leadership of the federation, as well as a discussion of the organization's efforts to change in response to the crisis.

We know from past transitional crises as well as the most recent one that the type of cadre to emerge in troubled times—especially in the upper ranks of local party organizations—is often a decisive factor in the party's eventual ability to survive and develop. Chapters 7 and 8 provide a detailed portrait of the apparatus of the Turinese PCI. Systematic interviews and observations of the full-time functionaries at work over a several-year period provided extensive information on how the leadership actually evolved at the end of the 1970s. Such information would be valuable in any event, but it is crucial with respect to the PCI, for the 1970s was a time of extensive leadership turnover amidst tumultuous change.

More specifically, Chapter 7 analyzes the changing role and profile of the communist functionary in Italy as the party has evolved and as some of the built-in organizational tensions noted in Chapters 5 and 6 have come into conflict with new types of party leaders. The impact of certain values not traditionally a part of communist organization—such as pluralism and feminism—is traced and assessed. Finally, this chapter includes a collective biographical sketch of the functionaries, which provides further insights into the often subtle recruitment mechanisms within the PCI. Among many other things, this information allows us to see whether and to what degree there are potential generations forming within the new leadership, and how these people were personally as well as collectively affected by the momentous mobilizations of the 1960s and early 1970s.

Chapter 8 draws on systematic interviews with the functionaries to establish their views on a number of issues related to the nature of the party and its strategy. Some questions ask the functionaries about their own experiences in the party: why they joined, what were the most critical moments in their own political maturation, and so on. Most of the questions were open-ended and drew on topics at the center of debate in the party at the time of the study. In other words, I tried to raise issues about which there was either open disagreement in the party or else no clear line that could be parroted back to me. Some of the major topics addressed are the role that Leninism or *any* doctrine ought to play in the party, what makes a good communist cadre or leader, the respondent's optimism or skepticism concerning a long-term agreement with the DC (agreement with the "historic compromise"), how far criticism of the Soviet Union should be pushed, attitudes toward the middle classes, and so on.

The goal of this chapter is to determine (1) the breadth and depth of different or similar views, within the apparatus, on specific items; and (2) whether *systematic* differences emerge along class, generational, or functional (i.e., headquarters vs. periphery) lines in the apparatus. Are there, in fact, nascent generations among the new leadership? Is there as much disagreement over fundamental issues, as is often alleged, in the very heart of the organization? Even if we find clear responses to many of these queries, we will hardly have unlocked the secrets of the PCI's future. We will, however, certainly have shed a good deal of light on how the recent past has affected the present—and that is no small achievement.

Finally, in the conclusions of Chapter 9, I return to the broader questions raised throughout the study to assess the overall impact of the crisis on the PCI, as well as where the party might be going in the future. This will not be an effort to generalize strictly from the case of Turin. As should be clear by now, Turin is hardly representative of the entire party. But what this single case will have illuminated much more sharply are the critical contours of the PCI's crisis. With Turin as one of the most socially homogeneous areas in the industrialized North of Italy, for example, the discovery of widespread and irreconcilable cleavages within the organization on key issues would suggest, at a minimum, that such differences would be equally widespread elsewhere in the PCI. Or we might find opposite conclusions that ultimately point in the same direction, such as fairly consensual views that reflect Turin's distinctiveness as a blue-collar bastion. It is even possible that plumbing this single case will point toward an embryonic new direction in the party's structure, strategy, or both. Naturally, it is far more likely that the findings will not be so clear-cut in any single direction. In fact, some of those who speak of advanced capitalist societies as too complex to be organized successfully by any mass party would predict an essentially random pattern to the major findings.

But if the crisis is as serious as I have suggested, informed speculation might be the most we should hope for. Especially since the transitional crisis is, in most important respects, still in progress, it would be premature and not a little arrogant to attempt to say with any degree of certainty what is the party's ultimate destination. It is both possible and essential, however, to provide a perspective on the PCI's past development and crises and a clear indication of where it has evolved most recently.

# 1

# Transitional Crisis and the PCI

## The PCI's Distinctive Characteristics

Among Western communist parties since World War II, and especially among those that have played a major role in their countries' domestic politics, the PCI's distinctiveness can easily be traced to the way the party emerged from clandestinity from 1943 to 1945.[1] Under Palmiro Togliatti, who guided the party from the 1930s until his death in 1964, the PCI emerged as a mass activist party intent on establishing as broad a presence as possible in Italian society. Its membership quickly rose to two million and beyond in the 1940s, and, as such numbers suggest, it actively recruited throughout society with little of the concern for ideologically "mature" members usually associated with communist parties. While it paid lip service to the tenets of Marxism-Leninism as its guiding doctrine, this party ignored these tenets for its mass membership, insisting only that those who joined agree with its political program for the war-torn country. Taking an unprecedented step for the period, the PCI invited everyone, regardless of philosophical or religious conviction, to join on this basis. This was clearly an open appeal to Roman Catholics—and it greatly annoyed the Russians.

Togliatti and those around him were well aware that a mass party of presence was a significant departure from the Bolshevik vanguard party concept, and there was initially considerable resistance to the idea from many leaders and militants. Nor did the top leadership try to hide the nature of the departure: Togliatti coined the phrase "new party" (*partito nuovo*) precisely to underscore its novelty. Although it never managed to attain the highly ambitious goals set in this period of greatest strength (e.g., a party section in every village and hamlet in Italy and a presence "in every fold" of the society), the PCI was irrevocably shaped by the mass party strategy.

This does not mean that the PCI abandoned the Leninist strictures on party organization altogether. Such a step would never have been tolerated by the Soviets, and it was unthinkable as well to the top party leadership. For the militants in the party, and this meant anywhere from a tenth to a quarter of all members, the PCI was still very much a *communist* party. This peculiar hybrid form would mark the PCI through the postwar period and be responsible for many of its greatest strengths and weaknesses.

What made Togliatti so adamant in his insistence on this particular organizational formula? The postwar realignment of Europe put Italy squarely within the West's sphere of influence, which ruled out any attempt at insurrection even if the leaders were so inclined (they were not). One could therefore argue that even if Togliatti had not been sincerely committed to the democratic rules of the game, he realized he was stuck with them and sought the means by which his party could exert maximum leverage within the system. Moreover, the postwar prostration of Italy, combined with a strong left and a widespread desire for change, provided what appeared at the time as a superb opportunity for the Communists to play a major, constructive role in the rebuilding of the country. Togliatti felt that although socialism was not on the immediate agenda, an advanced, "progressive democracy" was. He felt that the PCI could, in this context, generate important changes that would pave the way to a distinctively "Italian Road to Socialism," or *via italiana al socialismo*. The belief in such a radical reconstruction project as a realistic possibility would in itself probably have justified the mass party formula.

But what clinched the argument for Togliatti was the trauma of fascism. He was among the first to emphasize the movement's, and later the dictatorship's, mass base of support as an essential component of its success in Italy, and he consistently stressed the suicidal nature of the left's narrow-based policies before fascism's rise.[2] Thus a mass party, nonsectarian in its structure, base of recruitment and policies was an excellent defensive instrument against any potential resurgence of reaction in the postwar period. The direct link between the experience under fascism and the decision to make the "new party" a mass-membership organization is nowhere more evident than in the words of Togliatti as he reviewed early postwar achievements:

> Had we limited ourselves to being a party of 200,000 members, a very large part of the mass that we control would now be under the influence of the Catholic Church and of organizations led by it like Christian Democracy, because these are organizations with a tradition of legal existence even during fascism. . . . In countries where there was no long-term fascist dictatorship this need has not been felt so strongly.[3]

The *partito nuovo* was, then, the ideal instrument for realizing the PCI's postwar strategic goals, goals which were informed by both defensive and transformative considerations.

It is one thing to pose such a hybrid concept of the party as an ideal and quite another to put it into practice. An organization that attempts to merge two operational models—the Marxist mass working-class party and the Leninist notion of disciplined cadres—may not only find the task difficult, but it may then also find itself heir to the most severe problems of both traditions. Large mass parties, because they are deeply rooted in society, can be so slow-moving and caught up in self-perpetuating routines that their broader goals become difficult, if not impossible, to realize. To say, as the founders of the *partito nuovo* insisted, that party members ought to acquire the qualities of rigorously trained cadres may respond to a perennial problem in theory, but how is this to be realized in practice? Conversely, how is an extremely centralized *communist* party supposed to exercise the flexibility at the grass roots that is one of the hallmarks of a mass party? How can it reconcile the demands of a cadre party steeped in the traditions of the Communist Third International with its own simultaneous emphasis on membership based strictly on adherence to a much less inclusive political program?

Although it never fully resolved these tensions, the PCI did manage, for a considerable period of time, to carry out the basic tasks set by its leadership. And this relative success can be traced to the fairly good fit between the organizational forms and basic activities of the party on the one hand and the real shape of Italian society and politics on the other, until late in the postwar period.

Structurally, Italy was highly fragmented and unevenly developed. But, as very consistent electoral returns from the 1940s until the mid-1970s attest, the country was quite stably organized politically and culturally in many areas around the Communists and Socialists on the left and the DC on the center-right. These historical subcultural divisions stabilized during the polarization of the cold war. The PCI used its impressive organizational network and a strong oppositional posture to hold traditional areas of strength and make inroads into other areas.[4] The party lost members throughout the mid-1950s and 1960s, and the organization was riddled with problems—as we shall see later in this study. But it did manage to perform its basic oppositional and mobilizational tasks, and the PCI gained electoral support steadily throughout the postwar period.

It would be a serious error to underestimate the benefits to the PCI, and to Italian democracy, that flowed from the *via italiana* and Togliatti's "new party." But, with hindsight, it is fairly clear today that the setting to which the *partito nuovo* is best adapted lies more in the past than in the future. To cite but one telling example, even during its period of electoral expansion, the party lost votes in the area of the country where an advanced industrial society was taking root, the Northwest. For all its achievements, these and other considerations have led some of its most acute observers to characterize the *partito nuovo* as fundamentally premodern along many of its most crucial dimensions.[5] This will become especially relevant when we analyze its behavior toward new social phenomena in the 1970s.

Relative political stability for almost a full generation following World War II thus permitted the consolidation and evolution of the *partito nuovo* into a highly distinctive party with a unique mix of cadre and mass characteristics. Togliatti's vision ensured that it was less dogmatic and organizationally inflexible than one would expect of a communist party, but neither the vision of the top leadership nor the course of events permitted the PCI to stray too far from the classical vanguard model. It has not been hidebound, but tradition and ideology have strongly slowed and shaped the party's evolution. Historically, these factors are most apparent in the PCI's links to the USSR and its commitment to the idea of "democratic centralism." But they have also been present in much less obvious forms as well.

Two very important examples can be noted here; each is discussed at some length in this study. The first is the party's implicit and often explicit model of militancy, by which I mean the code governing cadres' behavior. This code, as anyone familiar with communist parties knows, consists of enormous doses of dedication and sacrifice, often at immense personal cost. Its origins lie in a semimilitary notion of service to the revolutionary cause. This idea undeniably persists for a host of functional reasons, but a major explanation for its persistence must also be sought in the survival, at least in diluted form, of a revolutionary ideal.[6] The special nature of this model of militancy, as well as its links to the communist tradition, were ably synthesized by Lucio Magri, a former PCI leader:

> By the term *revolutionary militancy* we mean here a particular relationship between the member and the party, which distinguishes Bolshevism from any other type of political formation. . . . [It] does not sanction the division between private and public spheres. . . . On the contrary, it is based on the involvement of the whole personality of the militant, involving his life-long conception of the world in the complex work of building the new society.[7]

Magri's reference to the bolshevik conflation of public and private and to the involvement of the militant's "whole personality" brings us to the second way that ideological traditions have shaped the PCI. In this case, we must contend with the legacy of Marxism itself. That is, Marxism does not simply provide a comprehensive worldview;

many—some would say all—ideologies do that. It also contains a key principle (the centrality of class relations), which it has refined over a century as a successful political movement, that permits it to organize and attempt to control the world as it understands it. Whereas the model of militancy provides insights into the PCI's *internal* code of operations, these factors explain why the party's historical attitude toward *external*, societal phenomena has so frequently been predictable, simplistic, and reductionist.

It is essential to understand how both factors can interact in the PCI. The party (i.e., its leaders, intellectuals, and activists) attempts to grasp, organizationally and ideologically, *all* social phenomena through established class-based categories. Obviously, things that do not easily lend themselves to the familiar economic, workers-versus-bosses framework may prove elusive. In some instances, when these new phenomena prove refractory to analysis and organization, the party may even dismiss them as irrelevant, immature, bourgeois, or irrational. The phenomena, and not the narrowness or inappropriateness of the PCI's own categories or methods, are blamed for their failure to conform to expectations.

One need only consider such recent developments as youth and student movements, feminism, the ecology movement, and, in the Italian context, many demands for secular civil rights to see that the above are not abstract considerations. In fact, they constitute some of the most vexing problems the PCI has been forced to face since the 1960s. The party's initial failures to comprehend these phenomena, along with its continuing inability to fit them comfortably into its traditional schemes of analysis or action, are eloquent testimony to the deep entrenchment of its established codes. It was, of course, precisely such phenomena which signaled the end of the relatively stable phase of Italy's postwar political and social evolution. That also happened to be the period during which the *partito nuovo's* underlying assumptions were in closest synchronization with the society and politics of the country.

## Strategic Crisis in the PCI: General Considerations

The strategy of the PCI, the *via italiana al socialismo*, has had a difficult history since Togliatti first enunciated its broad outlines in the immediate postwar period. Numerous leaders and apologists have argued, out of sincere as well as self-interested motives, that the line's evolution has been little more than subsequent elaboration of an analysis and strategy which were essentially complete by 1947. Others, including myself, have noted that while there is undoubtedly much continuity between the 1940s and today, the evolution of the *via italiana* has been less linear than is often claimed. Indeed, one of the party's great strengths has been the flexible fashion with which it has balanced dissenting and often irreconcilably opposed interpretations of the strategy. More often than not, it tolerated a fair degree of conflict, even if this generated a degree of confusion about exactly what the strategy might mean.

Such strategic fuzziness contained, until very recently, many more positive than negative payoffs for the party. These included (1) maximum appeal, as an oppositional force, to disgruntled groups in society; (2) a flawed but functional internal control mechanism that generated feedback to the leadership and consensus throughout the party; (3) a resultant image of relative openness to debate that was especially appealing to intellectuals. Finally, and importantly, this degree of intentional imprecision (4) permitted the PCI to hedge its bets and avoid making hasty or dogmatic decisions on numerous issues. An evasive style has allowed the leadership to assert a difficult position gradually, where brusque *pronunciamientos* may well have generated considerable resistance—primarily from the rank and file but, in earlier times, from the USSR as well. Vivid illustrations of this style at its most effective would be the PCI's edging away from its opposition to NATO or its almost imperceptible revision, over time, of doctrinal sore spots such as proletarian dictatorship or democratic centralism.

The drawbacks of this operational style can be severe at times, however. Events often do not permit the leisurely and painless assumption of a position; they may demand quick reactions. The PCI has been very quick to take firm stands when its position was earlier staked out clearly—condemnation of the invasion of Czechoslovakia in 1968 is a good example. But when events happen to involve ambiguous issues that the PCI has historically avoided clarifying, the entire party, starting with its top leadership, can waffle considerably. This was evident in heated debates over domestic strategy throughout most of the 1960s, and it became even more evident toward the end of the 1970s.

Related to the above is the point that the ambiguous style evolved in and best served the party's goals when it was in the opposition—and when few ever thought it would emerge from that role. When the situation changed dramatically in the mid-1970s, the PCI suddenly found itself in the classical dilemma of the evolving opposition party. But it was not just any opposition party in the throes of transformation. As a *communist* party, it aroused considerable suspicion even when it was quite clear on basic questions, and was especially vulnerable on issues it had left unclear. The PCI's position on the value of political pluralism, representative institutions, and the relationship between socialism and democracy had always engaged party intellectuals and students of modern Marxist theory. But when the party announced its serious intention to govern Italy, these suddenly became questions with far more than abstract theoretical implications.

## *The Evolution of the* Via italiana*: An Overview*

In the roughly four decades since it was first enunciated, the PCI's strategy has passed through several critical phases. Only the current crisis concerns us here, but it is important to summarize the party's strategic trajectory.

1. 1944–1947: The strategy and the *partito nuovo* are born. The cautiousness and limitations of the leadership, along with considerable international constraints, left the strategy incomplete. Possibilities for creative initiatives ended abruptly with the onset of the cold war.
2. 1956–1959: After the limbo of the worst period of the cold war, de-Stalinization allowed for the reemergence of the *via italiana*. The highly significant achievement of this period was the elimination, or at least marginalization, of the worst manifestations of sectarianism among almost all middle- and high-level leaders.
3. 1962–1966: Tensions internal to the strategy emerged and were extensively debated within the party. The proximate causes of the debates were Italy's impressive economic growth and the creation of the first Center-Left coalitions, for PSI participation in government threatened the Communists with isolation. Togliatti's death in 1964 contributed to the internal tensions, with proponents of varying interpretations of the line openly confronting one another in a struggle for the succession.[8]

4. 1977–1980: Although the 1969–1972 period marked Italy's turning point in social and political terms, and 1973 saw the emergence of the PCI's "historic compromise" strategy, the party's strategic difficulties were postponed until the end of the decade. This delay was a result of the favorable shift to the left of the country's electoral and political balance in the mid-1970s (the PCI jumped from 27 percent to 34 percent of the vote). Efforts to join a coalition that included the DC and to achieve serious (but by no means radical) reforms triggered the crisis.

This summary permits us to make a distinction between two types of strategic crisis. The first, embracing the two earliest periods, can be viewed as crises of emergence and/or consolidation. These saw the primary tension between the *via italiana* and unsympathetic resistance to its elaboration and realization. The second type of crisis can be called crises of articulation. In these cases, the tensions are internal. The basic tenets of the *via italiana* are widely accepted, although considerable conflict arises over how they can best be realized. In the 1960s, the problems were aired, but, by and large, they were successfully controlled by the top party leadership. Perhaps most important was the fact that the leadership preserved orthodoxy—not, as I have stressed, in the form of a clear line but rather as a set of boundaries which could not be breached. In the 1970s, for reasons already suggested, the crisis was more severe, for even the leaders soon realized that the traditional boundaries of debate could no longer be maintained. This most recent period is the context for the entire study, and it deserves more thorough treatment.

## The Strategic Dimension of the Present Crisis:
### from *Via italiana* to *compromesso storico*

What, exactly, is—or was—the "historic compromise"? In simplest terms, it was a *long-term* strategy put forward by the Communists which argued that profound changes in Italian society would only be possible if serious political polarization were avoided. And the only way to guarantee against such polarization was a pact between the major political forces in the country, starting with the PCI and the DC although understood to include the PSI as well.

From the very beginning, however, this proposal generated considerable confusion, for it also was framed with reference to very pressing *short-term* problems. Italy was in the midst of a serious crisis in 1973 when Berlinguer first mooted the *compromesso*, and he had been arguing for more than a year that only the Communists' inclusion in a governing coalition could set the country on the right track.[9] As the 1970s progressed, a series of crisis-specific proposals was put forward by the PCI; all projected a government of national unity in which "all constitutional forces" would participate.[10] These unity proposals were framed as steps toward the historic compromise, but even many sophisticated observers came to identify them with the long-term strategy. As a result, it became common to refer to anything in which the PCI asked for a national governing role as the *compromesso*.

However imprecisely the strategy may have been understood, its primary assertion— the PCI's bid for a full share of power at the national level—became the central issue in Italian politics in the 1970s. Some interpretations of the strategy saw in it a fairly cynical bid for power by the PCI, and some of the party's early words and actions did little to counteract speculation that the *compromesso* was really a way for the "two churches" to survive in symbiosis. Communist-Catholic collaboration, in this view, would represent a sort of consociational arrangement in which neither side would demand that the other change in any basic way. Several of the strategy's key assumptions generated nervousness and suspicion, particularly on the laical left. Especially disturbing was the idea that large—or overwhelming—majorities are "more democratic" than the proverbial 50 percent plus one, or the idea that numerous side effects of secular modernization, such as the erosion of traditional social forms and values, is a sign of decomposition, "Americanization," and general degradation. Many observers noted at the time that these views owed more to certain schools of Christian social thought than to either Marxist or even liberal democratic doctrine. Critics of the strategy were not at all surprised that Franco Rodano, who came to the PCI after World War II via the "Catholic Communists," was among Berlinguer's closest advisors through the mid-1970s.[11] Rodano was thought of by many as the party's *éminence grise* in this period.

Most people, however, including Berlinguer and the bulk of the top party leadership, realized that at a minimum the Communists would have to clarify many of the most ambiguous points in their strategy and policies. And throughout the mid-1970s they moved in precisely this direction, offering, among other things, reassuring statements about their respect for democratic institutions and processes as well as Italy's place in NATO.

What, then, were the more specific details of the *compromesso*; why was it presented in 1973, and to what extent did it truly represent a significant departure for the PCI? It is well known that the term was initially coined in a series of articles entitled "Reflections on the Events in Chile" written by Berlinguer in the wake of the bloody coup d'état that brought down Salvador Allende's Popular Unity government. This, combined with the obvious parallels between Italy and Chile—Christian Democrats led the opposition to Allende—almost make Berlinguer's overtures to the DC and concern about splitting the country down the middle self-explanatory. But even a superficial glance at official PCI pronouncements from 1972 will reveal that Chilean events merely precipitated what had long been in the works (see note 9 for this chapter). The Italian Communists were reacting to internal much more than to international events.[12]

What really lay behind the *compromesso* was Berlinguer's reading of the dynamics of Italy in the wake of the unprecedented labor and social militance of the late 1960s and early 1970s. The "hot autumn" had provided the Italian left with important victories, but it had also generated a powerful backlash.[13] The hegemony of the DC had appeared to be badly shaken during the high point of the movement, but the general elections of 1972 saw the ruling party's plurality emerge unscathed, while the left stagnated and actually lost seats in Parliament. Most alarming of all were the gains of the neofascist Italian Social Movement (MSI), which had done extremely well in earlier local elections, especially in the South. Its advance in 1972 was limited only by the DC's rightward shift. For the first time in the postwar period, there was good reason to fear a reactionary movement with true mass support. And if anything is guaranteed to give an Italian Communist nightmares, it is the specter of fascism resurgent.

Berlinguer thus saw a Christian Democratic party which enjoyed apparently unshakable support, and extensive mass agitation which had not produced immediate political benefits for the left but had helped destabilize a paralyzed system which now faced what he saw as a very serious threat of a reactionary backlash. Under these circumstances, he felt compelled to act quickly, and this accounts for the timing of the historic compromise's birth.

The boldest aspect of Berlinguer's proposal was the suggestion of Communist and Christian Democratic collaboration. This represented a dramatic reversal for a party which had vilified the DC for a quarter-century as the source of most, if not all, the country's ills. In terms of the never-resolved debates within the party over its basic strategy, the *compromesso* represented a sharp and largely unilateral resolution of some of the most hotly contested issues in the *via italiana*. These were (1) the relative importance of institutional, as opposed to mass-mobilizational, sources of change in reforming Italy; (2) the PCI's attitude toward the DC, and especially its assessment of the DC's relationship to Catholicism as a political force; and (3) the party's view of the Italian state.

When these points, among others, were hotly debated less than a decade earlier, the party had been unable to produce definitive clarifications on any of them. Now Berlinguer moved quite decisively—and, more often than not, explicitly—to what had always been the right-wing interpretation of the *via italiana*.[14] Events, as he and those in the leadership who shared his view saw them, seemed to leave open no other options. His underlying assumptions will become clear as we examine each issue in turn.

Clearly evident is the resolution of the tension between a reliance on institutions as opposed to mass mobilization in favor of the former. Berlinguer's proposal came on the heels of the most intense and extended extrainstitutional mobilizations in Italian postwar history. Yet this hot phase had done very little to improve the left's fortunes; if anything, the political balance of power had shifted to the right. We thus should not be surprised to find top priority given to formal collaboration between the leaders of the major parties in the political system. In practice, the PCI had always tended to come down on the institutional side of the balance at decisive moments. Until 1973, however, it had never done so in such unequivocal fashion, and it certainly had not enshrined this choice in its official strategy. On the contrary, Togliatti had often distinguished the PCI's approach from social-democratic reformism by pointing to the role played by mass pressure through mobilization in its vision of how to bring about structural reform in Italy.[15] Social-democratic parties, he argued, lost both critical leverage and their commitment to deep change by relying excessively on institutional maneuvering.

In view of the frightening backlash which had developed in reaction to the hot autumn, Berlinguer's emphasis on the need for a cooler arena in which to resolve disputes is quite logical. The entire party's caution in the face of the polarization of the early 1970s—long before the coup in Chile—is marked. Especially notable is the emphasis put on the risks of isolation faced by the workers' movement.[16]

The second resolution which the *compromesso* represented was perhaps the most dramatic and was unquestionably the most ill fated of all. This was the attempt to resolve the "Catholic Question" by identifying the *whole* DC with political Catholicism. Here, too, there had long been ambivalence in the PCI over precisely how to define the DC and fit it into the Communists' analysis of and projections for Italy. Italy was, of course, the home of the Vatican; it also was home to tens of thousands of clergy and millions of practicing Catholics. The PCI could ignore this formidable structure only at its peril. Togliatti was highly sensitive to the risks involved; as we know, he felt that a mass party could limit the extension of the social bloc of the church and DC. For the same reasons, he left party membership open to believers. The Communists also voted for Article 7 of the Republican Constitution, making the Lateran Pacts (which, among other things, make Roman Catholicism Italy's state religion) part of the basic law of the land. Even during the height of the cold war, when the church announced the excommunication of Communists, the party continued to make overtures to Catholics. The Catholic Question was not something the PCI discovered in the beginning of the 1970s.[17]

But, until the 1970s, the Communists always took pains to distinguish the DC from Catholicism and particularly from the Catholic masses. It was understood that the bulk of these masses supported the ruling party, but the PCI made clear that it did not accept this situation as permanent. It avoided anticlericalism in order to keep a door open to the progressive and "popular elements" who voted for the DC and helped keep it, with a steady 40 percent, Italy's dominant party. The "popular elements" were peasants and urban middle classes especially,[18] but also numerous Catholic workers.

Debates within the PCI had historically involved disputes over how best to separate the most progressive Catholics from Christian Democracy. Among those who felt Catholic support for the left was essential, the discussion centered on the merits of a left-Catholic party breaking with the Christian Democrats versus a shift in allegiance to the existing parties of the left which would severely reduce the DC's leverage. The PCI right wing, with its more institutional emphasis, chose to ignore the Catholic question almost entirely and assumed that the historic parties of the left would grow at the DC's expense—with ex-DC supporters presumably leaving their specifically Catholic ideals behind when they moved left. As we can see from this summary, the one alternative that no one in the PCI seemed to entertain seriously was an overture to the DC as a whole. Yet we know that this was precisely Berlinguer's *compromesso* proposal.[19]

To be sure, no one in the PCI proposed an unaltered DC as an acceptable short- *or* long-term governing partner. The ruling party would minimally have to adopt a truly reformist outlook and drop its most corrupt practices for there to be any hope of serious change. But it was now assumed that such alterations in the nature of the ruling party could come about without the dramatic changes in Italian politics that all earlier variants of the PCI's strategy had always insisted on. What led to this seemingly optimistic revision?

The answer, ironically, is a strong dose of pessimism in Berlinguer's reading of events. On a purely ideological level, his comments make clear that, for him, profound historical change is impossible without the support of an "overwhelming majority of the people"; alternatively (here we see the impact of Chile), positive transformation is most unlikely in a society split down the middle. Polarization is to be avoided, even if a mobilized majority is arrayed in the home camp. This broader view of change was obviously informed by the events of the early 1970s, especially the DC's demonstrated stability through the 1968–1972 struggles.[20] The DC held its own in the 1972 elections, and it did so in the face of challenges from clearly identified left-Catholic lists, which went down to resounding defeat. There was thus a hard-nosed realism which also lay behind the formulation of the historic compromise, and Berlinguer was absolutely clear about this.[21]

Finally, realism also compelled Berlinguer to come to terms with the DC as a whole because of the degree to which that party is identified with and in some respects indistinguishable from the Italian state. Once again, intractable circumstances and his own inclinations pushed the PCI's general secretary to embrace a position associated with the right wing of the party. Consistent with its more institutional perspective, the conservative version of the *via italiana* emphasized the importance of a PCI presence in government as a precondition for the implementation of serious change. Conversely, the PCI left's mobilizational perspective put primary emphasis on a movement "from below" (i.e., outside of and even opposed to formal institutions) forcing changes on society prior to any move by the PCI into positions of national governmental responsibility.[22] This is a far cry from the orthodox Marxist-Leninist tradition, with its emphasis on the seizure of power and smashing the preexisting state apparatus.[23] But it is also quite far from the conservative position within the party.

The PCI's dilemma was obvious. The DC's continued unity and grip on its constituencies showed how rooted that party is in civil society, but they also reflected its interpenetration with and occupation of all aspects of the Italian state machinery. Nor is this interpenetration surprising, given the DC's uninterrupted dominance of all Italian governments since the end of World War II, given the very large state sector in the Italian economy, and given the Christian Democrats' willingness to use the state for narrowly political ends.[24] Moreover, aside from its enormous patronage apparatus, there is a more sinister side to the DC's identification with the Italian state, and it was very evident in the early 1970s. By that point, many elements in the repressive state apparatuses—the armed forces, police, judiciary, and secret services—had shown an alarmingly weak commitment to the country's democratic institutions and openly hostile attitudes toward the left.[25] The relationship of the DC to some of the more obscure maneuvers of these "separate bodies" (*corpi separati*) was not always clear, but there was ample evidence of tolerance in high places and suspicion that at least part of the DC leadership was even more directly involved.

Against this background, even if the 1972 elections had been more favorable to the left, there were good reasons for anyone contemplating "throwing the bums out" to pause and reflect on the nature of the DC and state power. If in many crucial ways the DC *is* the state, how can a party that wants to avoid dangerous and possibly tragic polarization continue to think in terms either of splitting the ruling party or of driving it, dramatically and in one fell swoop, from the commanding heights of the Italian system? How would a party whose very lifeblood derives from its control of thousands of levers of power react to the sudden removal of these levels from its grasp? How prepared would it be—and how able would it be, from the opposition or debilitated by a schism—to restrain the more adventurous antidemocratic elements in the repressive apparatuses when they were threatened by radical changes in the balance of power in the country?

In the ugly atmosphere of the early 1970s, the absence of reassuring answers to these questions made the *compromesso storico* all but inevitable, given the predispositions of the top leadership of the Communist party. There were simply too many factors pointing in the same menacing direction. This explains the curious term *historic* compromise which clearly was intended in the sense of long-term, mutual guarantees. The emphasis on overwhelming consensus meant that the PCI would press neither for drastic social change nor for the dislodging of the ruling party, and it would, in the shorter run, restrain its own constituencies. The proposal of collaboration directed straight to the DC was a blunt but effective way of ensuring that the message was not lost in tortuous distinctions between Catholic masses and politicians. In exchange, the Communists were asking for full legitimation as a party acceptable in the government of the country (within, to be sure, a broad-based coalition). They would clarify their own position on the democratic rules of the game, but they also wanted to establish a framework in which everyone else would respect those rules.

It is a sign of the difficult times in which both the country and the PCI found themselves that Berlinguer's dramatic proposals did not result in an immediate firestorm of debate and protest within the party. This is partially a result of the peremptory fashion Berlinguer chose to put forward his proposal and to deal with initial criticism. But it is even more a function of the genuine impasse that seemed to have been reached by the end of 1973. The left within the PCI, from whom one would have expected the strongest protests, was badly weakened since the end of the 1960s.[26] But it also had seen many of its most cherished assumptions fail to materialize in the early 1970s. The largest and most militant mobilizations "from below" in Italy's history had strengthened not the left but the right. The long-awaited open challenge to the DC by left-wing Catholic organizations had ended in disaster. There were some efforts to give the *compromesso* a decidedly leftist reading almost immediately,[27] but it was really quite clear that this was not a reflection of Berlinguer's intentions. If anything, the most plausible interpretation of the strategy in the years immediately following 1973 was the previously mentioned consociational or two-church version.[28]

### The Long Agony of the Historic Compromise (1977–1980)

Shortly after Berlinguer outlined the *compromesso*, the PCI's fortunes improved dramatically. Much of this success was attributed to the new strategy, and there was at least some truth in these claims, as we will see in the next section. But as the 1970s wore on, the party's fortunes turned, and the *compromesso* was revealed as problem-ridden and, in many respects, simply wrong. By the end of the decade, Berlinguer was forced to redefine its goals in a very restrictive way, stating that it meant no more than a consensual framework to ensure respect for the democratic rules of the game even if the DC were relegated to the opposition.[29] By 1980, the party's official position on the DC had come full circle from seven years earlier: any solution to Italy's problems was held to be impossible as long as the Christian Democrats remained in power.[30]

What were the *compromesso*'s most serious weaknesses? One could start with the underlying theoretical assumption that profound changes are only possible when supported by an overwhelming majority of the population. Stated abstractly, this is merely a dubious proposition. Stated in Italy in 1973, it assumed that the bastion of the status quo in the country (the DC) could be recruited to undermine its own system of power. The longer the PCI stuck to this belief, which was counteracted every day by the DC's behavior, the more the credibility of the party suffered.

Similarly, there was at least one sense in which its proponents could correctly argue that the strategy showed profound continuity with the past. In many respects, in fact, it harked back quite explicitly to the tripartite collaboration between Christian Democrats, Socialists, and Communists in the Liberation and immediate postwar period. This has always been a favorite theme of some interpretations (including the most conservative) of the *via italiana*, and it makes the explicit assumption that the progress interrupted in 1947 by the cold war can somehow be resumed.[31] What this view has always chosen not to examine very carefully is the truly extraordinary and extreme nature of postwar collaboration: a generation of fascism, the devastation of war and foreign occupation, and the daunting tasks of reconstruction are, to put it mildly, historically specific circumstances. A dispassionate look back to the period suggests that the cooperation, and not the deep divisions (which surfaced almost immediately), should be seen as an aberration.

I have also argued that the historic compromise was marked from birth with a pessimism that soon was revealed as excessive. It was formulated when the left's fortunes were at an all-time low and the sociopolitical balance of power in Italy seemed depressingly frozen. It was, therefore, an overly defensive reading of a specific conjuncture, and not the profound analysis of society it pretended to be. In the very early stages of the strategy's ascendancy, this confusion probably caused only limited harm. But the longer the confusion persisted, the more it blinded the party to crucial changes that were erupting all around it, and these changes contradicted the fundamental assumptions on which the *compromesso*—and, indeed, much of the PCI's broader analysis, starting with the "new party" and the *via italiana*—rested.

The way the *compromesso storico* was imposed on the PCI, regardless of its substantive merits, also eventually came back to haunt the leadership. The lack of any serious debate, even though powerful criticisms were aired by 1976, and the silence of the rank and file and many intermediate cadres created the impression that the strategy was accepted by the party to a much greater degree than was actually the case. When serious problems arose, strong dissent erupted throughout the party. The fact that it had earlier been repressed, or at least discouraged, made the debate all the more forceful, while the lack of earlier discussion left even many proponents unable to defend their positions very skillfully.

But the real cause of the long-term strategy's collapse was the PCI's inability to propose a reasonable set of short-term reforms—or to get DC cooperation in generating any serious changes in the country. Had the Communists' austerity and National Unity policies worked, they might have provided an antechamber for the far more ambitious historic compromise, with its dream of long-term collaboration. Their dismal failure inevitably called the broader proposal into question.

Finally, because the PCI had tied its future so closely to the historic compromise, the agony and eventual demise of the proposal led to such serious disorientation that even party leaders began to use "identity crisis" to describe the PCI's plight. In the abstract, this is by no means a purely negative phenomenon; it can even be applauded as part of the necessary, and long overdue, adjustment of the party's general outlook and strategy to a changing reality. But such abstract musings were of little comfort to those who had to cope with the immediate consequences of the crisis.

## The Political Dimensions of the Transitional Crisis

Although Italian governments come and go with alarming frequency, there have been only a handful of truly significant shifts in either the voting patterns of the mass public or the coalition behavior of the parties in Parliament since World War II. Because it is the second largest party in the country, the PCI has always been deeply affected by these shifts. On three occasions, in fact, the party's role in the polity has either been altered or called fundamentally into question. These political crises have not always coincided perfectly with the PCI's strategic or organizational crises, but they usually have been related. The three political crises faced by the PCI can be summarized as follows, with Table 1.1 showing the parties' fortunes in postwar elections.

## 1946–1948

This was the sorting-out phase of postwar political alignments. The Communists and Socialists, with 40 percent of the vote and a strong commitment to united action, governed with the DC until they were expelled from the coalition in 1947. They presented a joint list in 1948, but schisms within the PSI and a ferociously antileft campaign saw them reduced to 31 percent. The left, which expected to do much better, was badly demoralized and appeared relegated to a permanent oppositional role. In the 1950s, the PCI consolidated its position as the dominant party of the left and even managed a very limited electoral expansion.[32] But the DC remained hegemonic: although unable to repeat its smashing success of 1948, it dominated "centrist" (center right) coalitions through the 1950s.

## 1960–1964

This period saw the birth of the "Center-Left," which was a mortal challenge to the PCI, for it lost the PSI as an ally. The Socialists' coalition with the DC gave the ruling party an apparently unshakable governing majority, but it had even more profound implications for the Communists. The long-range goal of the Center-Left was to bring modernizing

*Table 1.1.* Vote Obtained by Parties in General Elections, 1946–1987 (Percentage Obtained by Each Party List, Chamber of Deputies)

|  | 1946[a] | 1948 | 1953 | 1958 | 1963 | 1968 | 1972 | 1976 | 1979 | 1983 | 1987 |
|---|---|---|---|---|---|---|---|---|---|---|---|
| NSU/DP | — | — | — | — | — | — | 0.2 | 1.5 | 0.8 | 1.5 | 1.7 |
| PDUP | — | — | — | — | — | — | 0.7 | w/DP | 1.4 | w/PCI | — |
| PCI | 19.0 ⎱ 31.1[b] | | 22.6 | 22.7 | 25.3 | 27.0 | 27.2 | 34.4 | 30.4 | 29.9 | 26.6 |
| PSI | 20.7 | | 12.7 | 14.3 | 13.9 | 14.5[c] | 9.6 | 9.6 | 9.8 | 11.4 | 14.3 |
| PSIUP[d] | — | — | — | — | — | 4.5 | 1.9 | — | — | — | — |
| PR | — | — | — | — | — | — | — | 1.1 | 3.5 | 2.2 | 2.6 |
| PSDI[e] | — | 7.1 | 4.5 | 4.6 | 6.1 | [c] | 5.1 | 3.4 | 3.8 | 4.1 | 3.0 |
| PRI | 4.4 | 2.5 | 1.6 | 1.4 | 1.4 | 2.0 | 2.9 | 3.1 | 3.0 | 5.1 | 3.7 |
| DC | 35.2 | 48.5 | 40.1 | 42.4 | 38.3 | 39.1 | 38.7 | 38.7 | 38.3 | 32.9 | 34.3 |
| PLI | 6.8 | 3.8 | 3.0 | 3.6 | 7.0 | 5.8 | 3.9 | 1.3 | 1.9 | 2.9 | 2.1 |
| Extreme Right[f] | 8.4 | 4.8 | 12.8 | 9.6 | 6.9 | 5.8 | 8.7 | 6.1 | 5.9 | 6.8 | 5.9 |
| Others | 5.5 | 2.2 | 2.7 | 1.4 | 1.1 | 1.3 | 1.1 | 0.8 | 1.2 | 3.2 | 5.8[g] |
| Totals | 100.0 | 100.0 | 100.0 | 100.0 | 100.0 | 100.0 | 100.0 | 100.0 | 100.0 | 100.0 | 100.0 |

*a.* Constituent Assembly.

*b.* PCI and PSI together.

*c.* Reunited with PSI 1966 – 69.

*d.* Split from PSI in 1964.

*e.* Split from PSI in 1947.

*f.* Includes monarchist parties until 1972; Neofascists (MSI) thereafter.

*g.* Includes 2.5 for Greens.

NSU/DP = United New Left/Proletarian Democracy

PDUP = Initially "Il Manifesto"; later Democratic Party of Proletarian Unity

PSIUP = Socialist Party of Proletarian Unity

PR = Radical party

PSDI = Italian Social Democratic Party

PRI = Italian Republican Party

PLI = Italian Liberal Party

reforms to Italy and thereby to isolate and erode the PCI. The PSI, which hoped to become the dominant party of the left, had been moving steadily away from the PCI in the 1950s because of the Communists' continued espousal of Marxism-Leninism, as well as their maintenance of close ties to the Soviet Union even after Khrushchev's revelations about Stalin and the 1956 Hungarian uprising.[33] Now the Socialists began to dissolve many local left-wing coalitions and made serious overtures to the Social Democrats (PSDI), with whom they eventually reunited in 1966.[34]

Although serious strains developed between the Communists and the Socialists, and the PCI seemed genuinely paralyzed in the face of the challenge of the Center-Left, the experiment had largely failed by the end of the 1960s. Unity between the PSI and the PSDI proved short-lived and ended in 1969. Moreover, the Socialists had lost almost as much to their left when they joined the DC as they later gained to their right by uniting with the PSDI. But, most important of all, the reforms promised by the Center-Left never materialized. Social tension grew throughout the decade and eventually erupted in the "hot autumn" of 1969, which had as one of its after-effects a rapprochement between the PCI and the PSI. And, while the Socialists had stagnated and lost credibility, the Communists saw their support rise steadily from 22 percent in 1958 to 27 percent in 1968.

### 1974–1979

This marks the first period of marked electoral shifts since the 1940s. (The Center-Left came about because Socialist policies changed, not because of any notable realignments.) In 1974, a 60-to-40-percent victory in a referendum to retain divorce showed the degree to which the DC's hegemony had eroded. The next year's local elections saw the ruling party fall to 35 percent, while the PCI rose to 33 percent. Then, in the 1976 general elections, the Communists touched their postwar high of 34.4 percent. Already in power in the country's major cities, the PCI first abstained in support of, and then actually voted with, the governing coalition. It was recognized as part of the majority, but it was denied cabinet positions. Unable to obtain more leverage, and badly compromised by the government's ineffectual policies, the PCI forced the 1979 elections and lost 4 percent of the vote (the first drop in the postwar period). With the Socialists willing to enter a national coalition without them, the Communists were again relegated to the opposition.

The periods of crisis discussed above might seem arbitrary, but they do conform to the PCI's most dramatic phases since the end of the war. To cite but one omission, neither the hot autumn of 1969 nor the broader cycle of struggles between 1968 and 1972 is cited. This is not to suggest that the hot period was not a watershed in postwar Italian history, but it does underscore that its political impact was not immediate. Only after the right-wing backlash and the left's stagnation in the early 1970s did the electoral shifts occur. And between these two events, the PCI came forward with its substantial strategic revisions in the form of the historic compromise.

Here we can see the critical importance of timing in the PCI's future interpretation of events. Whatever the true underlying reasons for the voting shifts of the mid-1970s, the communist leadership read them at the time as vindicating the correctness of the *compromesso storico*. With hindsight, the most convincing interpretation of this period is that the *compromesso* turned out to be a brilliant *tactical* reaction to a very difficult phase of the post-1968 crisis. However, particularly in terms of the way it was put into practice, it was an inadequate *strategic* response to the crisis as a whole. The inability of the leadership of the PCI to distinguish between tactical and strategic advances—Berlinguer was, after all, committed to the historic compromise as a strategy—contributed to the immediate misreading of the political situation and helped dull the party's reaction to unfavorable events in the late 1970s.

This brings us back to earlier comments on the deep pessimism that lurked behind the original formulation of the strategy in the early 1970s. Communist leaders quite accurately perceived that the urban, and largely northern, mobilizations and militancy of the hot period had made the left particularly vulnerable among the urban middle classes everywhere and among large strata of southerners. These groups *did* need to be assuaged, and recent empirical work indicates that it was among the middle classes in particular that the Communists' biggest electoral gains came in the period immediately after 1972.[35] Thus, the *compromesso*, or some sign from the PCI that a more moderate set of policies was on the agenda, was certainly necessary as at least a tactical measure. At the same time, the very rapidity of the success should have alerted the Communists to the fact that the situation was far more fluid than their original calculations assumed. Instead, the party eagerly moved forward on the basis of previous assumptions—and in so doing it let slip through its fingers important opportunities to assess the changes that had occurred in Italy and what the political response to these changes might be.

## From Compromesso to Political Breakthrough (1974–1976)

The belief that the DC was entrenched in power, that it had a firm hold on the allegiance of its voters, and that Italy faced a potentially reactionary backlash convinced Berlinguer that the PCI had to pursue a rapprochement with the ruling party. As events began to suggest alternative interpretations of the sociopolitical dynamic in the country, PCI leaders held firm to their basic assumptions. This was clear from the very first development that signaled a fundamental change in Italy's political alignments, the divorce referendum of 1974.

Although Italy's divorce legislation, which was only passed in the aftermath of the hot autumn, is highly restrictive, it immediately incurred the wrath of conservative Catholics and the extreme right. They decided to attempt to repeal the law using the abrogative referendum; ironically, enabling legislation for this had also only been passed in 1970. Divorce would thus be its first application. The PCI had always been wary of issues which could generate religious polarization in Italy, and it was appalled at this prospect in view of the tense climate of the early 1970s. In fact, Parliament's early dissolution in 1972 had been precipitated by a general effort to stall the referendum (which cannot be held within a year of general elections).

To avoid what they—and everyone else—believed would be a crushing defeat for divorce, as well as a situation which clearly would not benefit PCI–DC collaboration, the Communists worked very hard to side-step the referendum.[36] To placate the right, they explicitly offered to rewrite the divorce law in even more restrictive terms. The latter, convinced that they had the PCI and the left on the ropes, were not mollified. And the secular left began to wonder about the lengths to which the Communists would go to strike a deal with the DC.

The referendum, held in April 1974, represented a clamorous failure for the right.

Only in the very Catholic areas of the Northeast did a comfortable majority vote to repeal divorce, while the percentages ran to 75 to 80 percent in favor of divorce in the North and Center. Even the allegedly backward South voted narrowly to retain the law. This was a mortifying defeat for both the church and the Christian Democrats, who had always claimed to speak for the vast majority of Italians: the 40 percent repeal vote did not even equal the electoral support of the DC and the neofascist MSI, the only parties to campaign for a yes vote.

This was, in short, an extraordinarily important watershed in modern Italian political history, and a clear sign that the 1971–1973 backlash was not the opening of a grim, regressive phase in which many of the victories just won would be rolled back. It began to appear, rather, as a circumscribed period during which the options open to the right were soon exhausted. As the electoral shocks of 1975 and 1976 confirmed, the referendum was the first clear indicator of the deep changes that had occurred in Italy since the end of the 1960s.

It would have been unrealistic to expect the leaders of the PCI to leap immediately to such conclusions, and they did not. On the contrary, although they were obviously delighted at the turn of events, the underlying assessment of the situation in the country did not show the slightest alteration. Berlinguer's cautionary and defensive tone following the referendum is striking: far from discussing dramatic breakthroughs, the secretary warns of the need to remain vigilant against further attacks from the right, which are sure to come.[37] As victory followed victory, caution gave way to triumphalism, but the party's basic posture remained unaltered. It was devastatingly critical of the DC leadership, which was both scandal-ridden and paralyzed by its characteristic immobility. Far from analyzing how the DC's social bases of support might be changing, the PCI's pronouncements in this period reaffirmed, against considerable evidence to the contrary, the assertions that lay at the heart of the historic compromise.[38] The DC, although it had desperately (and successfully) managed to maintain its electoral strength only by turning to the right after 1972, was portrayed as a party with a powerful progressive component that was held back by retrograde leaders. If they were replaced by a less self-serving, more realistic lot, serious collaboration and long-awaited reforms would be on the nation's agenda. The *compromesso* may have been formulated during a difficult moment for the PCI, but it was not going to be abandoned when that moment passed.

Had these been tactical moves, they would have been brilliant coming when they did. Here was the PCI, bolstered by the most significant political gains it had ever achieved, yet asking of the DC only that it put the national interest ahead of its own narrow concerns. Emphasis on corruption and inefficiency would appeal to broad sectors of society and reassure many of those who might fear the Communists' underlying motivations. In the 1975 local elections, the PCI had run with great effect on the slogan "Our Hands are Clean!" In 1976, far from calling for a radical platform, or even for throwing out the badly compromised ruling party, they asked for an emergency "Government of National Unity," in which *all* democratic parties would work together to pull Italy out of her crisis. The balance of power had shifted enough in 1976 to make it impossible to run the country against Communist opposition (especially with the Socialists refusing to join any coalition that excluded the PCI). Very astutely, the PCI pursued an extremely moderate line and put the ball squarely in the DC's court.

Yet it was obvious that the Communists were not simply maneuvering tactically; their pronouncements had suggested, and their behavior rapidly proved, that they were very much committed to collaborating with the DC. And they did this with such conviction that they quickly dissipated much of the new support they had gained. Arguing that they could not realistically obtain any more leverage under prevailing conditions, they propped up largely ineffective governments and accepted deeply flawed legislation in an increasingly immobile climate.

Why did the Communists persist so long in this behavior, discounting or ignoring mounting evidence that they were not achieving their goals and were in fact losing support? The leadership's commitment to the new strategy, as we have seen, was profound and perhaps unshakable;[39] events through 1976 seemed to confirm the wisdom of their strategic choice; finally, the political balance of power, after the 1976 general elections, did appear to leave no alternative options open. Taken together, these factors probably suffice to explain the doggedness of the party's commitment, especially if one adds that a large and traditionally slow-moving mass party such as the PCI is usually quite cautious and not given to dramatic turnarounds in its line. With the dust barely settled around the historic compromise, the moment was not propitious for another abrupt shift.

To these already compelling motives, I would add two others. They have in common the PCI's blindness to some of the most important recent changes in Italian society. For this reason they are doubly important, for they help us understand the party's miscalculations in a given period, but, even more importantly, they open a window on the entrenched patterns—one could even call them organizational reflexes—that make it so difficult for the *partito nuovo* to operate effectively in the waning decades of the twentieth century.

At issue is the PCI's (mis)reading of its own, and the DC's, mass bases of support. Between 1972 and 1976, the PCI gained three and a half million votes.[40] If, as I have argued, much of this gain was because of short-term or tactical considerations, one would expect the party to move swiftly to consolidate wherever possible, such as to press for immediate and concrete concessions. But if the party believed its gains were because of the correctness of its long-range strategy, it would view its new supporters in a very different light. It would see their allegiance as programmatic and stable, and it would interpret their vote as carte blanche to pursue the historic compromise.[41] In the past, with a more stable electorate, such assumptions were at least plausible. What the Communists now failed to see, because it conformed neither to their desires nor to past patterns, was that a significant proportion of their new support came from practically motivated and not ideologically committed voters.[42] There were probably too many disparate interests to satisfy with any single package of proposals, but the surest way to alienate a very large number was by treating them exactly as if their support could be taken for granted. And, in fact, in 1979, the PCI lost one and a half million votes—the first time its support had ever declined in a general election.

The PCI also studiously avoided serious analysis of the DC's own altered base of support or of its system of power. Any discussion of the real margins for change, let alone desire for change, in the ruling party was side-stepped. Because the *compromesso storico* was aimed at the entire DC, the strategy's proponents appeared to take that party's "progressive" potential for granted and therefore concentrated their critical fire on the leadership. Because it was not consonant with the goal of broad national unity, the very obvious polarization around the DC and the PCI that took place in 1976 was ignored or completely denied.[43] And only when the Communists had returned to the opposition did they once again acknowledge the most obvious point about Italy's ruling party: its very structure of power, built on thirty-five uninterrupted years of power holding and profligate patronage, makes it the sworn enemy of serious reforms.

## PCI Policies in the Standoff Period (1976–1979)

The most persuasive evidence of all of the leaders' commitment to the strategy is not found in their assumptions but in their behavior, especially when it became clear that the strategy was not working. For that reason, we must examine the party's activities after 1976. By 1978, the Communists could no longer ignore their policies' negative costs. Local elections saw the PCI vote drop everywhere in the country, including cities that were governed by the left. These alarming results caused Berlinguer to call party leaders to Rome. In his review of the situation, he noted, among other things, that the Communists had been much too lenient toward the DC. They had been "generous to the limits of ingenuousness—for our generosity and trust has not been paid back in kind, either by other parties or, especially, by the DC."[44] On the local level, national PCI practices had been slavishly imitated, even though conditions on the periphery were often far different from those obtaining in Rome. From mid-1978, the message became clear: recent preoccupation with political maneuvering on a purely institutional level would have to be balanced by much more attention to the streets and piazzas of Italy, that is, with mass struggle and propaganda.[45] At least in the abstract, some of the traditional left-wing aspects of the *via italiana* were being officially reasserted after a pause of several years.

Berlinguer's criticism of his party's actions, which contained a substantial dose of self-criticism, marked the hardening of the PCI line and a significant redefinition of the *compromesso storico*. It would take two more years for the leadership to conclude that progress would be impossible as long as the DC remained in power, but the real turning point was reached here, with the "clarification" that the strategy should be interpreted to mean a broad consensus which could permit the "alternation" of different governments in power. In short, such alternation was no longer viewed as necessarily leading to a dangerous polarization of society. Now the creation of a coalition of *all* major forces in Italy as an absolute requirement to change society also appears to have gone by the boards. The PCI had not done a total flip-flop to embrace the "left alternative" that the PSI and groups on the left had urged for five years, but there was a hollow ring in its insistence that this new clarification was really just a continuation of the older and more controversial strategy.

In essence, Berlinguer did reiterate the validity of the strategy, while arguing that it had been applied in erroneous fashion—the PCI had been too indulgent toward the DC. But closer examination reveals that this charge is as ingenuous as the local leaders' behavior, and for the same reasons. In the first place, debate within the PCI since the 1976 elections centered precisely—one could almost say exclusively—on how indulgent the party had been and on the degree to which it was subjugating its mass qualities and its long-term goals to a very narrowly defined notion of political bargaining.[46] Moreover, these complaints had led the leadership to take a number of initiatives designed to demonstrate that the party's long-range goals had not been abandoned.[47] They also led a new slogan, which stressed that the PCI was "A Party of Government *and* a Party of Struggle."[48] And these activities were directed toward internal dissatisfaction; the barrages aimed at the PCI from outside the party were, naturally, much more intense and continuous. Mid-1978 was very late indeed to be discovering the limits of the Communists' political activities.

But an even more basic reason to fault Berlinguer's criticism, particularly his attacks on the efforts of local leaders to apply the *compromesso* too slavishly, is that the national leadership had exerted enormous pressure after 1976 to ensure that the broadest possible collaboration with the DC was achieved on the local level. Whenever such broad alliances were achieved, they were publicized prominently in the party daily, *l'Unità*. Even in areas where the left had a majority without the DC, numerous concessions were offered to the Christian Democrats, concessions which frequently enraged the Socialists, who often correctly suspected the Communists of bypassing the PSI to make overtures directly to the DC. And the PCI took such initiatives in all areas of the country, including parts of the South where the local DC often was linked to the Mafia.

These efforts cost the Communist party time and the goodwill of traditional allies and newly won supporters alike. They also frequently led to demoralization and demobilization among the PCI rank and file, who were at best confused by the maneuvers and on many occasions actively dissuaded from any direct attacks on the local DC.[49] Nowhere are the original long-range ambitions of the strategy more apparent, in fact, than in these local actions.

However ill judged and ultimately unproductive the PCI's overtures to the DC on a local level may have been, they were totally consistent with the party's strategic goals. The DC's local power bases are an integral part of the Christian Democratic system of power. If the country's ruling party could not be forced to collaborate and change at that level, it is unlikely that a serious working relationship between the major parties could have been brought about nationally. Moreover, even if some formal arrangement was achieved nationally, it would have proven difficult, if not impossible, to implement against local opposition. Knowledge of this fact drove the PCI to press for local-level alliances with the DC after 1976, then, because such alliances were a necessary part of a long-term collaborative strategy. There is, naturally, room for more or less conciliation or aggressiveness within such a perspective, but there can be no doubt that this is a fundamentally conciliatory strategy, and that is how the PCI—very logically—attempted to apply it.

To argue that the *compromesso storico* failed to achieve its most ambitious aim is not to say that the PCI achieved nothing in the period of participation in the governmental majority between 1976 and 1979. It obtained a series of important symbolic institutional positions that had systematically been withheld since the Communists' expulsion from government in 1947. These included the presidency (i.e., the speakership) of one of the two houses of Parliament, a number of committee chairmanships proportional to the party's electoral strength, and the right to be formally consulted and to meet with the "constitutional parties" on important matters of government and state.

The Communists were also instrumental in forcing the 1978 resignation of Giovanni Leone, the scandal-ridden Christian Democratic president of the Republic. Their votes were decisive in the election of his extremely popular successor, Sandro Pertini, a Socialist. PCI firmness during the nearly two months when DC Secretary and former Prime Minister Aldo Moro was held hostage by the Red Brigades contributed, perhaps decisively, to the triumph of those who refused to recognize or negotiate with the terrorists. Finally, with the Communists in a strongly collaborative frame of mind,

Parliament functioned more effectively than it had for a very long time. Several serious reforms were enacted: rent control legislation was modernized (if not fully implemented) after thirty-two years, important powers were devolved to local governmental institutions, the secret services were reformed and reorganized, and abortion was legalized, to name only the most significant. These achievements followed hard-fought compromises, but most of them could not have been obtained before 1976.

Yet, in spite of a record that most neutral observers would have to call respectable, the PCI rapidly found itself in deep trouble. This was partly because of the unrealistically high expectations that accompanied the Communists' entry into the majority, expectations that PCI propaganda fueled by its lavish and extensive celebrations of even minor achievements.

But not all of the Communists' limitations were attributable to their sometimes careless propaganda. Some of the government's initiatives—especially in the critical area of economic policy—were devoid of real content. A 1977 economic program, a law on industrial reconversion, and a measure to provide jobs for young people all promised far more than they delivered. The PCI did not strengthen its position by greeting them with excessive fanfare, but the real problem was not one of image. Moreover, even those reforms which were substantial met with enormous obstacles and complications in their practical implementation: rent reform and abortion, predictability, proved much easier to set down on paper than to put into practice.

But the most damage of all was probably done by the fact that the PCI's presence in the majority did nothing at all to suggest a badly needed change in the *style* of Italian politics. The political balance of power and the decision to follow a policy of "small steps" (*piccoli passi*) to achieve full legitimation probably made stasis unavoidable. And it was certainly the case that the DC, fully aware of the PCI's goals, did all it could to stall and, in the colorful words of a communist leader, "roast us over a slow fire."[50] Still, for a party whose image had always depended on appearing to be different from the others, identification with "politics as usual" is extremely harmful. There had been numerous early-warning signs, but the PCI proved unwilling, or unable, to heed them.

*A Special Problem (I): The Unions.* The most dramatic of these early-warning signs took place late in 1977, when the militant metalworkers' union (FLM, *Federazione Lavoratori Metalmeccanici*) precipitated a governmental crisis against the PCI's wishes.[51] Consonant with their strategy, the Communists had strongly discouraged militant union activity following their partial inclusion in the majority. Indeed, the ability to guarantee a labor truce had been a strong communist bargaining chip, and the party had tried to play it in 1976–1978. But as it became clear that the Communists could not deliver economically, the most militant labor unions became restive. In spite of the presence of a strong PCI component in its ranks, the FLM brushed aside warnings against mass action and gathered in Rome to protest the government's economic policies. The presence of so many workers in the streets (estimates ranged up to two hundred thousand) forced the PCI's hand, and it demanded full participation in the governing coalition, namely cabinet posts. After a drawn-out governmental crisis in which the PCI was promised— and accepted—more limited concessions,[52] the DC simply re-presented a list of the same old faces for parliamentary approval. The Communists were humiliated; their only alternative at that point would have been to vote down the government and precipitate new elections. They decided to vote for the new cabinet and were given a reprieve of sorts by the Moro kidnapping, which occurred on the day of the confidence vote. But the party's image and confidence were badly bruised by the entire affair, which poignantly underscored the limitations of being caught between government and opposition.

*A Special Problem (II): "Red" Terrorism and the PCI's Reaction.* The Moro kidnapping pointed to an issue which haunted the PCI throughout the 1970s: left-wing terrorism. Here was a phenomenon that grew steadily worse as the decade progressed and that was guaranteed to hurt the Communists no matter how they reacted. For a long time, they refused to admit that such a thing as left terrorism even existed in Italy. Obsessed with their own legitimation, they claimed that it was a plot hatched by Fascists masquerading as leftists, by foreign (or domestic) intelligence services, or by combinations of the above. The aim of the plot was to discredit the left and to equate it with extremism. Since this is exactly what the DC was attempting to do, the charge did have a certain degree of persuasiveness. Unfortunately, long after the evidence had become overwhelming that organizations such as the Red Brigades, Front Line, and others really existed, the PCI continued to insist that the entire issue was a smokescreen.

On the other hand, once the Communists acknowledged that there really were "red" terrorists, they immediately staked out such a hard-line position that they alienated most of the left—while, of course, not really reassuring those on the right who lumped the whole left together and thus continued to hold the PCI at least indirectly responsible for terrorism. In each period, the party's reactions were mainly dictated by concern for its own legitimation. Its behavior in this second phase, which began late in 1977, was a conscious policy, in its leaders' own words, of "scorching the earth" around the terrorists. Whoever failed utterly and unequivocally to condemn terrorism with an enthusiasm equal to the PCI's was viewed as insufficiently committed to democracy and perhaps even suspected of harboring sympathies for the Red Brigades. Given the Italian political dynamic, this meant that many young people, left-wing unionists, and civil libertarians were tarred by the Communists' brush. Substantial segments of the Socialist party, as well as the smaller parties of the left and most independent intellectuals, were appalled by the zeal of the PCI's law-and-order campaign in the late 1970s.

It is highly ironic, but indicative of the Communists' dilemma, that on the one issue where the PCI could by no stretch of the imagination be called indecisive, it found itself in a no-win situation. What is interesting for our present purposes is that party leaders genuinely did not appear to recognize that they were caught in a cul-de-sac. PCI inflexibility was above all required by the domestic aims of the *compromesso*, but it also grew out of the party's "normal" way of orienting its rank and file. Leaders argued at the time that the PCI—because of its mass base—simply could not afford hair-splitting and excessive subtlety in the line it laid down. This might upset intellectuals, but they do not have to orient tens of thousands of activists and millions of voters. There is some truth in this argument, but even at face value, it assigns a rather limited reasoning capacity to party militants and supporters. In fact, with its return to the opposition in the 1980s, the PCI did begin to discuss issues related to civil liberties and due process in a more genuinely open fashion, but by then lasting damage had been done.

Taken individually, the party's many difficulties and blunders could easily be attributed to the extremely complex situation in Italy at the end of the 1970s, and no assessment of the period should ignore the limited options available to all the actors. There is, however, simply too much evidence of conscious policy choices that were either simply wrong, or else based on extremely limited readings of reality, to attribute the PCI's main problem to conditions over which it had no control.

Ultimately, the strongest evidence of the Communists' profound inability to grasp the new issues that faced them in the 1970s can be found in their reproposal of a thirty-year-old strategy as if events since 1947 had not radically altered the terms in which the problems of the country had to be understood. As it has always done, the PCI subjugated everything, from its alleged underlying analysis of society to its short- and medium-term goals, to its political goal—in this instance the creation of a government of national unity. For this reason, in spite of its profligate use of the term *crisis*, it remains unclear just what sort of crisis the PCI really perceived in Italy; we only know that it insisted that the only way out of the crisis was broad collaboration among the country's major political forces. As many astute observers have pointed out, such an approach, ironically, has the effect of understating the seriousness of the crisis by claiming that the basic solution is to be found in institutional rearrangements rather than deep structural changes.[53]

These considerations also help us understand why the Communists found it so hard to spell out and fight concretely for a limited (but clear) set of reforms. And the price the party ultimately paid for its inability to indicate its short-term goals, or to link its daily actions with any longer-range goals, was high indeed. New voters became disaffected and soon abandoned the PCI. And rank-and-file militants, initially confused, later became demoralized and demobilized, with predictable results for the operations of the party machinery.

## The Organizational Dimensions of the Transitional Crisis

Because so much of my study of the Turinese Federation will involve an in-depth analysis of the party organization, a discussion of the evolution and operations of the machinery of the PCI is best postponed until then (Chapter 2 and especially Chapters 5–7). For the purposes of this introduction, it will suffice to mention the most important contributing factors to the crisis of the late 1970s.

Particularly in the roughest period for the Communists (1977–1979), rank-and-file demobilization would be serious enough to impede the normal functioning of the party organization. But matters were compounded greatly by the fact that this was not a normal or stable period in the life of the party. Rarely, in fact, had the PCI's organizational structures been exposed to as many strains as they had to confront by the late 1970s. Ironically, many of these strains were the product of communist achievements, most notably the electoral victories of 1975 and the organizational advances of the mid-1970s.

How could undeniable successes produce severe tensions within the party structure? First, the growth of membership reversed a decline and stagnation that had not been significantly interrupted for a decade and a half (see Table 1.2). The waves of new members revitalized existing grass-roots organizations and caused many others to be created from scratch. All these structures required leadership, but experienced and available cadres were very few in number. In a relatively brief period, there was an enormous turnover of low-level leaders throughout the party, with the very rapid injection into the ranks of new people who were much more heterogeneous than had ever been the case in the past. The most extensive study of its kind has shown that more than two-thirds of the PCI's rank-and-file leadership at the end of the 1970s was recruited to

*Table 1.2.* PCI and FGCI Membership, 1955–1985

|      | PCI Members | PCI Recruits | FGCI Members |
|------|-------------|--------------|--------------|
| 1955 | 2,090,006   | 158,062      | 394,314      |
| 1956 | 2,035,353   | 156,698      | 358,126      |
| 1957 | 1,825,342   | 96,064       | 245,199      |
| 1958 | 1,818,606   | 115,767      | 241,747      |
| 1959 | 1,789,269   | 116,390      | 229,703      |
| 1960 | 1,792,974   | 141,965      | 211,634      |
| 1961 | 1,728,620   | 132,050      | 221,042      |
| 1962 | 1,630,550   | 105,159      | 182,916      |
| 1963 | 1,613,016   | 129,782      | 173,701      |
| 1964 | 1,636,416   | 139,386      | 173,699      |
| 1965 | 1,610,696   | 122,159      | 173,465      |
| 1966 | 1,571,335   | 108,206      | 154,485      |
| 1967 | 1,530,405   | 102,435      | 135,510      |
| 1968 | 1,495,662   | 98,067       | 125,438      |
| 1969 | 1,495,756   | 101,206      | 68,648       |
| 1970 | 1,498,367   | 105,867      | 66,451       |
| 1971 | 1,510,502   | 112,627      | 85,760       |
| 1972 | 1,573,956   | 151,118      | 111,735      |
| 1973 | 1,611,073   | 137,198      | 116,335      |
| 1974 | 1,643,716   | 132,774      | 118,972      |
| 1975 | 1,715,195   | 155,854      | 133,834      |
| 1976 | 1,797,597   | 170,966      | 142,200      |
| 1977 | 1,797,075   | 129,351      | 127,143      |
| 1978 | 1,772,425   | 100,438      | 113,509      |
| 1979 | 1,740,389   | 92,536       | n.a.         |
| 1980 | 1,732,487   | 88,913       | n.a.         |
| 1981 | 1,696,085   | 80,216       | n.a.         |
| 1982 | 1,657,344   | 66,365       | 55,037       |
| 1983 | 1,620,777   | 62,312       | 48,778       |
| 1984 | 1,605,929   | 63,704       | 44,920       |
| 1985 | 1,581,481   | 60,293       | 46,690       |

*Source:* Official published party statistics.

the party after 1969.[54] Because of the earlier stagnation, there had been only a limited leadership turnover at the intermediate levels of the party since the early 1960s.

Only in the aftermath of the hot autumn did large-scale replacement begin. By the mid-1970s, the normal aging process made a massive turnover imperative. While the party's growth provided the raw material for this process, the bulk of the new leaders was lacking in significant party experience. Thus, precisely when—because of the difficult strategy being assayed—a strong measure of continuity in the vitally important intermediate levels of the party structure would have helped ease tensions, the PCI found its resources doubly strained.

Finally, the local electoral victories of 1975 seriously exacerbated the leadership vacuum, as well as the other strains on the local organizations. The PCI suddenly found itself catapulted into governing responsibilities everywhere in the country, including the largest urban complexes with their intractable problems.[55] In these newly won areas, the most experienced cadres were almost always moved en masse out of their organizational posts and into local governmental office. And this shift further aggravated the already serious pressures on the local parties, for it created a near vacuum in their organizations. Extensive studies carried out by the PCI's own research organization testify to the rapid turnover and often disruptive generational differences that resulted from these moves.[56]

My examination of the Turinese party organization will show the degree to which leadership turnover was especially severe, for in Turin the PCI's electoral advances in 1975 were exceptional. But the whole party was affected by the problem of cadre formation and turnover. An indication of the seriousness with which this phenomenon was viewed is the fact that the National Party School Section of the PCI held three national conferences in the thirty years between 1945 and 1975 and then proceeded to hold two conferences between 1976 and 1977. The last of these specifically addressed the problems involved in creating cadres capable of handling the new burdens facing the PCI in the wake of its electoral victories and organizational expansion.[57]

Most indicative of the attention the problem was receiving is the extensive coverage of the new corps of middle-level leaders found in the party press from the middle of 1977.[58] A great variety of organizational problems was raised, but central to most arguments was the way the new leaders differed from their predecessors. Their largely white collar and intellectual origins implied diminished ties to the traditional rank and file, and particularly to the working class. These sociological differences often raised concerns about the potential for an identity crisis in the party's ranks. And different political experiences were seen as the harbingers of a possible "loss of historical memory" for the PCI: recent recruits did not go through the party's formative periods and therefore lacked a comprehensive sense of its history, struggles, and defeats. In the late 1970s, they had only directly experienced the PCI's and the left's victories, and concern was expressed that they might have little to fall back on when the going got rougher.

How do the Communists' organizational difficulties after 1975 compare to earlier troubled periods? Because organizational discontinuity or instability can take several forms, it is hard to single out discrete episodes in the party's history with the same facility that we were able to apply to ideological-strategic or political crises. Ideology, strategy, and domestic politics, by definition, occur on a single, partywide level. The organization, in contrast, exists on many levels, and these do not necessarily change simultaneously. Gross changes at the rank-and-file level are not always accompanied by the turnover of intermediate cadres. Or very significant changes might take place at the lowest reaches of the organization, but these can be spread over a relatively long time period, which obviously would mitigate their impact. Is it proper, in such cases, to speak of a crisis at all? If so, is it not at least necessary to qualify this crisis in terms of its intensity?

That this is not a purely abstract point can be seen with a glance at PCI membership trends. As Table 1.2 shows, total membership fell by roughly six hundred fifty thousand between the mid-1950s and the end of the 1960s (while the Youth Federation fell by more than three hundred thousand and all but disappeared). For the party, the drop was dramatic—two hundred sixty-five thousand—in the turbulent years of 1955 to 1957; over the next dozen years, the decline was more or less steady and totaled three hundred thirty thousand. It is technically accurate, but not very helpful, to speak of the entire decade and a half as an extended organizational crisis. It is much more accurate to speak of a true crisis in the mid-1950s, and of debilitating stagnation and decline for a decade beginning in the late 1950s. Thus, if we speak strictly in terms of the mass membership, there have been only two full-fledged organizational crises in the PCI: 1945–1947, when the mass party came into being and a million and a half new members flooded the organization, and then in 1956–1957 during the aftershocks of the Twentieth Congress's denunciations of Stalin, followed shortly thereafter by the Hungarian revolt. The net rise of three hundred thousand in the 1970s, concentrated in the middle of the decade, generated serious strains, but certainly not on the order of the two earlier episodes.

But if we define the party's organizational crisis in broader terms, and include cadre turnover as well as mass membership trends, the 1970s—and, for that matter, the 1950s—appear in a different light. At least where the recruitment and turnover of new cadres was substantial—this would especially include those areas where the PCI became a ruling local party in 1975[59]—a true crisis in the organization was likely. Historically, the greatest turnover period once again would appear to be 1944 to 1947, the truly formative years of the *partito nuovo*. The only other significant period of cadre turnover in the PCI's modern history before the late 1970s took place in the 1950s, when the party bureaucracy was de-Stalinized under significant pressure from the central leadership.[60] It is interesting and of great importance to note that this turnover did not coincide with the peak period of ideological turmoil and the huge drop in mass membership (1956–1957). It took place on a massive scale a few years later, peaking between 1959 and 1961. This lag drew out the impact of the de-Stalinization crisis, but it also obviously softened its impact on the party. Moreover, since the "new" leaders of the late 1950s were veterans of party activity who had joined the PCI during the Resistance or in the late 1940s, we can see that there was in fact a good deal of continuity within the organization in this troubled period. In the late 1970s, the various crises hit the party almost simultaneously; hence, while the net impact of this period was undoubtedly less traumatic than de-Stalinization, it was certainly very severe.

## Conclusions

This chapter has had three major goals. First, and most broadly, it needed to show that the PCI faced a transitional crisis in the late 1970s. On the heels, and to a great extent because of its own successes, the party was able to move aggressively to break out of nearly thirty years in the political wilderness in Italy. This move exacerbated the strategic crisis that had lain dormant since the 1960s and generated a political crisis that was a deeper reflection of the stalemate among the major parties in the country. Simultaneously, the PCI's organizational structures, obeying their own dynamic but deeply affected by these other developments, underwent excessive strains.

Secondly, I have tried to show how each aspect of the larger crisis was grounded not simply in the party's response to external forces and stimuli, which were numerous and powerful, to be sure, but in the inherent limits of the PCI itself. The demands of the 1970s called forth a strategic response—the *compromesso storico*—that the leadership faithfully followed until it proved totally unworkable. The depth of the leaders' commitment to the strategy is evident from the tenacity with which they followed it long after they received great quantities of negative feedback. The political conjuncture was extremely difficult, but the evidence that the party followed the strictures of the historic compromise is too systematic, and too overwhelming, to attribute its difficulties exclusively, or even primarily, to forces beyond its control. This is perhaps less true of the strictly organizational aspects of the crisis, where a very large number of stresses and pressures piled up simultaneously. But even here, some of the PCI's most ingrained (and unexamined) reflexes and practices deeply aggravated an already problematic situation.

Finally, this chapter was required as a national context against which events and developments in Turin need to be assessed. For all of Turin's special characteristics and exaggerated dynamics, the PCI there had to operate under the constraints of the party's national strategic and political choices. The local party organization has many unique qualities, but the guiding model, as everywhere in Italy, remains the *partito nuovo*, and most of the worst serious difficulties encountered in the machinery of the Turinese PCI were also experienced throughout the rest of the country. To forget this in an analysis of the Turinese federation is to fall into the classic error of neglecting the forest for the trees.

# 2

# Workers and Communists in Turin, 1945–1980

Anyone even passingly familiar with modern Italian history, and particularly the history of the Italian working class, needs little introduction to Turin.[1] Since the beginning of this century, it has been an obligatory reference point for Italian capitalism and for the workers' movement. Thus, its choice as research site hardly needs an extended justification of its importance to contemporary Italy. But it is also worth emphasizing at the outset that the one claim that cannot be made with reference to Turin is that it is representative of the rest of Italy. Of course, Italy's political geography is so complex and varied that no single province, or even region, is able to encompass the country's diverse levels of development and political traditions.[2] Yet even within the great variations that make up the whole of Italy, Turin is an exceptional case. It is the center of the most highly industrialized part of the country. Its industrial profile, moveover, is abnormally skewed, and this imbalance has had a profound effect on both its class structure and its politics. The dominant sector of the Turinese economy has represented the cutting edge of the entire Italian economy in the postwar period, thereby magnifying the area's importance and the intensity of its problems.

Turin, because of these qualities, is widely recognized as a social and political laboratory. Solid methodological arguments can be marshalled in favor of the extreme example as the best candidate for a case study,[3] but it is most of all the Communist party's trajectory here that makes it an excellent focus for our purposes. Reduced to an almost purely agitational role by the end of the 1950s and well into the 1960s, the local PCI was nearly swept away in the early phases of the hot autumn, which had one of its epicenters in the Piedmontese capital. The party eventually rode out the storm and went on to reap enormous political and organizational benefits, but its position was precarious. It had become the dominant political force, but it sat astride a society—and a labor force for which it allegedly spoke—that were extremely volatile and ill suited to the goals of the *compromesso storico*. Moreover, the Turinese PCI's own deeply entrenched traditions and experience as a classical oppositional force made this shift doubly difficult. If the inherent tensions in the PCI's strategy and organization came to the fore everywhere in Italy after 1975, few places would see them so clearly drawn as Turin.

Turin has been the site of extreme class polarization and conflict since the beginning of this century; in the period following World War I, it was known as "Italy's Petrograd." Much has changed since then, but the fact that Turin is the center of the Italian automotive industry remains the key to understanding its role. The auto industry was the engine that drove Italy's development after World War II. It did this impressively, but with devastating and ultimately explosive side effects. Runaway industrialization and urbanization were tied to immense waves of internal migration from South to North. The dominance of a single industry and, within that industry, of a single firm (Fiat) further exacerbated an already difficult situation. Italian capitalism's model of development probably triumphed here in its most distilled form by the 1960s. But this distillation also left as a legacy a middle class limited in size and importance and a disproportionately large and volatile mass of workers and subproletarians.

How was it possible to create such a volatile mass, and why did it take until the late 1960s for matters to come to a head, given the proud history of the Turinese working class? To understand Italian capitalism's triumph in Turin through the 1960s, one also must understand the defeats and failures of the workers' movement in the same period. At the end of the war, Turin was a bastion of the parties of the left and a redoubt of militant trade unionism. Within five years, the left had been chased from power; within a decade, its organization was crumbling, and militant unionism was routed in the factories. These disasters were the result of conscious policies of repression carried out by the most aggressive branches of Italian capitalism, aided considerably by the Italian state. They were also very much the product of the left's inability to abandon outmoded ideas and come to terms with the immense changes taking place all around it. The organizational forms, ideology, and behavior of the Turinese workers' movement were consolidated during the heady days of the hot autumn, which represented the high point of the movement's reawakening in the 1960s. But the earlier defeats were a prior, and powerful, shaping force as well.

## The *Città–Fabbrica* (Factory City)

> Turin is not the capitalist city par excellence, but the industrial and proletarian city par excellence. The Turinese working class is compact, disciplined, and *distinctive* as in very few cities in the world. Turin is like a single factory: its working population is of a single type, and it is strongly unified by industrial production.[4]

Turin after World War II did not, of course, bear much resemblance to revolutionary Petrograd, nor even to the Turin of the Factory Councils and Red Guards of 1919–1920. As Fiat's expansion into national and world markets led to the parallel growth of subsidiary and related industries, observers were increasingly likely to draw comparisons with an altogether different but far more appropriate model—Detroit. The purpose here is not, however, to go into the details of the political economy of Turin, or Italy, in the postwar period. It is, first, to provide some sense of the dimensions of Turin's growth and the effects this had on the socioeconomic and political fabric of the city and its environs. That, in turn, will permit us to comprehend why the fortunes of the Turinese left have followed a distinctive trajectory for the past thirty and more years.

Fiat had long been a dominant force in Piedmont, but only in the decade following the war did it come to be the colossus of the Italian economy.[5] By 1949, with seventy-five thousand vehicles produced, it exceeded its prewar high; by 1950, the figure rose to more than one hundred thousand. In the ensuing decade, specialization in the production of subcompact cars within the reach of middle-class, and then working-class, pocketbooks saw the total quadruple. As is also evident from these numbers, the 1950s witnessed the complete triumph of mass-production, assembly-line techniques, at the expense of the skilled workers and the unions. By the end of the 1960s, Fiat was producing nearly one and a half million cars a year, with more than a third destined for export. The company had become a multinational giant, and most of its two hundred thousand Italian employees were found in and around Turin. The massive Mirafiori works, a three-square-kilometer complex just inside the city's southern limits, alone accounted for sixty-eight thousand employees by the end of the 1960s, making it by far Italy's largest factory (and one of the five largest in the world). In the industrial suburbs of the capital, the Fiat Rivalta plant, with seventeen thousand employees, was the second largest in the country.

In citing these figures, we have not even mentioned the firm's involvement in aeronautical, marine, or locomotive production, machine tools, or metallurgy. Nor have we included the myriad industries which inevitably blossom in the shadow of a giant, either as subcontractors of specialized parts and accessories or as independent producers of related goods (in this case ranging from electronics through tools and tires). There are, of course, many other highly important corporations operating out of or close to Turin, and several of these have their own glorious traditions; some major textile manufacturers remain there, and Olivetti, a world leader in its own right, is nearby. But when one thinks of Turin, Fiat comes most prominently to mind.

There certainly is no doubt about this in the minds of the local population. In the midst of the boom, more than half the city lived directly from Fiat, with many others indirectly dependent.[6] Turin had begun as a strongly proletarian area, and this quality was reinforced throughout the period of greatest growth. Out of a total provincial population of two and quarter million, there were five hundred thousand industrial workers, three-quarters of whom were concentrated in the metropolitan area of the capital. Over half the active population of the capital, and nearly two-thirds of the active population of the industrial belt, were industrial workers. Seven out of ten were found in the metalworking sector of industry, and nearly eight out of ten were found in medium and large factories, those with five hundred or more employees.[7]

We have seen that industrial expansion went hand in hand with a demographic explosion. No large city in Italy grew faster than Turin in the 1950s, when its population increased by more than 40 percent.[8] By the 1960s, Southerners had become the large majority of new arrivals, exacerbating the cultural and semiracial aspects of an already grim set of urban problems. In the peak years of growth around the turn of the decade between the 1950s and 1960s, the capital city alone, with a population under a million, had to absorb between sixty thousand and eighty-five thousand new immigrants a year. Between the 1951 and 1971 censuses, the population of the greater Turin area (Turin plus the twenty-three cities in the primary industrial belt) doubled.[9] By the beginning of the 1970s, Turin had the third largest concentration of Southerners in Italy. The first decade of mass immigration had brought, primarily, single male workers; in the 1960s, migration predominantly involved entire families. There were grave problems associated with each wave, but the second, because it indicated more permanent population shifts, brought all of the latent social tensions to the fore. Italian capitalism needed masses of unskilled workers to grow, and it happily and quite openly recruited them from the more desolate regions of the country. But the big firms and the successive local governments who bragged so much about the march of progress in Turin provided very little housing, educational infrastructure, or any of the other social services that would have been required to keep pace with industrial and urban development.

## Party and Unions from the Reconstruction to the Hot Autumn

The dizzying expansion of Italy's leading firms and the geometric growth in output that led people to speak of an "economic miracle" obviously had to involve profound changes in the productive process. For the country as a whole, and for Turin in particular, these changes involved mass-production, assembly-line techniques, which were, of course, totally congruent with the flood of unskilled, politically unsophisticated workers who poured into the major cities in search of work. And these techniques, along with the entrepreneurial dynamism that promoted them, were anathema to the militant, skilled, and very proud workers who had always been in the vanguard of the Turinese working class.

Because of the strength of this class—reinforced by the Resistance and the bitter but heady struggles of the immediate postwar period—Italian capitalism faced a daunting challenge. The left, and the PCI in particular, was entrenched in the industrial centers of the North, especially in the largest factories. Left-wing unions dominated the shopfloors, left-wing governments ran the cities, and the PCI boasted a formidable presence indeed. In 1946, the Turinese Federation claimed more than eighty thousand members, 90 percent of whom were workers; in the same year, seven thousand of the sixteen thousand dependents of Fiat Mirafiori held PCI cards.[10] Although the party was at the time a member of the Government of National Unity, collaboration obviously stopped short of a policy that would consciously liquidate its own mass constituency. How, then, were the industrial leaders able to implement their plans in relatively short order, and how did the workers' movement, led by the Communists, react?

Part of the plan called for a direct onslaught. As the cold war generated extreme polarization, the Communists and Socialists were thrown out of the government in 1947. Within a year, schisms in both the PSI and the left-dominated united union movement, the CGIL (Confederazione Generale Italiana di Lavoratori) meant the secession of Social Democrats in the first case and Christian Democratic, Social Democratic, and other laical non-Marxist unionists in the second case. Whatever hopes the left may have continued to harbor were then definitively smashed in the 1948 elections, which saw the PCI–PSI common list soundly trounced (see Table 1.1). By the early 1950s, the left's domination of local governments outside the red regions of central Italy had been all but erased.

Although it was put on the defensive, the left remained strong in the factories of the North, and it was there that the next phase of the offensive took place. In some instances—and Fiat was one—systematic intimidation and union-busting became the order of the day quite early; this was a generalized policy in any event by the early 1950s.[11] It was obvious that the industrialists' plans could not be realized in the face of intransigent opposition from the unions, for whom most of Italy's captains of industry had little sympathy in any event. They willingly resorted to blatantly discriminatory actions against known or suspected militants, a great many of whom were Communists. These actions ranged from outright firings on the flimsiest of pretexts to systematic harassment. Activists who were not simply sacked found themselves placed in *reparti confino*, "exile shops" hundreds of yards from other areas where numbingly repetitive and meaningless tasks had to be performed all day, every day, in the hope that those subjected to this treatment would quit in disgust.[12] The bulk of the work force was constantly cautioned about the dangers of affiliating with or voting for the left-dominated union. Letters addressed to the relatives of workers would be sent out reminding workers and their families of the benefits that had been obtained without the need to resort to union activities—and warning of the fate waiting for those who actively worked for the union. Such warnings were probably redundant, for there was abundant firsthand evidence of the fate waiting for anyone who got involved in the union, let alone anyone who stood as a candidate in elections to the factories' Internal Commissions. And activists fired from one factory found it nearly impossible to find employment elsewhere. Thus, many of the previously dedicated soon found it prudent to withdraw from any sort of militance. It is not hard to imagine the effect of this atmosphere on new immigrants, many of whom had left their home towns with letters of recommendation signed by the local priest, attesting to the fact that they were good workers with no interest in politics or unions.

Open repression was, however, only part of the explanation for the left's clamorous defeat. The Communists contributed significantly to their own decline in the industrial Northwest in the immediate postwar period. Even before the cold war, their organizational practices were much closer to the classical Leninist-bolshevik model than one might have expected the *partito nuovo* to be. And, more importantly still, the party's overall strategic and ideological outlook was simply unequipped to deal with the new challenges which rapidly arose in postwar Italy. We shall see that organizational and strategic-ideological shortcomings are closely related.

One profound organizational flaw was in the type of local leaders the national party saw fit to impose on the provinces at the end of the war. The Resistance had brought hundreds of thousands of new, young, enthusiastic people into the PCI's ranks, but Togliatti and his collaborators fell back on older and more tested cadres to put the *partito nuovo* on its feet. With hindsight, we can see how the opportunity to avoid at least some of the later traumas of de-Stalinization were missed. Paolo Spriano notes that the overwhelming majority of all PCI federation leaders in the immediate postwar period were not products of the Resistance but had been members of the party since the fascist era, or even earlier. Other documentation from the late 1940s confirms this important observation.[13] In the Turinese case, firsthand testimony makes clear that Rome actively intervened at the end of the war to displace many talented young Resistance leaders from the upper rungs of the hierarchy. The trusted veterans who were installed at the summit were noted for a more sectarian and factory-centered outlook which quickly created serious problems in the Piedmontese capital, not the least of which was the brushing aside of "the partisan commanders and almost all the cadres of the Liberation."[14]

And these old-guard leaders carried out old-guard policies, the most significant of which was the Leninist "transmission belt" doctrine with respect to the PCI's relationship to all flanking organizations, including the trade unions. This tended to make the unions the party's political mouthpiece in the factories, deflecting energy and attention from many of the workers' more immediate concerns. As a communist trade union leader was later to put it, the party at the time viewed the union rank and file as a reserve to be mobilized for its own partisan political ends.[15] Many of the most significant changes introduced in Italian industry were largely ignored except in the most generic way (e.g., strikes against layoffs in one's own or another industry), and, as the cold war intensified, PCI-inspired agitations focused increasingly on broad issues of national and international politics.[16] Far from raising the workers' consciousness, these activities tended to alienate those who were not already persuaded—and even many of the already convinced felt the unions should be addressing industrial and shopfloor problems with more attention.

Finally, and importantly, this practice was the source of considerable division within the organized workers' movement, as well as a ready excuse for management in its savage campaign against militants.

But even had a less hidebound organizational practice and ideology been in force, it is doubtful whether the eventual outcome could have been avoided. For the movement in general, and the Communists in particular, were bogged down in an ideological outlook that made it impossible to grasp the changes that were taking place all around them. The dominant tendency, which could be traced both to vulgar Marxism and to an earlier (and not always accurate) reading of Italian events, was to view Italian capitalism "as pure stagnation and putrefaction," in the words of one leader's critical reflection on the period.[17] Thus, precisely when the work force and the workplace were being radically altered as a result of the dynamism of the industrial system, the left was looking elsewhere, absolutely convinced that Italy's decrepit ruling classes did not have the ability to make capitalism flourish. This helps explain why so many campaigns of the time were generically political and vague: overt political repression, and even reaction, were viewed as the only option open to the ruling class to provide breathing space for a capitalism believed to be in profound, even terminal, crisis.[18] Until the mid-1950s, this outlook dominated all but a few isolated pockets of the party and the unions.

In the mid-1950s, the full dimensions of the left's defeat became clear. The watershed is generally recognized as the elections to the Internal Commissions at Fiat in 1955. The Communist-Socialist Metalworkers' Federation, FIOM (Federazione Impiegati Operai Metalmeccanici), lost its absolute majority that year and even came in second to the Catholic-affiliated union. In the 1956 elections, the FIOM sank to a pathetically weak 24 percent (vs. 63 percent in 1954).[19] Equally significantly, unionism suffered a marked decline at Fiat, as it did in the entire country. For example, while the CGIL could still claim 5 million members in 1949—*following* the cold war schism of 1948—this figure had dropped to 4.2 million in 1954–55 and by 1958 it was down to 2.6 million. In Piedmont, while the work force was more than doubling between 1949 and 1962, the number of workers who joined the CGIL plummeted from more than half a million to just over one hundred and sixty thousand.[20] In roughly the same period, the Turinese PCI went from more than eighty thousand members to thirty thousand, a collapse unrivaled in the rest of the party. In the capital city alone, the drop was from sixty thousand to eighteen thousand; Table 2.1 provides data for the federation in the postwar period. Most significantly of all in terms of the health of the workers' movement in general, the period from 1955 to 1962, the most intense phase of growth for Italian capitalism, did not witness one successful strike in the firm (Fiat) that spearheaded the "economic miracle." In the words of one of the its most acute observers, this marked the worst crisis in the postwar history of the Piedmontese movement: for a time it was an open question regarding whether it would be viable again, or whether it would instead survive only as a sort of "residual organism."[21] The bleakness of the PCI's situation is vividly captured in Castronovo's summary of the Turinese federation at the end of the 1950s:

> The continuous replacement of the leaders of the Turinese organization, . . . the progressive shunting aside of numerous Resistance leaders, the losing strategy of the union as a direct instrument of the party, and the gradual disintegration of the grassroots machinery of the party following discriminatory practices in the factories

*Table 2.1.* Turinese Federation of the PCI: Membership in the Capital City and the Entire Federation, 1946–1984 (Even Years plus 1955 and 1969)

|  | Entire Federation | Capital City | (Pop./Memb.) | Rest of Province |
|---|---|---|---|---|
| 1946 | 81,799 | 60,464 |  | 21,335 |
| 1948 | 73,156 | 55,899 |  | 17,247 |
| 1950 | 63,287 | 47,416 | (15:1) | 15,871 |
| 1952 | 55,347 | 42,059 |  | 13,288 |
| 1954 | 49,424 | 39,323 |  | 10,097 |
| 1955 | 47,882 | 34,554 | (24:1) | 13,328 |
| 1956 | 44,235 | 31,516 |  | 12,719 |
| 1958 | 31,427 | 20,921 |  | 10,506 |
| 1960 | 30,249 | 19,587 | (51:1) | 10,662 |
| 1962 | 29,471 | 18,528 |  | 10,943 |
| 1964 | 32,123 | 18,663 |  | 13,460 |
| 1966 | 29,653 | 16,116 | (69:1) | 13,537 |
| 1968 | 30,255 | 16,011 |  | 14,244 |
| 1969 | 29,815 | 15,239 |  | 14,576 |
| 1970 | 30,900 | 15,089 | (79:1) | 15,811 |
| 1972 | 34,417 | 16,115 |  | 18,302 |
| 1974 | 37,964 | 18,117 |  | 19,787 |
| 1976 | 47,186 | 22,063 | (54:1) | 25,123 |
| 1978 | 46,123 | 21,337 |  | 24,786 |
| 1980 | 45,097 | 20,980 | (55:1) | 24,117 |
| 1982 | 41,208 | 19,020 |  | 22,188 |
| 1984 | 37,906 | 17,293 |  | 20,613 |

*Sources:* Federation Archives and published statistics.

and the repressive measures of Scelba [the Minister of the Interior] wore down, within a few years, the once-formidable force of the PCI in the factories, cooperatives, and social services. The cultural organizations, UDI [the women's organization], and the FGCI were broken, and an ever-deeper gulf between the Communist leaders and their electorate was created. The Turinese Federation continued to operate on a hand-to-mouth basis, reduced to a sort of isolated garrison, with its offices and functionaries, divided by bitter polemics over the causes of and responsibilities for the collapse of the FIOM, the loss of City Hall, and the meager results of too many purely propagandistic campaigns.[22]

We have certainly seen ample evidence to support the conclusion that, if the entire PCI stagnated organizationally from the mid-1950s through much of the 1960s, the party in Turin was nearly obliterated. And if the Center-Left with its reformist promises was a serious threat and led to the strategic paralysis of the party throughout the country, it was utterly traumatic for the Turinese PCI. In fact, while this was not the case in most of the country, it appears more than justified to conclude that the Turinese Communists' second transitional crisis ran from 1955 to 1962 (when renewed strikes at Fiat and throughout the industry signaled the end of near-total isolation). This point is crucial for an understanding of the federation and its institutional memory, for, although it was deeply scarred by the experiences I have been describing, these experiences imposed a rhythm of change on the local party that differed from that in most other places. To cite but one example, party and union alike realized how poorly they had been served by the sectarian leadership entrenched ever since the

Liberation. Wholesale changes in the leadership—alluded to above in Castronovo's quote—took place several years before the replacement of the old guard elsewhere.[23] If the Turinese PCI avoided the worst aspects of organizational de-Stalinization, this was because it attacked the problem earlier and for different—though related—reasons.

As this point alone should make clear, Castronovo's summary, although certainly accurate, perhaps exaggerates the wholly negative legacy of the 1950s and early 1960s in Turin. Another consequence of the stunning defeat was much greater sensitivity on the part of the local party than the national one to the potentialities of Italian capitalism. Although one certainly cannot claim that leaders of the federation leaped immediately to the appropriate conclusions, it is a fact that the Turinese party moved to the fore, within the PCI, in terms of attention paid both to changes in class composition and to the more dynamic aspects of modern capitalism.[24] In part because of the more clearly defined class divisions in Turin, but also reflecting the bitter lesson of the mid-1950s, the federation was squarely on the left of the party in the internal debates of the mid-1960s. Not surprisingly, it sided with those in the PCI who were less inclined to dismiss the reformist possibilities of Italian capitalism, and it also came down hard in opposition to the national party leadership's extremely vague and broad definition of alliances and reforms. As we will see, during the period of the *compromesso storico*, many local leaders continued to stress the importance of setting out a clear program based on a much more precise analysis than the national leadership was willing, or able, to produce.

Finally, although there is some danger in emphasizing what a party did *not* do or become, the Turinese case is worth the risk, in my opinion. A party with an over-whelmingly proletarian composition which suffers a crushing defeat could all too easily retreat, in consummate sectarian fashion, "into the fortress," to use Louis Althusser's memorable phrase in reference to French Communist behavior.[25] There was in fact a great temptation to retreat into an isolated working-class purity from the mid-1950s on in Turin, and some of the most charismatic leaders of the federation were known to hold this position. That this option did not prevail, and that the local party has espoused a more outward-looking perspective ever since the mid-1950s, is no mean achievement, all things considered.

## Summary: Class and Party on the Eve of the Hot Autumn in Turin

It should be clear by now that the Turinese Federation of the PCI has a distinct political-organizational personality that does not quite conform to most stereotypes. Given its environment and social composition (roughly 80 percent of the membership has historically come out of the factories),[26] there is, of course, a very strong strain of "workerism" (*operaismo*) in the party and in the workers' movement generally. This phenomenon can perhaps best be defined as the tendency to see all virtue residing in the factories and, further, to view labor-management relations as a model applicable to the entire society as well as the workplace.[27] But, as we have seen, it is not a hermetic, defensive, or essentially apolitical outlook. It reflects the union's and the party's broad, ambitious, and activist traditions.

It also reflects and has been reinforced over time by the notable organizational weakness in a volatile and competitive setting of both the PCI and the workers' movement in Turin.[28] Unable to count on the organized, organic adherence of more than a tiny fraction of the working class, workers' organizations in Turin are forced constantly to legitimize themselves to their constituents by proving they can lead struggles in defense of class interests. Their ideal operating conditions are highly conflictual in tone and strongly oppositional in content.

We have seen how the defeats of the 1950s forced party and union alike to shift their focus much more explicitly to the working class and its problems inside and outside the factory gates.[29] This meant an end to the idea of the "transmission belt," an obvious precondition before anyone outside the PCI would take seriously the notion of a reunited union movement. With some internal resistance to the idea, both party and union set out to lay the groundwork for future unity by guaranteeing maximum autonomy between their respective organizations. Moreover, in view of the alarming situation in the factories, reinforcement of the unions became the top priority wherever a working class of any size existed. This was a logical policy, dictated by necessity: the unions were in the "front lines" and in daily contact with workers and their problems. One of the major results of these twin policies, especially where the PCI was weak, was the creation of a severe identity problem for the party inside the factories. By design, the bulk of its working-class cadres moved into union activities, leaving the party proper with few militants and a very uncertain role on the shopfloor. One of the most acute observers of party-union relations has labeled this policy decision "the unionization of the PCI."[30] Even where the PCI enjoys a powerful organization and social presence, this policy created problems when the factories erupted at the end of the 1960s.[31] Where the party was very weak, as in Turin, its vulnerability was that much greater. To cite a single, telling statistic, in 1968, the PCI section in Fiat Mirafiori numbered a mere 216 out of a total workforce of well over sixty thousand.

The party's relationship to society as a whole was equally shaky through the 1960s in purely organizational terms, and this structural weakness helps us understand why it was necessary for the Turinese PCI to adopt a highly activist posture. In the capital city and the federation as a whole, the party is saddled with one of the highest voter-to-member ratios in all of Italy.[32] This means that the Togliattian *partito nuovo*, with its emphasis on a strong social presence, is a pipe dream in the Piedmontese capital. By PCI standards, the Turinese federation can barely be considered a mass organization at all, even though forty-five thousand members in an area embracing 2.2 million people compares favorably with other Western mass parties with voluntary membership enrollments.

This brings us again to the distinctive identity of the party in Turin. It is an extremely weak communist federation that does not behave like other weak federations (which are frequently much stronger in relative terms).[33] In areas where the PCI is chronically weak, such as most of the South and the Catholic Northeast, it has never gained more than a toehold in society, and it only manages to do so outside the working class among more marginal strata. In Turin and a few other large northern urban centers, the situation is quite different. Here, the party was forcibly *expelled* after being deeply entrenched and even playing a dominant role in society. The society itself was pulverized by the logic of advanced capitalism, which undermined the roots of many traditional modes of mass organization. And the party was also uprooted by force and as a result of its own misjudgments.

To appreciate the difference between these two sorts of weakness, one can consult the electoral statistics. Even at the time of its organizational nadir in 1968, the PCI obtained 30 percent of the vote in the general elections held that year. This was 5 percent more than its national average. In contrast, in the Catholic "white regions," where the vote-to-member ratio is far stronger than in Turin, the party has always commanded much less popular support. In 1976, it reached its all-time high, but that was 23 percent, more than eleven points below the national average (in Turin, the 1976 vote was more than 6 percent above the average). It should thus be clear that the extremely high voter-to-member ratio in Turin is not simply a sign of terrible weakness. It really reflects a very high degree of public acceptance in a society where such consensus cannot be translated—for many reasons touched upon above—into organizational strength.

All these factors combined to give the Turinese PCI a distinctive modus operandi that enabled it to survive the 1960s and then to flourish during the aftermath of the hot autumn—until the rise of the historic compromise and the policies described in Chapter 1. Rarely the initiator of union or urban mobilizations, the local party usually joined them and at least in part was able to direct their activities once they were under way. It made a special and largely successful effort to redirect those unions with strong ties to the PCI toward goals which were at least not incompatible with those of the party.[34] When mass mobilizations arose which it could not lead—and this frequently occurred in urban agitations in which the extraparliamentary left was prominent—grassroots militants of the party were almost inevitably in the thick of the action, at times in defiance of pressures from the federation leadership. In fact, in spite of their occasional discomfort at riding the tiger of social protest, the local party leaders did not mind emerging, time and again, as the most articulate and politically effective spokesmen of demands emanating from these mass movements. As weak as the local party may be, it has always been far more entrenched in society than any other political force; as the dominant actor on the left, it was clearly an obligatory reference point for demands for change.

The Turinese PCI moved ahead as a mobilizer and aggregator of dissent, becoming the central opposition to the way the city had developed since the 1950s and the way it had been governed by the DC. If there was ever a classical opposition party, this was it. The passage into a governing role at all levels in 1975 would create extraordinary difficulties under the best of circumstances. Add a national strategy that played down social mobilization and emphasized institutional solutions and collaboration with the DC, and thus clashed head-on with some of the most deeply rooted, defining characteristics of the local party and organized workers' movement, and the likelihood of a very severe test becomes even greater.

## Political Changes in Turin after the Hot Autumn

The details of labor's hot autumn of 1969 and the related mass mobilizations of the 1968–1972 cycle of struggles would take us far afield of our present purposes. These events have in any case been documented, analyzed, and interpreted extensively both for Turin and for the rest of the country.[35] We can limit our discussion here to a very broad overview, first of the way various pressures mounted and then erupted in Turin, and then of the way the political balance of the area was affected by the events.

In 1962, the long drought of significant labor militance ended with a vengeance during the renewal of the metalworkers' contract at Fiat. The Social-Democratic UILM (Unione Italiana di Lavoratori Metalmeccanici), which had been the major union at Fiat since the latter part of the 1950s and had often signed sweetheart contracts with the firm, ignored signs of increasing rank-and-file discontent and militance and signed a contract. After a highly successful series of strikes, militant workers, joined by many young people, stormed UILM headquarters in downtown Turin. Several days of violent clashes between the police and demonstrators ensued, signaling the end of the labor peace upon which so much of the Turinese boom had been built.[36]

These "Facts of Piazza Statuto," named for the location of UILM headquarters, were of immense significance. Most important of all, labor militance had returned to Fiat. But beyond this, many of the strikers and demonstrators were members of the younger generation which had heretofore been quiescent; moreover, significant numbers of Southerners joined both the strike and the protests. Finally, the demonstrations attracted considerable public support (because of extreme police brutality in one of the city's major public squares). As the 1960s proceeded, it was increasingly clear that the mass worker had become a protagonist of this new upsurge of militance. Unlike the traditional party and union vanguard in the factories, which was made up of the more skilled craftsmen and specialized workers, the unskilled or semiskilled mass workers put forward radically egalitarian demands and displayed a notable lack of patience with the cold war divisions that had obstructed unified trade union action for more than a decade.[37] In fact, by the mid-1960s, the drive toward union unity—or reunification—was unmistakable, and Turin, with the metalworkers leading the way, became the major center of united action.

The hot autumn, then, was by no means a complete bolt out of the blue, although its breadth and depth surprised everyone. Inside the factories, it was marked by extremely disruptive agitations which more often than not challenged the entire capitalist organization of the workplace as it then existed. In the broader society, highly successful general strikes in support of many of the workers' most basic demands—pension and wage reform, housing, political rights on the shopfloor—were seen for the first time since the cold war began. All over the country, this upsurge made the unions direct political protagonists, which was natural given the nature of the demands and the fact that the PCI had long since delegated its representative role on the shopfloor to them. In Turin and environs, where extremely weak party and union structures had to confront an exceptionally volatile work force and social setting, the mass actions of the period were more than usually spontaneous, fluid, and difficult to control. And if this was true with respect to the waves of factory-centered agitations, it was doubly the case with the even more amorphous mass movements which arose in the latter phases of the 1968–1972 period. In fact, although the traditional organizations of the workers' movement claimed to be the most authentic interpreters of these movements, they frequently had to scramble to keep up with events. The Communist Party and the unions were ultimately rejuvenated by them, but in the midst of the events themselves, there were times when the traditional structures seemed in danger of being swept away in the radical tide.[38]

While the Turinese PCI's organization continued to stagnate in the 1960s, the party's political fortunes took a turn for the better much earlier. As early as the 1963 general elections, the Communists had recovered from their sharp drop in the late 1950s (see Table 2.2). On the local political scene, the Center-Left never represented the serious threat that it did elsewhere, thanks to a Socialist party that remained strongly left-wing until the 1964 split which created the PSIUP. Only in 1966 was a local edition of the Center-Left finally put in place, and this occurred at high cost to the Socialists' credibility among the working class.[39] And the general elections of 1968, which many saw as the death knell of the Center-Left, certainly offered little comfort to its protagonists in Turin. The Unified Socialist Party (i.e., the PSI and PSDI combined) fell a full 7.5 percent short of its individual components' showing in the previous election. At the same

*Table 2.2.* Votes in General Elections, City of Turin, 1946–1983

(Percentage Obtained by Each List for the Chamber of Deputies)

| | 1946 | 1948 | 1953 | 1958 | 1963 | 1968 | 1972 | 1976 | 1979 | 1983 |
|---|---|---|---|---|---|---|---|---|---|---|
| PDUP/DP | | | | | | | 1.0 | 1.9 | 1.8 | 2.1 |
| PCI | 26.4 | } 37.1 | 27.4 | 22.6 | 27.2 | 30.0 | 30.5 | 40.0 | 34.1 | 34.3[a] |
| PSI | 28.6 | | 10.6 | 13.7 | 13.7 | 16.9 | 9.6 | 9.3 | 9.9 | 9.2 |
| PSIUP | — | — | — | — | — | 4.4 | 1.5 | — | — | — |
| PSDI | — | 13.2 | 9.1 | 9.2 | 10.9 | w/PSI | 7.1 | 3.6 | 4.0 | 3.5 |
| PRI | 0.8 | 0.7 | 0.6 | 1.5 | 0.8 | 1.6 | 4.6 | 4.9 | 5.5 | 10.2 |
| DC | 27.4 | 43.4 | 32.2 | 32.7 | 25.8 | 26.8 | 27.6 | 29.6 | 26.7 | 19.6 |
| PLI | 7.8 | 2.3 | 7.4 | 6.4 | 15.2 | 13.6 | 10.5 | 2.9 | 4.6 | 6.8 |
| MSI | 4.0[b] | 1.4 | 4.0 | 3.2 | 3.3 | 3.3 | 7.1 | 5.3 | 5.6[c] | 6.7 |
| Monarch. | — | 1.0 | 5.1 | 4.4 | 2.0 | 1.4 | — | — | — | — |
| PR | | | | | | | | 2.4 | 6.7 | 4.6 |
| Others | 5.0 | 0.9 | 3.6 | 6.3 | 1.1 | 2.0 | 0.5 | 0.6 | 0.1 | 3.0 |
| Totals | 100.0 | 100.0 | 100.0 | 100.0 | 100.0 | 100.0 | 100.0 | 100.0 | 100.0 | 100.0 |

*a.* Includes PDUP.

*b.* "L'Uomo Qualunque" in 1946; MSI thereafter.

*c.* Includes breakaway Democrazia Nazionale.

*d.* Monarchist rump joined MSI in 1972.

*Key to Abbreviations:* See Table 1.1.

*Sources:* Unione Regionale Province Piemontesi, *Cento anni di voto in Piemonte* (Torino: ILTE, n.d.), p. 53; Federation Archives and *La Stampa*, June 29, 1983, for 1976, 1979, and 1983 figures.

time, the PCI solidified its position as the largest party in the capital, and the PSIUP achieved its national average while maintaining disproportionate influence in the unions. The threatened erosion of the Communists' proletarian base had completely failed to materialize, as, of course, had the promised reforms which would have made that erosion possible. Those reforms, which had so frightened the PCI less than a decade earlier, now became a rallying point against the *Centro-Sinistra*. The frustrations apparent in the militance of the 1960s were being translated into votes for the left opposition.

Increases were most impressive in the industrial suburbs of the province. While the mobilizations were still under way, the undermining of DC electoral hegemony proceeded apace. The 1970 local elections saw the Communists advance everywhere in the province. In the capital, the PCI fell just short of driving the Christian Democrats from power. But in the "first belt" surrounding the capital, where the densest proletarian concentrations of all are found, a veritable rout took place. Prior to 1970, the PCI was in the local *giunta*, or government, of only three of the seventeen most important cities ringing the capital; after 1970, the figure had risen to fourteen, and people could speak of a "red belt" around Turin.

As dramatic as these advances were, they would soon pale when compared with the massive increases of the mid-1970s, when it appeared that the full consequences of the late 1960s came to fruition. The first sign, here as elsewhere, was the 1974 divorce referendum; the province of Turin had the highest no vote in the country (77 percent), and the capital likewise led all of Italy's major cities, with 80 percent. Less than a year later came the "electoral earthquake" of the 1975 local elections, and in Turin this term seemed more than apposite.[40] The Communists swept into power in the capital city and in the provincial and regional assemblies. They took over numerous cities in the hinterland and were returned to power greatly strengthened in the industrial belt as well. The PCI now had 40 percent of the vote in the capital, 37 percent in the province as a whole, and an absolute majority, give or take a few percentage points, in the major centers of the industrial belt. In 1976, the communist vote rose by an additional point or two.

Within half a decade, and hard on the heels of the most radical mass mobilizations of the postwar period, the Turinese PCI found itself thrust into a governmental role. In reality, even before the great gains of the mid-1970s, there had been warnings sounded within the party concerning the difficulties it could expect upon entering local government for the first time. In 1972, the newly elected mayor of an industrial suburb warned his comrades in the federation of the trauma suffered by the local party when it moved into City Hall.[41] The trauma, of course, would be much greater three years later when the entire party had to make a similar transition, and when it had to do so under the aegis of the *compromesso storico*. In 1972, the Turinese party was quite far from the historic compromise, although, as we have seen, Berlinguer was already moving toward it with his appeals to Communists, Catholics, and Socialists. The document that emerged at the congress of the Turinese federation that year reflected the party's leftist tendencies: it called for a "left alternative" that would displace the DC and radically alter the Italian state apparatus.[42]

After 1975, and especially after the PCI's dramatic move toward national power sharing following the 1976 general elections, the problems facing the Communists on a local level proved greater than the party's ability to deal with them. In a phase when new administrations and the party organization needed considerable time (and luck) to consolidate recent advances, they got neither. National considerations, quite understandably, constantly intruded into the local scene, and it was not long before the signs turned almost entirely negative. The strike led by the FLM in late 1977 had already told the party that some of its most presumably trustworthy constituents were restive. But the referenda of 1978 represented the first unmistakable warning to the Turinese federation that it had occupied very shaky ground.[43] The party had sided with the government in support of two contentious laws, and although neither law was actually abrogated, the strength of the negative vote could be seen as a moral victory for the opposition and a severe embarrassment for those, such as the PCI, who had campaigned hard against abrogation. In Turin, the results were especially embarrassing. The vote to abolish the "Legge Reale,"[44] a law on public order, was higher in Turin than anywhere else in north-central Italy except Trieste. And the vote to eliminate the public financing of political parties—which had put the PCI in the untenable position of joining with all other parties while claiming that it alone was different—actually carried in both the capital and the province as a whole.

By the 1979 general elections, Turin's weathervane status was still apparent, but this time the portents were very bad for the Communists. The PCI dropped 4 percent in Italy as a whole—the first time in the history of the Republic that the Communists lost votes between general elections—and 6 percent in Turin. This decline did not totally eliminate the gains of the mid-1970s, but it was a clear signal that the party was in a political crisis. By the 1980 local elections, the PCI was in fact once more in the opposition nationally, and the results were more mixed but generally positive. In the capital, the PCI obtained 39 percent of the vote, which almost equaled its historic high in 1976 and which upped its representation on the city council by two seats, to the surprise of everyone and the delight of the Communists. But this was the exception to a general trend in the province, which saw a partial recuperation of the losses of 1979 but a failure to equal even the 1975 local election results, let alone the high-water mark of 1976. Fortunately for the party, the absolute vote in the industrial belt was high enough to guarantee a continuing dominant role, even with a drop of a few percentage points. Strictly political headaches, in the form of highly contentious coalition squabbles with the Socialists, had begun in the period of the historic compromise and continued through the 1980s, but that is another matter.

## The Fluctuating Vote in the Capital: The PCI's Urban Dilemma

What generalizations follow from the sharp fluctuations in the communist vote in Turin during the period under examination? A study of this type cannot pretend to offer an exhaustive analysis of the evolution of the electorate in the most volatile decade since the war. But at least a limited sense of the party's electoral fortunes is required to fill in the broader picture of the PCI's relationship to Turinese society, especially in light of the very high voter-to-member ratio that has characterized the party since the 1950s. With the proper qualifications, the data at our disposal do provide a number of important insights into the broader picture.

Table 2.3 presents a summary of the PCI vote in the Piedmontese capital in the general elections of the 1970s. The smallest electoral unit available—the *seggio elettorale*, roughly equivalent to a small U.S. precinct or Canadian poll[45]—has been adopted for analysis. Homogeneous *seggi* have been clustered and compared over time to see if clear trends are apparent.

We can see immediately that the working-class vote for the PCI in Turin is quite high and also stable by Turinese standards. If we add the important qualification that the absolute weight of workers' votes in this classically proletarian city is also very high, it is clear that this is the group that has made the decisive contribution to the Communists' success in the capital. Not all workers live in the densely blue-collar districts from which our sample has been drawn, but it is clear where the PCI's most extensive and deeply rooted support is found. At the other extreme are the fluid white-collar categories, whose fluctuations have been much greater than average during the party's rise and

*Table 2.3.* City of Turin: PCI Votes in General Elections, 1972–1979, in Homogeneous Wards (*Seggi Elettorali*)

| | (N) | 1972 | 1976 | Variation 1976/1972 | 1979 | Variation 1979/1976 |
|---|---|---|---|---|---|---|
| Working class | (28) | 42.7% | 54.0% | + .265 | 46.9% | − .131 |
| Public housing projects | (67) | 36.6 | 50.0 | + .366 | 41.4 | − .172 |
| Total city of Turin | (1,667)[a] | 30.5 | 40.0 | + .311 | 34.1 | − .148 |
| White collar | (14) | 23.1 | 35.2 | + .524 | 27.5 | − .219 |
| "Upper class" | (11) | 16.5 | 22.2 | + .345 | 20.3 | − .086 |

a. The number of *seggi* has increased slightly with each election. The total of 1,667 refers to the 1979 general elections.

*Sources:* Calculated from mimeographed statistics and computer printouts of electoral returns provided, respectively, by the Federation and the City of Turin.

decline. When we discuss changes in party membership over the 1970s, we will find that this group—or, more precisely, "clerks and technicians"—has grown most rapidly in relative terms. Hence all the major electoral and organizational indicators point to the increasing importance for the Turinese party of these modern strata so typical of advanced capitalist development.

The table shows the significance to the PCI of another group, residents of public housing. Comprising a tenth of the city's population, these people do not show up clearly in official party statistics, but they certainly are of great importance. They tend to be primarily immigrant in origin and include large numbers of subproletarian and irregularly employed figures. Among those who can be classified as workers, skill, status, and wage levels tend to be much lower than average. As the table makes clear, their electoral volatility in the 1970s was second only to the white-collar groups. They were central figures in the early part of that decade, especially in some of the most radical and best-publicized urban agitations (e.g., housing occupations, nonpayment of utility bills, increased transit fares, etc.). Their support was clearly crucial to the Communists' great advance in the mid-1970s.

Immigrant tenement-dwellers, for numerous obvious reasons, are very difficult to organize; the PCI has had limited success with them even in those areas of the country where it boasts a gigantic organization and extensive social presence.[46] In Turin, the party has found it almost impossible to establish an ongoing presence in the sprawling and often desolate public housing districts which account for large parts of the city. But its major headaches in these areas unquestionably arose after 1975. Before that date, the Communists had been consistent champions of those who needed public housing, and they frequently took part in demonstrations against the city government and the public housing authority, the IACP (*Istituto Autonomo Case Popolari*). While it neither led nor condoned the most radical activities of the period, the party was quite content to be viewed as the most visible and politically important spokesman for the homeless.

After 1975, the PCI found itself in City Hall and at the head of the IACP as well. And it soon realized that even its best efforts, which were a great improvement over earlier administrations, fell far short of providing any real solutions to a truly crushing problem. The party inherited a massive debt and a creaking bureaucratic machine it was often unable to administer effectively. It also suddenly found itself confronted with a network of abuses and irregularities practiced by the residents themselves; the slightest efforts at reform met with stubborn and often openly hostile resistance.[47] By the middle of 1978, after introducing more rigorous eligibility rules and limited rent increases, the party's popularity had suffered notable reverses. The head of a party district which included numerous housing projects confessed to me at the time that the party sections in those areas were "demobilized in the most absolute sense." And militants from the same area reported that during the campaigns of 1978 and 1979, local hostility prevented them from holding even a simple voters' rally in a project where they had received 60 percent of the vote in 1976.

This brief summary permits a number of (cautious) conclusions regarding the Communists' electoral support in Turin. First and most obvious is that however impressive its gains among other social strata may have been, the Turinese PCI in the 1970s remained, in absolute and relative terms, solidly working class. At the same time, it found at the end of the decade that even its proletarian bastions could not be counted on to deliver massive majorities regardless of the party's general policies. That this is primarily a political and not an organizational phenomenon is shown by a similar drop in working-class votes elsewhere in the North-Center.[48]

We could make this statement even more sweeping by including public housing residents and speaking of a generic "lower-class" vote which is solidly but by no means exclusively communist in Turin. But the notably more fluid nature of the PCI vote in IACP wards suggests that more would be lost than gained by following that approach. For in local elections as well, the residents of public housing turn out to be much less predictable than almost all other categories. Between 1975 and 1980, for example, the PCI gained between two and three percentage points in working-class and upper-class wards—improving significantly, in 1980, on the showing in the general elections of a year earlier. Yet in public housing projects, the 1980 vote remained at 1975 levels and actually fell slightly.[49] This is not surprising in view of the housing policies of the local communist administration; at the same time, it points to different voting patterns among groups we might otherwise lump together under the same sociological heading.

The above suggests that there might well be additional distinctions that could further clarify the PCI's interaction with Turinese society and hence give us a better grasp of the party's recent problems. It is, after all, intuitively dissatisfying to put public housing occupants and upper-status white-collar workers in the same category simply because their support for the PCI has been volatile—or to lump together the proletariat and tenement-dwellers simply because both vote disproportionately for the Communists. Observation of these groups in society strongly suggests that there may be profoundly different motives behind their apparently similar actions. There must be different types of volatile votes involved when, to cite a pertinent example, lumpenproletarians, clerks, and middle-level factory managers all support the PCI in 1976 and then vote for other parties, or do not vote at all, in the next election.

In this context, a useful distinction proposed by Parisi and Pasquino can illuminate the situation in Turin.[50] They make a first distinction between a party's permanent and floating vote. The (more or less) permanent vote, in the Italian context, would be subcultural; it would consist of groups with strong historic ties and well-developed organizational links to a given party, who regularly provide that party with massive support at the polls. The stability of support for the dominant parties in areas with strong subcultures, such as the DC in the "white" Northeast and the PCI in the "red" Center of Italy, is, of course, the clearest illustration of this phenomenon. One would find the closest approximation in Turin in the traditional working-class neighborhoods of the capital and in the red suburbs of the industrial belt.

But this familiar observation is not the major novelty of Parisi and Pasquino's arguments. That comes when they turn their attention to the floating vote which became so important in the 1970s. They argue that the notion of a floating vote is simply too broad to capture the varieties of behavior witnessed in the decade, and proceed to distinguish two kinds of floating vote. The first they call *opinion votes*. These are delivered to a party on the basis of a reasoned assessment of its platform at a given time. Such rational calculation assumes a very high degree of integration into the political system on the part of the groups that behave in this fashion. This is the conditional vote of the privileged social strata, but also of the more qualified, educated, and integrated sectors of the working class. The second type of floating vote they label *exchange votes*. These involve much less positive integration into the system, or rational adherence to specific platforms. The classic "exchange," following this usage, is the clientelistic or patronage vote. Finally, if the opportunity for an exchange of this type does not immediately present itself, this type of vote can rapidly become a *protest vote*. It is characteristic of marginal social strata, and particularly the urban and rural subproletariat and the lower reaches of the urban petite bourgeoisie.[51]

This distinction is useful on its own merits, for it introduces much-needed precision into a discussion in which the electoral changes of the 1970s often led to the indiscriminate use of concepts such as floating or fluid votes. But it is especially helpful for our purposes, because the categories provided fit the Turinese situation so neatly. We can see how extremely different groups, for varied motives, can throw their support to the PCI—and then withdraw it. We can also see from these distinctions that there was probably little the Communists could have done to consolidate what was in all likelihood the protest vote of the occupants of public housing, short of stooping to blatant clientelism. A sizable portion of those in the projects voted in protest against the DC in 1975–1976, and a notable, if smaller, portion did the same thing in opposition to the PCI in 1979.

Finally, these distinctions help us understand the party's more generalized losses at the end of the 1970s. We saw earlier that at least one reason the party leaders pressed forward so vigorously with the historic compromise was their confusion of a tactical opportunity with a great strategic victory. Translated into Parisi and Pasquino's terminology, what they did was confuse protest or opinion votes with subcultural support. They did not understand the *new*, contingent, nature of much of their support; they believed, in line with past experience, that this new support was permanent. Because of this misreading, the importance of short-term and concrete achievements—which would at least have placated the opinion vote—was badly underestimated. The largely symbolic gains the PCI offered its supporters after 1976 may have gratified the most convinced, but they did little or nothing for those who were anticipating something more tangible. Of the many adjustments to a changing reality that the PCI would have to make, a key one would be an increased awareness of the complexities of society and hence of the political motivations of the different groups that make up modern Italy.

## Organizational Changes in Turin after the Hot Autumn

The major change that took place in the Turinese organization in the 1970s was phenomenal membership growth. This fact made possible the great expansion and turnover at every level of the party structure throughout the second half of the decade. I will analyze these structural changes and the organizational crisis they helped generate in detail in Chapters 5 and 6. This chapter is concerned with the broad sociopolitical context of the Turinese PCI, and the present discussion is limited to the most general implications of the party's growth. Where and among what groups was expansion greatest? Which problems did this expansion help resolve, and which did it create or aggravate?

A rapid review of Table 2.1 underlines several points made earlier about the PCI's organizational fortunes in Turin since World War II. First, the party was a very powerful, strongly rooted force which was almost obliterated by the end of the 1960s. Second, although the capital city continued to be the political and sociological center of attention throughout the postwar period, it had ceased to be organizationally dominant by the 1970s. The table, in fact, shows quite different trajectories for the capital and the hinterland, which really means the industrial belt. In the former, the party's decline was precipitous in the 1950s but continued steadily into the early 1970s. In the latter, the relative drop was initially equally severe, but it had bottomed out by the early 1960s. It then rose steadily, surpassed the capital by 1970, and has remained dominant even during the decline that began at the end of the 1970s.

Because both the capital and the suburbs grew greatly at the same time, these differences cannot be attributed to an automatic relationship between party organization and industrialization. They do suggest that the industrial suburb is a far more hospitable setting for organizational survival and growth than is a modern urban metropolis.[52] The figures in Table 2.1 also vividly underscore just how precarious the party's position had become in the capital by the time of the mass mobilizations of the 1960s.

These considerations, in spite of the decline that began at the end of the decade, make the party's gains in the 1970s appear all the more impressive. A discussion of the period of major growth (1969–1977)[53] will help us appreciate just how dramatic most of these advances were. For example, in expanding from thirty thousand to forty-seven thousand members, the Turinese federation increased its membership by 56 percent. This was nearly triple the rate for the PCI as a whole in the same period (20 percent), and, with just one exception, it was a growth rate exceeded only by the smallest and weakest federations in the country.[54] Moreover, as Table 2.4 shows, the PCI's growth in Turin saw a large jump in recruitment combined with a falloff in the proportion of those who did not renew their membership cards. This reversal of the typically high turnover rate that distinguishes large urban centers (and the South) dramatically altered

*Table 2.4.* Turinese Federation of the PCI: Members, New Recruits, and Nonrenewals 1965–1985

|  | Members | Recruits (%) | | Nonrenewals (%) | |
| --- | --- | --- | --- | --- | --- |
| 1965 | 31,272 | 3232 | (10.3) | 4083 | (12.7) |
| 1966 | 29,653 | 2365 | ( 8.0) | 3984 | (12.7) |
| 1967 | 29,655 | 2778 | ( 9.4) | 2776 | ( 9.4) |
| 1968 | 30,255 | 3715 | (12.3) | 3115 | (10.5) |
| 1969 | 29,815 | 3275 | (11.0) | 3715 | (12.3) |
| 1970 | 30,900 | 4532 | (14.7) | 3447 | (11.6) |
| 1971 | 31,188 | 3996 | (12.8) | 3708 | (11.9) |
| 1972 | 34,417 | 5582 | (16.2)[a] | 2353 | ( 7.5) |
| 1973 | 36,285 | 4994 | (13.8) | 3126 | ( 9.1) |
| 1974 | 37,964 | 4748 | (12.5) | 3069 | ( 8.5) |
| 1975 | 40,822 | 5293 | (13.0) | 2435 | ( 6.4) |
| 1976 | 47,186 | 7494 | (15.9) | 1130 | ( 2.8) |
| 1977 | 47,071 | 4665 | ( 9.9) | 4780 | (10.1) |
| 1978 | 46,123 | 3929 | ( 8.5) | 4877 | (10.4) |
| 1979 | 45,700 | 3714 | ( 8.1) | 4137 | ( 9.0) |
| 1980 | 45,097 | 3600 | ( 8.0) | 4203 | ( 9.2) |
| 1981 | 43,302 | 2791 | ( 6.4) | 4586 | (10.2) |
| 1982 | 41,208 | 2285 | ( 5.5) | 4379 | (10.1) |
| 1983 | 39,096 | 2015 | ( 5.1) | 4127 | (10.0) |
| 1984 | 37,906 | 1940 | ( 5.1) | 3110 | ( 8.0) |
| 1985[b] | 36,956 | 1846 | ( 5.0) | 2796 | ( 7.4) |

*a.* In 1972, the dissolution of the PSIUP brought many additional recruits to the PCI.

*b.* Figures for 1985 include the new federation of Ivrea.

*Percentage of recruits:* Proportion of current year's membership.

*Percentage of nonrenewals:* Proportion of previous year's membership.

*Sources:* Official published PCI statistics and archives of the Turinese federation.

the local PCI's age and seniority profile in a very brief time span. By 1978, fully 57 percent of the federation's membership had entered the party in the 1970s.

There were actually two distinct waves of recruitment into the PCI in Turin in this short span of time. The first came during and immediately on the heels of the most intense period of labor mobilization: it was disproportionately concentrated in the suburbs, among workers, and did not cause a sharp shift in the age profile of the rank and file. The first wave brought very few female recruits into the federation; in fact, the percentage of women members in the federation declined sharply in the early 1970s. The table also shows that nonrenewals of membership, and thus the over-all rate of turnover, remained high during the first wave of recruitment. The second wave, which was most concentrated in 1975–76, reaped the full harvest of earlier mass mobilizations and radically rejuvenated the federation. A single set of figures tells the story eloquently. Between 1973 and 1977, the federation increased by eleven thousand members, and this rise occurred overwhelmingly among those between twenty-six and forty years of age. In absolute terms, this single age group rose by seventy-eight hundred members, accounting for 70 percent of the total increase. The change in the relative weight of each major age group is presented in Table 2.5; the figures for the party as a whole show clearly that the dramatic shift that took place in Turin was not a generalized phenomenon. In fact, only where there was extensive mobilization in the late 1960s does one find large increases among this relatively young cohort in the mid-1970s.[55]

This disproportionate recruitment of a specific age group into the PCI wherever social mobilization and conflict were greatest during the intense cycle of struggles of 1968–1972 strongly points to a clear generational phenomenon. One cannot label this generation as youthful in an unqualified sense; it included people up to forty years old in 1977, and Table 2.5 shows that the very youngest cohort in the federation was not drawn disproportionately into the party at the same time. But if we refer to those who could be called young not at the time they joined the PCI but during the period of maximum social mobilization in Italy, it is evident that the twenty-six-to-forty group fits this definition very well. If party statistics permitted a more refined breakdown, we could be even more precise: those between twenty-six and thirty-five in 1977 would correspond almost perfectly to the "generation of '68," people in their teens and early twenties during and immediately after the hot autumn, a group which attracted attention even before the end of the period of most intense mobilization.[56] Party mem-

*Table 2.5.* Turinese Federation: Changes in Age Groups, 1973–1977

(in Percentages)

|  | | | Difference 1977 − 1973 | |
|---|---|---|---|---|
|  | 1973 | 1977 | Turin | Whole PCI |
| to 25 yrs. | 12.0 | 11.4 | − 0.6 | + 0.1 |
| 26–40 yrs. | 33.0 | 42.0 | + 9.0 | + 1.6 |
| 41–60 yrs. | 32.1 | 31.5 | − 0.6 | − 1.6 |
| 61 and over | 22.9 | 15.1 | − 7.8 | − 0.1 |
| Total | 100.0 | 100.0 | | |

*Source:* PCI, *Dati sulla organizzazione del Partito* (1975), pp. 40, 42; (1979), pp. 34, 37.

bership statistics do not allow for more elaborate breakdowns, so the twenty-six-to-forty age group is the best approximation available of that extremely important generation.

An analysis of the social composition of the members of the federation bears out the idea that the party was faced with two very different waves of recruits within the decade. As Table 2.6 shows, the increase between 1968 and 1973, which raised the membership by 20 percent, did not significantly alter the organization's general profile. The proportion of pensioners continued to rise, which is a clear sign that the party was not yet hit with a flood of younger recruits. In fact, the relatively "normal" profile that emerges at the end of this first wave of growth may help explain why the PCI was slow to appreciate the changes that took place in the 1970s. There were certainly very few signs of novelty in this first and rather large increase in members. Indeed, it is reasonable to hypothesize that the immediate effect of the climate of militance of 1968 to 1972 was to bring older ex-militants (or sympathizers) back into the organizational fold rather than to galvanize new groups into approaching the party for the first time.[57] The latter phenomenon evidently required the passage of more time and the sort of changes in Italy's political climate discussed above in Chapter 1.[58]

The data in Table 2.6 show how the social base of the party organization in Turin was altered in a single decade; the results are all the more dramatic when we see that most of the truly major changes occurred between 1973 and 1977. Changes for the party as a whole have also been presented to facilitate comparisons.

We have already discussed the influx of the "generation of '68," which shows up here in the radical drop in the proportion of pensioners. Especially noteworthy is the plunge of 9 percent between 1973 and 1977 in Turin, contrasted with the increase for this group in the entire party.

The traditional petite bourgeoisie, a group that has always figured prominently in the analyses of the PCI, made no headway at all in Turin during the 1970s. A slight

*Table 2.6.* Changes in the Social Composition of the Membership of the Turinese Federation between 1968 and 1977 (Major Groups)

| | 1968 | 1973 | 1977 | Difference 1977 − 1968 | |
| | | | | Turin | PCI |
|---|---|---|---|---|---|
| Workers | 58.5% | 58.3% | 58.6% | — | — |
| Clerks and technicians | 2.0 | 3.8 | 10.9 | +8.8 | +4.5 |
| Artisans | 3.7 | 2.7 | 3.0 | −0.7 | +0.8 |
| Entrepreneurs, shopkeepers | 2.7 | 2.1 | 3.3 | +0.6 | +1.7 |
| Professionals, intellectuals | 0.6 | 1.1 | 2.9 | +2.3 | +1.5 |
| Students | 0.2 | 0.4 | 1.6 | +1.4 | +1.5 |
| Housewives | 10.7 | 8.2 | 7.0 | −3.7 | −2.7 |
| Pensioners | 20.0 | 23.4 | 12.5 | −7.5 | +5.7 |
| Others | 1.5 | 0.1 | 0.4 | | |
| Totals | 100.0 | 100.0 | 100.0 | | |
| (N) | (30,257) | (36,285) | (47,071) | | |

*Sources:* PCI, *Dati sulla organizzazione del Partito* (1972), pp. 38, 42; (1975), p. 43; (1979), pp. 38–39, 42–43.

increase among shopkeepers is offset by a decline among artisans. More importantly, this stagnation took place against the backdrop of a 2.5 percent rise in the party as a whole, which brought the traditional middle strata to 9 percent of total PCI membership versus only 6.3 percent in Turin. With one exception, all other social categories in Turin follow the trends for the entire party, although usually in slightly more emphatic fashion.

The exception, which is dramatic, is clerks and technicians, the most important component of what many refer to as the "new middle classes." The absolute growth of these white-collar strata is even more striking than the table indicates. In 1968 they amounted to little more than six hundred members of the party in Turin, whereas by 1977 they had risen to more than fifty-one hundred—an eightfold increase. Regardless of whether one's framework is drawn from bourgeois or Marxist social science, these people are extremely difficult to categorize. As we will see in Chapter 5, the increasing presence of white-collar and other nonproletarian groups at all levels of the party structure has been the source of considerable debate among Italian Communists. Many worry that the party's historical class identity has been diluted or obfuscated by this development.

In Turin, even though their presence is much greater than the norm for the PCI, the problem is less acutely felt. This reflects the fact that in the Piedmontese capital, the great majority of white-collar workers are recruited out of the factories or out of "proletarianized" firms in the public or service sectors of the economy. In strictly sociological terms, therefore, they are much more easily classified as laborers (*lavoratori*) than in most other places in Italy. Although their abstract classification may not represent a serious problem for the party, at least some white-collar groups represent an important and growing *political* problem. An illustration of just what kind of problem they can pose was apparent late in 1980, when a mass demonstration of Fiat foremen, supervisors, and technical staff against a monthlong strike led by the union ended the strike and created serious problems for the entire workers' movement.[59]

Another reason why there might be less immediate concern about white-collar groups in the Turinese federation can be found in the fact that, for all the changes of the 1970s, this remained an overwhelmingly working-class party organization into the 1980s. Table 2.6 demonstrates the relative weight of the working class. In view of the other trends examined in this chapter, this means that there was a massive increase in the total number of workers—and young workers at that—in the party in the 1970s. In 1968, the federation counted roughly seventeen thousand seven hundred workers in its ranks; by 1977, this figure had risen to twenty-seven thousand six hundred. By almost every imaginable measure, this increase put Turin in the forefront of PCI federations which were revitalized in the wake of the struggles of the later 1960s and early 1970s.[60]

## Conclusions: The Ambiguous Legacy of the Hot Autumn in Turin

The Turinese PCI, seemingly on the brink of oblivion by the 1960s, had become one of the jewels in the party's crown by the heyday of the *compromesso storico*. It had not only undergone an organizational renaissance by the late 1970s, but it had also become the utterly dominant political force in practically every significant political assembly in the province. Yet within the span of a very few years, the waning fortunes of the PCI would be very much reflected, and in some instances even amplified, in the Piedmontese capital. It would not be reduced to its previous marginalized status, for its gains—along with changes in the Italian political and social system—were simply too great. But it would suffer stinging electoral losses and another dramatic organizational decline which underlined just how difficult it is to be a mass party of the left in the last quarter of the twentieth century. The underlying causes of the party's problems are not found in Turin, but the specific rhythms and forms of both its successes and its failures are clearly rooted in local conditions. A rapid summary and synthesis of the major points and findings of this chapter will help us better appreciate the constraints under which the federation had to operate as it faced the challenges of the post-1975 period.

At the risk of belaboring the obvious, it is vital to emphasize yet again the dimensions, trauma, and aftermath of the crushing defeat of the 1950s. To a degree unmatched anywhere else in Italy, a proud and very powerful party and labor movement was nearly annihilated. They were reduced to the status of helpless spectators as conscious political projects and the blinder forces of advanced capitalism irrevocably altered the world in which they operated. Largely because of the precarious state in which they found themselves at this time, party and movement alike adopted a highly conflictive, classically oppositional stance which would always be in a state of tension with their extremely limited organizational capacities. They would, in short, always be much better able to mobilize dissent than to organize or direct consensus into any sort of permanent institutional channels. This would represent a serious handicap for the Turinese PCI when the articulation of the *compromesso storico* in the mid-1970s and the local electoral victories of 1975 put a premium on its institutional capacities.

The eruption of the cycle of struggles of 1968 to 1972, which were a sign of deeply rooted social changes that could no longer be contained and of the failure of Italy's ruling parties to bring about serious reforms, represented a serious challenge from which the PCI ultimately drew immense benefits. But it hardly drew these benefits immediately; nor were its advances unilinear or unequivocal.

For this reason, it is appropriate to speak of the ambiguous legacy of the hot autumn in Turin.[61] The party was able to absorb the bulk of the energy that had generated the most explosive mass mobilizations in postwar Italian history, but this process was not automatic. It revealed a party-society dynamic with its own distinctive tempos, and the Communists' successes also meant, ironically, that many demands that had previously existed outside the party would henceforth represent internal problems as well. It is, in short, a gross oversimplification to assume that "the movement" was a solid or monolithic entity which followed an easily traced route through Italian society. Because it was a *mass* movement of considerable duration and complexity, its legacy was, by definition, a mixed one.

Let us first examine the tempos of the dialectic of party and movement. The PCI certainly did not simply gobble up the mass movements. On the contrary, much of the evidence in this chapter indicates two distinct stages in the PCI's postautumn growth, with the major influx only taking place five or more years after the peak period of mobilization. This suggests that the PCI only absorbed these energies in a mediated fashion. Not only did a significant portion of the movements have to trace their own parabola before coming closer to the PCI, but the party itself had to alter its own image and practices before enjoying its greatest successes. As I argue in Chapter 1, it is difficult to understand either the genesis or the success of the *compromesso storico* without an appreciation of the stalemated situation that prevailed when it was first proposed.

In addition, and related to the above, many of the problems the party would eventually have to confront were outgrowths of a political dynamic that was not at all easy to understand. One can, for example, criticize the Communists' slowness to grasp numerous changes in Italian society, including alterations in the party's own social bases of support. Here is where the misreading of the *compromesso* as a strategic breakthrough would prove so costly. But one must also recognize that these were often difficult messages to decipher, especially in settings such as Turin. In the earliest stages of the party's victories, for instance, we saw that both electoral and organizational advances came much more from traditional constituents than from new ones. Only after 1973—and especially after 1975–76—did the party make impressive headway among younger people, white-collar strata, and other new actors. The electoral conquest of the industrial belt in 1970 and the membership figures through the first wave of recruitment suggested increased legitimacy and popularity for the party but offered little evidence of inroads into new areas. This cannot excuse the persistence of old orientations and behavior patterns throughout the 1970s, but it does make the PCI's slowness to react much more comprehensible.

A similar complexity and ambiguity is apparent when we turn our attention to the groups that were brought into or close to the PCI in the wake of the *autunno caldo*. The earliest waves of recruits and voters seem to have come primarily from the party's traditional sources of support, but by the middle of the 1970s the membership and electorate alike had become much more heterogeneous. The "generation of '68" is useful shorthand, but it undoubtedly includes a multitude of diverse and perhaps even opposed motivations. Some of its members wanted nothing more than an immediate payoff; many probably hoped for a measure of good government and an end to corruption or political paralysis; others were undoubtedly committed to radical social change. It is easy to see how any one of these constituencies might quickly become disillusioned with a party that devoted itself to the desires of the others, however legitimate these might be. Moreover, the personal experiences these people brought into the party were immensely varied, in spite of the shared generational experience. Many were direct protagonists in the struggles of 1968 to 1972, while others must have been more marginal participants or perhaps were only politicized later. A good number lived these tumultuous events as Communists, or at least as sympathizers of the party, while many others were involved in or at the fringes of the extraparliamentary groups which were so active from the end of the 1960s until the middle of the 1970s. Many of these groups were openly in conflict with the PCI. The diversity of political experiences that the party would find in its midst by the end of the second wave of recruitment would therefore be as great as at any time in its entire history.

Finally, as we will see in Chapters 5 and 6, even the great organizational advances made by the PCI in the 1970s would pose serious problems for the Turinese federation. Some of these problems were on the order of growing pains which unquestionably reflected the party's dramatically improved situation. Nonetheless, the earlier legacy of organizational weakness made them so acute in Turin that it is necessary to speak of an organizational crisis. Compounding these more positive causes of the crisis, however, were problems that derived directly from the party's policies of the period, or those that had long been latent in the concept of the *partito nuovo* but for a variety of reasons had not represented serious threats to the party's operations and identity until it had to face the challenges of the 1970s.

With the background provided so far, we can now turn to a more detailed examination of the period from 1975 to 1980 in Turin and how the federation experienced the political, strategic, and organizational aspects of the transitional crisis.

# 3

# The Political Dimensions of Transitional Crisis in Turin: Three Cases

What specific forms did the transitional crisis take in Turin in the critical period of 1975 to 1980? How did the Turinese federation of the PCI experience the contradictions between its own history and the demands of the national party strategy? How did the latent contradictions of the *partito nuovo* manifest themselves in the party, and how, in turn, did the party respond? These are the questions to which we turn in this and the following chapters, beginning with the political dimensions of party activity.

A detailed study of developments on a local level will allow us to escape the often abstract generalizations that accompany discussions of broad party strategy, for on this level party strategy is not merely enunciated but must be implemented. We can therefore see, from a firsthand perspective, which policies were followed and the degree of success with which they were carried out. At the same time, this closer perspective also enables us to understand which options were *not* taken by the PCI. One of my central arguments about the transitional crisis is that it must be understood as more than the party's reflexive response to blind objective forces  although these forces and responses are certainly present, and important—therefore, it is essential to understand the interplay between national and local conditions and the extent to which conscious choices, however circumscribed, shaped the PCI's fortunes after 1975.

This discussion of the political aspects of the party's crisis is not intended as a survey of the political history of Turin since 1975. Such a study would be far beyond the scope of this work and would require its own monograph. The objective here is far more limited. We will examine three situations in which the party's relationship to different dimensions of the political sphere were put to the test in the late 1970s. Each issue selected illustrates a distinct level of party theory and activity, as follows:

1. The PCI's place in the tension between political institutions and social movements.
2. The PCI's conceptions of how to mobilize its own rank and file, and the broader society, in the altered conditions of the late 1970s.
3. The PCI's vision of democracy and the measures required to defend it when the state is viewed as seriously threatened.

As is evident, these three cases embrace a very wide range of issues, but their political implications for the party are broadly similar. Each shows how the PCI either misread specific cues or else moved ahead because of national strategic considerations or ingrained behavior patterns and ultimately alienated many of its traditional and new supporters. They also show how the party alienated and hastened the demobilization of its own militants in the same period. I will begin with an overview of the party's general dilemma and then proceed to an examination of each of the three cases.

## Party, Institutions, and Movement: A New Way of Governing

> We're a party of government and of struggle. As a party of government, we
> lose to the left. As a party of struggle, we lose to the right.
>                     Comment circulating at the grass roots in Turin (Spring 1978)

The electoral victories of 1975 and 1976, in spite of the profound satisfaction that accompanied them, generated two separate, if related, shocks to the Turinese PCI. By far the most traumatic adjustment was on the local level, for the assumption of such an extensive governing role would have taxed even a less weak and inexperienced organization. Then, from 1976 on, this adjustment had to take place against the backdrop of a national policy of outright collaboration with all other parties except those of the extreme left and right, especially the DC, heretofore the Communists' archenemy. From the beginning, the PCI's behavior in Parliament drew fire from every quarter, including within the party, with respect to the amount of tolerance shown the Christian Democrats.[1] Nor were such accusations limited to the party's behavior in Rome. Because the national strategy was predicated on broad collaboration at all levels, local Communists also had to hold out an olive branch to their Christian Democratic counterparts—even when, as in Turin, the left had a clear majority and therefore did not need DC support.

In view of the militant setting of Turin and the local party's orientation to mass mobilization, it is not surprising that the federation was giving serious thought to its own situation even before the general elections of 1976. Almost immediately following the quantum leap in the party's local governing responsibilities, the Communists in Turin found themselves faced with a dramatic falloff in organizational and mass political activity, as well as a rise in criticism from the grass roots. To counteract these worrisome trends, the federation organized a conference of the party in the capital city early in 1976 which had the explicit goal of reasserting the PCI's traditional identity. The message was that the party remained one of "struggle and combat," for this had brought it success and thus had to remain the fundamental task of the party organization. The requirements of governing could not be allowed to obscure the party's basic character; nor should they generate passive expectations for PCI initiatives to originate from within the public institutions now controlled by the party.[2] "A new way of governing," in the Turinese context, had to mean maintaining the historically strong relationship to mass movements and to a policy of mobilization.

This approach was probably unrealistic from the start. Even if the local party decided to mobilize its members or the masses, how would it do so? Given the organizational weakness of the federation, it would have been impossible to galvanize tens of thousands of people or get them into the streets in support of the generic demands made by the Communists at the time. And the only proven technique of mobilization in Turin, which was oppositional, was out of the question now that the PCI was the party in power.

But in any event, the mobilizational approach was never seriously attempted, for two overriding reasons. One was that after the 1976 vote, the national strategy of the party called for and practiced a policy which was exclusively one of institutional mediation. No local organization would have dared buck this tide even if it were inclined to do so, and the top Turinese leadership was strongly committed to the national line of the party. The second reason, given the conditions prevailing in Turin, was equally decisive. By conscious design, the federation had moved almost all of its most seasoned cadres into local governmental or bureaucratic positions after 1975. This created a vacuum in the party organization that was enough to make any sort of sustained effort a moot point. It also had the largely unintended consequence of focusing party attention on the institutions to which the most experienced and charismatic leaders had been shifted. This meant, in spite of the desire to the contrary, that PCI initiatives were inevitably shifted to public institutions wherever the party recently took power.[3] The high expectations that followed the 1975 sweep into power might have turned all eyes to the new left-wing *giunte* in any case, but it is important to underline that the shift of personnel left the party not only unwilling but also incapable of undertaking sustained mass initiatives.

As untenable as the situation had become, the federation continued to grapple with it as it faced increased demobilization and confusion at the rank-and-file level. Following the general elections, the Turinese leadership attempted to define more clearly the respective roles of party organization and mass movement on the one hand and public institutions on the other.[4] Mass movements and their struggles, it argued, are governed by internal dynamics which are quite different from those that concern political institutions. The former—the reference to the labor movement is unmistakable—are primarily conflictive and make demands on or strike bargains with a clearly defined opposite number (*controparte*). Institutions, in contrast, are "the site of mediation for the comprehensive interests of society."[5] One can hardly transfer the logic of mass movements into them and expect them to operate effectively. Movements must, therefore, follow their own logic. But they should understand that institutions (i.e., those run by the PCI) have to act in the interests of society as a whole and cannot simply be the spokesmen for a single group or class.

At first blush, this sounds like a tortured effort to squirm out of a difficult situation, especially when the point is also made that public institutions are automatically on the side of the working class if they are "progressive" in structure.[6] But although this appears to be a hastily composed rationalization of the Communists' behavior after 1975, these arguments do have a lineage that can be traced all the way back to the earliest formulations of the *via italiana al socialismo* and the Togliattian vision of progressive democracy. And they do attempt to address the increasingly disturbing phenomenon of the fragmentation of politics in the late twentieth century: if various groups try to "capture" political institutions, it becomes impossible to address general problems, or to undertake serious reform projects.[7]

The problem is that despite its pedigree or the effort to restrict special-interest politics, this remains a profoundly flawed formulation given the nature of the PCI. Although it was prepared to assume a wider governmental and institutional role, it was not about to abandon its traditional organizational and political characteristics. Movements and institutions may well obey different dynamics, but in practice the party ended up favoring the mirror image of the fallacy it wished to prevent. While arguing against the introduction of a conflictive "movement logic" into political institutions, the behavior of the PCI after 1976 led to the de facto infliction of a mediating institutional logic onto the party and mass movements. The social, not to mention the mobilizational, side of the equation was preempted by the party's National Unity policy of austerity and sacrifices. The signal sent to the rest of the political system was that the PCI would moderate its constituents' demands in exchange for a larger share of institutional power and a reform program (purposely left open-ended) which could then be hammered out in Parliament among the major parties. The union confederations' adoption of a very restrained line under the strong pressure of communist union leaders showed how seriously this approach was taken.[8]

This may be part of the normal give-and-take of politics, but it created an intolerable situation for the PCI as a party of mass mobilization. In spite of adopting the slogan "We are a party of government and of struggle,"[9] it is clear that the PCI intended to play down the latter and favor the former. The national leadership probably felt that there were no other alternatives in view of the precarious balance of political forces in Parliament. But it was extremely risky to put all its eggs into the single basket of institutional maneuvering. The gamble, which did not pay off, was that the positive results of these maneuvers would prove adequate to offset the demobilization which was bound to occur at the grass roots.

In the mid-1970s, there was only one area of the country in which the party's strategy might have been implemented successfully, and that was in the "red belt" of central Italy. But in the central regions, the social, organizational, electoral, and political components of communist hegemony grow out of specific historical circumstances which do not apply to any other areas. Only where the PCI has *always* been exceptionally strong does it command the organizational and political instruments that can orient its mass base and electoral support around moderate policies. Put in slightly different fashion, only in its historic strongholds does the Communist party have both the enormous organizational resources and a general environment which enable it to mediate social conflict through its control of political institutions. The social structure is relatively stable and was in any event never pulverized by large-scale industrialization and massive immigration. The PCI in these areas is a well-oiled machine profoundly rooted in society; it is surrounded by an extensive network of highly articulated mass organizations. If a "red subculture" still exists anywhere in Italy, it is in the party's strongholds in large areas of Tuscany, Umbria, and Emilia-Romagna, which have been totally dominated, socially and politically, by the PCI since the end of the war.

For all these reasons, the PCI in the red belt evolved a distinctive political style in the postwar period. Most social conflict and much of the normal trade-off of politics are generally handily managed between the myriad of organized interests or within the formal political institutions. Indeed, conflict is frequently nipped in the bud because the bulk of the party's initiatives originate *within* the institutions it controls: consensus is first reached among the leaders of organized interests; the party and mass organizations then move in society to mobilize mass consensus around prearranged goals.[10] This highly structured modus operandi evolved in the 1940s and 1950s, when mobilizing mass constituencies around the PCI's accomplishments—inside or outside local government— served ideological and political ends which were far from moderate. But as time wore on and the party became less interested in mobilizing its strongholds against central power in Rome, the moderate temper prevailed to the point where observers often spoke of an "Emilian road to socialism."[11]

Before the electoral shifts of the 1970s, when Italian voting patterns seemed to be

*Table 3.1.* Selected Indicators of Communist Party Strength (1978)

| | Turinese Federation | Industrial Triangle[a] | Red Regions[b] | All of Italy |
|---|---|---|---|---|
| Adult population in 1971 | 1,708,233 | 11,048,520 | 6,194,281 | 38,533,788 |
| (% of total) | | (28.7) | (16.1) | (100.0) |
| PCI members | 46,123 | 391,740 | 712,446 | 1,772,425 |
| (% of total) | | (22.1) | (40.2) | (100.0) |
| Female PCI members | 9,515 | 89,369 | 224,620 | 437,979 |
| (% of total) | | (20.4) | (51.3) | (100.0) |
| Pop. provincial capitals per PCI member | 41.4 | 31.3 | 9.9 | 25.2 |
| PCI votes/PCI members (1976) | 13.2 | 8.9 | 3.9 | 7.0 |
| PCI members/subscriptions to *L'Unità* | 39.6 | 30.2 | 18.5 | 30.1 |

*a.* Industrial Triangle = Piedmont, Lombardy, Liguria.

*b.* Red regions = Emilia-Romagna, Tuscany, Umbria.

*Source:* Calculated from PCI, *Dati sulla organizzazione del partito* (1979).

rigidly fixed, the red regions represented the dominant, and indeed practically the only, model of how the PCI exercised local power. But however much this style of operations recalls the most ambitious formulations of the *compromesso storico*, it should be clear that few of the conditions found in the red regions are typical of Turin. More often than not, conditions in Turin are the opposite of those found in central Italy. Table 3.1 provides a useful, but only partial, comparison of indices of organizational strength. The table cannot show the equally impressive differences in the general organization of civil society or, of course, the radically different political traditions that prevail in the different areas. To cite just one telling example, in Turin, local political institutions were until very recently under the control of "the enemy." The party's identity was consolidated in opposition to these institutions, not by mobilizing support around them.

As we know, the course of events after 1975 drove the PCI, in Turin and elsewhere, to adopt a pattern of behavior whose reliance on institutional mediation paralleled the Emilian model. For all the reasons outlined to this point in our analysis, such an approach was bound to encounter great difficulties. For a perspective on these difficulties and the particular ways they contributed to the party's crisis, we now turn to the examination of specific cases.

## From the Mobilization of Dissent to the Mobilization of Consensus: The Case of Neighborhood Councils

Like most of Italy's major cities, Turin had been the scene of the sporadic rise and fall of spontaneous neighborhood councils (*consigli di quartiere*, or CdQ) from the late 1960s well into the 1970s. In the wake of the hot autumn, the Turinese CdQ became more permanent, mainly agitating over urban issues like housing, schools, health services, public transport, and recreational facilities—all of which were terribly inadequate under the Christian Democratic government that was in power in the Piedmontese capital until

1975. The *consigli* also were often highly effective focal points for grass-roots resistance to unpopular policies (fee hikes by the utilities or transportation authorities). And they frequently represented the only political outlet for the frustrations of public housing tenants, whose bleak housing projects otherwise isolated them almost totally from the surrounding society.

In the late 1960s, both the PCI and some of the budding groups of the New Left actively and effectively agitated around most of the urban issues spelled out above. By the early 1970s, however, as the CdQ took on a semi-institutional character, the influence of the New Left overshadowed the more established parties. Under the leadership of groups such as Lotta Continua, more confrontational forms of politics, such as fee or rent strikes, often unruly demonstrations, and occupations in public housing projects became more frequent.[12] The Turinese Communists often reacted to such events in schizophrenic fashion. While the leadership of the federation generally condemned "excesses," most party militants active in the urban struggles participated in them. And since some protests enlisted the support of an astonishingly large number of citizens, even the party's formal condemnations were often quite muted.[13]

This was the turbulent backdrop to the question of councils when the Communists took over the government of Turin in 1975. Because the history of these institutions had been so politicized, their formal status had not been definitively resolved. In most large cities, CdQ with at least a degree of autonomous power had been put in place by the mid-1970s. But the Turinese *giunta*, led by the DC, had dragged its heels in an effort to avoid legitimizing a very painful thorn in its side.

Under considerable pressure, the *giunta* finally proposed councils which would be indirectly elected. This meant their members would be appointed by the City Council in proportion to the vote received by each party in the city's twenty-three formally decentralized neighborhoods (*quartieri*).[14] This stratagem was designed to avoid an embarrasing election which would necessarily focus on the shortcomings of the local government. It also would limit the powers of the CdQ which were established. For, by law in Italy, directly elected councils have some decision-making powers and must be consulted by their city councils on designated issues. Those that are indirectly elected have much more restricted, consultative functions. Finally, the local DC, following the lead of that party throughout the country, hoped to render the councils as innocuous as possible. Appointment from above would fill the CdQ with the party faithful, rather than with grass-roots activists who were often among the local government's most severe critics.[15]

This position was understandably opposed by local activists and by the official parties of the left. Since the late 1960s, the rank and file had been strongly in favor of direct elections and at least a measure of true decentralization of power of the CdQ. The intense activism that had been an integral part of their own experience made this an article of faith for the Turinese urban militants. In fact, many Christian Democrats with links to the neighborhoods shared the activists' point of view, as has already been suggested and as is clear from the following comments from the DC commissioner of decentralization in 1975:

> there has never been acceptance [in Turin] of the principle, in force in other cities, that the Neighborhood Committees should be designated and regulated by the City Council. We have always wanted a new experience here, one which in particular avoids that the Committees slavishly repeat the political configuration which exists in City Hall.[16]

Studies of the same phenomenon elsewhere in Italy show that this sentiment is common wherever there has been a large measure of grass-roots activity.[17]

Quite slowly, action was taken in Turin to institutionalize the CdQ. In 1974, a bill passed by City Council was ruled to have devolved too much financial discretion to the *consigli* under the legislation in force·at the time. In 1975, new laws passed by Parliament permitted more real powers to be handed over to directly elected bodies; obligatory consultation between CdQ and *giunte* was also mandated for the delivery of specific services. Within a year, Turin had drawn up a new decentralization bill in the wake of extensive and quite lively grass-roots consultations—by now the city was governed by the PCI. Following the usual political and bureaucratic delays, the stage was finally set for direct elections, which were to coincide with limited local elections scheduled for the fall of 1977.

The Turinese Communists' true position on the institutionalization of the councils was never as one-sided as their public pronouncements in favor of direct elections suggest. There was certainly always a commitment to the principle of decentralization. And the local party was aware of the debt it owed the neighborhood movements, which had helped galvanize dissent against the DC and thus contributed to the PCI's own victory in 1975. Indeed, as early as 1972, Diego Novelli, who would become the Communist mayor of Turin three years later, acknowledged that groups such as Lotta Continua had been able to outflank the Communists and organize the homeless because the party had ignored the critical housing issue for too long.[18]

But it was precisely the powerful representation of a number of extraparliamentary groups and tendencies, with their frequent inclination to adopt highly militant or occasionally illegal actions, that contributed to PCI wariness vis-à-vis the CdQ even before the 1975 electoral sweep. Through the early 1970s, there was considerable debate within the party about the advisability of becoming too closely associated with protests that might tarnish the Communists' public image.[19] Militants active in the *quartieri* tended to feel that the party should take part in and attempt to direct local actions. The leadership of the federation, along with most city councilors, took a much dimmer view of the more radical activities that occasionally broke out at the grass roots. Militants often complained that interference from party headquarters had been heavy-handed in what looked like efforts to undermine the CdQ. One veteran of these struggles candidly told me that the leadership wanted to keep local-level activities centered around the sections of the PCI, "which could be much more easily controlled than the less malleable *consigli*."[20]

If this debate was frequently heated *within* the party, the PCI's *public* position in Turin never went much beyond a ritualistic denunciation of the worst excesses, such as fee strikes or the occupation of previously assigned apartments in public housing projects. Some excesses, and many inflammatory slogans, were rather casually tolerated by militants and leaders alike. The PCI was by no means a totally irresponsible opposition party, but it certainly did not go to great lengths to relieve the pressure on the DC-led *giunta* when this pressure served its own ends.

When the Communists eventually won City Hall, and with it the administration of the local utilities, transportation, and housing authorities, they found themselves reaping a whirlwind of demands and forms of mobilization they earlier had done little to dissuade. Well into the end of the 1970s, party administrators would complain about the earlier collective failure of the PCI to denounce many past "stupidities."[21]

This is a classic illustration of the limits of a model of party activity based on the mobilization of dissent. When the conquest of local power led to efforts to change the party's established patterns of behavior, almost no one was satisfied. The mass participation and "new way of governing" so central to the PCI's platform and local identity quickly went by the boards. The party, in the surge of enthusiasm following the 1975 vote, was able to use public institutions to generate massive citizen participation. In its first year in power, people flocked to highly publicized grass-roots consultations in the *quartieri*. But as time wore on and neither new institutions nor concrete policies were forthcoming, participation fell precipitously. A PCI commissioner put the situation in starkly numerical terms: in 1975, the city government's consultations drew twenty thousand citizens; a year later the figure was down to four thousand; by 1977, only three hundred people, almost all of whom were die-hard PCI activists, bothered to show up![22] A party militant once active in the CdQ provided a slightly different perspective on the same problem when he described how the local movement simply collapsed following the 1975 elections. This occurred, he said, when the PCI tried to "transform itself into a consensus machine (*macchina di consenso*)."[23] The Turinese Communists had neither the organized presence in civil society nor the organizational strength to put anything like an Emilian model of consensus into practice. The top leadership was increasingly preoccupied with limiting the pressures on Turin's beleaguered political institutions, while the few activists still to be found in the sections after 1975 could hardly afford the luxury of putting the *consigli* high on their own list of priorities, given the immense number of other demands with which they were faced.

## The Institutionalization of the CdQ: 1977–1980

The degree to which institutional, mediating logic dominated the concrete actions of the Turinese PCI after 1976 is evident from the way the CdQ were finally established. It was very much in the Communists' interest to act quickly on this matter, given the earlier foot-dragging of the DC. Indeed, now that the DC was in opposition, it suddenly became a vocal champion of directly elected CdQ. This blatantly self-serving maneuver increased the pressure on the *giunta* to act. It was also part of a broader DC plan to put the PCI immediately on the defensive as it groped its way through the initial adjustment to governing Turin: the DC hoped that a direct election would turn into a referendum on the PCI and prove embarrassing to the Communists.[24]

The DC's turnaround left all major parties in Turin in favor of elections as quickly as possible. But it soon became clear that the public facade of unanimity hid a lot of behind-the-scenes activity. For example, we recall that the CdQ elections were set for late 1977, a date when a series of partial local elections was to be held. But these elections were then put off until spring of 1978, which meant that representations would again have to be made to Parliament to allow this special vote to be held in Turin. With all parties publicly in favor of a quick vote for the CdQ, it was assumed that the request would routinely be granted. Oddly enough, the parliamentary committee to which the amendment was presented voted it down unanimously even though Socialist and Christian Democratic MPs from Turin had put it forward. These same deputies re-presented their amendment on the floor of the Chamber of Deputies while, simultaneously, Turin mobilized to press its own case. In November, City Council unanimously approved a *giunta* motion asking for direct elections at the earliest possible date.[25] When Parliament delayed its vote on the request, the entire leadership of the Turinese Coordinating Committee of Neighborhood Councils resigned in protest.

In spite of this pressure and the unanimous stand of all parties in Turin, Parliament voted down the amendment in December 1977. This meant that the CdQ could only be directly elected in the next round of regularly scheduled local elections in the capital— and these were set for 1980. If Turin were to have any councils at all before that date, they would have to be chosen by City Council on the basis of the 1975 local vote in the *quartieri*. But then, in the strangest twist of all, Parliament promptly turned around and approved a Communist amendment which assigned powers to indirectly elected councils that normally could only be obtained through direct elections.[26] In other words, Turin's request for special consideration was initially denied, but then all the perquisites of direct elections were provided even though the direct vote was avoided! Clearly, some sort of deal had been struck in Rome. It is equally clear that the resulting arrangement would be most satisfactory to the Turinese Communist leadership.

One can only speculate about the trade-offs that went on in Rome, but the PCI's actions in Turin can be documented with firsthand evidence. While the Communists were busy addressing grass-roots assemblies and passing motions to be sent to Parliament demanding direct CdQ elections, they had already decided in private that direct elections would not be held. The PCI position was spelled out to militants from the *quartieri* in a meeting held in October 1977, much earlier than the flurry of activity described above. The way the meeting was set left no doubt that the basic decision had been worked out in Rome, since the scheduled main speaker was the member of the PCI National Executive in charge of the section that deals with problems of local government.[27]

How did the party justify a decision that ran counter to all it had fought for in Turin for years, and which moreover belied the position it had publicly assumed at that very moment? Five separate arguments were presented to the party rank and file, and three (or even four) of them indicate the importance of the PCI's institutional calculations and preoccupations.

A member of the Secretariat of the federation spelled out the rationale in the following terms, cautioning the audience that the decision to avoid direct elections was to be kept strictly confidential. First came the desire to avoid polarization and "excessive problems" among the major parties in Turin. Following the PCI's national line, the federation was sparing no effort to reach an accord with the Turinese DC. An electoral campaign would force all parties to accentuate their respective differences and would in all probability create a climate in which rapprochement would be undermined. Second was the time factor: rapid action in City Council could have functioning CdQ, albeit via indirect elections, within a few months. Spring elections, aside from costing the city two million dollars, would mean that at least another year would pass before any institutions were truly functioning in the neighborhoods. Third, the Communist members of the local government were not eager to go to the polls for the same reasons the local DC wanted a quick popular referendum on the PCI. The Communists knew that the *giunta* had been slow to produce highly visible results, largely because they had taken up a great deal of time in their efforts to build a consensus that included the DC. Fourth, the PCI was in deep trouble nationally and feared any result in Turin that might further erode its already slipping credibility. Turin was simply too important a symbol for the party; a setback here would deal a heavy blow to its national strategy and further strengthen the hand of those Christian Democrats who were intent on undermining any accord.

Finally—and this was the only reason provided that had nothing at all to do with strictly political calculations—there were serious doubts among the hierarchy of the federation about the party organization's ability to stand up to the strains of an electoral campaign. The PCI's National Festival of *l'Unità*, a prestigious but daunting undertaking, was scheduled to be held in Turin in the summer of 1978. A debilitating campaign immediately before the festival might well prove to be beyond the local party's physical capabilities. The leadership knew all too well that the transition to a governing role, combined with the gross organizational turnover since the early 1970s (see Chapter 6), had left the federation in a terribly weakened state.

In the debate that followed the presentation of the leaders' reasoning, there was, as is characteristic in the PCI, the understanding that what had been presented was now official party policy. Only one of the ten militants who spoke (roughly seventy-five were present) totally opposed the decision. But several other activists condemned indirect elections as a negation of everything the party had stood for and fought for in the past. In an atmosphere which can best be described as one of resigned, grumbling acceptance, the militants' comments centered on the price the PCI would have to pay for its efforts at institutional rapprochement with the DC.

Many said that while they were personally upset with the decision, they at least judged positively the fact that something had finally been decided. If there was a leitmotif running through all the comments, it was in fact this sense of urgency that an untenable situation needed to be unfrozen. The militants obviously considered the argument about a speedy resolution to the situation to be the most persuasive one put forward by the leaders.

A number of comments from the floor revealed serious doubts about the effect this decision would have on the party's *compromesso storico* strategy. Supporters of the strategy felt that the only way to force the DC to assume more progressive positions was via direct elections. If it had to go to the people to win popular support, the DC would be compelled to fill its lists with Catholic activists with good ties to their parishes and experience and high visibility in the *quartiere* in which they lived. And these were precisely the people with whom local Communist activists had good working relationships and with whom more lasting bonds were at least plausible. If, on the other hand, the CdQ were to be filled by nomination from above, the DC could stack them with hacks and careerists who had little interest and even less experience in the neighborhoods. These people would be poor candidates for unified action with the PCI. In fact, given the local DC's persistent attacks on the PCI since 1975, they could even represent serious obstacles to unity of action, let alone the more ambitious goals of alliance building called for by the historic compromise.

In the conclusions to the meeting, the Secretariat member agreed that this was an extremely serious problem. He added another concern: indirect elections would further alienate young people from the political process, whereas a direct vote would have gotten neighborhood youth actively involved and established valuable contacts between them and party activists. Appointments from above were the worst possible start for a new set of institutions and would further convince young people that politics, even under the PCI, continued as usual. These proved to be prophetic comments, for it was evident to all observers in the wake of the electoral disappointments of 1978 and 1970 that massive defections of young people from the PCI had in fact taken place.

The meeting's conclusions also made clear that the *consigli* issue had dragged on for so long because the national leadership had been engaged in very hard bargaining with the DC. "We have been on pins and needles awaiting word from Rome on this," was the way the local leader put it. He did, however, voice optimism that the local Christian

Democrats would now prove willing to cooperate in the indirect elections and hasten matters to an acceptable conclusion.

But we have already seen that things did not go as the party leaders had planned in the months following the October meeting. A very strong groundswell in favor of direct elections forced the PCI to join, even though it had privately decided otherwise. Militants who attended the meeting had been assured that the party's real position would quickly be made public, but this proved impossible—since it would have been mortifying—in the heated debate at the end of 1977.

By far the greatest miscalculation involved the optimistic assessment of what the local DC would do. From late 1977 on, the Turinese Christian Democrats consistently denounced the PCI's intention to suppress grass-roots democracy and break its promises to the city. Far from quietly going along with indirect elections, they publicly attacked the Communists for their one-hundred-eighty-degree switch on the question.[28] And then the DC did everything it could to obstruct the implementation of the councils, for example, by ignoring deadlines agreed upon earlier for the submission of lists. The PCI had argued to its militants that direct elections would have made it impossible to have working councils before the end of 1978. Thanks to the DC's delaying tactics, the indirectly elected CdQ were not operational at the end of 1978.[29] Well into 1979, many still existed only on paper. In fact, they only became fully operational after the direct elections of 1980—which had been the federation's worst-case scenario in late 1977. But by the time of the 1980 vote, which coincided with municipal, provincial, and regional elections in most of the country, the campaign for the councils was a very minor part of a much broader political event.

As everyone expected, the PCI and the left utterly dominated the Turinese CdQ vote, taking twenty-one of twenty-three with an absolute majority. But by 1980, this overwhelming victory took place in an atmosphere devoid of significant mass participation or enthusiasm, for in those same elections the PCI lost ground in most places compared to its great showing in 1975.[30] And few people, even among the party's staunchest supporters, could point to the outcome with pride as evidence of "a new way of governing."

On balance, the course of events on the CdQ must be considered as a setback for the Turinese PCI. The party did manage to buy some time and alleviate additional pressure on this organization and officeholders by putting the elections off. And it is worth pointing out that even without the direct elections, the federation eventually had to back out of its commitment to host the National Festival of *l'Unità*. This was a stinging blow to the local party's prestige and gives a sense of how overloaded its agenda was in the period under study.

But it is also clear that the Turinese Communists missed one of the rare opportunities available in this period to implement a concrete reform that was well within even the limited capabilities of an overburdened federation. In view of the profound problems facing it and the era of fiscal restraint in which it had to operate, it would have been wildly unrealistic to expect dramatic breakthroughs or profound structural reforms. However, it was reasonable to expect fast action where the costs were not so high and where a great deal of political capital could be gained simply by doing things with which the party had long been identified. More streamlined, democratic, and participatory forms of local governmental institutions were exactly the sorts of reforms that PCI *giunte* everywhere had implemented to prove that the party was in fact different from others. But in this period, the PCI was so obsessed with institutional concerns of a different nature—building vaguely defined "accords" with the DC—that it found itself paralyzed and unable to deliver the goods even on a relatively limited level. It is also clear that the PCI was staggeringly naive in its expectations of how the DC would behave. This susceptibility would be demonstrated all too frequently in the late 1970s.

One vivid illustration is available from the same period in which the CdQ drama was taking place. Late in 1977, elections were held for school districts throughout Italy. Again following the national directive to collaborate with the DC and Catholics wherever possible, the PCI entered into lengthy negotiations in an effort to produce single lists for these elections. This, of course, meant that the creation of the left-wing lists in which the Communists normally participated were badly delayed, much to the consternation of the Socialists, moderate extraparliamentary groups, and independent leftists who were the PCI's usual collaborators. Only when the campaign was already well under way did the Communists fully realize that the DC and allied conservative Catholic groups had no intention whatever of joining a single list with the left; they were delighted to see the PCI tie itself up for weeks in this vain effort. They also had a field day denouncing what they called the PCI's one-party ambitions.

The left ultimately patched together its own lists, which fared very badly in the school vote.[31] In the Turinese federation, militants (mainly teachers) who had been active in the campaign complained bitterly, as did several functionaries. They were dismayed at the unfortunate image the party had projected in its effort to present a single list of candidates, and they wondered aloud how it could have lost so much time in such a wasted effort.

## The Referenda of 1978: The Costs of the Institutional Strategy

After a campaign that was alternately lackluster and nasty, the Italian public went to the polls on June 11, 1978, to vote in a twin referendum. The two laws being challenged[32] were important for a number of issues discussed in this study. One regulates the public financing of political parties in the country; a strong vote to abolish this law would have to be read as a negative judgment on Italian parties (and hence on Italian politics). With the PCI in the majority and in favor of the law, any such judgment would necessarily reflect on it as well. The other, the so-called *Legge Reale*, governed police powers and public order.[33] In a period dominated by Red Brigade terrorism (Aldo Moro's murder had occurred a month earlier), it was clear that this law stood no chance of being abrogated. But the vote was considered important for two reasons. First, it would measure law-and-order sentiment in Italy at a difficult time. Second, the left was predictably divided on the issue, with only the Communists strongly in favor of the existing legislation. An analysis of the vote would thus indicate more clearly the nature of the left's—and the Communists'—difficulties.

The no's carried the day in each case, but the final results embarrassed the governmental majority, and especially the PCI. Nearly 44 percent of those who voted were opposed to the public financing law, and this reached an absolute majority in the South and in the large urban centers of the North, including Turin. And while only 23 percent voted to abolish the *Legge Reale*, the yes vote was higher in Turin than almost anywhere else in the North.

As we saw in Chapter 1, the PCI's self-criticism, which had just begun before the referenda, was accelerated by these results. There will be ample opportunities to examine these reactions in the next chapter; I will focus here on the way the PCI carried out its campaign and on the results of the vote in Turin.

## The Communists' Campaign

The various cross-pressures to which the PCI was exposed in the late 1970s emerge clearly in the way it chose—or felt compelled—to present its case to the public. Most evident, with reference to the issues already introduced in this study, were (1) the straitjacket represented by the PCI's institutional strategy and emphasis on national legitimation and (2) the appalling thinness of communist arguments when an issue under discussion fell outside the party's traditional or preconceived categories. Combined with organizational inertia, these two factors led to behavior that alienated significant portions of the left while failing to make inroads into public opinion in other parts of the political spectrum. Perhaps most importantly, these factors prevented the party leadership from grasping how isolated it had become. In its behavior toward its own rank and file, the leadership seemed to assume that skeptical militants would eventually be won over to whatever decisions were taken. In its orientation toward the external world, it acted as if formal agreements with other parties, however tenuous, guaranteed mass support for the policies in question.

The public financing law was passed in the wake of terrible scandals involving the parties but was never well received by public opinion. Its generous provisions—forty-five billion lire (fifty-six million dollars) was distributed in 1978, when the referendum was held—were a further cause for resentment amidst all the calls for austerity at the time. The PCI supported the law when it was proposed in Parliament, in the name of the need to improve public morality. It did this even though it was least touched by scandal *and* most economically self-sufficient of all Italy's major parties. While the PCI received fourteen million dollars from the public fund in 1978, this only accounted for a fourth of its income that year.[34]

However public-spirited the PCI's actions may have been (not that fourteen million dollars is a risible sum), its support for the law undermined one of its most valuable assets by making it appear to be just one more greedy party grubbing at the public trough. Since one of the PCI's most effective slogans is "We are *not* a party like all the others," its stance hurt its credibility among the public and its own militants. The party did not express much concern with the very lax accounting the law required of the parties receiving aid; these limits were well known to informed opinion, because the press regularly criticized harshly the inadequate annual budgets the parties were required to publish.

The PCI's position on the *Legge Reale* was in some ways quite embarrassing. When it was originally proposed, the Communists had voted against it. Now, three years later, the party had to explain its support for a law many considered highly repressive and which had given the police much greater freedom to use their firearms, often with lethal results.[35] But none of the technical, legalistic explanations offered by the PCI[36] could hide either the profound divisions on the left or the true motivations for the forceful and often strident position the Communists assumed on this issue.

These motivations were exquisitely political. The PCI had always taken a dim view of referenda, seeing them as a threat to parliamentary supremacy. In the late 1970s, having expended so much energy to arrive at the threshold of formal power sharing in Rome, the party was not about to allow what it viewed as purely disruptive and obstructionist tactics to complicate or even thwart its goals. These inclinations were strongly reinforced throughout the 1970s by the fact that the major proponent of the referendum as a political tactic was (and remains) the Radical party. The PR, led at the time by the flamboyant and sometimes bizarre Marco Pannella, is an extremely libertarian group which did not hesitate to accuse the PCI and the DC of teaming up to suffocate popular participation and stifle Italy's budding civil liberties. Very small in size, the PR took its allies where-ever it could find them, and in 1978 this was on both the extreme right and the extreme left of Parliament. For very different reasons, the leftist PDUP and the neofascist MSI were strongly opposed to both the *Legge Reale* and the rapprochement of the PCI and DC, and they teamed up with the radicals. Thanks to governmental blunders and its own parliamentary adroitness, this extremely odd coalition, which had received less than 10 percent of the vote in 1976, managed to force the referendum on the *Legge Reale*.[37]

Given this background, a nasty campaign was a foregone conclusion. But even those who expected hostility and mutual recrimination were shocked at the scurrilous level to which the rhetoric often descended. The Communists were especially abusive toward the Radicals and, of course, the Neofacsists. But they were no less harsh in their criticism of the PDUP and others on the left with whom they had frequently had good or at least proper political relations (e.g., many unionists and also numerous Socialists). They thus tended to lump all their adversaries together not as opponents of one or two pieces of legislation but as enemies of Italy's republican institutions.[38] More sober critics wondered why the PCI was intent on a "hysterical crusade" that would divide the left and terrorize the petite bourgeoisie and concluded that the party leadership was simply desperate.[39]

The Communists' ham-fisted old-style campaign was all the more embarrassing because they were the only major party in the country to campaign actively for the no position on either issue. The Socialists and Christian Democrats both understood the depth of negative sentiment over public financing and maintained very low profiles on this question. On the *Legge Reale*, the PSI was so internally divided that it directed its supporters to follow the dictates of their conscience. The DC took a hard-line stance on law and order and tried to portray the Communists (because of their Marxist heritage and Italy's often violent labor relations) as linked to the country's present troubles. The PCI thus barged on practically alone. Only five days before the vote, the absence of the other parties led the Communists to ask pathetically, "Where Are They?"[40]

The final embarrassment suffered by the PCI in this episode was that the party's zealous campaign caused a delay in the cautious reassessment of its behavior that was just beginning. Only a month before the referenda, the PCI had suffered a stinging setback (its vote fell 9 percent) in partial local elections that involved 10 percent of the population. The national leadership read these losses as a condemnation of the party's overly indulgent behavior toward the DC and its inclination to identify itself too strongly with the other parties in the ruling coalition. Its future actions would therefore have to emphasize the differences between the PCI and the other parties.[41] The referenda followed on the heals of this reassessment, but, as we have seen, the PCI carried out a campaign that made it an aggressive apologist for the government's acts. It simply was unable to take a position that was less than totally committed.

This heavy-handed style carried over in the immediate aftermath of the vote. The PCI's first reaction to what was at best a mixed and problematic result was one of crowing triumph. It was claimed that the Communists had held their supporters with only minor and insignificant exceptions.[42] This was only true for the red regions and flew in the face of reality elsewhere, especially in the South and the large cities of the North. In fact, the PCI quickly backpedaled. In Turin, where the campaign and the vote had been a disaster and where some of the most troubling results were registered where the PCI was strongest, the period of wishful thinking and self-delusion came to an abrupt end.

*The Referenda in Turin.* From the vantage point of Turin, the analysis presented above is confirmed but with two qualifications. First, there was full awareness within the party that its positions were very unpopular. Hostility was not limited to the mass public: on the public finance law, it was endemic among rank-and-file militants as well; on the *Legge Reale*, party intellectuals and even some leaders and high-ranking militants were opposed to their party's position. Second, the degree of internal confusion in the party was immense. This grew out of the national leaders' slowness to decide what the PCI's position would be (especially on the *Legge Reale*) and out of the unexpectedly high losses in the partial local elections.

At a meeting of the party apparatus held just one month before the date set for the referenda, a leader who had just returned from Rome informed his comrades that the public finance vote was certain, but it remained unclear whether it would be necessary to vote on the public order law. Several leaders complained that they did not even know what arguments they were supposed to prepare in the event this vote was held, thanks to confusing messages from party headquarters in Rome.[43] And at a meeting less than two weeks later, the federation's leaders had to reverse their earlier strategy, which had been for a very quiet campaign; it had been hoped that a single issue such as public financing would bring out a low number of voters. This would permit the PCI to carry the day for the no's by turning its own supporters out in great numbers. Now the leaders felt that a low-turnout campaign would be used by the Radicals and their allies as further proof of the gulf between Communist leaders and supporters shown in the local elections. For that reason, "the Party's initiative must be capillary."[44] But this was only decided three weeks before the voting was scheduled!

Even had the local elections not jolted the party, reports coming from the base soon made clear that the PCI was about to inherit a whirlwind on the party finance question. At every meeting in which intermediate cadres reported on the orientation of the rank and file, a very bleak picture was painted. Even the active cadre of the party was reported to be "unreliable," for the militants were furious that so much money was being given to corrupt parties and that the PCI was not doing more to set itself apart from other parties.[45]

The fact that the *Legge Reale* was above all a problem for the left was clear from the course of discussion in the federation before the alarming reports from the base on the public finance issue. Until then, the party devoted much more time to *Reale* and its own deep discomfort. Using the law, the police had made some obvious fishing expeditions on the left in Turin in search of presumed terrorists, and these apparently haphazard raids and arrests—which in the past the PCI would have instantly denounced—were mobilizing the opponents of the law. The secretary of the federation agreed that the police's actions were causing problems but cautioned, "Woe on us if we denounce this too strongly."[46] Other meetings saw leaders and militants alike denounce the party's demagoguery, especially when it frightened the middle class and vilified other leftists.

One rank-and-file militant waved a particularly offensive flyer (it contained photos of bloody corpses) in the air and proclaimed it unworthy of the PCI; most of those in the room angrily agreed.[47] On another occasion, a regional party leader said that even his own vote on *Reale* was not a foregone conclusion, and leaders in the federation were openly talking at this time of party militants who were active in the yes campaign.[48] Finally, and not at all surprisingly, the unions were badly divided on this issue, as they were on the broader question of how to deal with the question of terrorism. At one apparatus meeting, communist trade unionists informed their comrades in the party that little help would be forthcoming from the CGIL or the FLM because of these divisions.[49]

But as the campaign wore on, the public finance law became the major worry for most Communists. There was a general sense of a campaign which had never really gotten off the ground, and some leaders even began to speak hesitantly about a possible defeat in Turin. A big provincewide meeting of cadres, followed by a mass public rally, was acknowledged by federation leaders to have been a failure.[50] This was a painful admission to have to make, because national leaders had come from Rome to act as drawing cards for these gatherings and would obviously report back to Rome on the local situation. Every meeting of the leadership dwelled on the lack of grass-roots involvement, and it was candidly acknowledged that PCI spokesmen regularly lost public debates to the yes forces.[51] Because of their own ambivalence on both questions, many local leaders hoped national party headquarters would send material to the federation that could be used to strengthen their arguments. But no "miracle packets" arrived, and dissatisfaction with Rome's low level of involvement in the practical aspects of the campaign continued right up to voting day.

The results of the voting confirmed most of the pessimism, especially with respect to the party finance law. Turin's showing was especially dismal: a modest victory for the no's in the working-class suburbs was not enough to offset the 54 percent garnered by the yes vote in the capital, and thus the whole province voted to abolish the law by a 51.3 percent to 48.7 percent margin. Moreover, the more closely the vote was studied, the more alarming were its implications for the party.

For example, although the left, led by the PCI, dominates twenty-one of the city's twenty-three *quartieri*, the no vote only carried three of these, and one case was essentially a dead heat. In the industrial belt, where the PCI was in power almost everywhere since 1970, often with an absolute majority of the votes, the no vote carried by the extremely narrow margin of 51.3 percent.[52]

A similar pattern is evident in the capital city. Where the PCI is extremely strong, it was able to squeeze out a very narrow victory for the no's on the public financing referendum. Data to support this conclusion came from the precincts with the most lopsided general election results in the city.[53] Those (thirty-six) precincts where the PCI vote exceeded 60 percent in 1976 were examined as a distinct group. For comparative purposes, thirty precincts where the DC obtained more than 45 percent were also analyzed. The results are presented in Table 3.2. And they show that the margin of victory for the no vote was razor thin even where the PCI has a crushing majority in dense working-class districts. The no vote is, in fact, more than 10 percent below the party's popular vote. The table also shows that the DC, although less strong and practically absent from the campaign, had an equally modest level of success in its strongholds. The other noteworthy finding is the high level of blank and spoiled ballots and the somewhat lower turnout in the areas of greatest Communist strength. These data

*Table 3.2.* Results of Referendum on Party Finance Law in Turin Where PCI and DC Electoral Strength Was Highest in 1976 Elections

|  | Voter Turnout | | Blank or Void Ballots (%) | Yes Vote (%) | No Vote (%) |
|---|---|---|---|---|---|
| PCI strong | 14,507 | (79.6%) | 6.2 | 49.7 | 50.3 |
| DC strong | 11,691 | (83.2%) | 3.6 | 48.7 | 51.3 |
| City of Turin | 732,268 | (81.9%) | 4.3 | 53.8 | 46.2 |

can never be interpreted with complete confidence, but the contrast with DC strongholds does suggest a higher level of general dissatisfaction in the red areas.

In the public housing districts, where we would expect to find the purest expression of a protest vote, we in fact do. These precincts had the highest vote in the city in favor of ending the public financing of political parties (57 percent).

These results are a sobering reminder of the PCI's tenuous links with civil society in Turin. They forced the party to recognize that a protest against the entire political system had been registered by the electorate, although the Communists went to some lengths to dissociate themselves from the other parties in the aftermath of the vote.[54]

The outcome of the vote on the *Legge Reale* is in many ways even more interesting, even though the final result was never in question. The total abolitionist vote in the capital was a high 27.4 percent, as opposed to a national average of 23.4 percent. And the very highest yes vote was in public housing areas, where it hit 37 percent. In the most famous and volatile of all these districts, Via Artom, the yes vote arrived at 43 percent. And yet, in spite of the very high abrogationist vote in the areas of greatest urban disintegration, the difference between the capital and the provincial hinterland was not marked: the provincial average was 26.5 percent, with the capital roughly one point higher and the rest of the province a point lower.

But there are two ways in which the vote for the abolition of the *Legge Reale* differs notably from the party finance vote. One is in the impact of voter turnout. I compared the one hundred precincts with the highest and lowest turnouts in the city and found that turnout made no appreciable difference on the public finance referendum.[55] On the *Reale*, however, turnout was quite important. In the fifty precincts where the greatest numbers of voters went to the polls, the result was roughly the same as the citywide average (26.8 percent to abolish). Where the turnout was quite low by Italian standards, the abolitionist vote was much higher (30.7 percent).

But the most interesting contrast is found in areas of greatest strength for the two major parties. We saw in Table 3.2 that both obtained better-than-average, if not outstanding, results in their strongholds. But as we can see from Table 3.3, these same strongholds show radically different tendencies on the *Legge Reale*. Where the DC is strongest, the vote to abrogate is extremely low. In fact, it is on the level of the vote in the Veneto, the "white" region of massive DC strength. For the PCI, in contrast, the yes vote is extremely high in the densely working-class districts where it garners more than an absolute majority in general elections. And this trend is precisely the opposite of that found in the red belt, where the lowest vote in the entire country (between 14 and 16 percent) was cast to abrogate the *Legge Reale*. To the extent that there is a red subculture in Turin, it seems to be a long way from the easy-to-orient society of

*Table 3.3.* Results of Referendum on *Legge Reale* in Turin Where PCI and DC Electoral Strength Was Highest in 1976 Elections

|  | Voter Turnout | | Blank or Void Ballots (%) | Yes Vote (%) | No Vote (%) |
|---|---|---|---|---|---|
| PCI strong | 14,547 | (79.8%) | 6.1 | 32.1 | 67.9 |
| DC strong | 11,691 | (83.2%) | 3.8 | 19.0 | 81.0 |
| City of Turin | 732,309 | (81.9%) | 4.2 | 27.4 | 72.6 |

central Italy. This undoubtedly reflects the weak organization of the party and all other organizations of the left in Turin and is also a commentary on the vastly different culture of the large urban centers.

For the Turinese PCI, as for the party in general, this vote was extremely important. Until June 1978, abundant warning signs could be, and largely were, written off by party leaders because of extenuating circumstances. Even the alarming drop of 9 percent in the local elections—which had nevertheless been taken seriously enough to call the leadership to Rome—had been the result of partial elections in which the unpredictable South was overrepresented and the great urban centers were underrepresented. Now the entire country had spoken, and only in the red and white regions had the result been close to that desired by the PCI. Once again, the South proved almost impossible to orient. But, most alarming of all, the areas of the greatest triumphs of the mid-1970s, the large urban centers, had produced results that were embarrassing in the immediate sense and potentially disastrous in the longer run. And just as Turin had led the party's advances in 1975 and 1976, it was now leading the decline a scant two years later.

## The PCI, the Strong State, and Civil Liberties: The Problem of Left-Wing Terrorism

The *Legge Reale* referendum showed the problems that a law-and-order orientation created for the PCI, especially among its most natural constituencies on the left. We turn here to the issue that really generated the problem, or at least so seriously aggravated it that the party was forced to take a clear stand: left-wing terrorism. The stand it took was very clear and very hard-line. Because Turin was one of the major focal points for actions by the Red Brigades and other groups through the 1970s, and because the party assigned such importance to "the defense of the Republic," terrorism all but dominated the federation's agenda and paralyzed its actions for much of 1977 and 1978.

Why did the PCI adopt such a hard line, and why did it choose to act in a way that all but guaranteed that it would be unable to carry out most of the other tasks it set for itself in this period? As already suggested, there is no single, simple answer to this question; in reality, a number of independent factors combined to push the party in a relatively coherent direction. Aside from the immediate press of events in Turin, these included the party's earlier positions, the trajectory of extremist politics in Italy in the 1970s, and the Communists' very particular reading of events after 1975–76.

To speak of the party's earlier positions is, first of all, to situate the PCI squarely within the traditions of the European left in its deep suspicion of the "forces of order" and the way the state (especially in Italy) often used them against the labor movement. In the Italian context, this historical distrust was aggravated until quite recently by evidence that various security and/or military services were involved in cover-ups of right-wing activities or indeed in outright plots agains the Republic.[56] As long as terrorism remained of the right-wing variety—and it did through the early 1970s—it was easy to oppose it in the name of the "antifascist Republic, born in the Resistance." Needless to say, this was an extremely comfortable position for the PCI.

These predispositions were further reinforced by the DC's political use of terrorism after the late 1960s. Most terrorist acts through the early 1970s, and without doubt the most serious threats to democracy, came from the right (in the form of bombings or outright plotting). But the DC found it politically expedient to assign the blame equally to right *and* left extremism. This reasserted the DC's centrality and moderation in a period when its hegemony had been badly shaken. And it also created an atmosphere of guilt by association that would plague the left-wing parties and the unions in a period when they were using militant and often disruptive strikes and demonstrations to great effect. The DC's willingness to capitalize on the very ugly atmosphere that followed the hot autumn was a powerful contributor to the "strategy of tension," which met with a predictable response from the PCI and those to its left. The suggestion that terrorism came from the left was seen as an attempt to discredit the left in toto, to undermine the victories it had achieved since the hot autumn, and—this was critical for the PCI—to keep the Communists out on the margins of the political system. It was thus easy and convenient to deny the existence of *any* red terrorism under these conditions. Even after the appearance of actions with an unmistakable left-wing signature (around 1972–73), the PCI therefore continued to ignore the phenomenon and to claim that the perpetrators were Fascists in disguise or foreign agents.

Left-wing terrorism escalated notably after 1976 as the PCI assumed a more important political role in the country. By 1977, groups such as the *Brigate Rosse* and *Prima Linea*, to name the most active and infamous, had switched their targets from the extreme right to much more moderate political figures, factory managers, and police officers; they also began to murder some of their targets rather than kidnap or wound them. Leftists, including Communists, appeared among the terrorists' targets.

Events in 1977 also escalated as mass demonstrations, often violent, took place against communist unionists (at Rome University) and local governments (in Bologna).[56] In these and other incidents, young demonstrators were shot dead by the police or armed forces. And armed individuals began to appear among the violent fringes of demonstrators, indicating yet another stage in what began to appear to many as a very serious breakdown of order. These so-called *autonomi* (their autonomy was to be understood as independence from all groups) might be hard to classify according to the usual political spectrum, but they certainly were not right-wing.

Communist concern over mounting evidence of the alienation of young people from politics grew considerably in this period.[58] But the PCI still would not admit that such a thing as left-wing terrorism actually existed. It is difficult to point to an official position in the party at the time, but the prevalent tendency was to be extremely generic: quasi-military actions, violent and less violent demonstrations, and the mass disaffection of young people were all considered indicators of a general moral and political crisis in Italy. The PCI presented itself as the one political force that could lead the country out of this crisis, and it did so by frequent recourse to the comforting but shopworn slogans and symbols of antifascism. A typical tactic drew parallels between 1977 and 1919, when fascist squads began their activities, frequently recruiting university students with great success. But although the charge of *diciannovismo* ("nineteenism," after 1919) might have had a vague and superficial applicability to the armed *autonomi*, it begged the much more important questions of organized terrorism and the mass disaffection of young people.

This was unquestionably a difficult period for the PCI; the options at its disposal were extremely limited. But if this survey of events shows anything, it is that the party's own conscious and unconscious choices automatically blinded it to most of the alternatives it might have considered. The party's unswerving dedication to its own political legitimation, combined with elements in its cultural baggage, simply did not allow it to admit that unwelcome phenomena existed. It fell back on convenient symbols and concepts ("moral crisis," antifacism, National Unity, the Resistance) not only because they served its immediate short-term goals but also because it did not have adequate tools available to analyze a new and admittedly complex situation. It would seem that especially where generically "postmodern" issues are involved, the old Jacobin inclination to guide society becomes much more pronounced. Phenomena that do not fit preconceived ideas are considered immature or, as we have seen, confused and morally defective; the presumably more rational political sphere will have to lead the way out of this confusion.[59]

The PCI finally acknowledged the existence of left-wing terrorism late in 1977, after it was formally admitted to the governmental majority. Once it did so, it rapidly integrated this change into its preexisting analysis. The basic goal of terrorism was still viewed as the thwarting of the PCI's efforts to be accepted as a legitimate partner in a national coalition. And the party's position on all forms of terrorism remained very hardline; all forms of violence were unequivocally condemned, and no de facto recognition of any terrorists (e.g., by negotiation) was to be tolerated.

As is often the case, considerable differences could be found within the PCI on the issue, although only a few intellectuals openly criticized the general line. The hardest position in the party argued that the violence that had spawned terrorism and other aberrations such as the *autonomi* was a pathology rooted in the mass movements of the late 1960s.[60] One of the PCI's best-known "moralists," no friend of the New Left, struck a more painful (because accurate) chord when he attacked the labor movement's uncritical adoption of some of the less tolerant types of protest of the 1960s.[61] Many leaders of the party did not wish to go so far as to "incriminate the hot autumn," but all agreed that Italy's democratic institutions were under direct and serious attack.[62]

Were this merely an abstract debate, it would represent little more than an interesting footnote in a troubled period for the PCI. But the party was forced by circumstances both to formulate a position and to act on it, and that proved to be fraught with costs. Its drive for legitimation reinforced the tendency to defend the existing order and call for a "strong state." Then the kidnapping of Aldo Moro by the Red Brigades in March 1978 further aggravated the situation; the Communists, in fact, ended up as the strongest opponents of any negotiations with Moro's captors. The party's unwillingness to delegate law-and-order questions to the DC and the right reflected an effort to circumvent the growing backlash in the country, which was calling for capital punishment and emergency legislation to counter the terrorist threat. The PCI knew it would ultimately be hurt by a strong turn to the right. It thus tried to hammer home the theme that the instruments to deal with terrorism already existed, if the political will could be found to use them.[63] Needless to say, the best way to express that will would be to form an all-party emergency government which gave the PCI a full share of power; this had been the PCI's position before the eruption of the terrorism issue as well.

But taking the hard-line stand cost the PCI dearly, and not only in terms of the referendum on the *Legge Reale*. Whatever its intentions, in practice the party emerged as a zealous defender of repressive measures, and then had to construct elaborate rationales and explanations that left almost no one satisfied.[64] And its stated policy of "scorched earth" around terrorists deeply alienated many leftists and civil libertarians, who often found themselves attacked as soft on terrorism—or worse—when they raised questions about police behavior or procedures. Moreover, because it was simply unable to act subtly on these matters, the PCI treated its own intellectuals in a very heavy-handed manner, forcing them to adopt its agenda and framework with disastrous results for the broader dialogue they were seeking with others.[65] Many young people and all sorts of intellectuals were profoundly alienated by the PCI's behavior in this period. The party's intolerant actions were once again generating grave doubts.

The party was also upsetting its own militants and supporters at an increasing rate because of what it was *not* doing. In this period of strategic floundering for the PCI, pressing for an all-party coalition based on the lowest common denominator (the defense of democracy) must have appeared to be an easy line to follow. It obviously allowed the leadership to fall back on comfortable formulas when they were demonstrably unable to spell out even their medium-range goals.[66] The soft-pedaling of criticism of the DC, which had begun in the post-1976 period, greatly increased late in 1977 when the PCI joined the governmental majority and its position on red terrorism crystallized. Then, with the kidnapping of Moro, it became even more difficult for the Communists to be openly critical of Italy's ruling party.

The waters were further muddied because "defense of the Republic born in the Resistance" was a classically antifascist rallying cry, and thus most successful as a mobilizing tool against the right. To the extent that the party was successful in employing this line against the extreme left (and it was usually only able to do so by preaching to the converted), it seemed to imply that the real enemy was still on the right and that the Red Brigades were a right-wing phenomenon. Here one sees the limits and perhaps even the exhaustion of the usefulness of the party's traditional symbols in the drastically changed reality of the late 1970s.

## The Antiterrorism Campaign in Turin, 1977–1979

The Piedmontese capital was a center of left terrorist activity throughout the late 1970s. During the period when the bulk of the fieldwork for this study was carried out, attacks on people and property in the Turin area occurred on an average of twice a week.[67] A highly publicized trial of leading Red Brigade figures early in 1978 saw four thousand troops stationed in and around the city when the group threatened to disrupt the proceedings. Roadblocks and military patrols, along with constant press coverage, made it impossible to ignore the phenomenon.

Turin was thus much more than a microcosm of the larger society in this period. In fact, events in Turin helped precipitate the party's national line on left-wing terrorism in November 1977. The key event was the murder by the Red Brigades of Carlo Casalegno, an editor and columnist of the Turinese daily *La Stampa*. Casalegno, an ex-partisan but by no means a man of the left, had consistently denounced the terrorist threat to Italian democratic institutions. His murder was doubly shocking, for it left no doubt that the *brigatisti* were now shooting to kill and that they were no longer limiting their targets to narrowly defined "oppressors of the masses" (e.g., policemen or Fiat managers).[68] This was itself an alarming escalation, but what really pushed the Communists to a more forceful stand was the very poor response to the call for a short protest strike when Casalegno was shot. National press coverage made much of the workers' nonresponse, and indeed of their general indifference to or garbled understanding of the terrorist threat.[69] The Turinese PCI, openly admitting that it was reacting to this disturbing situation, called a flurry of high-level assemblies within a week, all of which focused on left terrorism and the need for a mass campaign, especially in the schools and factories.

These assemblies were at first largely confined to organizations of the PCI, for the rank and file's orientation was scarcely more sophisticated than that of common citizens. They soon became public initiatives in which representatives of the major parties would go to the piazzas, schools, and factories of Turin to defend republican institutions and denounce terrorism. The federation was already very busy at the time preparing for a National Conference of Communist Workers and holding regular congresses for a good number of its sections. Throwing itself into the antiterrorist campaign thus resulted in (1) a strong infusion of the terrorist theme into activities which had been planned to focus on organizational or economic issues and (2) a stretching of the federation's capacities beyond their physical limits.

Events conspired to ensure that the Turinese PCI always had terrorism on its mind (and agenda). By the end of February 1978, it became evident that Red Brigade threats against anyone who "collaborated" in bringing the group to justice were effective: of the first ninety-one Turinese citizens called for jury duty in the upcoming trial, only five accepted.[70] Then, in mid-March, Aldo Moro was kidnapped. Both of these events caused the party to escalate its already frenzied activities. But in the entire period between November 1977 and May 1978, the federation frequently canceled much of its regularly scheduled activity whenever anything related to terrorism occurred. On some occasions, it brought strong pressure to bear on its own youth group or on flanking organizations to ensure that their activities were canceled and that they joined demonstrations, funeral corteges, and the like. In a period in which the PCI's political position was already quite precarious, the road taken by the Turinese federation guaranteed that its regular activities would be severely hampered, if not paralyzed.

Given the tension in the city and the indifference shown by militants as well as by common citizens, the party's obsessive concern is understandable. And given the size and problematic orientation of the Turinese working class, the local PCI would find it difficult to present a subtle, civil libertarian defense of democracy even if it were able or inclined to do so (it was not). A campaign of this type had to be limited to a few strong and unequivocal arguments, and PCI meetings and documents leave no doubt about what these were to be.[71] First, the party's general line was to be defended: PCI-DC collaboration was identified as the major target of the terrorists. Second, mass attitudes had to be oriented, both to sensitize people to the threat to democracy and to avoid the right-wing backlash that inceasingly seemed to be taking shape in the country. Third, attitudes on the left that stressed the negative qualities of the Italian state also had to be condemned. Whatever its shortcomings, the "democratic state born in the resistance" was a great achievement of the Italian labor movement which had in the past decade brought impressive gains to the PCI and the workers; thus, those who argued "neither with the state nor with the Red Brigades"[72] were not only wrong but played into the terrorists' hands. And those on the left who claimed that terrorists were "comrades who have erred" were, at best, naive fools.

If clear in theory, this position created many problems for the federation when it attempted to put it into practice. As important as the question of terrorism was, it was not the only challenge facing the PCI at the time, and one could even argue that it was not really worth the extraordinary attention the party devoted to it. Yet, in the real world of limited resources, this topic became practically the only one the badly strained organizational machine in Turin could address systematically. And this raised serious reservations at all levels of the party, even among some of the top leaders most strongly identified with the party's hard line. Some openly confessed their pessimism to me; they felt that the rounds of assemblies were mainly affecting only those already convinced, and they sensed that the party might better spend its time on other issues.

Unfortunately, neither the content nor the format of the party's attack on terrorism left much room for other issues. The emergency government theme, the defense of collaboration with the DC, and the physical presence of Christian Democrats in many public assemblies all militated against the development of a more independent position by the PCI. In fact, I frequently observed Communist speakers forced to defend the DC from scathing attacks from the floor in many assemblies. The issue, they would say (often with embarrassment), is not any party's past corruption or responsibilities but the defense of democracy *now*. And while Communists frequently tried to link the need for economic change with the mobilization to defend democratic institutions, they did not do so very convincingly, because the party itself had provided no clear-cut policy initiatives that were logically or directly linked to the campaign in defense of democracy.[73]

The result was a classical de facto two-stage approach to social reform: first we defend the existing state of affairs, and then, when things have improved, we try to change them. The PCI had argued against this approach since the days of Togliatti, but after 1976, it was increasingly accused of abandoning its commitment to change.[74] Hostility to the two-stage approach, as one might imagine, has always been especially great in Turin, given its militant traditions.

It will thus come as no surprise to learn that the party encountered the stiffest internal criticism of its antiterrorism line from Communist trade unionists. Immediately after the Piedmontese Regional Committee of the PCI set out its position, a joint meeting of functionaries from the party and the CGIL was held in the federation.[75] Almost every unionist who spoke made clear that the party's position had complicated an already delicate relationship in the factories. The united union confederations had accepted the principle of austerity and would formally endorse the idea early in 1978.[76] But it was no secret that the Turinese union leadership was much more hostile to the proposal. Communist unionists had been under a constant barrage of criticism from those in other parties or organizations in all three confederations ever since the austerity line had been enunciated. And if they had been made uncomfortable by their party's economic moderation, they made clear that they found it even harder to stand by it on the question of terrorism. Many members of the CISL (*Confederazione Italiana di Sindacati Liberi*: originally Catholic, in Turin it included many members of extraparliamentary groups) were in fact advocates of the line that supported neither the state nor the BR. They in particular found the Communists' arguments offensive and saw in them an effort to tar any working-class militance with the terrorist brush. Their position was, in essence, "What has the state done for us that justifies such a fierce defense?"

These criticisms did not fall on deaf ears. Why, wondered the (Communist) head of the Piedmontese CGIL, was there suddenly so much emphasis on terrorism in the factories? Equal attention to centers of white-collar employment, or the schools, was nowhere in evidence, although *brigatisti* could obviously be found in such places. He and many of his comrades said they were wary of "sticking a 'red' label on the terrorists." They also felt the PCI was deeply alienating many groups whose allegiance was already at best tenuous (especially young people) by its posture of "arrogant preaching."

The federation leadership, in contrast, tried to emphasize the importance of defending democratic institutions, and the danger in appearing to support them only if an adequate economic trade-off could be obtained. In his concluding remarks, the secretary of the federation put it bluntly:

> Do we defend this democratic state *only* if we get rapid changes in the direction that we want? Or do we defend democratic institutions in any event, even if we have to suffer some defeats?

When he concluded, "We have to defend this state unequivocally," a unionist interrupted him with a question already raised several times. Did he really think that the party could commit itself to the state just as it is? Wasn't this a signal to the DC and the bosses not to give an inch on anything, since the PCI's support was a foregone conclusion? At this point, the secretary had to back off somewhat, and he apologized for putting the matter in such a crude (*grossolano*) way. But he immediately returned to his central theme, and the lack of consensus on terrorism—along with a strong sense of union dissent on austerity—remained.

Had the PCI's general position in the give-and-take of Italian politics been stronger at the time, the party's own unionists might have been more sympathetic, or at least less hostile. But this was late November of 1977—just a few weeks before the mass rally of the FLM in Rome that would force the Communists temporarily to withdraw their support from the government of Giulio Andreotti. And the FLM is, of course, the dominant union in Turin. Moreover, the rapidly deteriorating relations among the various components of the presumably united union movement made it nearly impossible for the Communists in the movement to give their party's hard-line position much material support. The leftists—in the CISL, but some were also in the CGIL—were already a problem. Far more serious, however, was the opposition of the Socialists, who dominated the Turinese UIL (*Unione Italiana di Lavoratori*) and remained a significant, if minor, presence in the CGIL. They were extremely suspicious of anything that looked like Communist favoritism of the DC over the PSI, and many, if not most, of the PCI's actions in this period fueled such suspicions. The Socialists, in any event, were likely to resist Communist initiatives out of pure political rivalry.

It was thus quite clear to federation leaders that, regardless of Communist unionists' reservations about the line on terrorism, the imperatives of unity within the movement meant that the party could not count on much support for its positions from the unions inside the factory gates. This realization pushed the PCI toward undertaking the exhausting round of party-led assemblies in the factories (as well as in schools and in public *piazze*). These constraints on the PCI may surprise those who continue to think in terms of communist dominance of the CGIL, or that the latter's acceptance of the austerity line demonstrates its slavish adherence to party dictates.

Hence, in spite of its effort directed toward the factories, the party could not count on much of a support structure for its positions once a meeting ended. Few shopfloor militants put the antiterror campaign at the top of their list of priorities, and the general climate was one in which Communists were markedly on the defensive. People in the federation would eventually speak of having reached eighty thousand workers in hundreds of meetings. Although far less than this number actually attended the assemblies held in their plants (or listened very attentively when they did attend), this is still no mean achievement. But party leaders were still reporting serious problems in getting their own militants to accept that left-wing terrorism truly existed late in April 1978.[77] And the base of the party remained deeply distressed by the PCI's apparent willingness to absolve the DC of past wrongs. Thus, the federation's actions did little to counter, and in some ways they reinforced, the general demoralization and demobilization of the party rank and file, especially in the factories.

Nor could the federation claim great progress outside the factories on the terrorism issue. It was there, and especially in contact with intellectuals, that the costs of the hard line could be seen. At a meeting of Communist high school teachers, serious reservations were expressed at the party's "Prussian" posture.[78] Absenteeism at high school assemblies was massive, and those who did attend were described as indifferent. But many reservations, especially those concerning the party's often intolerant pressing of its position, fell on deaf ears in the upper reaches of the federation hierarchy. Indeed, because the top leaders in Turin—following the national party's lead—were clear about their indifference to the theme of civil liberties, most functionaries filtered the reservations they had heard out of their reports to the leadership. Under these circumstances, only those lower-level leaders who felt strongly about the matter would bother to do more than mention this in passing, if they did so at all.

The party's zeal to vilify terrorism and to isolate sympathizers often alienated more than intellectuals. On more than one occasion, PCI statements or initiatives appeared to sanction a witch-hunt mentality. Following the Moro kidnapping, the Communists announced that they would use their significant presence in the country's workplaces as eyes and ears to seek out terrorists and their supporters. This did not go down at all well with grass-roots militants, who balked at playing policeman. The prevailing sentiment seemed to be that it is one thing to witness criminal acts or extremely suspicious behavior, which should be reported to the authorities, or at least to party leaders. But it is quite another matter to be expected to report on generically defined suspects.[79] This position was not a libertarian objection to party policy; it grew out of class solidarity. But it showed how unpopular the party's approach was among the rank and file and how badly out of touch with the sentiments of its own base, not to mention public opinion, the party had become on this question.

And it remained out of touch, sometimes moving from insensitivity into the realm of whopping political blunders. A full year after the Moro kidnapping, some leaders of the federation and the Piedmontese Regional Council of the party decided to use the newly established *comitati di quartiere* to fight terrorism. Against considerable resistance among the rank and file and in headquarters, they used the CdQ of several neighborhoods to circulate a "mass questionnaire" on terrorism. As is often the case with such undertakings, the questionnaire itself fell far short of anything a serious social scientist would view as a reasonable research instrument. Worst of all, however, was the inclusion among the questions of a section asking whether the respondent had any suspicions to report. Any such suspicions would be kept in strict confidence (the questionnaire was anonymous to begin with) and relayed to the authorities by the survey's administrators.[80]

It is easy to imagine the outcry that greeted this initiative and the doubts that were publicly reiterated concerning the PCI's commitment to pluralism and civil rights. Although there was a "debate" within the party on the question, the fact that the top leaders' minds were already made up meant that no useful exchange of views or altering of positions resulted. It is once again striking how easy it proved for the top leadership of the federation to take a position that violated public sensibility and, more importantly, common sense.

It is extremely difficult to gauge whether even the PCI's more modest goals were achieved in its campaign in Turin. The party did alter its own position late in 1977, but it is unclear whether it was truly able to communicate this to militants, and especially to the public. In large meetings and mass assemblies throughout 1978, Communist orators generally received chilly receptions when they spelled out their party's positions. They inevitably encountered the warmest reactions when they dwelled on Resistance and antifascist themes. As good orators do, they were quick to read the crowd and therefore tended to elaborate on parallels between the *brigatisti* and Fascists. As already noted, this approach obscured more than it clarified, and I personally saw it occur time after time.

The extensive exposure of the federation's intermediate cadre to the public in this period also does not seem to have been a very useful learning experience for the apparatus. I accompanied many functionaries to assemblies and spoke with and observed many more as they returned to headquarters after such gatherings. They were generally appalled at the low level of concern they found, especially among workers and students, and saw it as evidence of antipolitical attitudes among the masses. It did not seem to occur to them that the reaction signified a fairly diffuse apoliticism that one might expect when the mass public is confronted with fairly abstract ideas.[81]

Terrorism, in sum, appears to have created a no-win situation for the PCI. It faced obstinacy among some of its own militants and leaders over whether red terrorism even existed; the unionists are a good case in point, although their own situation was complicated. Its national strategy and ingrained ideological predispositions further pushed the party to assume positions that were, to say the least, unsubtle. And once it put terrorism at the top of its agenda, the issue's pervasiveness, at least in Turin, meant that the federation's limited resources would be badly overloaded. From another vantage point—Rome—dwelling on the threat to democracy may have represented a comfortable way to side-step more pressing matters for which the party had no ready responses. But even on a national level, as events showed, this proved to be a gross miscalculation. The PCI ended up with the defense of democracy as practically its only program in this period, and it quickly found that it did not have the credibility to compete head-on with the DC on that terrain.

Although the cases examined here range widely in their subject matter, they are clearly bound together by the systematic weaknesses they reveal in the PCI's orientation and actions in the late 1970s. In each instance, the interplay of three basic factors emerges strongly: the party's institutional strategy, its organizational inertia, and its underlying theoretical or ideological inclinations.

The ideological factor can be a contentious one, suggesting something of a residual category to be called in to mop up behavior or attitudes that are not otherwise easily explained. For the sake of clarity, I am using the concept in the way many observers employ the notion of the party's "culture." It does not imply a coherent set of beliefs or orientations to action so much as a series of strong remnants or residues left over from the Leninist past. When confronted with new situations, the party often falls back on them by default, because they offer reassuring (even if outmoded) ways to understand reality and to act in unified fashion. There is abundant evidence of this above all in the party's style of relating to its own militants and even its supporters: the tendency to pose issues in black-and-white terms, a highly pedagogical attitude taken toward the masses, a recurring lack of sensitivity to civil libertarian positions, or a manipulative attitude toward representative institutions have appeared too systematically to be mere happenstance. I repeat that this does not imply a secret agenda on the part of Italian Communists; it does suggest that they are strongly conditioned by their own past.

But it was the present that actually dictated policy options, and in that sense the determining element among the three was undoubtedly the PCI's single-minded pursuit of wider legitimation and rapprochement with the DC. It would take a long time, and a crushing setback, before the party undertook a thoroughgoing reassessment of its behavior and of the strategic underpinnings of its actions. The motives behind and the nature of this reassessment are examined in the next chapter.

# 4

# The Strategic Dimensions of the Crisis: *Autocritica* and Change (1978–1980)

Five years after spelling out the *compromesso storico* and two years after committing itself to a national unity government that would have brought it fully into a coalition in Rome, the PCI began to reexamine its behavior. More slowly, it began to restate its strategic goals. Within a year, as the DC continued to block its efforts to obtain ministerial responsibilities, the PCI forced national elections. And by the end of 1980, back in the opposition, the party abandoned its efforts to form a national unity coalition, and the *compromesso* was, in effect, dropped. The transitional crisis was not over, but it had reached a strategic juncture.

This chapter will examine how the party struggled to extricate itself from the most serious and painful contradictions that had emerged in the period of national unity. Two major questions will be addressed: Why did it take two years to arrive at a point that was clearly indicated in 1978? How does a change of strategy take place in the PCI, and how is that change experienced at a local level? The major focus will remain the Turinese federation. But since I have argued that the national strategy was most responsible for the difficulties of PCI local organizations, we must examine national developments as well. Any effort to avoid discussing what took place at the summit of the PCI would be misleading. Local conditions seriously aggravated the federation's problems, but the most basic problems did not originate in Turin.

## False Starts: Reactions to Electoral Losses in 1978

We have seen that even before the results of the referenda, the regional and provincial leaders of the PCI were called to Rome to discuss the serious losses suffered in the partial local elections of 1978.[1] Berlinguer chastised local leaders for seeking agreement "at any price" with the DC and saw this as a major reason why the party had lost so much support. Local events, and hence the party's actions, had to be viewed "in terms notably different from those that arise at the national level." Too much emphasis on institutional maneuvering had led the party to ignore "the direction of struggles, work among the masses, and cultural and ideological battles." Henceforth the PCI would have to reassert its combativeness and identity as a mass party by distancing itself from the governing parties, particularly the DC.

Though this might have sounded like a clear set of marching orders, we know that the party then turned around and behaved very differently during the referendum campaigns, to the chagrin of many militants and low-level leaders. Six weeks after the referenda, Berlinguer spoke to the Central Committee using the same concepts and criticisms that had been employed two months earlier.[2] Most significantly, he repeated the strategic revision first heard in May. The *compromesso storico* was strongly defended, but its meaning was immediately qualified. As a broad strategy, he said, it had nothing to do with a coalition formula—indeed, under the rubric of the *compromesso*, one could even imagine the "possible alternation" of governments.

The strategy had thus been reduced to a search for a broad consensus on the demo-cratic rules of the game, which would avoid a possibly destructive polarization of society. Missing from this new definition of the party's strategic goals is the transformation of Italy through the creation of a vast bloc of forces, far in excess of 51 percent; this had been a central pillar, if not the very heart, of the original formulation. This restricted definition was clearly a response to recent frustration. It was undoubtedly also meant as a signal to the DC that the Communists' patience—and their support of an increasingly immobilized government—was coming to an end. An even stronger version of the same message was delivered by Berlinguer in his speech at the National Festival of *l'Unità* in September, which most observers agreed was the most militant statement of PCI principles and priorities in more than two years.[3]

And yet, in spite of toughening its stance over the summer of 1978, the PCI's practice remained unaltered for another six months. This is not really surprising, since its immediate goal—a government of national solidarity, with ministerial posts for Communists—had not changed. That goal set sharp limits on how far the PCI could push the DC, because it remained a prospective coalition partner. Moreover, too strong an ultimatum would probably have led to early elections, which the Communists, given their recent track record, were not eager to precipitate.

In addition, developments from mid-1978 have to be seen within the context of internal party maneuvering. The PCI was preparing for its Fifteenth National Congress, scheduled for spring 1979. The party's problems had led to considerable speculation about the Congress, including anticipation of a possible reshuffling of the top leadership.[4] Given the critical but also disoriented atmosphere within the party, there was a consensus not to push matters too far before various positions were clarified and debated. In fact, however, the precongressional debate revealed so much disillusionment within the party that the top leaders felt compelled to deliver a very strong ultimatum to the DC at the beginning of 1979. The PCI announced that its fence-straddling period was over. Its new slogan became "Either in the Government or in the Opposition." The DC, of course, refused to countenance the inclusion of the Communists, and the result was a full-fledged governmental crisis that eventually saw early elections called for June 1979. The Fifteenth Congress was held late in March and early in April, after the PCI's break with the government but before elections were actually set. Berlinguer was thus able to address the Congress from a strongly reinforced position vis-à-vis internal dissatisfaction in the party. And while his criticisms of the DC (and others) were harsh, he continued to repeat the call for a government of national unity.[5]

It is thus evident that, in spite of a much firmer tone and the ultimatum to take the PCI into the government or see it return to the opposition, the next step—which party organizations in the provinces needed as a guide for their actions—remained unclear. Berlinguer's initiative had undercut calls for an outright alternative to the DC, and nothing that might replace the policy of national solidarity had crystallized. With early elections about to be called and a sense of foreboding about their possible outcome, the party's agenda would be full until well into the summer. It is not clear whether Berlinguer and those closest to him genuinely believed that the ultimatum might produce a result that could avoid the election. It is clear that they were unwilling to move any farther in their revision at this point than they already had, and the practical result of that decision was the continuation of earlier political and strategic paralysis.

## Autocritica *in Turin: Phase I*

The leaders of the Turinese federation had been, on the whole, strongly committed to the general lines of their party's strategy since 1975.[6] It is therefore not surprising that, lacking any clear directives from the center as to what could be done in the wake of the defeats of 1978, the local party achieved no notable breakthroughs in the opening stages of its *autocritica*. It did, however, witness a very lively debate within its ranks. And a number of highly important issues, long bubbling below the surface, came fully to light. The way the process unfolded is instructive.

In the earliest stages of the debate, it was evident that the leaders of the federation were quite disoriented. The exceptionally poor showing in the referenda opened the party to a charge that could not be brushed aside: it clearly had lost touch with its own base, even in its strongholds. And yet, because the *compromesso* had been touched up but also placed beyond serious criticism, discontent was inevitably channeled against specific recent actions, not underlying assumptions. At the very top of the federation, the *autocritica* was a carbon copy of Berlinguer's May and July speeches, down to parroting his exact phrases (perhaps the clearest sign of widespread confusion). Somewhat lower down in the federal hierarchy, where belief in national solidarity and the historic compromise had been less profound from the start, more extensive attacks on the party's past and present actions were heard. And at the rank-and-file level, the tone was even more extreme; it is no small matter when militants designated to speak by several party sections pronounce their "extreme lack of confidence [*sfiducia*] in the leaders of this federation."[7]

But it would be an error to assume that the federation only divided vertically in this debate. It would be even more incorrect to assume that craven careerists at the top defended party orthodoxy against the righteous rage of the base. There was a vertical division, but this hardly means that all justice resided in the lower rungs of the hierarchy, many of whom simply wanted to return to the opposition while ignoring the broader issues that had been put before their party since the mid-1970s. At the same time, there were also strong horizontal divisions among different groups in the party in Turin. Each division had its own logic and conditioned the course of the debate.

Vertically, the fundamental issue was party strategy, even though it rarely was articulated in so many words; the PCI has developed an elliptical vocabulary precisely to avoid direct confrontation on critical issues. Thus, the most common criticism was that the line had been handed down from above for several years, with no apparent concern for rank-and-file views. Consistently voiced warnings about the difficulties confronting those who had to explain the PCI's positions had been brushed aside. This criticism was accepted by the top party leadership, with the open acknowledgment that "the leadership [of the federation] tends to orient before it discusses or listens."[8] And leaders—particularly the secretary of the federation—were candid about being strategically at sea, with no doctrinal anchors to provide reassurance. "The certainties of the past simply cannot return, and there's nothing to be done about that," was the way it was put.[9]

A number of grass-roots militants and even some middle-level leaders did not want to accept this line of argument, although most did. The bulk of those who did accept the argument also emphasized a theme that had been present in the party and especially strong in Turin for years. They stressed the need, precisely because the PCI no longer can claim to hold a transcendent truth, to spell out clear priorities—and, better yet, a concrete program—that would clarify the party's broader ideals and orient its day-to-day activities.[10] In Turin, as elsewhere, this tended to be a left-wing critique of the national leadership: a project or set of priorities would force the party away from broad and vague formulations and lead to the specific targeting of some groups in society to the exclusion of others.

The vertical *autocritica* thus put two perennial problems for the PCI on the front burner. One is the question of internal organization and democracy, to which I shall return at length in subsequent chapters. The other was the perceived need for a program or project to serve as a modern substitute for the ideological certainties of the past. Just below the surface, however, and occasionally in full view, was a more sectarian, workerist position that was quite strong in Turin, as we would expect. This held that the party should throw out the historic compromise, *all* mediating activity in public institutions, and march gloriously into the opposition (and, one might add, the past) with red flags unfurled. For supporters of this view, there were still plenty of certainties that the Turinese Communists could fall back on. And when this view was put forward, full of combative and workerist rhetoric, at a major party meeting immediately following the referenda, it received the loudest applause of the evening.[11]

Here we see the real dilemma for the federation's leaders. Even had they not been committed to the *compromesso*, they would have to hold on to what remained of it in the absence of a clear line emanating from the center. A strategic vacuum in Turin posed at least the threat of a return to hard-line—and, in 1978, sterile—oppositional attitudes of the past. Turinese traditions were strong enough and the rank and file were restive enough to make that kind of backsliding a very real possibility.

What could be done under these circumstances? Obviously, not a great deal. On one occasion, simply as an effort to boost the battered morale of the common militants, the leadership proposed a full-scale march through the capital as a way of showing the party's colors. But functionaries more in touch with the grass roots quickly shot down this idea. They argued that the turnout was likely to be so low as to represent yet another demoralizing experience for the federation, and the top leaders let the idea drop.[12] When initiatives of this type are the only ones that come to mind, the underlying confusion (if not desperation) is all too obvious.

The horizontal divisions that emerged in the federation were equally intense and in many ways more interesting, for they underscored the PCI's general dilemma in the period after 1975. Since that time, the party had become terribly fragmented and sectorialized. As it moved into governmental posts locally and as it addressed an increasing number of specialized problems generally, it became increasingly difficult to formulate any sort of broader synthesis, which is one reason why it was so difficult to spell out a clear set of priorities, let alone a more ambitious project. Each group within the party was increasingly cut off from others. This is the case when we define groups by sector (e.g., schools, middle classes, factories) or functionally within the broader movement (party, unions, local government). It had even become difficult to get various components of the party together physically, which only reinforced the tendency of each to act more as a pressure group on behalf of its own constituency.[13]

This is not a purely Turinese problem, although the massive assumption of governmental responsibilities, with the requirement of demonstrating expertise in many new areas, definitely aggravated the federation's difficulties. The underlying problem is really one of the basic ones that the *partito nuovo* in transition faces. How is it possible to be a mass, highly articulated structure with a nondoctrinal (or "agnostic") outlook and avoid degenerating into a federation of pressure groups? The new situation represents an important step forward from the centralization of the past, but it is likely to produce disharmony, if not cacophony.

If this horizontal cleavage was recognized and lamented by everyone in the federation, a second horizontal cleavage was the source of open conflict. This involved the proper relationship between the party and public institutions where the PCI held local power. Conflict was inevitable here, for at issue was the PCI's actual behavior since 1975 and hence the assessing of responsibility for recent losses. Tensions existed on this issue in Turin from the very beginning, but only the aftermath of the referenda permitted them to be fully aired. When they were, a dramatic polarization emerged in the federation.

The most clearly articulated positions are quite familiar by now. On one side, the PCI was attacked for having become too closely identified with institutions at the expense of its mass-mobilizational, activist identity. When Berlinguer chastised the local leaders in this fashion in mid-1978, he was expressing (and legitimizing) sentiments that had long been simmering in the party.[14] When articulated at a local level, these views contained stinging rebukes.[15]

The "institutional party" was most strongly criticized for treating the regular party organization as a mere support system for its own initiatives. And these initiatives were usually decided without any real discussions with the rank and file, who were then nevertheless expected to support them unquestioningly. The phrase most often heard in this attack was "Do not disturb the driver," which was the base's shorthand way of saying the public officials wanted things entirely their own way. This high-handed treatment had led to a loss of interest, and thus a drop in participation, along the lower rungs of the party hierarchy. It was no surprise at all that the party had badly lost touch with reality, even in its working-class bastions.[16]

Organizational cadres were not alone in expressing this criticism. Many of those who had taken up institutional posts had argued forcefully, long before 1978, that a dangerous trend was emerging in the federation. After the referenda, one of the most prestigious political figures in Turin put it succinctly: "[institutional] mediation is the road to disarming the movement."[17] And many other administrators' voices joined the chorus, pointing out that public officials (most of whom had recently been organizational cadres) ended up as confused as party organizers when neither group was able to keep its own tasks clearly in mind. If former party organizers continued to use public institutions to mediate social conflict as much as they had in the post-1975 period, there was a serious risk that the institutions would become overloaded and unable to perform their primary tasks.

At the other end of a spectrum which contained many intermediate positions is what we might call the purely institutional position. This was most forcefully expressed, as would be expected, by a number of prominent administrators and elected officials, including the very popular mayor of Turin, Diego Novelli.[18] These people had not hidden their views earlier, but the 1978 *autocritica* also provided them with the opportunity for a direct confrontation. The gist of the institutional position was that the party's recent losses were best understood as a whirlwind the PCI was reaping for not having been more courageous when it was in the opposition. Demagoguery had been tolerated with a wink in order to galvanize all forms of protest and opposition. Now the party had to govern in a state of chaos for which it bore considerable responsibility. It had failed to tell several groups what they needed to hear in the past: "Listen, comrades, some of the things (free rent, free transport) you are asking for are just stupid."[19] If there was demobilization and passivity abroad, it was because the party had built up unrealistic expectations among the masses, many of whom now expected the Communist-led *giunta* to hand them whatever they demanded. Furthermore, it was quite appropriate and necessary for local government to fill the "political and cultural vacuum" that was created after 1975.[20]

These contrasting positions generated very heated feelings following the referenda and for some time afterward. Militants as well as some federation leaders strongly resented what they saw as a very superficial analysis of the party's problems and a moralistic, preachy tone which seemed to suggest that the unwashed masses were in need of a good education in civics and little more. Others felt that the "institutional party" had a hidden agenda: to discredit the mass movements of the 1960s and 1970s. In one exchange, a high-ranking public official insisted that the PCI, far from being demagogic, had more often than not directed protest into constructive channels. He concluded, "You can't exorcise 'sixty-eight: it is the flesh of our legs."[21] On other occasions, party leaders criticized some members of the "institutional party" by name— a rarity in the PCI—and stated that it might be wise not even to invite them to a planned assembly, because their contribution would be predictable and of little value.[22]

The more extreme positions attenuated over time, but the underlying tensions were very real. These exchanges reflect radically different interpretations of the PCI's experience in the 1970s and two entirely understandable defenses of different aspects of party activity. The real problem was that each position expressed an important aspect of the truth. The PCI *had* occasionally stooped to demagoguery while in the opposition, and it had blithely ignored the importance and complexity of public institutions when it did not have to run them. And, in power, the party *had* closed itself off in these same institutions as it attempted to master them, often merely tolerating or manipulating its own militants. Although this debate brought the issues into unusually sharp focus, the exchanges themselves mainly consisted of people talking past one another. The party had become more complex and differentiated after taking local power in 1975, and this accounts for some of the tension between its institutional and organizational personalities in 1978. But that tension was also rooted in the party's very nature, and it is only logical that it came more fully forward in a period of strategic confusion. At a local level, the PCI's identity crisis was no abstraction.

It was even more strongly felt in some of the other issues that the referendum results stirred up. We have seen that a constant leitmotif of the *autocritica* was the gulf that had opened between the party and its strongest constituency in Turin, the working class. Returns in the capital's proletarian districts and in the industrial suburbs spoke for themselves. The very poor relations that now existed in the unions had also been aggravated by recent Communist actions. Finally, the massive support among younger voters for the yes position in the referenda had deeply upset most of the federation's leaders. Many of the direst warnings of the campaign appeared to have come true, and there was a growing fear that the party was losing touch with an entire generation of new citizens, a fear that would be confirmed in the 1979 elections.

And yet, although the basic themes had been raised in Turin in the summer of 1978 and continued through the autumn as the federation prepared for its own Congress early in 1979, little came out of the first stages of the *autocritica*. Significantly, party leaders would later speak of the 1979 Congress as a rather dull affair, with lively debate in the sections and zones but with more filtered discussions heard at the top level of the organization. Yet this was only to be expected. The national party leadership had side-tracked most strong criticism by taking a tougher position on the DC by the beginning of 1979, leaving little room for sectarian recrudescences by emphasizing the continuity of the main points of party strategy. But the lack of additional cues from the center certainly did not help the Turinese federation, although it is doubtful that Rome could have done much for Turin's most pressing problems at the time. The federation therefore did what it could, which was not much: it mainly tried to make some organizational adjustments while, like the rest of the party, it waited to see what would happen in Rome.

### Either in the Government or in the Opposition: The Campaign and Aftermath of the 1979 General Elections

> I repeat that only imbeciles can argue that the political line was correct, but that it was put into practice in a mistaken way.
>
> Gian Carlo Pajetta, after the 1979 elections [23]

Close to a year elapsed between the first strong signs of change in the PCI and a break with the parliamentary majority. And even when the break came—it led to general elections—the Communists were not eager to burn all their bridges. The PCI precipitated the elections with its call for an increased governing role within the framework of national solidarity, and it continued to insist that this was the only way out of Italy's crisis following the vote as well.

We have seen that the PCI's Fifteenth Congress fell between the governmental crisis and the setting of the election date. Although the Congress had been expected to be quite lively,[24] it did not turn out that way. There had even been rumors that the party might begin to ease Berlinguer out of office by flanking him with one or more vice-secretaries. But aside from the carefully prearranged elimination of "Marxism-Leninism" from the Party Statute, the Congress contained few new departures. When the announcement of the new leadership of the PCI came, a full month after the June elections, it too contained no surprises.[25] No vice-secretaries had been chosen, and both the Secretariat and the National Executive (*Direzione*) continued to consist mainly of people closely associated with the general secretary.

Here again is evidence of the extreme caution with which the PCI would move, even after the drubbing it took at the polls in 1979. It had learned that seeking agreement with the DC at any price did not pay. But when it tried to press the issue, it was punished by the electorate (though it appears to have been punished more for its past sins than for its recent boldness). It was returning to the opposition, but it needed to keep its options open, and these were rapidly dwindling. A "left alternative" was only deemed desirable by a small part of the PCI, and its preconditions no longer existed in any event, for the Socialists were edging ever closer to a more active governmental role. Under these conditions, the entire party elite was understandably worried that momentum could carry the PCI into an intransigent posture that might leave it profoundly isolated. News of the bitter and often nostalgic criticism coming from the base only intensified these anxieties.

The 1979 election results did not ease the situation at all. Voting in 1978 had produced disappointing but ambiguous outcomes: the local elections were partial and geographically distorted, while the referenda were by their nature unclear in many important respects. In 1979, there were no escape clauses. The results were not catastrophic—the communist vote fell from 34.4 percent to 30.4 percent—but they did represent the PCI's most serious setback at the polls in the postwar period. The greatest demoralizing factor was that this was the first time the party had lost votes in a general election. The most important results can be summarized as follows:

1. The protest vote, in the broadest sense, was quite high and most pronounced among younger voters. Voter turnout hit a record low of 89.9 percent (it was over 93 percent in 1972 and 1976). Spoiled ballots doubled (to 2.2 percent) over 1976. The Radical party rose to 3.4 percent from 1.1 percent. And the New Left formations, PDUP and NSU, which together had obtained 1.5 percent in 1976, received 2.2 percent in 1979.
2. The PCI lost one and a half million votes. With the Socialists static at just under 10 percent, the traditional left-wing parties lost roughly 4 percent. This is nearly offset by the gain of the Radicals, PDUP, and NSU combined, but only if one considers all Radical votes as coming from the left, and that is a dubious proposition.
3. Contrary to expectations, the DC lost half a point and fell to 38.3 percent. Only big gains in the South offset heavy losses in the North, especially in the big cities. The minor laical parties gained roughly 1 percent, thus giving the center bloc a net rise of just under half a point. The neofascist MSI declined by nearly a point (from 6.1 percent to 5.3 percent).

Unlike 1976, then, when notable shifts occurred between the left and center, 1979 saw realignments which were basically confined within the major voting blocs. But this general picture was really much more complex, with significant interbloc shifts offsetting one another in different areas of the country. The Communists, for example, lost very heavily in the South.

If the PCI's numerical losses were distressing, the state of relations within the left must have been even more so. Indeed, one must force the issue considerably even to speak of the left as a block after the 1979 vote. PCI–Radical relations were hostile, and the attitude of the NSU toward the Communists was extremely negative. The NSU was in fact a cluster of all the extraparliamentary groups most opposed to the PCI; they had refused to repeat the 1976 expedient of running on a single list with the more flexible PDUP precisely because of their differing assessment of the Communist party. (The PDUP, with many ex-communist leaders, would eventually run with the PCI on joint lists in 1983.) With nearly 6 percent of the vote on its left—an unprecedented figure— the PCI knew that barely 1.5 percent could be considered friendly.

But the Socialists would deliver the most serious blow to the left. Under Bettino Craxi's dynamic leadership, the PSI had maneuvered constantly since 1976 to avoid being crushed between the PCI and the DC. Communist arrogance since the formulation of the *compromesso storico* fed Socialist suspicions and worsened a strained relationship.

But even taking hurt feelings and legitimate political calculations into account, Socialist behavior had been blatantly opportunistic. The PSI had, for instance, loudly championed a left alternative to counter the *compromesso* but immediately dropped the idea the moment the PCI edged away from the DC. Basically, the PSI was groping, as it had since 1956, for a well-staked-out ideological position and constituency. By the late 1970s, Craxi was convinced that this was the laical-left area which the PCI's eager courting of Catholics and the DC had left uncovered.[26]

The Socialists ran a campaign in 1979 that was evasive and disturbing to the Communists. The PCI had always rejected the left alternative outright, so it is not surprising that the PSI did not press the issue, even though it might, for once, have been viable. What was surprising was the abrupt about-face on a position held firmly since the early 1970s: the PSI dropped its insistence on the PCI's collaboration as a necessity for any solution to the Italian crisis. Capitalizing on the PCI's difficulties, Craxi announced that his major obligation was to ensure that the vote led to a "governable" Italy. To many this sounded suspiciously as if the Socialists were edging back toward direct collaboration with the DC in some new edition of the Center-Left. And this was in fact the case. By the end of the year, the PSI was governing in a five-party coalition, and the PCI, more isolated than at any time since the 1960s, was back in the opposition. (By 1983, Craxi had forced the DC, which was battered in the elections that year, to accept him as the first Socialist prime minister of Italy.)

Political isolation was thus the most serious and pressing problem that faced the Communists after the elections. But it was far from the only important issue on their agenda. The 4 percent drop was a serious psychological blow, a brutal punctuation mark after two years that had brought little good news. Some loss had been expected, but the extent of the damage was a surprise to most party leaders and militants. And the loss of many young voters and considerable working- and lower-class supporters as well added to the shock. Compounding the misery was the Radicals' stunning success, especially among young people.

The postelectoral period saw the PCI undertake considerable soul searching on the theme of its strained relationship with young people. The methods usually employed to calculate the youth vote can be controversial, but no one doubts that the Communists lost heavily in the eighteen to twenty-five age range.[27] Experts within the PCI estimated this loss to be roughly 10 to 12 percent of all young people, which means that for every four of them who voted PCI in 1976, only three did so in 1979.[28] Many voices in the party which had been muted during the referendum campaign now ripped into PCI policy toward the Radicals. The Communists were criticized in particular for their insensitivity to the libertarian issues championed by the PR and also for the moralistic and insulting tone that had usually been adopted when addressing young people's aspirations.[29] The PCI had ended up in a situation, as one leading intellectual put it, "where our relations with an entire generation are at stake."[30]

Once considerations of this type were put on the agenda, the party's strategy could no longer be considered immune from open criticism.[31] As the comment by Pajetta at the top of this section revealed, the much-used explanation that a perfectly appropriate strategy had been systematically misapplied in practice was beginning to tax the patience of many party leaders as well as militants. This was particularly true of those who had long been upset about the damaging impact of the *compromesso* on relations within the left, which by this point had deteriorated dramatically.

Finally, it seemed, the doubts within the party would get a full hearing; as we know, none of the issues raised after the elections was new. Most, including problems with young people, were depressingly familiar by then and had originally been thoroughly publicized in 1976–77.[32] And yet, at the very peak of the 1979 *autocritica*, an observer outside the PCI prophetically anticipated that the Communists would not push their revisions very far precisely because they were in so much trouble. The "incomplete" Fifteenth Congress had just gone the same way and for the same reasons: self-preservation was a much stronger instinct that the search for truth. It is interesting that this insight into the party's internal workings came from an ex-Communist.[33]

The prophecy was quickly proven true. At the July 1979 Central Committee meeting, Berlinguer reiterated criticisms of party behavior that were now more than a year old, especially the PCI's excessive softness toward the DC. But he dug in his heels on the question of the party's underlying strategy and basically blamed the electoral losses on the steady ( and "concentric") attacks suffered by the PCI for more than a year. Following two days of often stormy debate, he made the same point again in his conclusions. He also made clear, in a comment widely reported in the national press, that he was prepared to resign as secretary if that was the will of the Central Committee.[34] At the end of this meeting, the new Secretariat and Executive were chosen. Some of the new leaders were known to be critical of the way the line had been applied since 1977, but all were well-known *berlingueriani*. The historic compromise had been powerfully diluted, and the PCI was now fully back in the opposition, but the broad strategic (and many of the tactical) goals of the party remained unaltered. A government of national unity, with full Communist participation, remained the top priority.

## Autocritica *in Turin: Phase II*

> We responded to the *compromesso storico* in the same way you react to the Holy Trinity in church: everyone nods and goes on believing whatever he wants.
>
> A Turinese Communist militant[35]

The situation in Turin, in the absence of strong initiatives from national party headquarters, continued for some time as it had in the period between the referendum and the governmental crisis. Because this was a period of uncertainty, with no one able to provide hard evidence of the superiority of any of the differing positions in the party, there was a tendency for the earlier positions to crystallize. In most instances, this also meant that the conditioning effects of many of Turin's most distinctive traits were more evident as well.

By tradition, social structure, and recent history, the Turinese federation was always on the left wing of the PCI. Even in the late 1970s, with almost all the federation's top leaders staunch backers of Berlinguer, most insisted that the party needed a much clearer program or project. Only this, they believed, could consolidate the PCI's identity and provide the foundations for mass mobilization in a period when the tendency to seek agreement at any price with the DC had diluted the party's mass and radical identity.[36] But open hostility to party strategy increased dramatically as one moved down the party hierarchy; it was strongest of all at the grass roots and in the trade union movement.

Several events in 1979 make clear the top leaders' commitment to the *compromesso* and the pursuit of a unity government. They also suggest why there was less open criticism of party strategy heard in the higher reaches of the federation even at this

relatively late date. Late in 1978, Bruno Ferrero, PCI regional secretary for Piedmont—
a critic of party policy and definitely not an insider in the Turinese hierarchy—was
interviewed in a noncommunist paper.[37] Ferrero's criticism of his party's analysis of
modern society and its internal organizational practices were especially biting. Several
months after this event, in a move that everyone saw as a kick upstairs, Ferrero was
made a candidate for the European Parliament. When elected in June 1979, he was
compelled to resign his organizational position in Piedmont. His removal was not a
vindictive reaction to this single incident, but a member of the Secretariat candidly
admitted in a private conversation that this troublesome leader was replaced "at our
suggestion." Ferrero's fate was a signal to others in the apparatus (who were equally
candid in private conversations) that there were limits to acceptable criticism in the
federation. The top leadership may not have intended to chill debate, but this episode
definitely had that effect.

Another episode witnessed firsthand provides further evidence of at least some
leaders' commitment to Berlinguer's very strong continued reiteration and defense of
party policies through the end of the 1970s. The Central Committee meeting of July
1979, which discussed the losses in the 1979 elections, was considered so important
that Berlinguer's address was broadcast on Communist-affiliated radio stations all over
Italy. Following the broadcast (see p. 101), I was personally surprised at the hard-line
tone Berlinguer had assumed in light of acknowledged widespread dissatisfaction with
party policies by this time. I was even more surprised to note the deep satisfaction of two
members of the Secretariat I met in headquarters immediately following the broadcast.
One of them went so far as to say that while he agreed with Berlinguer's arguments,
he was even more pleased with the secretary general's methods. It is far better, this
Turinese leader said, to lay down a strong and clear position than to patch together a
"mosaic" which makes everyone happy. In the next few days, other leaders in Turin
had far less enthusiastic reactions. They felt that Berlinguer's resignation threat and his
arguments about concentric attacks on the party would probably establish a defensive
tone that would preempt much of the criticism that might otherwise take place.

These incidents illustrate the constraints put on a local PCI organization when the
national leadership stubbornly sticks to its guns, but they also show that the top leadership
of the federation was not passively buffeted by outside stimuli. Most of the real decision
makers in the Turinese hierarchy remained deeply committed to the *compromesso*, in
spite of mounting evidence of the strategy's costs. The dilemma for these leaders was
especially acute, given the very difficult situation in party, movement, and society in
the late 1970s.

The 1979 general elections provide a clear example of the dilemma. There was deep
dissatisfaction everywhere in the federation with the feeble nature of the party's campaign
slogans. After so much emphasis in the 1978 *autocritica* on the PCI's distinctiveness, it
was distressing to find the party's major slogans restricted to "Either in Government or
in the Opposition" and "The PCI Must Govern." Functionaries and activists complained
throughout the campaign that it was nearly impossible to rally the masses around such
slogans; they felt that the campaign had been condemned from the outset to become a
tediously ritualistic propaganda exercise.[38]

But these reservations did not keep the party from running its campaign at the usual
frantic pace. For six full weeks, the federation threw itself into an unending round of
speeches, meetings, and public assemblies. On the eve of the vote, the secretary reported
that 1,269 separate initiatives had been undertaken, an increase of 25 percent over the

historic 1976 elections.[39] Yet all this activity could not save the Turinese PCI from losses much worse than the national average. The party's total fell 5.9 percent in the capital and an equal amount in the province. The hated Radicals enjoyed one of their greatest victories in Turin, garnering 6.7 percent of the vote, a whopping 4.3 percent increase over their 1976 showing. The only bright note in this dismal panorama was the sharp fall of the DC (by nearly 3 percent, to 26.7 percent), marking the start of a precipitous decline that would continue into the 1980s. The trends in eight consecutive elections can be seen in Table 4.1.

These losses jolted the federation. The Radicals' success was disturbing in itself, but most upsetting of all was the fact that a lot of PR support had clearly come directly from those who had earlier voted for the PCI. Notable shifts from the Communists to the PR could be seen in public housing and solid, traditional working-class districts. This latter phenomenon was the source of greatest distress; as the campaign wore on, most of those involved in it had agreed that the party's initial weaknesses had been overcome in the proletarian bastions. Several leaders publicly expressed their shock, pointing out that no better indicator existed of the party's loss of touch with reality.[40] Not only had it fallen from 54 percent to 47 percent in its strongholds, but it had done so unexpectedly. Communist losses were somewhat contained, but still notable, in the reddest working-class *barriere*, while they were highest of all—between 9 percent and 14 percent—in the public housing districts, where the Radicals and extreme left did best.

The voting results provided additional evidence of gross misjudgments. Throughout the campaign, pessimism had been greatest concerning the various white-collar groups, in which a strong malaise had been apparent since the referenda of 1978. It was here, and in upper-income areas in general, that many Turinese Communists feared the greatest losses would occur, to the advantage of the center-right, which had always done well in middle-class areas. Although PCI losses were indeed high, it was the radicals who did best in the white-collar precincts, averaging nearly 8.5 percent of the vote. The DC and the extreme right lost as heavily in such areas as they did in the rest of the capital, and only a recovery by the minor laical parties over their 1976 results keep the centrist bloc

Table 4.1. General and Municipal Elections, City of Turin, 1970–1985
(Percentage Obtained by Each Party or Grouping)

| Year and Vote[a] | Smaller[b] Left-Wing | PCI | PR | PSI | PSDI | PRI | DC | PLI | Extreme[c] Right-Wing | Others |
|---|---|---|---|---|---|---|---|---|---|---|
| 1970 (M) | 2.7 | 28.9 | — | 10.5 | 9.0 | 4.0 | 27.9 | 10.8 | 6.2 | — |
| 1972 (G) | 2.5 | 30.5 | — | 9.6 | 7.1 | 4.6 | 27.6 | 10.5 | 7.1 | 1.6 |
| 1975 (M) | 1.3 | 37.9 | — | 12.8 | 7.5 | 4.5 | 24.1 | 5.6 | 6.0 | 0.4 |
| 1976 (G) | 1.9 | 40.0 | 2.4 | 9.3 | 3.6 | 4.9 | 29.6 | 2.9 | 5.3 | — |
| 1979 (G) | 1.8 | 34.1 | 6.7 | 9.9 | 4.0 | 5.5 | 26.7 | 4.6 | 5.6 | 0.1 |
| 1980 (M) | 1.8 | 39.3 | — | 14.4 | 4.5 | 3.8 | 23.5 | 6.6 | 5.3 | 0.8 |
| 1983 (G) | 2.1[d] | 34.3 | 4.6 | 9.2 | 3.5 | 10.2 | 19.6 | 6.8 | 6.7 | 3.0 |
| 1985 (M) | 1.5 | 35.4 | 3.4[e] | 11.5 | 3.4 | 7.1 | 23.5 | 6.0 | 5.9 | 1.5 |

a. (M) = municipal election; (G) = general election.

b. PSIUP in 1970 and 1972, PDUP and DP in 1975–1980, DP alone afterward.

c. Monarchists and Neofascists (MSI) in 1970, Neofascists 1972–1985.

d. PDUP ran with PCI in 1983 and dissolved afterward.

e. "Greens" in 1985.

roughly at its previous levels. Far from generating a moderate backlash, the middle class punished both major parties and cast a sizable protest vote in addition to rewarding, as everyone expected, the secular minor parties. In the very richest neighborhoods, the DC suffered its greatest losses, while the minor centrist parties made their greatest advances (−9.4 percent vs. +7.8 percent). The Communists' drop was most contained here, while the Radicals approximated their citywide gains (see Table 2.3).

These results stunned the party, but they were not really bolts out of the blue. Public-housing and working-class districts had delivered unpleasant messages in the 1978 referenda, but federation leaders had chosen to ignore the evidence of strong support for the PR and the extraparliamentary left in Communist bastions. One plausible explanation for this blinkered reaction is the difficulty of interpreting the referendum results clearly. Another is the leaders' ideological unwillingness to admit that there was a serious risk of losing votes, especially young people's votes, to the left of the PCI; to admit to this was to admit that the strategy was clearly not working. It is significant that in the 1978 *autocritica*, some of the most heated exchanges revolved around whether Communists ought to be more concerned at the prospect of losing middle-class support or that of the party's more "natural" constituents. Party leaders most identified with the *compromesso storico* had brushed aside the latter concern, perpetuating the erroneous idea that only a moderate backlash could be expected from the middle class.[41] In the wake of the 1979 elections, these old disagreements again came to the surface and could not be brushed aside so easily. Harsh criticisms of the Communists' high-handed treatment of young people and their contemptuous dismissal of the Radicals as right wing or *qualunquisti* were now earning the loudest applause at assemblies called to analyze the vote.[42]

Even more urgently than in 1978, the federation was again faced with having to explain and remedy Communist losses among key supporters. Because this was not the first round of criticism, exasperation was beginning to run high as identical arguments were repeated after having been ignored earlier. Logically, the earlier arguments were pushed even farther, and the entire strategy increasingly came under fire, especially, but by no means exclusively, from the rank and file. With the PCI now clearly scheduled for a return to the opposition, the risks of withdrawing into the citadel of a splendid and sterile isolation were greater than ever. It was thus vitally important for the party as a whole, and especially for the party in Turin, to stake out not simply a position that was critical but one that proposed some sort of constructive alternative that would help the PCI strengthen its weakened ties to society and begin to regain the support it had obviously lost. (This explains why even most of the *berlingueriani* in Turin were simultaneously proponents of a clear "project" or "program.")

But the only unequivocal signal that came from the July 1979 Central Committee meeting was that even from the opposition the party's goal remained the pursuit of a government of national unity. This made clear that sectarian opposition was not on the agenda, but it furnished neither tactical nor strategic guidelines. With the top leadership of the federation equally committed to the broad strategy of the party, there were not many areas in which meaningful changes could be initiated.

Constrained as it was, the Turinese federation at least began to act on some problems where its freedom of maneuver was not totally hampered. Most of these changes are in the organizational realm and will be discussed in the following chapters. But a number of them are such patent reactions to the political problems being discussed here that they deserve at least brief mention now.

The basic problem, apparent since 1978 and acute since the 1979 vote, was the PCI's loss of contact with and diminished support from even its strongest constituencies. In Turin, we know that the party's ties to society have always been tenuous for endemic structural reasons, but we also know that these links were dramatically weakened after 1975 for political and organizational reasons as well. The PCI's policy choices demobilized the working class and underclass, alienated young people, and discouraged the opinion voters of the more educated middle strata. Organizationally, the party co-opted its best cadres into public institutions, leaving its structures weak and transparently irrelevant to the real decision-making processes in the party.

The move back into the opposition in 1979 permitted the federation to begin to seek closer ties to its social environment and to the grass roots of the party. The most notable, least cosmetic steps were aimed at reinforcing the peripheral organization. Countering the post-1975 trend, experienced cadres were moved from the central apparatus in party headquarters out into the zones of the capital and the provincial hinterland; by the early 1980s, these personnel shifts, combined with a number of ambitious institutional reforms undertaken throughout the party, indicated a seriousness of purpose that was frequently lacking in the earlier period. But by the early 1980s, the PCI and the Turinese federation in particular were faced with a new series of problems (e.g., a drastic decline in members and recruitment) which left the ultimate outcome of these changes very much up in the air.

## 1980: End of the Historic Compromise?

The year 1980 saw the PCI settled into an increasingly clear oppositional role on a national level. As the new decade began, the party's fortunes continued to be mixed enough to ensure that no easy solutions to its transitional dilemmas would miraculously appear. The recruitment of new members fell off dramatically, and, as a result, overall party membership continued the decline that had begun toward the end of the 1970s. Pressures for internal organizational change, and especially for more internal party democracy, ultimately resulted in a dramatic and wide-ranging Central Committee meeting (in January 1981) that set important reforms in motion.[43] Among the many pressures that led to this development, a crucial one was the general resentment in the party against the way policies had consistently come down from a restricted leadership group in Rome that rarely, if ever, consulted the party before committing it to a course of action.

Electoral trends into the 1980s were rather more reassuring in the sense that the sharp drop of 1979 was not immediately followed by a continued severe erosion of PCI strength. In fact, in the 1980 nationwide local elections, the total Communist vote rose more than a percentage point (to 31 percent) over the results of the previous year, and the party even improved its showing over the 1975 local elections, but only in the North and Center. In the South, the PCI did much less well, falling significantly almost everywhere and aggravating the North-South scissors that had appeared to close in the 1976 general elections but had reopened again in 1979.[44] By the 1983 general elections, the Communist vote seemed to have stabilized at around 30 percent.[45]

By far the greatest difficulties awaited the PCI in the political realm, both broadly and narrowly defined. The party did not really have a clear strategy. The *compromesso* had been altered and put on a back burner, but the leadership continued to insist that a government of national unity was on the agenda. The Communists were both organizationally and electorally stronger in 1980 than they were a decade earlier (though not by very much), but the Socialists were no longer adamant about the PCI's inclusion in a governmental majority.[46] And without the critical leverage of PSI support, even a strengthened PCI could not make a very strong case for its own indispensability in running the country. The Communists had to walk a very thin line between conflicting pressures in 1980, and they did not always succeed.

In March of that year, there was an especially dramatic development. An estimated forty Communist deputies broke party discipline to vote against a foreign-policy motion supported by all major parties in Parliament.[47] This totally unprecedented move had its origins in many grievances, but they all boiled down to the same general complaint: the PCI was continuing in its old ways and failing to distance itself from the parliamentary majority in spite of assertions from party headquarters to the contrary. The deputies reportedly were incensed by the high-handed fashion in which the leadership had simply ordered them to vote for the motion without even a cursory explanation beforehand. The national leadership at first tried to suggest that the forty-plus "snipers" did not come from within Communist ranks (secret balloting in Parliament makes it impossible to identify with certainty those who break discipline), but this effort was short-lived. Eventually admitting that the motion itself left a lot to be desired, Berlinguer acknowledged that the party had been damaged by this serious breach of discipline.[48]

## The Thirty-Five Days at Fiat: Autumn 1980

By far the most dramatic development of a very dramatic year, especially with regard to the party's problems in Turin, involved labor relations at Fiat. This was, by definition, not only a Turinese problem. A top party leader was surely exaggerating, but not by much, when he referred to the events of September and October 1980 as "the most difficult and bitter workers' struggle of the entire postwar period."[49] In terms of both symbols and content, "the thirty-five days" was without doubt the most important labor confrontation since the hot autumn.

The basic outline of the conflict is straightforward enough.[50] Fiat, with most auto producers, was suffering badly from the worldwide recession by 1980. Strong hints had been dropped during the summer that the firm would seek relief via the long-term layoff of upward of twenty thousand employees.[51] But early in September, notice was given to fourteen thousand that their jobs had been totally eliminated; two thousand more outright firings were announced as imminent. The metalworkers' union (FLM) immediately called an all-out strike at Fiat. As the battle went on, the PCI, the national union confederations, and the government all attempted to mediate; there were supporting strikes from the national FLM and eventually a national general strike. In the wake of the general strike, the government fell, and Fiat announced that the firings were suspended for three months. The unions at this point called off a scheduled general strike, but the Turinese FLM continued its complete shutdown of Fiat. A few days later, on September 30, Fiat laid off, for periods of up to two years, twenty-three thousand workers, and these layoffs were not negotiated with the unions as they (and the PCI) had demanded.[52] Another general strike was called for October 10, and the FLM's shutdown of Fiat continued. On October 14, a massive counterdemonstration, dubbed the "foremen's march" and involving between twenty thousand and forty thousand mainly white-collar participants, took place in the heart of Turin. After thirty-five days, the strike abruptly ended on Fiat's terms; both the PCI and the national union confederations exerted very strong pressure at this point to accept what they called an honorable compromise.

The identity of the basic protagonists, Fiat and the FLM, and the intensity of the struggle ensured from the start that this could not be a normal labor-management disagreement. It really represented the establishment of a more promanagement equilibrium in large industry after the impressive gains racked up by the workers' movement during the 1968 to 1972 battles and the electoral advances of the left in the mid-1970s. Management had been chafing under the limits on its freedom of maneuver, and particularly the need to negotiate everything with the unions, which had been one of the legacies of the hot autumn. This is why Fiat acted unilaterally, and it is also why the unions behaved so intransigently. In the mid-1970s, the Agnelli family (Fiat's owners) had been in the forefront of industrialists who felt that a modus vivendi was necessary with the workers and the PCI. Now, with their firm in trouble, with the unions weaker and divided—by the recession and by the presence of the Socialists in the government—and with the PCI much less a factor in national politics, the Agnellis moved decisively.

Fiat's gamble, born of desperation and shrewd calculation, paid off brilliantly, though it was by no means guaranteed from the start. Once the FLM took a (predictably) radical position in favor of an all-out shutdown of the company, the assumption was that divisions within the work force would prove greater than the solidarity that was sure to emerge in a classical capital-labor confrontation. Naturally, Fiat did all it could to play on these divisions—between the very militant delegates who called and tried to enforce the total shutdown and more moderate workers, between blue- and white-collar employees, and, in some observers' views, between Piedmontese and immigrant workers.[53] The firm emphasized picket-line "violence" that was keeping honest workers from their jobs, and it also noted that it had not randomly targeted the work force but had chosen to fire (eventually to lay off) those with the worst attendance records. In spite of these efforts, it is doubtful whether the march, which was the decisive event of the strike, could have been as successful as it was had the Turinese FLM not insisted on continuing the complete shutdown once Fiat announced that the firings had been suspended. Both the national union confederations and the PCI had tried very hard to get the local FLM to take a more moderate position at the end of September, without success.

The Communists' situation, as is evident, was extremely difficult. They would later argue that although not in favor of the all-out strike, they had to show the workers that at least one party stood solidly behind them on so basic an issue as the right to work.[54] And here we have a motivation that goes beyond simple class solidarity and the need to reassert its recently obscured identity: the PCI wanted very much to embarrass the Socialists and send a clear message to the governing coalition. This was the opposite side of the coin of collaboration and social peace that "national solidarity" implied. In the opposition, the Communists could make life difficult indeed for those in power.

But even taking these factors into account, the party's behavior during the thirty-five days appears extreme. The Turinese federation was completely mobilized in support of the strikers, and so were all levels of local government controlled by the PCI. Diego Novelli, whom we have seen criticizing past excesses, made inflammatory workerist speeches reminiscent of the earlier era he had so consistently denounced in party meetings. The pièce de résistance, however, undoubtedly was Enrico Berlinguer's visit to Turin late in September. Speaking several times at various Fiat plants, he not only gave the party's unconditional support to the strike, but he also made clear that the PCI would support an outright occupation of factories by the workers.

Some would conclude that the PCI's behavior was simply an example of dema-goguery from the opposition; the Socialists widely held this view, and almost everyone outside the party (and many within it) judged Berlinguer's visit and speeches as a serious error in terms of building up unrealistic expectations in view of the struggle's eventual outcome. A more measured analysis would emphasize that given its problems from 1976 on, the PCI felt it important to shore up its identity among its strongest constituency, and it did this very consistently from the time it entered the opposition.[55] But however true this latter position may be, it cannot account for the many elements that suggest a good deal of moderation in the party's behavior even during the thirty-five days. It is notable that after the strike, most of the party's time was spent trying to explain to the workers—and to PCI militants—that it had not sold the unions out in October 1980. The party's failure to persuade large sectors of the movement is apparent from the fact that more than two years later, at the 1983 Provincial Congress, the same arguments were still being repeated.[56]

In fact, if one discounts the PCI's rhetorical excesses in the heat of battle, the party's behavior during and after the thirty-five days was very close to the moderate form that had been its hallmark since the mid-1970s. Indeed, the author of the most perceptive account of these events goes so far as to argue that the party consciously went to extremes in the symbolic realm in order to fend off criticism from the left when it ultimately delivered its highly critical message to the unions.[57] I would not go quite so far, for there were signs of profound disagreement in the leadership of the Turinese federation at the end of these events.[58] It is noteworthy that Berlinguer's visit seems to have created a division that ran exactly opposite to what one would have predicted on the basis of many leaders' earlier positions. Those most clearly identified with moderate past policies recounted the visit in glowing terms and did not see it as exacerbating tensions in any way. Others, including most of those who wanted the party to take a more militant and clear stance, felt that the visit and speeches had been unnecessarily inflammatory because the PCI obviously was not really in favor of an extreme solution. It is evident that personal loyalty to the secretary general contributed strongly to and may even have shaped some of the leaders' attitudes on this occasion.

The Communists' behavior during the strike provides an excellent case study of the party's dilemma in general, and especially in Turin, while it remained committed to the broad outlines of the old strategy under the new conditions of being in the opposition. It had to side with the working class and hoped that a militant posture would also remind the governing coalition of the costs of isolating the PCI politically. But it also believed that the workers had been poorly served by their own unions. From the mid-1970s on in Turin, it was not uncommon to hear party leaders rail against the "obtuseness" of unionists, from the regional level down to the shopfloor. Many federation leaders were exasperated by the prevailing view in the Turinese FLM which considered any discussion by management of economic crisis, low productivity, and the need to take steps to improve competitiveness as a smokescreen. These attitudes had made the Turinese unions unsympathetic to the party's position on austerity and sacrifices ever since it was first enunciated in the mid-1970s. In the late 1970s, when the national union confederations adopted a similar line, it was well known that their Turinese comrades did not agree.[59] The irony for the PCI was that the thirty-five days showed that the most intransigent unionists (a good number of whom were party members) did not, in fact, speak for the overwhelming majority of the work force, even at Fiat. But while the events of 1980 may have vindicated the PCI's vision of events—that the crisis was real and could not be addressed by militantly denying reality—they did so in circumstances which allowed the party precious little leverage on either the economic or the political system.

On balance, the struggle was clearly a serious defeat for the workers' movement. Within the movement, the PCI probably lost least, while scoring some gains. The party had shown, in the early stages, a mobilizational capacity that many had doubted it still retained. In the later stages, it had shown that it could intervene forcefully in a labor conflict that might have produced even more disastrous results for the movement. There was also, as noted, a sense of vindication about the seriousness of the economic crisis in Italy. Moreover, "the march of the forty thousand" provided evidence for the PCI that even at Fiat one would have to view the work force as far more complex and multiform than had previously been the case.[60] The divisions underscored by the march called for alliances that were more broad-based, however one chose to read the event, and this was also seen as a confirmation of its own positions by the party. Finally, the PCI obviously took pleasure in the way the various weaknesses of the most militant unionists had been exposed. Party spokesmen used every possible occasion to point out how badly out of touch with the rank and file the Fiat *delegati* (shop stewards) and many union leaders had become in this period, and how strongly this pointed to the need for a dramatic reform of union structures and practices.[61]

But the PCI also paid a heavy price in the aftermath of the strike. Its approach to problems might have been vindicated, but the party remained as devoid of concrete proposals for the movement after the events as it was before them. Moreover, its immediate reversion to more moderate positions after its initially enthusiastic support for the strike deeply alienated large sectors of the movement, including many of its own members. Finally, the massive layoffs not only badly demoralized the movement, but they directly undermined the party's organization in the factories, since many of those furloughed by Fiat were party (and union) militants. None of these developments would make the party's lot easier in the 1980s.

## The Second Svolta *of Salerno*

In spite of a tougher stance since moving into the opposition, the party's official strategy altered very little through November 1980. This was evident in PCI behavior during the strike at Fiat, but also in a number of formal party meetings. It was now two years since Berlinguer's redefinition of the *compromesso storico* to the status of a broad consensus that could even allow the alternation of different coalitions. But the secretary general had obviously not abandoned the idea of a government of national unity. There was a strong sense that grass-roots resistance and poor results had forced the top leadership to make numerous adjustments, but there was certainly no show of haste to clarify new positions or to deepen old analyses. Thus, at the June Central Committee meeting, Berlinguer explicitly restated the idea of a national unity government, although he did say that the PCI would be much more rigorous in its demands before the formation of any such government; this would avoid the paralysis that had so badly hurt the country (and the party) from 1976 to 1978.[62]

At the November Central Committee, the same argument was reiterated in even less hypothetical terms in response to the criticism of a noted left-wing party leader who pronounced himself unconvinced by the PCI's continued wooing of the DC.[63] This meeting, like innumerable conferences, publications, and similar gatherings over the previous two years, was a great disappointment to many people in the party. Once more it had been rumored that some long-awaited clarifications might finally be forthcoming, and once more this turned out not to be the case. It was hard to disagree with the observation of Giuseppe Vacca, a leading party intellectual, that the meeting was "insufficient in its indication of objectives, priorities, alliances, forms of left-wing unity, and programmatic proposals."[64] It was harder still to disagree with the (anonymous) party leader who, late in 1980, concluded that "there was a total vacuum of ideas" in the party over the last two years.[65]

The situation changed very dramatically at the end of November, and it took, literally, an earthquake to alter the party's proposals. When large areas of the South were devastated in November, with the loss of three thousand lives, the inefficiency and corruption of the Christian Democrats was revealed in appalling detail. Nonstop live television reports showed villages that had been "forgotten" by state officials, DC hacks who shamelessly tried to use relief distribution to their own advantage, and a degree of incompetence that even an immense natural disaster could not excuse. The very popular Socialist president, Sandro Pertini, made a moving public appeal and denunciation which left little doubt as to the DC's responsibilities. The terrible tragedy, the surge of public outrage, and a dose of pure political calculation finally pushed the Communists over the edge. The PCI Executive met on November 27, 1980, and issued a communique, the most important parts of which read as follows:

> It appears illusory, inadequate to the gravity of the situation, and in particular to the acuteness assumed by the moral question to seek solutions which are framed within the context of the parties that have governed Italy over the past decades. . . .
>     . . . at a time when the DC demonstrates that it is not capable of guiding the moral healing and renewal of the state, it is objectively the task of the PCI to be the promoter and main guarantor of a government which expresses and brings together the best energies of Italian democracy, honest and capable men from within but even from outside the various political parties. The exceptional character of such a proposal is evident.[66]

Within a few days, Berlinguer elaborated the party's position in a press conference in Salerno, earning for this shift the label *la seconda svolta di Salerno* (the first "shift" was Togliatti's, in 1944). Now yet another term, *democratic alternative*, would enter the Communist lexicon. This was to distinguish the proposal from the left alternative that the party had been eschewing for more than five years. As vague as this proposal was, it finally and clearly ruled out any variant of an emergency or national unity government that included the DC. It was also quite evident that this was not intended to be an immediately viable option; even those most sympathetic to the shift knew that the PCI would have to do more than appeal to honest folk to change the direction of government in the country. But in spite of qualifiers about the exceptional nature of the proposal, there was a genuine strategic departure in the *seconda svolta*. That was the assertion that Italy could be governed with a majority that was not overwhelming and that did not include the DC.

For these very reasons, not everyone in the party was pleased by the change. The most vociferous supporters of the historic compromise tried to rephrase the *seconda svolta* in terms which echoed the *compromesso*, such as, "We cannot collaborate with *this* DC." But articles in the party press and the next Central Committee meeting soon made clear that a genuine change in party policy had taken place.[67]

Even some longtime opponents of the historic compromise were upset at how the shift had taken place. Above all, people were annoyed that once again party policy had been dictated from on high, and in this instance only a few weeks following a meeting of the allegedly sovereign body of the party which had decided not to change the party line. The vagueness and lack of any programmatic content in the proposal reminded many Communists of how the *compromesso storico* had evolved, and this refusal to tackle specific issues frustrated many observers. With the Socialists in government and a rapidly deteriorating situation in the unions, even those who had called for some variant of an alternative knew that much remained to be spelled out. The long period required for the leadership to evolve its position on the DC after 1978 offers a clue to the gradual future evolution of the line. As of this writing (1987), little has been clarified in terms of the specific policies, or social alignments, in the PCI's alternative vision, even though by now the post-*compromesso* period has lasted as long as the entire period during which the historic compromise was the official party strategy.

## The Svolta in Turin

The *svolta* was initially greeted with both shock and distress in Turin, at least in the upper reaches of the federation where support for the historic compromise had always been strong. There was concern that the shift would be viewed as an opportunistic response to a tragedy. Moreover, with the thirty-five days barely behind them, the Turinese leaders were especially worried about presenting a coherent facade to the workers' movement and to the outside world in general. There was the fear that such an abrupt change might generate further confusion or a momentum that would push the party into more intransigent positions than anyone wanted. Whatever its problems, the period of collaboration had forced the party to face the realities of a modern capitalist society in ways that had not been attempted earlier. Now the party risked losing much of the ground that it had recently gained.[68] And the leaders of the federation knew that if there is any local party organization in which the risks of backsliding are great, it is Turin.

But the general reaction of most of the local party was one of decided relief. Whatever the limits of the new position, it pointed away from collaboration with the government and the DC and toward the parties and social forces that were more clearly identifiable with the left. This would remove a source of deep distrust that had divided the left and the workers' movement for five years. Although relations with the PSI were difficult in 1980, they were better in Turin than in most places, though this situation would change dramatically in 1983 when a local scandal deeply implicated many leading Socialists (and a few Communists). Thus, those leaders who had long wanted to see the party move in the direction of a real alternative, most of those who favored a clear program or project, and almost the entire rank and file all saw the *svolta* as a necessary, if limited, step in the right direction.

These themes and the open admission that the party had been paralyzed by its policies since 1976 were sounded constantly in a meeting held at the end of 1980, and they were still being repeated, albeit with more pessimism concerning the PSI, three years later.[69] At the end of 1980, one of the Secretariat's most consistent critics of recent party actions fashioned a tombstone of sorts for the period of national unity. He said that the party's actions from 1976 to 1978 had helped legitimize it as a democratic force in the country and thus were positive for that reason. But the party's failures had been tremendous, and almost all of them derived from the PCI's unwillingness and inability to understand what was really going on in Turin and in the country: it constantly confused its desires with reality. He saw its recognition of the impossibility of achieving change in collaboration with the DC as positive but warned that the party still had a very long way to go, beginning with a better understanding of its own bases of support and the changes that had taken place in Italy during the 1970s.

## Conclusions

It is a commonplace that communist parties are organizations with a high and even extraordinary degree of tactical flexibility. But as this discussion of the PCI in the 1970s has shown, such a view has little to do with the reality of Italian communism. Nor should this be surprising: twists, turns, and abrupt reversals of line may be part of the history of the communist movement, but they are increasingly part of its ancient history. Moreover, those parties, past or present, that have most successfully made sharp turns have been able to do so because they were not encumbered by large mass memberships and myriad relationships linking them tightly to their environments. When larger parties have made such turns—one thinks of the French Communists in 1939[70]—the costs have been crippling.

But even this caveat cannot really explain the plodding slowness with which the PCI registered and then reacted to the flood of negative messages from 1977 on that told it just how badly it was faring. A mass party cannot be expected to react with blazing speed, but its presence in society should permit it to appreciate its dilemma and act to change it more rapidly than the PCI did. Otherwise, what is the advantage of being a mass party? How, then, can we explain the PCI's delays?

A number of plausible explanations emerge from the material examined in this chapter. Two of the most obvious, especially in combination, are organizational inertia and an extremely constrained political setting that allowed few, if any, realistic options to be mooted. Without suggesting that either of these explanations does not contain important aspects of the truth, I would say that the evidence at hand enables us to be a good deal more precise and provides answers to more interesting questions: Why was inertia and paralysis so typical of the party organization in this period? And why did no other strategic options appear as realistic long after the dominant strategy had so manifestly failed to produce positive results?

The most fundamental responses to these questions can be found in two factors. The first is the very strong ideological commitment by national (and many local) party leaders to the policies that were followed in the late 1970s. The second is that this period found the party, with its very high priority on unity, divided to a point where it was difficult to articulate a clear and unequivocal position on anything. In other words, regardless of the many serious external and internal constraints acting on the party, the bulk of the leadership was unwilling, and the party as a whole was unable, to reexamine basic assumptions and spell out a coherent alternative line any earlier than it did. Only the constant negative hammering of events and the overwhelming accumulation of one-sided evidence generated the painfully slow changes we have witnessed.

It is interesting in this regard that the plight of the Turinese federation was quite similar to that of the party as a whole. Administrators, organizational elites, and rank-and-file militants tended to pull the party in different directions and to articulate (at times only implicitly) radically diverse strategies. Turin's very distinct qualities generated some consensus on a few points, for instance, that too much had been conceded to the

DC, the party badly needed a project or program, and the industrial working class had to remain the key group around which any program would be built.[71] It is doubtful whether many other federations could even have gone this far. Most could only agree on the first point, which helps explain why the top leadership in Rome, when it did move, altered the party's posture more than its policies. Yet, as we have seen, the fact that the national leadership held so tenaciously to the old strategy actually helped the Turinese organization hold the line against some of the more sectarian pressures from the base. If we project the Turinese situation on the rest of the party, it is easy to see the organizational advantages in sticking to one position rather than opening up a free-for-all.

Another way to appreciate the same point is to try to visualize what sort of situation might have impelled the party to change its line more rapidly. Such a situation might have materialized if one could imagine some of the more important federations speaking with a single voice. But if it was difficult, as we saw in Turin, for even a single federation to spell out an unequivocal alternative, it would have been all the more problematic to get numerous local party organizations to agree on a single desirable course of action. It is easy enough to demonstrate this point for the PCI in the late 1970s, for the federation of Milan was notable in this period for its secretary's outspokenness against national party policy.[72] And while he expressed some views that echoed those heard in Turin (criticisms of too many accommodations, the need for a project), other views reflected Milanese peculiarities that contrasted with the concerns of the Turinese party and were even seen by some Turinese leaders as proof of the greater "reformism" and "social-democratization" of the party in Milan.

The Milanese Communists, for instance, worried much less about the PCI's loss of a traditional class identity, for the perfectly sound reason that the class structure in Milan is far more articulated than in Turin. Hence, the project hoped for in the Lombard capital would be more responsive to the complexity of advanced capitalism. More specifically, it would drop the idea of the blue-collar factory worker as the central figure of a new society and aim at bringing together a multiplicity of new groups, with urban middle strata as a crucial new target.[73] Some events in Turin might be seen as confirming the wisdom of this view, but it would hardly be a popular position there. Thus, even the need for a project, which was (and is) far from unanimously accepted within the party, has quite different meanings to its supporters, even when they come from the large urban areas of the North.

With such deep differences scattered throughout the party, the national leadership would have had a formidable task ahead of it even if it had been much more inclined to change course. Under these conditions, the limited and cautious nature of the *seconda svolta* becomes much more understandable, for the only clear consensus, except among the most die-hard proponents of the historic compromise, concerned the futility of endless overtures to the DC. But if this is an understandable reaction in terms of organizational preservation, it is one that reveals a party leadership that is unable to make crucial strategic choices at a time when the transitional crisis demands them. Broad indications for strategy might emerge from the lower levels of the party; clear and synthetic formulations must come from the center. If the party cannot provide these, it should at least provide, as an interim measure, guidelines or cues concerning the directions in which the party is expected to move: What are the central problems, reforms, and social groups the party intends to address? This is the area in which the PCI's national leadership has shown itself least capable (or least courageous) since the late 1970s, perhaps because it is here that it was most convinced, but most in error, in the early 1970s.

But what can be said in defense of the national leadership, even in the realm of strategy where it is most open to criticism, is that once the party moved definitively back into the opposition, the leaders did not follow the line of least resistance. A much tougher stance in domestic politics was not part of a more inwardly turned sectarian trend. On the contrary, the long-awaited clean break with the USSR came much closer (and some would even argue that it occurred) with the PCI's denunciation of the military coup that crushed the Solidarity movement in Poland.[74] And from 1981 on, the party not only addressed its internal organizational practices but actually began to change some of them in more than token fashion.[75] The PCI's greatest weakness remains its difficulty in spelling out a clear strategy that corresponds to the realities of Italy in the 1980s. And the party often gives the impression of groping much more slowly than most critics would like along a number of other strategic dimensions. But it at least appears to be groping in the right direction while avoiding withdrawal into a secure—and sterile— shell. On balance, particularly in light of the fate of other communist parties in the 1980s, that is no small achievement.

# 5

# The Organizational Dimension of Transitional Crisis: The Turinese Federation's Broader Context

At the end of Chapter 1, we saw that by the late 1970s the PCI's difficulties had led at least some communist intellectuals to ask whether the mass party is capable of grappling with the problems of a complex advanced capitalist society. Not surprisingly, the leaders of the party answered this question with a resounding yes. But the depth of the PCI's crisis is evident from the fact that, for the first time, the party officially acknowledged that at least some of the basic assumptions of the *partito nuovo* needed to be revised.[1] This does not mean that the PCI then boldly moved to rethink its entire structure. In fact, it quickly showed great reluctance to implement several measures aimed at democratizing decision making and opening up internal debate.[2] But it had at least begun to move in a new direction, albeit with little sense of what it would find over the horizon.

The aim of this chapter is to provide background material adequate to understand the most important aspects of the organizational side of the PCI's transitional crisis, and sufficient as well to situate the Turinese federation within the broader picture. That is no small task, for the organizational problems faced by the PCI embrace a broad range of issues. The progression of the discussion here and in the following chapter represents an effort to minimize the complications. This chapter begins with the deeply rooted determinants of the crisis of the *partito nuovo* and then examines the major organizational issues that came to the fore in the mid-1970s. The bulk of this examination will be set within the broader context of the prevailing model of party organization in the PCI, with specific reference to Turin. Finally, we will examine the party's identity crisis with regard to the nature of its cadres and leaders, again focusing on specific aspects of the Turinese case. A more detailed analysis of how the Turinese federation experienced the organizational side of the transitional crisis will be presented in Chapter 6.

## The Partito Nuovo in Crisis

One of the PCI's most distinguishing characteristics has surely been the deep entrenchment of the *partito nuovo* concept. As noted in Chapter 1, de-Stalinization could never have taken place so rapidly or thoroughly without party leaders' ability to fall back on a very clear image of the organization they wanted and the broad policies it was to carry out. The PCI has clearly benefited immensely from its hybrid character. It has never been a true cadre party (in which all members are activists) with a mass membership, but it has emphasized the importance of both activism and mass presence so consistently that both are ingrained in its ideals and practice. Hence, while the dominant strain in this hybrid new party historically has been the vanguard tradition of the Communist Third International, the need to operate as a genuine mass party (generally associated with the Socialist Second International) has always tempered the worst sectarian tendencies, ideological as well as organizational.

But the very fact that it is a hybrid has at times left the PCI in situations which have simultaneously brought out the worst aspects of the socialist mass-party and the communist vanguard-party traditions. Such a hierarchical chain of command means that indecisiveness or sharp changes of direction at the top can create disorientation and paralysis at the grass roots. Moreover, although it represents an unquestioned advance over more orthodox heirs to the Marxist-Leninist tradition, the Togliattian mass party has frequently revealed a closed, ideological outlook that perpetuates sectarian traditions in form if not in content. The historic compromise, to cite the most recent example, assumed and indeed insisted that Italy had permanent political subcultures (and a DC with a popular soul) just as these phenomena were markedly declining. Until the end of the 1970s, Communists who raised questions about the DC and spoke of its system of power were dismissed as not understanding reality.[3] And on the labor front, the PCI's reading of the economic crisis—a reading which had to dovetail with the party's own political ambitions—emphasized centralized, national-level solutions to an extent that ran counter to the thrust of the entire labor movement since the mid-1950s.[4] Attention to local developments was put aside at a time when profound industrial crisis and restructuring required detailed information about trends in the work force and in management strategies.

In parallel fashion, precisely because PCI leaders have always been so committed to the *partito nuovo*, they have often been quite blinkered in their approach to many of the organization's most persistent problems. From the 1950s on, it was an article of faith in the PCI that the root cause of most serious organizational problems lay in the failure to implement fully the tenets of the *partito nuovo*. For more than a generation, the same problems were called to the party's attention, and, with monotonous regularity, the same "solutions" were proposed. This is not to suggest that the analysis and remedies were totally off the mark, particularly when they raised questions about the internal operations of the party and whether these hampered or facilitated its ability to act effectively in society. But all too often, fairly acute descriptions of structural changes in the country led to moralistic and generic denunciations and concluded with equally generic exhortations to "build the party" which indicated less an analysis than a ritualistic restatement of received truths.

Illustrations drawn from the issues that run throughout this study are abundant. On the crucial question of the party's difficulties in recruiting among key social groups, the gap between identifying important trends in society at large and connecting these trends to the PCI's structures and model of militancy has always been great. Giuseppe Berta has shown how the party has been quick to note changing technology in industry but much less swift to connect these changes to how real workers' perceptions, motivations, and behavior have altered over time. Hence, long after the deskilled assembly-line worker had become the typical figure in the great northern factories, the PCI—which had noted and denounced his "massification"—continued to appeal to the working class using concepts and terms appropriate to the skilled craftsmen of an earlier era or to a totally idealized worker who probably never existed at all.[5] It is not altogether surprising that the party's generic assertions about the value of organizing the factories largely fell on deaf ears until the early 1970s, when the hot autumn finally made it impossible to ignore mass workers.[6]

In the same way, the PCI has regularly catalogued the social changes responsible for the emergence of a modern youth culture, and it has even analyzed that culture with some subtlety.[7] But here, too, it has generally denounced what it has found, as if it cannot quite forgive young people for no longer flocking to the party or Youth Federation as they did through the 1950s (see the figures in Table 1.2, herein). As long as the PCI remains locked into a framework that is essentially Leninist, it continues to think in terms of bringing all significant social phenomena under its control. It thus strikes out at the manifestations or symptoms of social change as if these were the causes of its organizational problems.

A consistent theme in this regard is the crisis, often expressed as the Americanization of modern society, which is inevitably described as having reached pathological proportions. Public aversion to organized mass politics is presented as self-evident proof of the pathology.[8] Critical party leaders have perceptively pointed out that this kind of analysis is informed by a Third International vision of common citizens as "incomplete militants" who are treated as irrational or "prepolitical" simply because they do not identify with existing parties or political institutions.[9] The critics argue that it is proper to attempt to understand a changing society and address the concerns of new political actors. But, they note, solutions framed in terms of traditional political structures are doomed from the start, for these traditions have revealed themselves to be inadequate as Italy has evolved into a more complex society.

Entrenched assumptions which are products of the immediate postwar period have also done little to help the party understand those organizational problems whose "objective" causes are less easily understood. It is obvious, for instance, that there have only been two periods since World War II when the PCI was able to recruit a mass of new members large enough to change its overall profile dramatically. The first was right at the end of the war, and the second was in the aftermath of the profound changes of the late 1960s and early 1970s. The rest of the time has mainly witnessed a holding action or, even more often, a gradual decline in members with the Communists' fortunes much less relevant to increases in growth than even common sense would suggest.[10] A recent study of PCI recruitment has shown, for example, that in the most triumphant year in recent history, 1976, the monthly recruitment pattern did not depart from the norm: 90 percent of all new members had joined the party by June, *before* the stunning advance in the general elections. The PCI's decline, or at least stagnation, actually began in the midst of its greatest victory, before any of the deleterious effects of its policies were evident.[11] The inference is that the party had largely drained the potential pool of new recruits while its fortunes were still on the rise.

This phenomenon is not very well understood by anyone, but it strongly suggests that organizational breakthroughs are exceedingly rare and rather independent of the party's actions. Yet the PCI's attitude toward recruitment seems to be that breakthroughs are perhaps not the norm but certainly always on the agenda. The party's annual recruitment drives, reflecting this (ritualized) conviction, absorb by far the greatest amount of time and energy of all normal organizational activities. Conversely, small drops in membership are usually viewed in alarmist terms and generate lengthy discussions, although there is overwhelming evidence of a consistent and fairly extensive turnover everywhere in the country except the red belt of central Italy. This is probably an intractable problem, but the way the Italian Communists address it does not allow that conclusion to be drawn. As a result, the idea that there might be more efficient ways to utilize militants' energies cannot seriously be entertained. A number of leaders in Turin privately confessed their suspicion that the federation could probably arrive at the same membership figures each year while expending much less energy and scarce resources, but no one felt that the local party could afford such a gamble. "How would we explain ourselves to Rome," they said in essence, "if we eased off on our recruitment drives and then did worse than the rest of the party?"

## The Evolution of the Party's Structure: An Overview

The same considerations as those made above often apply to the way the PCI has discussed its internal structural arrangements. But here the situation is complicated by purely organizational factors, the most important of which is a direct outgrowth of the party's hybrid nature. That is the tension that exists between the demands put on the PCI as a party of cadres and those that arise because it is simultaneously a mass party of presence. In more sociological terms, cadre requirements such as organizational maintenance, cohesion, and solidarity are often in conflict with presence requirements such as external projection into the social and political system. As we will see, at some levels of the party structure, this conflict is constant. Such tension is common to all parties that depend to some degree on grass-roots activism, but it is especially acute in the PCI because its Third International heritage remains most pronounced in its model of militancy, while it may well be, simultaneously, the most compulsively active of all mass parties of the left.

The need for an active cadre at the grass roots has never been called into question in the PCI. The number of cadres, their major tasks, and the most appropriate base-level structures for their activities have, on the other hand, been the subject of continuous debate since the 1940s. Through the worst period of the cold war, when it was isolated domestically and totally identified with the USSR internationally, the party's attentions turned almost exclusively inward. With ideological rigor and reliability at a premium, centralization and a strong emphasis on maximizing the number of cadres became top priorities. However, there is evidence that from the beginning the classical communist grass-roots structure—the cell—proved difficult to adapt to a party the size of the PCI.[12] It is also quite clear that even in the depths of the cold war, Togliatti favored a more flexible, outward-looking structure than some of the more hard-line leaders.[13]

But it would be a gross oversimplification to explain the entrenchment of the classical bolshevik model of militancy strictly in terms of ideological indoctrination and hard versus soft(er) liners in the leadership. It is evident that in a highly defensive period such as the cold war, intense and inward-turned activities by a core of cadres (roughly 10 percent of the membership) kept the party organization from being eroded. Yet even in the much less grim period that preceded the cold war, there was a very good fit between many of the *partito nuovo*'s organizational structures and practices and the reality of a country that had just emerged from a generation of fascism and the devastation of a war fought on its own soil.[14] The PCI's social base was poorly educated, lacking in political skills, and not highly differentiated; the party's reconstruction strategy was relatively straightforward and could be readily encapsulated in a limited number of broad marching orders. Under these circumstances, the party's basic political goals were also well served by the organizational structures (e.g., cells and high levels of centralization) and the pedagogical style that were an intimate part of its bolshevik heritage. If it took an inordinately long time for the PCI to rethink many of its most basic arrangements and practices, that is because there were very real political and organizational as well as ideological reasons for the earlier persistence of these traditions.

## The PCI's Grass-Roots Structure

Cells still exist in the PCI and even obtain pride of place in the Party Statute.[15] But in reality, the much larger section has officially been recognized as the basic grass-roots unit since at least the early 1970s; in practice, this recognition came much earlier.[16] More suited to a cadre party in the true sense of the term—that is, one whose entire membership is active—the cell remains operational in limited contexts. One is the extraurban hamlet (*frazione*) which is geographically distinct from its parent city or village; there are not enough party members to make a section feasible, but there are good reasons to bring the members together on their home ground. More often, and more importantly, cells are found in factories or workplaces; this is the case for Turin. Cells, rather than sections, are constructed in workplaces when the party's presence or the size of the work force does not permit the larger aggregation. It may also be the case that a factory section can rationally be subdivided into cells on the basis of shifts, production departments, or the division of labor. But in all cases, cells must be affiliated to a workplace or territorial section. The limited importance and presence of this unit is probably most eloquently documented by its neglect in official party statistics since the 1960s (for the territorial cell) and 1970s (for workplace cells).[17]

With the section, we arrive at the universal rank-and-file unit of the PCI and at extensive documentation for both the party as a whole and the Turinese federation. Ideally, the section should enroll between one hundred and three hundred members.[18] Because of the relatively low levels of participation in the PCI (very rarely do even a quarter of the members attend section congresses; 10 percent is closer to the average for regular meetings), these dimensions allow general assemblies of the membership. They also provide a pool of cadres large enough to carry out the section's basic tasks but small enough to maintain the face-to-face environment that seems to be necessary to sustain militants' commitment. Like cells, sections may be based on territory or workplace, but unlike cells, the territorial aspect has become totally dominant for the section. In 1982, there were more than twelve thousand five hundred sections in the PCI, a considerable advance over the late 1960s, when the total had fallen below eleven thousand. Less than 10 percent of these sections were found in factories or other workplaces.[19] In Turin, the federation reported 339 sections at the beginning of the 1980s, of which 68 were in workplaces. This latter figure was the second highest in the entire PCI.[20]

There is no unanimity in the PCI concerning either the ideal territorial extension or the ideal size of the "standard" party section. In fact, there is a growing awareness in the party that it is counterproductive to impose standards on the extremely disparate political geography of the entire country.[21] Moreover, the sections provide a vivid illustration of how the party's hybrid nature affects even the most mundane organizational issue. There is a consensus in the PCI that the larger sections function best in terms of activities projected out into society. But there is an equally strong sense—backed up by empirical evidence—that levels of strictly internal activity decline in linear fashion as section size increases. The smaller the section, the higher the proportion of members who turn out for party meetings.[22] This is not a totally automatic phenomenon, but it does pose a vexing dilemma for a party that wishes to maximize both internal participation and external involvement at the grass roots.

In Turin, where increases in membership and in the number of sections—of both types—far outstripped the national averages in the 1970s, two totally opposed strategies have been followed. In the early stages of rampant growth, the party's organizers tried to stimulate the creation of as many new, relatively small sections as possible by subdividing older, larger sections. They felt this practice stimulated recruitment and the participation of eager young activists. The practice certainly met with success; between the end of the 1960s and 1978, the federation jumped from 260 to 349 sections, of which 100 were located in the capital. In the process, the number of sections that met the minimum standard of at least one hundred members doubled, bringing them to nearly 60 percent of the total.[23] After the party began to encounter serious political problems toward the end of the 1970s, and especially when these were followed almost immediately by a severe decline in membership, the emphasis swung rapidly, wherever possible, toward larger sections and, indeed, suprasectional structures.

As great an improvement as this was, it hardly converted the Turinese PCI into a strong party organization capable of mobilizing the general population and intervening decisively as a social force. The growth of the 1970s did resuscitate a moribund party organization, but the party still found itself in a situation where it had far too few resources to cope with far too many demands, especially in the urban sprawl of the capital. And in smaller towns or in small cities where the PCI is weak, organizational choices continued, even in the peak period, to be dictated by objective conditions. In these locales, the party is lucky if it can establish a single section that can perform basic organizational tasks; rare indeed are the cases in which such sections can play a significant political or social role.

The most impressive organizational advances of the 1970s in Turin were unques-tionably in the factories and firms of the capital city and its hinterland. By the end of the 1960s, the party's presence in the workplaces of "Factory City" was negligible, and even most of the very weak organizations it possessed could barely function. By the mid-1970s, something of a renaissance had taken place, at least until the PCI's political problems, followed shortly thereafter by economic dislocation, intervened. By far the greatest gains were registered in the largest factories of the capital and its province, which is where the federation quite logically concentrated the bulk of its efforts.

As we saw in Chapter 2, the defeats of the 1950s had made the Communists concentrate on rebuilding the unions, often at the expense of any organized party presence in the factories. Ironically, the revival of militance and the move toward trade-union unity in the 1960s made the need for the party's autonomous presence all the more imperative. Where unions have ideological identities, cooperation (not to mention unity) requires that no union be too closely affiliated with any party. Hence, by the 1960s, any direct Communist contact with the shopfloors and offices of Italy had increasingly to come from an organized *party* linkage. Given the importance of its class identity for the PCI generally, and especially for the Turinese federation, that linkage was an absolute necessity.

The dimensions of the growth of the party in the workplaces of Turin are impressive. In 1967, there were only thirty-two factory and eleven workplace sections in all of

Piedmont (six provinces), regardless of the size of the sections.[24] In 1980, in the single province of Turin, the PCI could boast forty-four factory and ten other workplace sections with more than one hundred members.[25] The total number of all party cells and sections in all workplaces reached 283, with 146 in the capital.

The impact of this degree of organization can best be appreciated with reference to another set of figures. In 1967, the federation enrolled just over eighteen thousand blue- and white-collar workers in its ranks (17,700 blue, 600 white). A decade later, at the peak of its post-1960s growth, the total was nearly thirty-three thousand (27,600 blue, 5,200 white). In the earlier period, the number of workers who were organized in their place of work numbered roughly five thousand, just over a quarter of all workers in the federation. By 1977, the figure had risen to seventeen thousand, or just over half. Thus, the working-class component of the federation nearly doubled in a decade, and the party also doubled its ability to organize this work force in its place of employment. Indeed, at the high-water mark, one-third of the entire membership of the Turinese party was signed up in workplaces.[26]

The federation's structural reinforcement in the wake of the hot autumn was thus in many ways even more impressive and organizationally important than the striking quantitative growth registered in the same period.[27] The quantitative growth was, of course, a necessary precondition, but the structural data show how the new energies that were drawn to the PCI were actually utilized. Generational analyses of the data leave no doubt at all about the rejuvenation of the PCI in the factories of Turin. By the end of the 1970s, 57 percent of the entire membership of the federation had joined the party after 1970, but 76 percent of members enrolled in factory sections had done so. And whereas 41 percent of the total membership was in the age group between twenty-six and forty years in 1978, this group accounted for 61 percent of the membership of the factory sections.

A final set of figures, this time pertaining to the party in the largest factories in the province, further underscores the truly remarkable rebirth of a once moribund organization. In 1969, the Turinese PCI had a single section in each of the six largest plants or complexes in the province, for a total of just over one thousand members. In 1973, following the creation of new sections where none had existed and the subdivision of those which had been in place (e.g., to cover different shifts in the same department), the total had risen to thirteen sections and thirty-nine hundred members. By 1978, the figures for the same six establishments were twenty-four sections and more than sixty-three hundred party members.

Because of its limited resources, the Turinese PCI soon found itself facing the negative, unintended consequences of its largely successful efforts in the factories. Within the factories themselves, militants join the party but tend to be preoccupied with shopfloor issues. While they thus increase the party's presence, their activities are concentrated in the unions. These militants are very hard to recruit to the PCI's more specifically party-oriented activities. Circumstances have changed dramatically since the 1950s, but the phenomenon of dual militancy remains, and with predictable results.[28] Outside the factories, ironically, the party's success in rebuilding the workplace organizations has severely cut down the number of cadres available for general activities in the sections' territories and in the broader society. As demands on the party rose after 1975—especially as many activists were drawn into political office—the shortage became acute.[29] We will see in Chapter 6 that both these problems have been severe in Turin.

## The Federation's Intermediate Structures

The PCI has been committed to organizational decentralization since 1956 and has considered it a top priority since at least the early 1960s.[30] Frequent guidelines have emanated from central party headquarters, but the ensuing two decades have seen all but a handful of federations grope for arrangements that can work in practice. The underlying idea is clear enough: effective intervention in society *and* greater rank-and-file participation should result when the party is organized or coordinated within boundaries that reflect socioeconomic reality and not often arbitrary administrative acts (e.g., the province). Yet the gap can be great between a good idea and its implementation. With their highly centralized traditions and practices, PCI federations have been extremely reluctant to surrender any of their considerable powers. Moreover, the Statute of the PCI does not grant autonomous decision-making power to structures located between the sections and the federation.[31] But there also has been a number of very real constraints that have prevented local party organizations from implementing effective zonal structures over the past two decades. Three of these are particularly important.

The first constraint involves the party's way of defining itself. How does it view reality? What are the criteria by which it wishes to organize in society? In the earliest stages of decentralization, when the PCI was more explicitly Marxist-Leninist, its organizational criteria were also more traditional: smaller and relatively homogeneous zones were viewed as desirable. In practice, this never worked very well; local militants tended to get encapsulated in their distinctive milieux. Particularism and local patriotism thrived, providing strong reasons for the federations to intervene heavily in local party affairs. More recently, with the PCI's emphasis on the complexity of society and its problems, it has favored much broader boundaries which embrace the range of issues it must confront. This recent tendency was accelerated in the mid-1970s, especially in places (such as Turin) where the local party suddenly found itself with governing responsibilities.

A second constraint is narrowly organizational. A zone, like any other fairly complex level of the party structure, requires a minimal permanence in staffing to function satisfactorily. A restrictive definition of zonal boundaries means more zones and hence a more thinly spread apparatus and active cadre. There is a certain attraction in avoiding militants and leaders whose focus is too narrow, but when arrangements permit little if any specialization, one of the zones' major justifications is undermined. Larger ones, in contrast, permit the concentration of numerous militants and several full-time party workers in one area. This permits an organizational division of labor, and some specialization as well: the federation-level commissions that deal with specific issues (e.g., factories, propaganda, women, culture) at least have the possibility of functioning when reproduced in the more peripheral territory of the party.

The final constraint is also organizational, but this one emanates from the sections and tends to generate pressures for smaller zones. In spite of, or indeed because of, the federations' habit of centralizing their authority, grass-roots militants tend to take a dim view of further levels of organization inserted between themselves and local party headquarters. Experience has taught them that such "coordinating" structures tend, in practice, to impose centrally defined objectives more often than they solicit input from below. And the larger the intermediate structures, the more pronounced the phenomenon tends to be. Difficulties in this regard are most keenly felt in the largest urban centers, where the sections are least able to function satisfactorily.[32]

If one adds the Turinese federation's chronic organizational weakness to these considerations, it will come as no surprise to learn that the potential tensions indicated above have materialized frequently. This has been most notable in the capital city, where a variety of alternative arrangements were attempted before, during, and following the fieldwork for this study. The basic principle that took shape during the 1970s was to group together several populous *quartieri* of varied social composition into single zones. There were as many as a dozen in the earliest phase of experimentation, and half that many in the late 1970s; by the 1980s, the number seemed to have settled at nine. But coordination continued to prove extremely difficult, and at the end of the 1970s an additional intermediate structure which is often found in the PCI—a City Committee (*Comitato cittadino*)—was established in the capital, to the dismay of most zonal leaders and militants (see Chapter 6). In large measure because of this lukewarm reception, the *Comitato cittadino* never really became operational, although it continues to exist on paper. The zones, in contrast, appear to have their future assured as the party increasingly comes to understand the inherent limitations of the section as an effective grass-roots unit.

In the Turinese hinterland, zones consist of clusters of cities and towns. The present configuration (nine zones) had evolved by the late 1970s after considerable experimentation. When the party is fairly strong and well entrenched in society—that is, in the industrial suburbs and in the more peripheral area centered around Ivrea, headquarters of Olivetti—one tends to find the more successful experiments in decentralization. Local leaders from these areas point out that they have a near-ideal situation: a milieu in which the party functions well,[33] "friendly" local governments, and enough distance from federation headquarters to enjoy a real measure of autonomy. Other outlying areas are much less fortunate, most notably those in the least industrialized, least populated mountainous parts of the province. On one of Turin's rare clear days, the Alps loom dramatically just outside the capital, reminding the observer that there are nearly half a million people in more than two hundred fifty towns and cities who do not live either in the capital or in the industrial belt that rings it. And, as is the case almost everywhere in Italy, the PCI's support drops precipitously with the size of the inhabited center.[34] With few exceptions, the truly peripheral areas of the province are weak and largely ignored by the rest of the party. Figure 5.1 shows the territorial dimension of the federation's organization in 1978. Note the special status of the Fiat Mirafiori organization, which is treated as a zone and has a direct link to the Factory Commission in party headquarters.

With reference to the national party, there is evidence that it is now taking the zones more seriously after numerous fits and starts. For example, most zones now are staffed by full-time party workers.[35] The precise meaning of this trend is, however, open to differing interpretations. Gori's analysis of Florence concluded that the zones had to be staffed by paid party workers (often part-time) because the drop in rank-and-file participation had made this the only way to keep the organization operating. He also argued that the zonal apparatus represented a "minor league" separate stream for militants who otherwise had no hope at all of a party career.[36] This latter point may be an exaggeration, or it may simply reflect the state of the zones at a different period of party history. But the party's top organizer admitted, toward the end of the 1970s, that the zones were understaffed, poorly equipped, and their functionaries "are often the first to be dropped in times of financial difficulties."[37]

If the general, although still embryonic, trend that began to emerge in the 1970s continues—namely the PCI's increasing awareness of the shortcomings of its tradi-

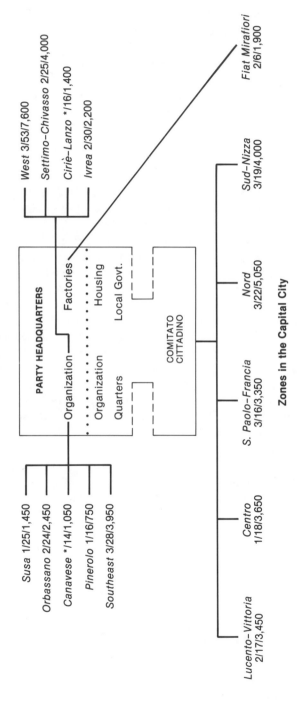

**Zones in the Provincial Hinterland**

Figures following zones indicate number of
functionaries/sections/party members (rounded).

Susa 1/25/1,450
Orbassano 2/24/2,450
Canavese */14/1,050
Pinerolo 1/16/750
Southeast 3/28/3,950

**PARTY HEADQUARTERS**

Organization — Factories
Organization — Housing
Quarters — Local Govt.

COMITATO
CITTADINO

West 3/53/7,600
Settimo–Chivasso 2/25/4,000
Cirìè–Lanzo */16/1,400
Ivrea 2/30/2,200

Fiat Mirafiori
2/6/1,900

**Zones in the Capital City**

Lucento–Vittoria
2/17/3,450

Centro
1/18/3,650

S. Paolo–Francia
3/16/3,350

Nord
3/22/5,050

Sud–Nizza
3/19/4,000

*Part-time functionaries only

**Headquarters:** 17 functionaries (only full-time party workers counted)
**Capital City:** 14 functionaries, 6 zones, 103 sections, 21,337 members
**Provincial Hinterland:** 13 functionaries, 9 zones, 232 sections, 24,776 members

*Figure 5.1.* The Territorial Decentralization of the Turinese Federation, 1978

tional, highly centralized structures—the most dramatic organizational innovations will undoubtedly occur at the intermediate level of the party structure. But such innovation would involve a redefinition of the role of the federation, most likely by subdividing most existing federations on the basis of clusters of present-day zones. (And, in fact, Ivrea became a new federation in the mid-1980s.) To put the issue more within the terms that have informed discussion in this chapter, a dramatic process that emphasized the outward projection of the PCI as a mass party would necessarily involve further undercutting of many cadre-party qualities that remain embedded in the *partito nuovo*. A fuller discussion must await the end of this chapter and of this study. For now, it is sufficient to conclude that the party's record does not provide much evidence that it is prepared to experiment radically, given the cautious and inconsistent way in which it has addressed much more innocuous forms of decentralization to date.

## The Federation's Central Structures

Broadly speaking, communist federations are free to structure their own affairs. The local party decides on the functional subdivisions, personnel assignments, and salary schedules of its functionaries. It may even decide to subdivide the territory of its province into two or more federations, although this must be approved by national headquarters in consultation with the regional leaders.[38] This latter option is not altogether rare; there were 109 federations in Italy's 94 provinces in 1983, and 115 by 1985.[39]

Although there is thus considerable variation among federations, there does remain a central organizational model to which all federations adhere. The configuration of decision-making bodies may be determined locally, but their functions and responsibilities are statutory. Even more important is the fact that the federations must copy the organizational pattern established in Rome to carry out their day-to-day operations. Experts are grouped, information is organized, and materials are distributed along lines determined in national party headquarters. Access to party resources and efficient two-way communication require that federations follow the national lead in the way they divide their activities, both functionally and by sector.

These organizational subdivisions have historically been called working commissions (*commissioni di lavoro*), although toward the end of the 1970s the term *departments* came increasingly into use.[40] Ideally, party federations attempt to maintain functioning commissions in all areas considered important to the local organization. Turin's highly industrialized profile has made an Agricultural Commission unnecessary for some time, for instance; hence the Piedmontese Regional Committee of the PCI generally concerns itself with agricultural policies and initiatives in the capital. Conversely, Turin's special problems caused the federation to create an Immigration Commission in the 1960s, even though there was no exact national counterpart. The priority areas common to all PCI federations are Administration; Problems of the Party (Organization); Information and Image (Press and Propaganda); Culture, including Schools; Local Institutions; and Factories. In Turin, as expected, urban problems have made it imperative to emphasize housing and general health and welfare issues as well, and each of these areas also has its own commission.

While the broad outlines of the local parties' organization have remained fairly constant over time, a closer look often reveals much adjustment and adaptation from one year to the next. Even the changing titles of the commissions (now departments) are not always cosmetic: they may reflect important changes in outlook and indeed in practice. For instance, whatever the other motives may have been for changing "Press and Propaganda" to "Information and Image," the latter label certainly corresponds better to a party that is now deeply involved in radio and television broadcasting. Similarly, at the end of the 1970s, an umbrella Department of Economic and Labor Problems was created, incorporating the Factory Commission. This reflects a strong effort not to isolate the party's focus on the factories but to integrate it with other issues (planning, political economy, and the middle classes, to name the most significant).

A ready measure of a federation's priorities is not only whether a commission is created but how solidly it is staffed. If a full-time party worker, or functionary, heads the unit, one can safely assume that this sector is considered quite important by the local party. In fact, of the top-priority areas noted above— excluding housing and health— all had at least two full-time party workers in headquarters when this study was being carried out. Each commission has a formal head (*responsabile*) and some division of labor. But these divisions usually break down entirely when work pressures are great. In the late 1970s, the Organization Commission in Turin had two full-timers who shared the work load quite indiscriminately. By 1980, the situation had reverted to an older scheme of one *responsabile* for the party in the capital and one for the rest of the province. In the Factory Commission, logically, there has been a general coordinator and also one who oversees all organizations in Fiat plants.

On rare occasions, highly reliable volunteers with specific expertise are found running a commission or one of its divisions. Such arrangements lighten the federation's payroll. They also slim down the party bureaucracy, something the PCI constantly preaches for both fiscal and ideological reasons but finds it hard to implement in practice. In the wake of the economic crisis of the 1980s in Turin, volunteers were increasingly placed in positions previously occupied by functionaries in headquarters and in the zones. Some were truly volunteers who held other jobs, but many were ex-workers subsidized for the moment by the *Cassa Integrazione Guadagni*. This is clearly an exceptional situation, making it hard to say if a more lasting change may be under way. In any event, the Turinese party was forced to trim its budget sharply at the start of the 1980s, for the very large drop in membership that began in the late 1970s bit deeply into the federation's finances as well as its other capacities.[41] The availability of so many militants with time on their hands may help the federation through a difficult period of organizational transition.

The party apparatus, about which much is said in Chapters 7 and 8, does not even exist on the PCI's formal organizational charts. Hardly mentioned in the Statute, these people are nonetheless the critical permanent components of the party machine.[42] In Turin, as in most federations with a sizable group of full-time functionaries, the apparatus meets frequently, usually in response to the ebb and flow of events. Full-time members of the apparatus vary in number according to the individual federation's budgetary decisions, but a general rule is one functionary for every thousand members of the local party.[43] At the time of this study, there were approximately forty-five functionaries in the federation as the membership varied from forty-five thousand to forty-seven thousand.

This, then, is the permanent operational structure of the federation. It is not, however, a description of how any federation is actually governed. Formally, the Statute assigns sovereignty to the Federal Committee (*Comitato Federale*, or CF), which is the local equivalent of the national Central Committee.[44] It is elected at the federations' congresses, which are normally held every three or four years. Because of its unwieldy size in most places—it has hovered between one hundred and one hundred twenty members in Turin for more than a decade—the CF is not even expected to be a true decision-making body. Everyone understands it to be a representative organ which brings together the top-ranking Communists from the party, mass organizations, and public institutions as well as many of the most distinguished rank-and-file and intermediate activists from the whole range of the party's presence and activists. It is a useful subject of study for this very reason: its composition quite faithfully reflects the local party elite and hence the party's collective self-image.

From time to time, efforts have been made to make the CF a more genuine decision-making body by reducing its membership to more manageable size. Pressures for streamlining and more democracy tend to come from the grass roots after periods of intense mobilization or marked successes.[45] But when implemented, these changes have inevitably produced a backlash at both the rank-and-file and the elite levels of the federation: even sixty people cannot govern effectively, and there is no way a group this small can perform a representative function. There has been something of a pendulum in Turin, but recent trends suggest a continuation of larger numbers. Federation leaders are convinced that the CF can never really be sovereign, and they are naturally loath to anger various geographical areas, sectors, or individual "notables" by excluding them.

The other formally sovereign organ of the federation is the Federal Control Commission (*Commissione Federale di Controllo*, or CFC). Its national counterpart is the Central Control Commission. Limited to no more than one-third the size of the CF, the CFC carries out oversight and auditing functions to ensure compliance with PCI regulations and customs. It is also responsible for overseeing the creation and education—the Italian term is *formazione*—of cadres.[46] As these various tasks suggest, the CFC's past functions gave it a heavily disciplinary cast. This coincided nicely with the party's organizational needs in the past in a double sense: the CFC, like its national counterpart, was an honorable place to shunt older leaders who, at the same time, would be sure to interpret the party's rules and regulations in strict fashion. The CFC still tends to be somewhat more conservative (and senior) than the CF throughout the country, but today its auditing and educational functions predominate. When the federation calls a general meeting, particularly to discuss major issues, it invites the CF and the CFC to a joint session.

Following each Congress, the CF and the CFC together elect the real decision-making bodies of the federation; between congresses, the elite groups co-opt new members. Since the end of the 1970s, proposals for co-optation are supposed to be ratified by the CF and the CFC, but to date this has been carried out in pro forma fashion. The true elite of every federation are the federation secretary, the Secretariat, and, "in cases where it is not possible to delegate the tasks of effective direction to the Secretariat alone" (art. 30), an Executive Committee (*Comitato Direttivo*, or CD). At the time of this study, the federation of Turin had a CD of twenty-five members, which included several prominent Communist administrators and elected officials. It mainly consisted of functionaries who head the main commissions or who are the *responsabile* of important zones in the capital city or province. The Secretariat, which varied between five and ten members and was recognized as the true pinnacle of the federation hierarchy, was composed entirely of top-ranking party functionaries.

Figure 5.2 presents a simplified summary of the federation's major functional divisions at the time of the fieldwork for this study. Note that the linkage shown between specific zones or the *Comitato Cittadino* and various *commissioni* in headquarters is not an exclusive one, with the exception of the subcommission on the quarters of the city. The basic link of the provincial zones is to the Organization Commission; that of the zones in the capital is to the *Comitato Cittadino* (which has several commission and subcommission heads on it). But whenever a zone or a section establishes a specific commission, militants who work in that sector of party activity will frequently be in direct contact with their counterparts in party headquarters.

The most up-to-date study of PCI federations in print concluded at the end of the 1970s that the major structural innovations at this level of the party had really been put in place on paper with the decisions to decentralize in the late 1950s. The party's subsequent organizational history consisted of a search for ways to implement decisions taken a generation earlier.[47] Much of this chapter has been concerned with why it took a full generation to implement, often incompletely, earlier proposals. And as we have seen, significant organizational changes in the 1980s, to the extent that they occur at all, will likely involve the sections and zones rather than the federations (unless, of course, the role of the zones is enlarged to such a degree that federation size is radically reduced and the number of federations is thereby greatly augmented).

But the organizational evolution of the PCI has not only involved the party's structures in the narrow sense. Indeed, as noted in the first chapter of this study, discussions about changes in the party's active cadre were probably the central organizational theme in the PCI during the second half of the 1970s. This issue brings up yet again the hybrid character of the *partito nuovo*: because of its cadre-party legacy, but also because its ability to act as a mass political party depends so much on the nature of its activists and leaders, the PCI is by definition deeply concerned with this dimension of its organization. The next section examines both the framing of the problem and the evidence for the Turinese case.

## Identity Crisis? The Changing Profile of Cadres and Leaders

It is not surprising that mass parties of the left would be concerned about and even preoccupied with just who their cadres and leaders are and from which social class they are drawn. The parties' representative function, in society and toward their own membership, is enhanced when activists and leaders come from the classes whose interests they claim to serve. For a highly activist mass party, and especially for one that continues to emphasize its cadre-party qualities, the concern is not only to mirror reality but to act on it. Experience has taught the PCI that concrete examples galvanize mass action far more than abstract appeals. The classical illustration of this phenomenon is the highly regarded militant whose personal dedication wins the respect, often the support, and on occasion even the deeper commitment of his coworkers.

Finally, for potential activists with a measure of personal ambition, party leaders also know that it is important to show that it is possible for people of humble origins to rise within the ranks of the organization. Giorgio Galli noted long ago that this was the only party in Italy whose elite, at least up to the provincial level, came significantly from the lower classes.[48]

Yet it was not simply general considerations but a potent combination of immediate factors that put the question of cadres and leadership on top of the Communist agenda in the latter part of the 1970s. Recalling (from Chapter 2) the situation that faced the PCI at that time, membership had expanded greatly, and more so in Turin than almost

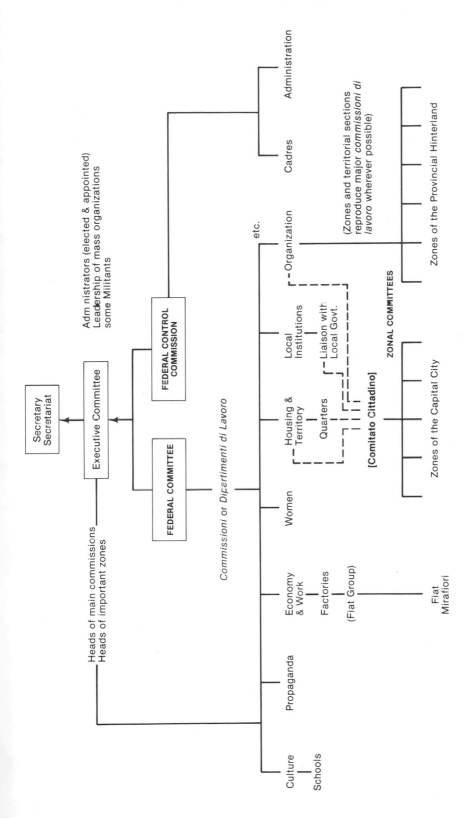

GRASS ROOTS: Sections (and cells) elect delegates who elect zonal committees. CF and CFC
All sections are grouped into territorial zones except for Fiat Mirafiori.

*Figure 5.2.* Basic Organizational Structure of the Turinese Federation, 1978

129

everywhere else. This expansion, especially in the mid-1970s, had brought a dispropor-tionate number of younger and white-collar members to the party. Simultaneously, those leaders and cadres already in place were aging and would soon have needed replacement in any case. But the electoral victories of the PCI in 1975 drew many of them out of the organization and into public office more rapidly and in greater numbers than had been anticipated. Finally, as shown in this chapter, the very rapid expansion of the federation's organizational structures—most notably at the grass roots—created an even greater need for leaders at lower levels.

The PCI was fortunate to have an immense new pool from which to recruit, but it now found itself literally flooded with cadres of varied background, disparate formation, and a notable lack of experience within the party. Responding to the press of events, federations were forced to draw constantly from this pool, whose freshness was at once its strongest positive and negative asset. The party's plight at the end of the 1970s underscored the shortcomings of the new cadres. A vague strategy and a set of tactics which called for a great deal of patience while "small steps" were taken nationally were hardly the ideal conditions under which this heterogeneous mass could be stabilized and consolidated.

Local party organizations thus experienced an identity crisis in highly specific ways, and top party leaders were quick to open a general discussion of what they considered the most serious problems. These were, first, the growth of white-collar and intellectual cadres at the expense of the party's traditional constituent classes. The risk in this development was viewed as a loss of contact between the party and the daily concerns of the masses. Moreover, the recruits of the mid-1970s only knew a victorious PCI. Their "lack of historical memory" was seen as cutting them off from the party's history, from its bitter struggles, and from important insights into how the organization works even in times of adversity. And finally, the heterogeneity of the new cadres made it even less likely that they would be able to formulate the much-needed unifying vision that the PCI had to provide in a very challenging period.[49]

Some of these criticisms are patently unfair, such as the implication that the key obstacle to a unifying or synthetic vision is the heterogeneity of new cadres. The party itself had no such vision ready to impart to anyone; the cadres' only fault in this regard is that they mirrored all too well the complexity of the broader society. And while there was concern about the heterogeneity of the new generation of leaders in the rising phase of party fortunes, complaints were soon heard that local elites were too restricted and homogeneous in the next, more consolidated phase, meaning they had squeezed out older cadres excessively.[50] But these criticisms do reflect the PCI's most pressing concerns in a turbulent period. We can assess their accuracy and gain additional insights into the evolution of the Turinese federation in the 1970s by turning our attention to the broadly defined cadre of the local party. An abundance of material provides a fairly solid image of several levels of the leadership of the federation in a crucial transitional juncture, and it can even offer some indications of how this leadership has changed over time.

## The Federation's Cadres

The most accurate approximation of the activists in any federation is the executive committee (*comitati direttivi*) of the sections. At this level of the party organization, cadres are supposed to be chosen on the basis of their specific contribution in a given area. Yet a common complaint is that cadre selection at all levels of the party, from section executives upward, is "unorganic" and "even chaotic at times." In practice, selective criteria break down, and the tendency is to include everyone who makes a regular contribution as a militant.[51] In Turin, the party gathered data on nearly three thousand members of section executives in 1977, an optimal year for comparative purposes, coinciding with the maximum expansion of the federation's membership.[52]

At this most basic grass-roots level, the working class composition of cadres is identical to that of the general membership. But even here we find what Italian Communists call *terziarizzazione*. The term derives from the "tertiary sector," but it is used in a broader sense. It refers to the presence of clerks, technicians, students, professionals, and teachers and intellectuals, all white-collar groups, loosely defined. Representing about 15 percent of the total party membership, their presence in section executives is twice that figure. Another group that is similarly overrepresented is young people. This is in fact the only level of leadership, however defined, where those under twenty-five are overrepresented; they account for 24 percent of the cadres. Women also do very well at the grass roots, although they generally are not found in the highest positions of the *direttivi*. Nevertheless, with 18 percent of the total, they come close to reflecting their weight in the membership of the party. Finally, the age group of twenty-six to forty, or the "generation of 'sixty-eight," is as strong here as it is everywhere else, accounting for over half (54 percent) of all cadres.

As we can see from this rapid review, the Turinese PCI's rank-and-file cadre reflected the general membership quite accurately toward the end of the 1970s. If any groups were overrepresented, they tended to represent the more dynamic new subjects in society with whom the party most wants and needs to make contact. There is little evidence here of distorted representation or an identity crisis.

One step farther up the ladder of the federation's hierarchy, the picture changes markedly. Considerable evidence is available on the delegates elected by the sections to the party's provincial congresses from 1969 on (sources are cited below in Table 5.1). This is a much more restricted group, less than 2 percent of the membership, as opposed to nearly 7 percent in the section executives. It is also a largely formal artifact, only coming into existence every two or three years. But it is quite important, for it includes the entire true elite of the federation as well as the most outstanding cadres, who are rewarded for their commitment by being chosen to represent their sections at the local party congress. Delegate selection always involves considerable discussion and input from activists, so these figures provide a fairly reliable self-portrait of the local party.

The age distribution of the delegates was unfortunately only available for 1979, with the mean age recorded at earlier congresses. The mean dropped steadily, from thirty-eight to thirty-three, between 1969 and 1977, after which it began to rise again.[53] By 1979, there was no evidence of any overrepresentation of youthful militants as the younger recruits of the 1970s grew older and were not replaced by an influx of fresh blood; one delegate in nine and one member in nine was below twenty-five years of age in Turin. But the "generation of 'sixty-eight" strengthened its dominance of the federation's cadres through the 1970s, and by the end of the decade two-thirds of all delegates were in the group between twenty-six and forty years of age.

The data on the delegates do include information about when they joined the PCI, which is very helpful in tracing how their profile changed during the 1970s. Here we can clearly see how the older generations of leaders was replaced. In 1969, the largest group (29 percent) was made up of those who joined the party in 1945 or even earlier. And the other "glorious generation" was also present in significant numbers: those who had entered the PCI between the Liberation and 1955 were 21 percent of the total. As noted earlier, these two generations dominated the party in Turin more than the figures indicate. On the eve of the hot autumn, they still accounted for half the delegates. In 1972, they were a high 37 percent, and even in 1975 they were just under a quarter of the total. By 1977, when the second wave of recruitment after the hot autumn had taken place, they had dropped to one in nine.

The delegates' profile thus indicates, as expected, the weight of history in the PCI. But it also points out how quickly the party can react to new stimuli, especially when these come from the factories and mass struggles. In 1972, for instance, a fourth of the delegates to that year's congress had joined the party between 1969 and 1971. In 1975, half the delegates had joined after 1969. Hence, while the "generation of 'sixty-eight" did not enter the party rapidly on the mass level, this was *not* the case for the cadres and the broadly defined elite of the federation. At these levels, it became the largest group in the mid-1970s and remained such into the 1980s.[54]

The social composition of the delegates also reveals a number of interesting developments over time. The most significant relative changes, as seen in Table 5.1, involve white-collar groups and students. The presence of students in 1969 was still very limited, in spite of the strength of the Turinese student movement between 1967 and 1969. By 1972, although still less than one percent of all party members, their presence among delegates had already risen to the level at which it would remain through the 1970s before dropping off in the 1980s. But by far the most interesting change took place midway through the 1970s, and this involved the ratio of blue- to white-collar workers.

The total weight of both groups has been very stable over time while remaining roughly equivalent to their weight in the general membership of the federation. But the relationship between the two shifted from three-to-one in favor of the blue-collar workers in the late 1960s to near parity by the 1980s. Technically, clerks and technicians were even more overrepresented among delegates in the past (see Table 2.6), when they were a minuscule proportion of the entire membership. But it was clearly the rise in the mid-1970s, combined with the displacement of the blue-collar workers from leadership

*Table 5.1.* Social Composition of Delegates to Provincial Congresses of the PCI in Turin, 1969–1983 (Major Groups)

| Class or Group[a] | 1969 | 1972 | 1975 | 1977 | 1979 | 1983 |
|---|---|---|---|---|---|---|
| Workers | 57.8% | 52.3% | 43.8% | 42.2% | 43.5% | 39.4% |
| Clerks and technicians | 17.4 | 18.7 | 30.6 | 31.9 | 29.1 | 34.1 |
| Intellectuals, professionals, teachers | 8.8 | 8.9 | 11.9 | 13.3 | 13.7 | 9.6 |
| Students | 2.5 | 6.3 | 5.9 | 6.8 | 6.3 | 3.2 |
| All women | 8.0 | 10.3 | 12.2 | 13.5 | 11.5 | 12.7 |
| (N) | (477) | (662) | (523) | (810) | (678) | (657) |

a. Full-time functionaries from the party, unions, and other mass organizations are classified according to employment immediately prior to becoming functionaries.

*Source:* Calculated from typewritten minutes of provincial congresses' *Relazioni della Commissione per la verifica dei poteri dei delegati.*

positions, that made many people in the party increasingly uncomfortable. The combined weight of students and other professional and intellectual categories doubled to 20 percent over the course of the 1970s, although it then dropped notably in the 1980s. Still, all white-collar groups rose from a quarter at the time of the hot autumn to nearly half in the early 1980s, even with the recent drop.

For reasons noted earlier, these trends cannot be seen as a sign of the creeping embourgeoisement of the Turinese party leadership, nor can one even interpret them as an indicator of the growing distance of the leadership from the masses. Federation leaders pointed out that many changes in the elite in fact reflected the evolving nature of the working class. The most marked changes have been the downgrading of blue-collar factory workers and the expansion of more educated and skilled white-collar workers. The latter may not wear coveralls, but they are the new skilled workers in the current phase of capitalist development.[55] In Turin, at least, white-collar groups come overwhelmingly from factories and other firms, and few ranking party leaders were worried about any loss of the PCI's class character.

But everyone knew, even before the thirty-five days, that there are considerable differences between blue- and white-collar workers and at least some differences between an increasingly white-collar leadership and a mass membership still largely composed of blue-collar workers. It is significant that the most recent party statistics for the first time distinguish between clerks and technicians instead of lumping them together.[56] But the problem remains a difficult one which even the best definitions will be unable to resolve. It is the political behavior of these groups, and not their objective location inside or just outside the working class, that remains problematic and therefore leaves many Communists uneasy.

A final point is worth making about the rise of clerks and technicians among the delegates, and that is that while the big increase in this group occurred in 1975, it was not because of the local electoral victories of that year. Those delegates were in fact elected at the end of 1974 to attend a congress held early in 1975. The elections, however, took place in June of 1975. The group that does show an increase right after the elections consists of teachers, intellectuals, and professionals. In this instance, it is probably true that growing technical demands on the PCI because of the party's increased administrative responsibilities explain a significant part of the rise. The clerks and technicians, in contrast, most likely rose as a function of their greatly increased weight in the party membership.

The last level of the party hierarchy to be examined here can only be considered cadre in the broadest sense: it is the formally sovereign *Comitato Federale*, half of which consists of party professionals or other full-time activists in mass organizations or public office. But, for this very reason, it represents an important subject for analysis. As we will see, although this group is only a sixth the size of the delegates, there are many more similarities than differences between the two, except for the question of professionalism. Hence, however one judges the issues discussed in this section, it is important to realize that at the level of the federation the really sharp sociological and generational breaks come quite far down the organizational ladder, just above the sections.

We have information on four of the five CFs elected between 1969 and 1979. Data are unavailable for 1975, and that is a pity, for at least some evidence examined from lower levels suggests that this was a watershed year. But since the primary concern here is to indicate trends in the evolution of the organization, the best place for a gap to occur is right in the middle of the period under study. One of the most interesting trends is the changing age distribution of the federation's elite, and this can be seen in Table 5.2.

The table confirms many of the phenomena already observed elsewhere and shows how thoroughly the changes that took place in Turin penetrated the party at all levels. Most obvious is the way in which the impact of the cycle of struggles rolled though the upper reaches of the party by the end of the 1970s. At this level, we would expect the youngest age group's trajectory to be as shown: it expands steadily and then contracts sharply, corresponding to a large influx of youth, a delayed promotion to the elite level, and then the effects of the natural aging process. The next youngest group follows a similar route. By 1977, fully 40 percent of the CF had joined the party in the first half of the decade, indicating, as anticipated, that the party absorbed new energies into its upper reaches more slowly than at the grass roots, but that it eventually did so in thorough fashion.

Finally, because we have complete biographies of the members of the 1977 CF, the analysis can go beyond the simple aggregates we have been constrained to work with for other years. By far the most important finding to emerge from a more detailed study of the leaders' career patterns is the direct impact of the 1968–1972 cycle on the federation elite. When we break down chronological generations by political generation, we find that more than half the leaders between ages twenty-six and forty—the "generation of 'sixty-eight"—actually joined the PCI between 1968 and 1972. Moreover, a third of the youngest generation also joined the party in the same very limited time span, which, as we saw earlier, was not a period that brought a great influx of younger people into the general party membership. The mass flood of youth only took place after 1973.

This is a logical sequence of events when viewed from the perspective of the party organization: militants who entered the PCI with the first wave of recruits in the hot period would have more experience inside the party by the mid-1970s and thus be more likely to be promoted rapidly to the top of the federation hierarchy. But it does show how solidly the veterans of 1968 were entrenched in Turin by the late 1970s. Their strong position in the federation is one reason for the spirited defense of the hot autumn when it was under attack from national party leaders and several exponents of the "administrative party" during the difficulties of 1978–79.[57]

Information on the social composition of the CFs in Turin over time is incomplete. There are satisfactory data for 1977, the first year that falls clearly on the far side of the massive membership increases. The evidence indicates that, like the delegates

*Table 5.2.* Age Distribution of Federal Committees of the Turinese Federation, 1969–1979

|  | | 1969 | | 1972 | | 1977 | | 1979 |
|---|---|---|---|---|---|---|---|---|
| to 25 years | | 6.9% | | 9.3% | | 11.2% | | 5.9% |
| 25–30 years | 19.0 ⎫ | | 26.9 ⎫ | | 20.6 ⎫ | | 27.7 ⎫ | |
| | ⎬ 46.6 | | ⎬ 51.9 | | ⎬ 61.7 | | ⎬ 68.3 | |
| 31–40 years | 27.6 ⎭ | | 25.0 ⎭ | | 41.1 ⎭ | | 40.6 ⎭ | |
| 41 and older | | 46.6 | | 38.9 | | 27.1 | | 15.7 |
| Total | | 100.1 | | 100.1 | | 100.0 | | 99.9 |
| (N) | | (58) | | (108) | | (107) | | (101)[a] |

a. Data missing for nineteen cases.

*Source:* Archives of the federation.

who elected them, the CF members were 40 percent working class. And, while the strictly defined white-collar groups were less present (21 percent) in the CF than among the delegates, the professional and intellectual categories, with one-third of the total, were nearly as numerous as the workers. Most notably of all, the trends noted here accelerated radically among the most recent recruits. Viewing only those who joined the party in the 1970s, the workers were nearly equaled by clerks and technicians and badly outnumbered by professionals and intellectuals.[58] Here it really is possible to speak of *terziarizzazione*. It will come as no surprise to note that nearly three-fourths of the 1977 CF were high school graduates, and a very high 30 percent had university degrees. These figures are a good deal higher than for cadres and the rank-and-file membership, in Turin and in Italy as a whole.[59]

In reality, however, the great weight of the party's full-time apparatus at this level of the hierarchy means that functionaries and other political professionals are the truly dominant category among the elite. In Turin, as elsewhere, the CF has consistently drawn half its membership from professional ranks. For instance, twenty-six of the forty-three "workers" in the CF had actually moved out of the factories into professional political activity, most frequently in the PCI organization. And the weight of the party machine in other social groups is even more crushing: eight of ten "students" listed in the 1977 CF were really party workers. The presence of functionaries in the party leadership is certainly no cause for scandal, but their utter predominance in the upper reaches of party federations has been subject to constant criticism since the difficulties of the late 1970s.

This criticism is rooted in several sources, all of which find the party apparatus to be a handy target. One is narrowly political and reflects (justifiable) resentment at the way the party line was placed beyond effective criticism through most of the 1970s. Another source is more general and reflects the same issues that fuel concerns over *terziarizzazione*. Here, too, is the belief that many of the PCI's mass qualities are diluted or subverted by too large a professional corps of leaders. Functionaries were increasingly criticized for being closed off in a world of their own and inclined to impose their own priorities and rhythms on the entire party.[60] But in spite of increased attention to this issue since the end of the 1970s, the ratio of professionals to volunteers has remained the same into the 1980s.[61]

## Conclusions

The party's problems in the 1970s brought a wide range of organizational issues to the fore. A few, such as those relating to cadres, were new to the PCI but are among the oldest of all those that have historically plagued mass parties of the left.[62] The others, as noted, have long been discussed within the PCI, but for a variety of reasons the party proved unable or unwilling in the past to move to remedy widely acknowledged shortcomings. Nor is it certain that the solutions discussed at the beginning of the 1980s will prove adequate or be acted on decisively in the future. What does appear clear, however, is that the party's strategic and political difficulties and the profound changes in Italian society that precipitated (or at least aggravated) them finally brought the most serious tensions embedded in the very concept of the *partito nuovo* to a point where they could no longer be ignored.

By far the most recurrent tension, from an organizational point of view, relates to the dualistic or hybrid nature of the party, to the often conflicting demands of an organization of cadres versus those of a mass party of presence. The discussion in this chapter shows that the balance appears to have shifted decisively in the 1970s in favor of the mass party. Almost every force acting on the PCI in this period pointed toward the need to reinforce the party's ability to establish links to, and to move within, society. At the same time, these and other forces—including natural attrition—were attenuating the party's classical cadre characteristics. As the data on Turin demonstrated eloquently, the weight of the leaders and cadres of the "glorious generations" (primarily the ex-workers of the Resistance and postwar periods) faded rapidly in the 1970s. Among other things, these groups had represented a living bridge to the past and thus to the *partito nuovo* in its heyday. The "lack of historical memory" so often referred to in this period was in many ways a lament for this aging generation, which had few answers for the future but a very solid patrimony on which to fall back in times of trouble.

This is the fundamental tension, and its ramifications are extremely serious for the party. On one level, the PCI's official position has been to recognize the problem and opt in favor of updating and adapting the mass-party aspects of its structure and practices. It has acknowledged the need to jettison the most oppressively centralistic, antidemocratic remnants of the Stalinist past. And it may even be moving in the direction of a more truly decentralized mass organization with a grass-roots and intermediate structure that corresponds much better to reality and is therefore inherently more capable of acting effectively in its surroundings.

Unfortunately for the PCI, however, many of the qualities that make it effective as an activist mass party are intimately linked to its more desirable cadre characteristics. The dilemma of the size of sections is one illustration of how internal operations can be at odds with the need to project the organization into society. If smaller units at the grass roots are required to enhance rank-and-file participation, but larger aggregations are needed to intervene effectively in society, no amount of institutional tinkering can eliminate the contradiction. As the real weight of the zones (or some other intermediate structure) grows, common militants will inevitably sense that their own input remains minimal. And discouraged militants are not the best candidates for carrying out the everyday tasks that are largely responsible for keeping the organization going. In the future, the party's foot-dragging over serious structural reform of its own organization may well continue, not because of a commitment to outdated ideals but out of the need to balance demands which, in the final analysis, cannot really be reconciled.

# 6

# The Organizational Dimensions of the Crisis in Turin in the 1970s

The organizational problems of Turinese communism, as we have seen, have diverse roots. Some are found in the *partito nuovo* itself. Others reflect the inability of this particular type of mass party to take hold in an urban context, especially one with the postwar political and socioeconomic characteristics of the Piedmontese capital. Then there are problems, such as generational turnover, that would have come forward in any case at this stage of the party's life cycle but were exacerbated by a series of special events in the 1970s. Finally, there were the events of the 1970s themselves. These events, including the profound strategic confusion in which the party found itself, signified important breaks with the past and therefore must be seen as positive. Some, such as the PCI's significant organizational growth and its transition to a governing role, were extremely positive.

This chapter describes and analyzes the impact of this ensemble of problems on the Turinese party organization in the period under discussion. The main goal is not to trace the roots of each aspect of the party's crisis or to assign weights to each component of the crisis. Such issues can hardly be ignored in a study that argues that it is the underlying model of the mass party that is in part—but only in part—the source of the PCI's difficulties. But excessive attention to such issues would obscure the central question, which is how the crisis manifested itself in Turin.

## Transitional Crisis at the Grass Roots

At the base of the Turinese federation, two issues had an especially heavy impact on the operations of the party organization. The first was leadership turnover and its numerous disruptive effects. The second was the maturation of long-standing tensions in the division of grass-roots organizations into workplace and territorial units.

### Organizational Expansion and Leadership Turnover

Recall from Chapter 2 that while party membership rose 20 percent between the hot autumn and 1977, the jump was nearly 60 percent in Turin. And the impact on the local organization was even greater than these figures suggest, for most of the growth was compressed into a very limited time span. Indeed, an important internal document reveals that the federation had to absorb thirteen thousand new recruits between 1975 and 1977 alone, an astonishing figure for a party that limped through the last half of the 1960s with barely thirty thousand members.[1]

These were exciting results and seemed to bring within reach the once fantastic goal of fifty thousand members. But at this point, old and new problems combined to generate difficulties that would plague the party into the 1980s. As already noted, one of the most common complaints concerned the rapid pace at which cadres were being inserted into the party structure. In Turin, the themes of "renewal without continuity" and of the development of cadres without "historical memory" were in the air by 1975 and were widespread by 1977.[2] By 1979, a document prepared for the provincial congress argued that the party had not successfully integrated its different generations of activists.[3]

These complaints actually cover a multitude of phenomena and past sins of the local party organization. It did indeed prove difficult to integrate new and old cadres in the 1970s, but this had much to do with the older cadres themselves. Grass-roots leaders of an earlier generation all too often had an oppositionist and even a sectarian notion of the party: reflecting their own experience, they tended to see society not as a terrain to penetrate but as an entity organized against the PCI. Their activism consequently was turned inward.[4] Leaders and activists who joined the party during and after the hot period told me how difficult and unwelcoming many veterans had been. Some new leaders encountered episodes of sabotage, and a few were even threatened by the old guard with expulsion.

Viewed from this perspective, renovation that appears to have been too rapid reveals itself as a double-edged sword. It certainly cannot be put down only to brash newcomers insensitively shunting aside their more venerable comrades. The organizational history of the Turinese PCI actually required a fairly brutal approach at the outset, and this is what it got, with the full support of the federation's leaders. Hundreds of painful battles had to be fought in the party's rank-and-file organizations to displace the old leaders and, frequently, many of their followers. The harshness of this changing of the guard might later be regretted, but it is hard to see what alternatives existed for a party that badly needed to gear up for an entirely new series of challenges in the 1970s.

And generational turnover was only one source of organizational instability. Another, noted in Chapter 5, was the conscious decision, sanctioned by central PCI policy, to divide existing sections as soon as their membership grew to about three hundred.[5] The party in Turin, following these directives and additionally building factory organizations wherever it could, found itself with hundreds of new and untested leadership groups at the grass roots by the end of the 1970s.[6]

But most destabilizing of all was the brief tenure in organizational posts of most new grass-roots leaders on account of the Turinese PCI's greatly increased role in local government in the 1970s. National policy and sheer necessity, reflecting the lack of qualified cadres, combined to create this situation, and its effects on the organization were devastating. Promising new leaders were snatched out of the sections and into party headquarters or public office, almost as rapidly as they emerged at the base. Constant turnover completely disrupted the party organization at a critical time, while it also undermined the section's role in the federation. This was recognized as a disaster almost as soon as it began.[7] One local leader told me how all five sections in an industrial suburb with one thousand members were "decapitated" when the Communists won the 1975 local elections: of twenty-one PCI councilors elected, seventeen were the organizational elite of the city's sections. All of them became involved frenetically in local governmental affairs, leaving the sections floundering in their wake. Where the

PCI was weaker organizationally, the trauma could be even greater. Another leader related how the entire active cadre of the party (a dozen people out of a few hundred widely scattered members) was suddenly thrust into a governing role in a small city following the 1975 vote. In this case, the party section simply ceased to function as an autonomous political structure in society.

## The Nature of the New Recruits: The View from Turin

As we have seen, the infusion of new blood into the PCI generated concern throughout the party, even though most leaders knew that renovation was long overdue. Because the turnover of members and cadres was extensive, and because it occurred at the same time that the party was undergoing so many other trials, many of the criticisms raised against the new low-level leadership were extremely broad. It is obvious that party veterans frequently blamed new cadres for all the PCI's difficulties. Lurking behind accusations of a lack of historical memory or an inability to roll with the punches, for example, is often dismay at the party's general plight—and wishful thinking that seasoned veterans would somehow find ways to cut the PCI's losses.

Chapters 2 and 5 documented massive organizational changes. How were these actually experienced by the grass-roots structures of the federation? A partial response can be provided by a study of the sections in the capital, which the Turinese party itself carried out in 1980.[8] The federation generously gave me access to the completed questionnaires. They provide a good, if somewhat overstated, summary of the health of the sections in the city of Turin.[9]

By most of the generally accepted criteria, a remarkably consistent 20 to 25 percent of Turin's sections were barely able to function in 1980. That is the percentage that reported either no meeting place at all or else a meeting place that was "absolutely inadequate." The same proportion reported meetings of their executive committee that were "irregular" or, at most, monthly (70 percent met on a weekly basis, which is the recommended norm). These proportions come close to the one section in three described as "on the margins of survival" by the head organizer two years earlier.[10]

We can obtain a very graphic sense of the impact of leadership turnover at the base from these same questionnaires, for they asked how long the serving section secretary had been in that position. They also asked how long his or her predecessor had held the job. Table 6.1 summarizes the responses.

The table shows how dislocations that began in the mid-1970s were still evident five years later: less than half the city's sections had enjoyed continuous leadership for more than two years. Moreover, if we analyze the same data in a slightly different way, we discover that turnover was very extensive indeed. In the period from 1975 to 1980,

*Table 6.1.* Period in Office of PCI Section Secretaries, City of Turin, 1980 (Absolute Figures)

|              | Less than one year | 1–2 years | 2–3 years | 3 or more years | NA |
|--------------|--------------------|-----------|-----------|-----------------|-----|
| Incumbents   | 18[a]              | 18        | 15        | 13              | —   |
| Predecessors | 4                  | 20        | 15        | 20              | 5   |

*a.* Includes two vacant posts at the time of the survey.

*Source:* Calculated from questionnaires in federation archives.

just over two-thirds of all sections in the sample had undergone at least two changes of leaders. Hence, no matter how the figures are interpreted, it is clear that most grass-roots organizations in Turin had had multiple changes of leaders in the few years following 1975.[11]

Such extensive turnover, especially in view of repeated comments in meetings and documents about the loss of experienced cadres at the section level, might lead us to expect the section secretaries to be overwhelmingly made up of newcomers to the PCI. There is a large contingent of secretaries who joined the party in 1975 or later; they account for 42 percent of all those in the sample. But almost precisely the same number (37 percent) joined the party during the 1968–1972 cycle of struggles. What explains the presence of so many relative veterans in such a fluid situation?

A closer look at the data reveals that the high proportion of veterans is actually further evidence of high turnover. Two-thirds of these "veterans" had only served as section secretaries for two years or less, while the remainder had been in office for a year or less. They may have joined the party in 1972 or earlier, but they were also newcomers to leadership positions in 1980.

Political and organizational factors once again interacted to create a distinctive profile. Politically, the more veteran activists are primarily the products of the great mobilizations that started in the late 1960s. Organizationally, the very high turnover at the grass roots of the federation after 1975 took a heavy toll of local leaders. It was so heavy, in fact, that by the late 1970s many of the most talented—or simply hardworking—newcomers had moved out of the sections to other positions. Those with less skills or those more easily discouraged by the barrage of problems after 1977 probably fell by the wayside. By the end of the 1970s, many sections were desperately in search of leaders, any leaders with a modicum of organizational ability and experience. And many veterans, often by default, were drawn into this vacuum. The federation's new *responsabile* of organization summarized this situation quite bluntly in an apparatus meeting at the end of 1980. He described the current group of section secretaries as "simply those who have stayed in the sections, or who cannot find an adequate excuse to avoid the job."[12]

## Workplace versus Territorial Organizations and Dual Militancy

The PCI has always assigned great importance to an organized presence where its members work. In an industrial center of Turin's size and importance, this goal was paramount even though it could not be realized throughout most of the 1950s and 1960s. Economic change, repression, and the party's policy of concentrating its (limited) energies in union activities meant that the Communists had all but vanished from the workplaces of Italy's major industrial areas by the end of the 1960s. But PCI commitment to extending and reinforcing the party in the workplace has never wavered.[13]

As Chapter 2 showed, it is against this backdrop that the hot autumn's importance for Turinese communism must be understood. Intense industrial and social mobilization triggered a great organizational renaissance which far outstripped the national party's growth. Workplace organizations increased by a factor of six, and the end of the 1970s saw half the federation's membership directly organized in these structures. The Turinese PCI could by no means organize all the factories within its territory (nine hundred plants in the province had more than fifty employees, and more than two thousand had at least ten),[14] but it had finally reestablished a serious presence in the most important ones.

Communist parties have always been distinguished by their emphasis on factory organization, but the PCI's commitment to a strong presence in the workplace is much more than a vestige of bolshevism.[15] Workplace organizations are especially well suited to an activist mass party of presence. They force party militants to confront reality: identified as Communists by their fellow workers, activists are compelled to grapple with common problems and to defend and carry out party policies. Ideally, the hard work and good example of the party militant can orient the entire working class and its organizations.

This, of course, is how the organization is supposed to work. In reality, even during the high points of the 1970s, difficulties were rampant. For one thing, after 1976, Communist militants were in the uncomfortable position of having to defend highly unpopular austerity policies. Hard put to respond to critics, many militants eventually became demoralized; a great number ceased to be active altogether.[16] Here is the flip side of the coin for the mass party: when things do not go well, its grass-roots presence acts as an early-warning system. This happened in the factories of Turin in the 1970s. PCI militants became lightning rods and carried working-class and trade-union divisions into the federation.

But even if we ignore political problems, the federation had to confront structural contradictions that, ironically, grew out of the PCI's *success* in organizing its members where they work.

One of the most powerful contradictions for an organization such as the Turinese PCI is the sharp demographic imbalance that must work against territorial sections if workplace sections become widespread. Even before the territorial units are exposed to debilitating turnover, they will have to contend with a drastically limited pool from which to draw potential activists. This is an unintended but unavoidable side effect of building up an extensive presence in the workplace; it was noted in Turin as soon as the first breakthroughs were achieved in the early 1970s, even before the local elections of 1975.[17] Table 6.2 shows how marked the imbalance can be. The data are drawn from a

*Table 6.2.* Social Composition of Membership of Turinese Federation: Workplace and Territorial Sections Compared (1971)

|  | Workplace | Territorial | Entire Sample | Whole Federation |
|---|---|---|---|---|
| Workers | 80.3% | 43.8% | 53.5% | 58.6% |
| Clerks, technicians | 14.2 | 10.7 | 11.6 | 10.9 |
| Students | 2.2 | 1.2 | 1.5 | 1.6 |
| Intellectuals, professionals | 1.6 | 3.6 | 3.1 | 2.9 |
| Self-employed | 0.2 | 8.3 | 6.2 | 6.3 |
| Housewives | 0.5 | 9.3 | 6.9 | 7.0 |
| Pensioners | 1.0 | 22.6 | 16.9 | 12.5 |
| Others | — | 0.5 | 0.3 | 0.4 |
| Total Percentage | 100.0 | 100.0 | 100.0 | 100.0 |
| Number in sample | 4,584 | 12,814 | 17,398 | — |
| Number in federation | 23,400 | 23,700 | — | 47,100 |

*Sources:* Sample of 125 sections with 20,272 total members; PCI, *Dati sulla organizzazione del Partito* (1979), pp. 38–39.

sample of 125 sections embracing more than two-fifths of the members of the federation. Thirty of these sections are workplace organizations, and ninety-five are territorial.[18]

Two things immediately strike the eye. The first is the presence in the territorial sections of a very high proportion of social groups that are less active in party life. Pensioners and housewives account for nearly a third of the membership, and the self-employed, whose long working hours frequently permit little time for party activities, bring the total to 40 percent. These groups naturally account for a minuscule proportion of the workplace sections.[19] The second striking, if unsurprising, finding in Table 6.2 is the overwhelmingly working-class character of the workplace sections—and the low percentage (for Turin) of workers in the territorial sections. The rank-and-file organizations in the territory of "Factory City" have a proletarian component that differs little from the PCI's national average, which was just under 40 percent when this survey of the sections was carried out. Another way of summarizing the data enables us to appreciate the absolute dimensions of the difference: out of a total pool of twenty-eight thousand working-class members of the federation in 1977, roughly eighteen thousand were in workplace sections, leaving ten thousand scattered in the much more numerous territorial organizations of the province.

It follows from both these factors that workplace sections would have a preponderance of members who were more active and younger and who also had joined the party more recently. And, in fact, the data from the sample confirm these assumptions: more than two-thirds of those in factories and firms were forty or younger in 1977 (vs. 46 percent in territorial sections); nearly three-quarters had joined the PCI after 1969 (vs. 47 percent). With a smaller pool of fresh energy to draw on, the territorial sections suffered more from the turnover and burnout that were endemic at the time.[20]

The irony of the situation described here is that while it put the federation's territorial sections at a disadvantage, it did not guarantee a good bill of health to the workplace organizations. I have already mentioned the political cross-fire in which PCI cadres were caught because of the PCI's austerity policy and its general foot-dragging as it tried to woo the DC. A more profoundly rooted problem for the party exists, however: dual militance (*doppia militanza*). This refers to the fact that almost all party militants in the factory are also union militants, and the very top cadres are inevitably union delegates—rough equivalents of shop stewards—who are deeply caught up in union affairs.[21] Because the unions have operated at arm's length from the parties in Italy— and particularly in Turin—for many years, there is by no means a harmony of interests or activities implicit in dual militance. On the contrary, party and union compete for the militant's limited time and energies, and the union almost inevitably wins, given the immediate and pressing relevance of union activity for a working-class activist.

In fact, *dual* militance is really something of a misnomer, given the predictability with which communist militants in the factories tend to favor trade-union activities. Party leaders regularly complain that even when shopfloor cadres participate in party activities, they bring the union's concerns and perspectives into the sections. This is a complete reversal of the Leninist/bolshevik model of the union as a "transmission belt" for party policies, but it does follow logically from several developments discussed in this study: (1) the conscious decision, following the rout of the 1950s, to pour the PCI's limited resources into (re-)building a shattered union movement; (2) the trend, starting in the 1960s, toward a more unified union movement that reinforced greater autonomy vis-à-vis the party; (3) the fact that the resurgent militancy of the late 1960s brought more PCI cadres into politics via the unions, rather than vice versa. If their initial socialization came from outside the party, they would obviously be less inclined to see party activity as the most important form of "real" political activity.[22]

What this really points to is a failure to think through the full implications of the *partito nuovo* in a late-20th-century setting. The dilemma was succinctly summed up by one of the functionaries assigned to the Fiat Mirafiori complex: "Our most basic problem is that we really don't know what the party organization in the factories is supposed to do. We know it must be different from the unions, but how?"[23] Given the centrality of the workplace—and especially the factory—in the history and collective consciousness of Turin, it is only logical that the local party threw itself into the expansion of its workplace organizations as soon as this became feasible in the 1970s. Recalling the tumult of the period, it is evident that this was a political necessity as well as an organizational reflex.

Yet even when such efforts met with success, it soon became clear that the workplace-territorial division of the party organization—formerly taken for granted but never effectively implemented in Turin—was the source of serious structural differences. Official federation documents were soon acknowledging that this long-hallowed formula actually institutionalized "a very serious vertical gap" between grass-roots organizations in Turin. Where steps were taken to bridge the gap, such as formally linking territorial sections with factory cells or sections, it was admitted that these links were "purely administrative"; they did not really change the way the sections worked.[24]

Naturally, the more general crisis of the PCI's grass-roots organizations, discussed in Chapter 5, was also having its effects in Turin, but the purpose here has been to focus on the more distinctively Turinese aspects of the organizational crisis at the grass roots. It is especially important to underscore the speed with which these problems came to the fore: the federation was nearly paralyzed by 1977; by mid-1978, the head of the organization commission told a gathering of militants that the party had reached the end of its tether (*il Partito a Torino non regge più*).[25] These are important dates, for they show that long before the organizational collapse and economic crisis that struck Turin in the early 1980s, inherent structural tensions combined with the political difficulties of the post-1975 period had already taken a punishing, decisive toll on the federation.

## Transitional Crisis between Base and Summit: The Zones

By the latter part of the 1970s, Turinese Communists at the grass roots often found it difficult to carry out the party's supposedly routine functions. But a full understanding of the pressures exerted on the base of the party and an appreciation of the general search for more effective arrangements within the federation cannot be reached if we focus only on the base.

The general picture in the zones at the time of this study was extremely fluid, especially in the capital. In 1975, they attained their numerical high point, with twenty-seven in the entire federation. In 1977, there were nine in the capital, including Fiat Mirafiori, and nine in the rest of the province. By 1979, three of the smaller zones in the capital had been joined to others. Of the six zones in the city, one had one full-time functionary; the others had at least two, and some had as many as four or five. (By the mid-1980s, unsuccessful combinations were broken up, and the total stood at thirteen.)

In the rest of the province, the situation was more stable. Nine zones existed throughout the late 1970s, and only one of these lacked a full-time functionary. The other eight varied greatly. Those in the dense industrial belt approximated small federations, with four thousand to seventy-five hundred members, at least one full-time office worker, and three or four full-time party workers in relatively well-equipped zonal offices.[26] Furthermore, in the industrial belt, the PCI was in power in almost all the largest cities. In the hinterland, with a few important exceptions, this was not the case. In strictly organizational terms, in the periphery one often finds only one functionary, part-time secretarial help, more modest physical plant, and a smaller, more scattered membership.

This intermediate level of the party was seriously buffeted, directly and indirectly, by the PCI's transitional crisis. Here, as everywhere else, leadership turnover reached pathological dimensions. We also see, at this level even more than elsewhere, how the crisis undermined effective decentralization—or, if one prefers, how it reinforced centralizing tendencies—in a traditionally centralistic federation. Finally, the crisis also exacerbated the local party's fragmentation and sectoralism, which are also phenomena felt with special acuity as one moves up the organizational ladder (where coordination and synthesis are supposed to take place).

## Cadre Turnover and the Frenetic Work Pace

One would expect the turnover phenomenon to be very keenly felt in the zones, for, as intermediate-level structures, they are subject to especially intense cross-pressures. In the capital, where the boundaries of the zones were in constant flux throughout the 1970s (and later), the disruption of the party's coordinating structures was continual in many places.

The zones' susceptibility to disruption is, above all, a function of the fact that at this level of the party, several different layers of cadre meet: zones embrace the grass roots, a zonal cadre which partially overlaps the sections, as well as the lowest level of full-time party workers. Turnover at the lowest levels is immediately felt at the next stage up in the hierarchy, and one can easily imagine how the sections' fluid situation impeded any serious consolidation of the party organization in territorial entities that embrace many—often upwards of twenty (see Figure 5.1)—sections. Throughout the fieldwork for this study, zonal leaders I met referred to themselves as firemen who only had time to rush about in response to one emergency or another. Rarely, if ever, did they feel that they were seriously able to build the party, let alone intervene actively in society. Zonal cadres may well be the most overworked and pressured of all activists in the federation, with those who survive the overloading of responsibilities generally co-opted into activities higher up in the party structure, setting the zones back to their point of departure.

And high levels of turnover reach to the very top of the zones. Table 6.3 shows how the experienced functionaries were massively concentrated in headquarters in 1978: seven of ten members of the zonal apparatus had been full-time party workers for three years or less. Even this proportion does not tell the full story, for let us remember the extensive redrawing of boundaries and shifting of personnel that went on in the zones. In fact, of the twenty-three functionaries in the zones in 1978, only one remained in the same locale, within the same geographical boundaries that he had occupied before 1975. A broader definition of "personnel change" in the apparatus would make the turnover figure in the zones nearly 100 percent for the period from 1975 to 1978—and, as the table clearly shows, these were mostly inexperienced cadres being shunted from place to place.

*Table 6.3.* Experience of the Apparatus of the Turinese Federation in Party Headquarters and Zones, 1978

| | Number of Years as a Full-Time Party Worker | | | | |
|---|---|---|---|---|---|
| | 3 or less | Between 4 and 6 | 7 or more | Total (N) | |
| Headquarters | 22% | 17% | 61% | 100% | (18) |
| Zones | 70 | 17 | 13 | 100 | (23) |

Personnel shifts are often needed, but they can be quite disruptive of relationships that are frequently highly personal and may have taken a good deal of time to develop. At the grass roots, and even more so in the zones, informants inevitably emphasized the importance of the single individual around whom the *gruppo dirigente* of any unit of organization in the PCI eventually forms. Militants and functionaries alike complained constantly and bitterly to the higher levels of the party in Turin that constant personnel changes were creating chaos in the lower ranks. The strongest critics pointed out that these policies showed the federation's basic priorities to be profoundly incorrect.[27] There were, it was granted, intense pressures on headquarters, but this did not excuse the high-handed way people were moved about and zonal lines redrawn. "[The leaders] may call this consultation," said one militant, "but all they are doing is just coming and telling us what they have already decided."

It has been noted many times that the PCI's distinctive hybrid qualities take a terrible toll of its cadres. Here we see the costs of a small militant cadre, with the simultaneous ambition to be present and active throughout society.[28] Compulsive activism is the rule rather than the exception, even in normal periods; when demands increase, the most active cadres are soon "devoured," in the words of one, by party activity. In a period of extreme pressure on the PCI, militants find themselves forced "to fly over everything at a very low altitude," as a functionary in one zone expressed it. He also pointed out that this kind of superficiality undermines any hope of a truly effective intervention by the party in society, for it compels local organizations to relate to their surroundings in a limited and generally purely propagandistic fashion.[29]

This period of crisis allowed many Turinese leaders to see that the party's inability to function was the result of far more than an inadequate corps of intermediate cadres.[30] Many, especially those in the zones, accurately singled out the headquarters tendency to rain directives on the lower ranks of the party as a major cause of the problems. This practice provided no guidance at all, but, as several middle-level leaders caustically noted, it "covered" the top leaders. And during such a difficult time for the PCI, when signals from Rome to Turin were anything but clear, it is not surprising that the top leadership fell back on established—if ineffective—patterns of behavior.

## Centralism and the Undermining of Decentralization

Yet the higher-ranking members of the federation were not unaware of the shortcomings of the party's actions. Even before the eruption of the worst organizational problems, the chief organizer in Turin stressed that far too much power and too many resources were concentrated in headquarters, leaving the zones overworked, understaffed, and without effective direction. In fact, he concluded bluntly, "the whole mode of organization in the federation is fundamentally wrong."[31] The problem was not unique to Turin, but it was felt more strongly there: references can be found in the national party press to headquarters behaving in "ministerial" rather than collegial fashion toward the periphery in the federations.[32]

Nowhere was this sort of imbalance more apparent in Turin than in the working commissions (see Chap. 5 and Figure 5.2). As a result, nowhere did one find more bitter or more frequently expressed complaints within the apparatus. The most that one could find of these commissions in the zones were skimpy structures—and often even these were lacking. In headquarters, in contrast, the situation was (and remains) fairly adequate. Resources are concentrated in the center, with little incentive to maintain or nourish two-way contact. Simultaneously, the (better-off) units in headquarters generate documents, directives, and projects which only add to the zones' problems. The result is a situation in which the federation's central commissions are frequently described sarcastically as "beautiful" or "well fed," while the zones remain, in one leader's phrase, "a desert."

Of course, commissions that only exist in headquarters are doomed to failure; they can achieve little if they have no functioning counterparts in the federation's territory. As the zones constantly reminded the higher levels, it is the periphery of the party organization that is in direct contact with society, and it is there that initiatives must actually be put into practice. There is some truth in complaints from the zones that the commissions mainly tend to produce documents written by specialists to impress other specialists. I witnessed one debate in a zone in which the secretary of the federation tried to demonstrate to skeptical militants that the document they had pronounced illegible was in reality quite comprehensible.[33]

The zones also heavily criticized the other form of centralization, which is the tendency to concentrate authority, as well as resources, in very few hands in party headquarters. The totally predictable result was the reliance of the periphery on both the good will and the physical presence of the *responsabile* in the center. As one functionary from the periphery put it, "When the *responsabile* is not around, you're just out of luck."

A final major source of tension that derives directly from the federation's centralizing practices is financial. Although the public funding of parties now gives the PCI millions of dollars each year, between 75 and 80 percent of the PCI's income is still self-generated.[34] And the bulk of this income passes from the grass roots to the center in the form of membership contributions and income generated at *l'Unità* festivals, to name the most prominent entries in the party's budget.[35] The zones thus see a sizable sum of money pass through their hands on the way to party headquarters, while a much smaller amount finds its way back to meet operating costs. The actual proportion varies greatly from zone to zone: the larger zones receive about 10 percent of what they raise, while the smaller, poorer outposts receive 25 percent. But everyone agreed that the sum the zones receive is terribly inadequate. As one local leader told the apparatus, the zones often have to make do with locales that are not even hygienically acceptable, let alone aesthetically attractive.[36]

Everyone knows the financial constraints under which the PCI must operate and that certain operations have to be centralized (e.g., salaries, administration, much published material). Still, it is not difficult to see how this situation fuels resentment in the periphery, for it reinforces the impression of a top-heavy federation that refuses to find the resources to make serious work possible at the grass roots.

Hence the vicious circle that spawns much resentment and job dissatisfaction. The federation, badly pressed for funds, makes constant demands on the lower levels of the party to generate more money. These demands reach a peak in the summer, when *l'Unità* festivals are held, and in late autumn, during the main membership drive. Each campaign becomes so time-consuming that it effectively eliminates all other initiatives except the most urgent. And while neither campaign is exclusively a fund-raising affair, this aspect is constantly emphasized, especially with regard to the *Festivali dell'Unità*. Some disgruntled militants criticized the PCI's drift toward what they considered commercialism. Similar complaints are common within the zonal apparatus, where resentment of the festivals can run very deep.[37]

A common wisecrack in the federation had it that the brains were concentrated in the Palazzo (headquarters), while the arms were found out in the zones where the dirty work got done. The discussion above shows how much truth lurked in that ironic comment. Moreover, just as all the direct observation and testimony cited support the contention of an imbalance, so do the raw figures, as Table 6.3 showed. In 1978, just over 40 percent of the apparatus of the federation was located in party headquarters. On the limited information available, this was a somewhat higher proportion than had been in the center fifteen years earlier.[38] Any trend in Turin was not in the direction of decentralization.

The centralization that obstructed and at times crippled the zones' operations was by no means caused by post-1975 events, for we know that the PCI has been saddled with organizational traditions and a model of militancy that have never been indulgent toward lower levels of the party structure. The significance of developments since 1975 is that they aggravated centralizing tendencies and undermined most of the forces working for decentralization in spite of this having been the PCI's declared policy for more than two decades.

## Organizational Fragmentation and Sectoralism

Chapter 4 showed that one of the worst problems for the federation in the late 1970s was that its internal divisions had gotten out of control. This problem had been brewing since the early 1970s, but it became a crisis after the organizational growth and electoral victories of 1975.[39] By the time of the postreferendum *autocritica* in 1978, one of the most frequent laments in Turin was that the party found it increasingly impossible to bring together—in the literal, physical sense—its numerous constituencies and internal components. There was also a feeling that the PCI was rapidly losing any general sense of where it stood in society, or of the interests its policies were supposed to represent.[40] Several of the factors that contributed to this state of affairs have already received ample attention in these pages. Two of the most important structural contradictions of the Turinese federation, however, deserve further mention in our discussion of the zones' organizational problems.

*Workerism and Dual Militance.* From what has already been said, we can expect these two phenomena to combine in the zones in especially potent fashion. Indeed, the late 1970s saw such a shortage of working-class cadres in all territorial organizations that some leaders were speaking of a sociological division of labor in the party. Territorial tasks had become the province of middle-class and student activists, while workers stuck to union and shopfloor activities. Leaders in every zone expressed dismay about the unwillingness and inability of shopfloor militants to look beyond the gates of their factories. In some areas, conditions had deteriorated to such a degree that some activists openly questioned the wisdom of the PCI's commitment to workplace organization. That one even heard such things in Turin is perhaps the strongest evidence of how bad things had become.

An example can suffice. When the *Comitati di quartiere* were finally about to be established, the federation set about putting together candidates' lists for the twenty-three *quartieri* in the capital. As the party of the working class, Turinese Communists felt it their duty (and to their political advantage) to include a reasonable proportion of workers on each list; the federation therefore issued explicit instructions to this effect. The number of workers included among PCI candidates quickly had to be scaled down, and even the rather meager 25 percent the federation was forced to settle on often proved impossible to achieve.[41] I personally witnessed what one functionary later described as the "agonies" of his zone over several weeks as efforts were made—mainly in the form of an endless round of telephone calls to sections and individuals—to come up with four or five working-class candidates for each CdQ in the zone's territory. At the time, this zone had nineteen sections, five of which were in workplaces, and a total of four thousand members, half of whom were workers!

Similar "agonies" were repeated everywhere in the federation when other new public institutions, elective or appointive, came into being in the province or city in this period (e.g., local school districts and local public health boards). Dual militance was not the only cause of the shortage of cadres, but its impact was obvious whenever blue-collar militants could not be found.

The entire organizational history and workerist practice of the federation greatly aggravated its factory-centeredness at times like these. As many leaders candidly acknowledged, the party in Turin was paying a price for its historic failure to encourage the workers to consider anything but their own struggle as central to PCI goals. While stressing social struggle in a very broad sense, the federation had badly ignored what was really going on in society. This left it with immense organizational and theoretical lacunae when in the 1970s it eventually had to address a range of problems that went far beyond the factories.

*The Sectoral and Corporative Fragmentation of the Party.* From the perspective of the zones, the sectoral phenomenon is felt in a number of ways, and all of them create serious problems in terms of even the simplest coordination of activities. Cadres with specialized interests, as we have seen, are drawn into sectoral activities which leave little time for more general party activities. It is revealing, for example, that the term *quartieristi* was used at the grass roots to refer to Communists active in the CdQ. The regular rank and file would in fact assume that a comrade was lost to the party proper when he or she became involved outside the section. And this assumption was reinforced by the behavior of the activists in question. More than one zonal leader pointed out that there appeared to be a new kind of cadre attracted to the PCI on the crest of its successes in the mid-1970s. Their motivations for joining the party were seen as personal and sectoral; this helped the PCI achieve a more diversified base than it had ever enjoyed in the past, but it also guaranteed that a broader sense of the party's goals and tasks would be deemphasized. A functionary from the largest zone in the federation had no doubts at all on this score when he referred to the new type of activist: "As, say, a teacher or a professional, he is perfectly happy with the Party as things stand today. He just wants to pursue the interests of his own category, and sees the PCI as the best way to do this."[42]

But whenever the topic of sectoralism and horizontal fragmentation arose in the 1970s, the discussion inevitably turned to local governmental power, which had grown so much in that decade. What we see at the zonal level is not only the loss of qualified personnel to local administration but the structural consequences of local power-holding on the party organization.

This takes two major forms, each of which undermines the zones and the party organization in general. The first form is the development of what many activists and leaders now call "the administrative party," which amounts to a separate party elite composed of officeholders who act as if their responsibilities, and their real power base, lies entirely in their institutional position.[43] This often resulted in high-handed treatment of those in the party organization, usually in the form of inaccessibility or the open assumption that the party structure existed to serve the aims of local government. Both of these attitudes were deeply resented at the grass roots, where the epithet *notabile* ("local notable"), which has very negative connotations in the PCI, was frequently used to describe such behavior. The ill will I witnessed appeared to be greatest in the capital, where government is, of course, much larger and more impersonal to begin with. Local militants often complained that Communist administrators did not even bother returning their telephone calls; they scornfully remarked that Socialists and Christian Democrats were accorded more courteous and prompt attention than PCI members.[44]

But the zones were also undermined in a more subtle yet still serious way when the PCI moved massively into local government. The party's electoral victories rapidly led to the expansion and reinforcement of the *Commissione Enti Locali* in headquarters. Two full-time functionaries were assigned to it, while a third occupied himself exclusively with liaison work between the party organization and the governments and Communist representatives in the capital city, province, and region. This is a large chunk of the apparatus in headquarters, and, from 1977 to 1979, it included some of the most impressive members of the top leadership. This concentration of expertise and information had a predictable result. It created what one functionary aptly dubbed "the unofficial leadership for administrative problems" within the party hierarchy. And the very effectiveness of this group meant that militants with questions about local politics in their home territory soon found it more convenient to bypass their zonal or other intermediate structure and address themselves directly to headquarters.

Peripheral leaders did not like to be bypassed in this fashion, but they made clear that it was not, in their view, a willful usurpation of power by the center. "But what can you expect," said a zonal functionary, "since I myself am always telling the comrades to call the federation for the information they need? After a few experiences like that, the next time they won't even bother checking with me, and will call headquarters directly."[45]

Regardless of intentions, it is apparent that sectoralism invades the party structure, reinforces centralism, and thus undermines the role of intermediate and grassroots organizations. At the same time, as the evidence shows, it generates formidable centrifugal forces within the party, making any broader overview of problems, let alone a grand synthesis, increasingly elusive. In the ideal organizational scheme, the sections and their zone would work together and develop their own political and organizational initiatives within a framework that reflects the PCI's policies and central goals. This occasionally took place in Turin in the late 1970s. In general, however, with information emanating from party headquarters (along with strong suggestions about which specific initiatives would be most appropriate at a given time), the zones were bypassed. Both their own capacities on the ground and their ability to coordinate and direct autonomous initiatives were not given much opportunity to develop. They, and the sections, were maintained in a state of chronic weakness as they carried out tasks decided on and transmitted downward to them from the center of the federation.

## Organizational Problems in Federation Headquarters

As one rises higher in the party structure, organizational problems multiply. Those that exist at lower levels persist, becoming matters that the higher levels, charged with coordination, must try to resolve. At the same time, the higher levels have their own structural difficulties. This accumulation of problems itself creates a new problem at the peak of the party hierarchy: organizational overload, the existence of so many issues requiring attention that any hope of addressing problems or setting priorities rationally is diminished. This is a formidable additional source of stress, especially for a chronically weak and understaffed party. It should be kept in mind when reviewing the federation's individual difficulties, for it helps us understand in part why problems clearly recognized as such, and for which solutions are at least thought to exist on paper, are nonetheless allowed to fester long after having been identified.

### *Leadership Turnover*

It would indeed be strange if a problem identified as critical at all levels of the party did not have especially serious repercussions at the top of the federation's command structure. This is where the pick of the crop is found, where proven leadership ability and expertise are in great supply. The loss of a leader at this level can be especially disruptive to the entire local organization—doubly so if the loss is unanticipated and opens a gap in what may be a key part of the party's coordinating structures. With extensive turnover at lower levels the order of the day, continuity at the summit is especially desirable both practically and symbolically. (The national leadership of the PCI furnishes an example of such continuity through the 1970s.) But there was no such continuity in the upper ranks of the Turinese PCI. As occurred elsewhere in the federation, a combination of natural attrition and movement from organizational to administrative positions at a time of expansion, along with a considerable amount of shuffling within the organizational elite, created a turnover problem which was, if anything, even more acute in headquarters than elsewhere.

As we know from Chapter 2, by the end of the 1960s, the top leadership of the federation had a number of qualities. It was charismatic, it had been deeply entrenched in power for fifteen years, and, as its modal age approach forty-five, it was soon going to need to be replaced. But a strongly homogeneous, hegemonic leadership is rarely concerned with its own succession, and the evidence was clear throughout northern Italy on the eve of the 1970s that this was the case within the PCI.[46] Almost everywhere in the party, the "renovators" who had wrested control from the Stalinist "old guard" had their own federations well in hand, but they had usually ignored the issue of transition. Thus, a marked gap existed between the entrenched leadership and their much younger eventual successors even prior to the great influx of new members and cadres in the 1970s. Figure 6.1 shows graphically that this was the case within the elite of the Turinese party organization, and it also shows the dynamic that followed as the composition of the elite altered during the 1970s.

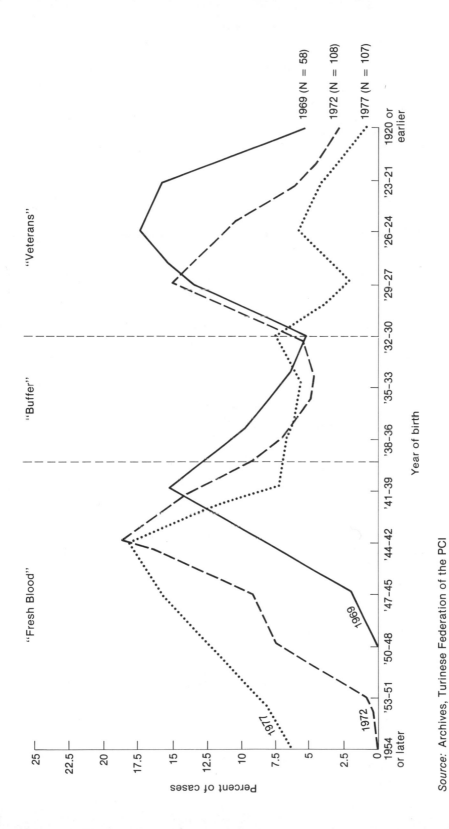

*Figure 6.1.* Age Distribution, Federal Committee of the Turinese PCI. 1969, 1972, 1977

*Source:* Archives, Turinese Federation of the PCI

151

The solid bold line represents the leadership on the eve of the hot autumn and is dramatically bimodal. This reflects the summary above: the dominance of people in their forties, a strong influx of youth just moving into the party hierarchy, and the near-total absence of a "buffer" or transitional generation of thirty-year-olds. By 1972, the "heroic generations" had already been reduced, although even in the first wave following the late 1960s the presence of this group was still pronounced. In fact, it fell from 52 percent to 34 percent of all members of the Federal Committee. The buffer generation remains around the 20 percent mark, and the younger leaders rise sharply from 26 percent to 49 percent of the total.

The growth of the organization after 1975 had a powerful effect on the leadership, as the curve for 1977 shows. Here we see the heroic generation's presence all but eliminated: it was reduced to a mere 12 percent of the federal elite. Equally importantly, the figure furnishes evidence of the "loss of historical memory" in the PCI, not at the grass roots but at the very peak of the federation. One need not mythologize the older leaders to appreciate their stabilizing influence throughout the 1960s and the early part of the 1970s. It is not hard to imagine the disruptive effect of their relatively rapid departure in the late 1970s.

But even this was only one part of the turnover at the top of the federation. When the PCI took on extensive local governing responsibilities, most of the older leaders who remained in the party heirarchy in the broad sense—as members of the CF and CFC— really shifted their attention, with very few exceptions, to the elective or appointive offices to which they were moved after 1975. This was, after all, official party policy in Turin (and elsewhere). Hence, in very short order, the bulk of the federation's veteran organizational leadership found itself in regional, provincial, or municipal governmental roles.

The dimensions of the shift involved can be appreciated by examining some data relevant to the turnover within the apparatus, which is the most direct measure of impact on the central party structure that we have. By combining biographical data from different sources, we can compare full-time public officials who used to be party functionaries with active functionaries in the party organization. The age profile that emerges from this distinction is shown in Table 6.4. It demonstrates the degree to which federation policy was put into effect and the impact of this policy on the age profile of the apparatus. Whether one focuses on the rows or the columns of the table, the older leaders' concentration in public office is evident. More detailed breakdowns of the biographies of these leaders confirm the overwhelming concentration of experience in public rather than party positions.[47]

These biographical data also round out the picture of the very heavy turnover that took place within the apparatus after 1975, which was already glimpsed in discussion of

*Table 6.4.* Age of Former Functionaries Holding Public Office Compared to Active Party Functionaries in Turin (1978)

|  | Forty-plus | Thirties | Twenties | Total |
|---|---|---|---|---|
| Public office | 9 | 6 | 1 | 16 |
| Apparatus | 4 | 18 | 19 | 41 |
| Totals | 13 | 24 | 20 | 57 |

the zones. There was more job shifting in headquarters than in the periphery, while there was much less hiring of people in the center with no previous experience. In 1975 and again in 1977, half the posts in headquarters changed hands. In the apparatus as a whole in 1978, eighteen of forty-one functionaries (44 percent) had held their jobs for a year or less. Only two had not changed jobs since 1975, and most of those in headquarters had seen their responsibilities shift more than once since the electoral sweep. Job rotation is viewed positively inside the PCI, but this can hardly be considered normal or desirable.

It is therefore evident that the same situation found in the rest of the party obtained at the top of the organizational hierarchy of the Turinese PCI. The rejuvenation of the leadership at this level was not a dramatic affair, for there were ample and indeed highly prestigious public offices into which older leaders moved after 1975. But while this minimized bruised personal feelings, it could not lessen the disruption that the party organization suffered: Just as the PCI sailed into the stormiest waters it had encountered in two decades, it had to do so with a terribly inexperienced crew. Structural consolidation was an urgent priority, but the potential consolidators were drawn out of the organization and into public office.

Only very slowly did the top leadership of the federation begin to question the wisdom of the way in which the party organization had so brusquely been decapitated. But the conviction remained that there was really no alternative to the course of action that had been followed. Many of the offices that had to be filled were simply too visible, too sensitive, or both, to be entrusted to less proven cadres. Even leaders who were critical of the process—and there were several—acknowledged this point.

At the same time, they also cited as evidence of poor personnel planning several cases in which proven party veterans had egregiously botched their public jobs. Moreover, although several older leaders were doing well in their new public position, they were obviously very uncomfortable outside the narrow party milieu in which they had spent their entire adult lives. Simultaneously, many promising young leaders were floundering as party organizers, whereas they might well have made excellent public officials. The scandal that hit the left-wing municipal and provincial governments in the early 1980s was nearly five years off when these criticism were leveled, but it eventually showed that even putting veterans in public office could not absolutely guarantee that no shadow would fall on the PCI.[48]

In any event, the degree of leadership turnover in the federation after 1975, particularly because of very low turnover earlier, was a serious problem in its own right. But it also aggravated every other serious organizational problem the federation faced in the late 1970s. Nowhere is the linkage to turnover more clear than with regard to the related problems of compulsive, frenetic activism and the issue of the training of cadres.

## Compulsive Activism and Cadre Formation

The PCI lexicon contains the euphemism "spontaneous cadre formation," which means both (1) filling leadership positions with whomever is available at the moment and (2) not seeing to cadres' formal training, whether on-the-job or before the assumption of responsibilities. Such "spontaneity" is least desirable organizationally when the new leaders have highly varied backgrounds. Add the normally frantic work pace of the PCI, intensified by nonstop crises, a steady barrage of undifferentiated directives (all of them urgent), and considerable strategic floundering, and it is easy to see why this issue had become a very serious matter for the party by the end of the 1970s. In Turin, nearly everyone viewed it as one of the PCI's most serious problems. Complaints, often brutally worded, were voiced in private interviews and conversations, in documents, in closed and open meetings, and by top party leaders and common militants alike.

Of course, such ubiquity raises suspicions. As with many of the complaints levied against new cadres' presumed shortcomings, the plea for more rigorous training often is an indirect way of saying that the party's situation is untenable and maybe *this* will make an important difference. For some Communists unhappy with a vague strategy and official denials of any party doctrine, it is a way of suggesting that the PCI get back to basics (i.e., Marx and Lenin). For many others, it is really a complaint lodged against compulsive, mindless activism—and thus many of the unexamined routines of the PCI's organizational life. Frenetic activism does more than burn out militants; it is also a deeply frustrating, unpleasant experience. But it is ideologically less acceptable to complain about having to carry out endless grubby tasks. Thus, dissent tends to be voiced in a more "noble" context, such as against spontaneous cadre formation.

If complaints about cadre formation are not always what they seem on the surface, there can be no doubt that this is a very serious problem for the PCI. The national party felt strongly enough about the issue to convene two conferences in the last half of the 1970s, after having held only three others in the entire postwar period. And no one in Turin could possibly plead ignorance of the problem. Yet when we look to the specific initiatives undertaken by the federation in this area, the results are meager indeed. The most devastating indicator of how far the situation had deteriorated was the admission of the relevant commission that it could not even say with certainty how many courses had been offered at the grass roots in 1978.[49] Clearly, if the simple ability to monitor formal activities had broken down, the implications are grim with regard to such activity as did take place. What explains this parlous state of affairs?

One obvious explanation is that the federation did not consider cadre formation to be a top priority, in spite of the extensive lip service paid to the problem in formal documents. Evidence of this lack of commitment is easy to provide: no one in the apparatus was exclusively charged with the job of overseeing or coordinating the training of cadres. The *Commissione Formazione Quadri* in Turin was headed by a functionary. He was assisted by the president of the CFC (which is formally charged with educational matters in the party) and a volunteer who held a university position. But the functionary was also the full-time head of the very important Press and Propaganda Commission, and he additionally was the coordinator of the party's increasing involvement in the mass media. This latter activity alone—the federation supported a radio station that grew notably in the late 1970s—soon became a full-time job. Similarly, the president of the Control Commission had to supervise all activities of that body, which has no apparatus of its own. At the same time, he held public office with a fair amount of responsibility in a mountain district far from headquarters. He was not often in Turin, and when he was, he had many party-related matters to attend to. Under these circumstances, a sustained educational effort could not possibly be generated in the federation.

But why didn't the federation see fit to address the problem in a more satisfactory fashion? One response is that the party in Turin was chronically short-handed. Another is that, consistent with the behavior of any overloaded bureaucracy, the party leadership put off anything that could be postponed in the interest of coping with problems that demanded immediate attention. Yet another is undoubtedly the awareness that the true underlying causes of a shortage of good cadres cannot be remedied by even the most ambitious efforts within the party. Dual militancy, the constant shift of cadres into institutions, and compulsive activism are all issues that go to the heart of the way the PCI functions. The conviction that little can be done in any event—the acceptance of the party's operational code as it exists—is almost never articulated, but it is surely a constraint that limits significant remedial action.

Finally, and crucially, although there is general agreement that new cadres are heterogeneous, there is no consensus at all about what they require by way of a common educational base that could remedy the PCI's problems. This lack of consensus goes so deep as to involve the ideological and theoretical underpinnings of the PCI—the very nature of the party is in dispute. How can a mass party which has recently renounced the very idea of party doctrine, let alone dogma, expect to give newcomers to its ranks a relatively uniform and coherent worldview? Assertions that the PCI is laical and agnostic and that Italy is a society far too complex and pluralistic for a single synthesis (based on Marxism or anything else) to be possible seem to be the party's official position. But the fact remains that as long as any serious political program is thought possible, some form of synthesis must be implicit in the party's general orientation.

## Overcentralization in Party Headquarters: Centripetal Forces

This last point should remind us of the many diverse pressures that are at work in any PCI federation, especially one as besieged as Turin, to centralize and concentrate authority. We have already touched on some of the problems the zones encounter because of this tendency, but a broader discussion of centralism (or overcentralization) can by definition only take place with reference to headquarters.

This is not the place to discuss democratic centralism in depth,[50] but we can note in passing that many of the federation's practices added to the problems of the Turinese PCI in the 1970s. The leadership of the federation was in fact fully aware that its own behavior deeply upset many new arrivals to the party—arrivals whose previous experiences in social movements made them especially keen on true participation in decision making within the PCI; most new cadres were believed to feel very strongly about the question of internal democracy in the party.[51]

As we have already seen, there were ample grounds for resentment in the lower ranks of the party organization in this period. Militants often complained openly of heavy-handed interference from above when low-level initiatives met with disapproval from headquarters.[52] The top leadership was not so overbearing as to attempt to stifle open discussion at the grass roots or even every attempt at autonomous activity. Rank-and-file resentment tended rather to focus on the fact that while opinions could be expressed freely, they were rarely solicited and even less often acted on in the higher reaches of the federation.

Interestingly, only in the higher reaches of the federation were intimations of real intolerance heard. At least some functionaries felt they could not even speak freely in closed meetings. One spoke of a "Palazzo mentality" that pervaded the federation: there was an inner group of perhaps ten leaders (the Secretariat plus four or five others) followed at some distance by everyone else. And in his words, "if you aren't part of the Palazzo, you're cut out of the real action [*sei tagliato fuori*]." Others confessed that they often felt compelled to state their positions in very nuanced fashion for the same reason, citing the "inner group's" rigidity once it made up its mind. They also pointed out, with specific examples, how more critical spirits found themselves marginalized in the federation if they were too insistent. These criticisms parallel those heard from rank-and-file militants, but it is one thing for a volunteer to feel more or less ignored, while it is obviously a much more serious matter for a full-time cadre, whose job may be on the line.

Some of these complaints may express personal frustration, but the same point was made far too often to be ignored. Moreover, as someone who heard functionaries express themselves in apparatus meetings and in numerous private discussions, I can state that the chilling effect they described was indeed a reality in the upper reaches of the federation. None of this is surprising; it helps to explain, at least in part, why some of the party's feedback mechanisms did not work as they were supposed to between 1975 and 1979. The PCI has moved considerably from the classical model of democratic centralism, as well as from the type of internal practices still found in, for instance, the French Communist Party.[53] Still, a number of important pressures—some limited and conjunctural, others much more rooted in the party's structures and practices—helped entrench a very high degree of centralization in the Turinese PCI at the end of the 1970s. The most important of these deserve at least a brief review.

1. Tradition is, of course, a fundamental explanation when one speaks of centralization in a communist party. The specific traditions of the Turinese party are especially significant in this regard: in Turin, for decades, a very weak organization has sat astride an environment that was both hostile and hard to control. Defensiveness rarely makes for openmindedness, or for an experimental attitude toward the world outside, and this is a federation that has been on the defensive far more often than not.

2. As a rational response to new demands on the party, centralization—especially in the form of concentrating resources in headquarters—was reinforced in the course of a barrage of events in the short run. Whole areas previously ignored in Turin had to be addressed urgently, and frequently the only reasonable way to establish links was from the center out.

Even if we define centralization as the concentration of power in few hands, we can see why the events of the late 1970s reinforced the tendency. Extensive turnover as the party tried to put its audacious strategy into practice made everyone—in Rome as much as in Turin—sensitive to the need to consolidate a new elite in the federations. The top leadership in headquarters felt this pressure very strongly, and it undoubtedly contributed to the more extreme forms of the "Palazzo" phenomenon mentioned earlier.

3. From a strictly structural perspective, many highly centralized practices are organizationally efficacious. (They are also extremely problematic, not to say oppressive and antidemocratic, but that is another matter.) Highly structured routines characterize all but the smallest informal party gatherings, from section meetings all the way up to local and national congresses. Whether the setting is a section assembly or a national congress, the format is the same: a *relazione* or introduction focuses discussion and announces the major themes; interventions follow from the floor; conclusions are then presented, generally by the highest-ranking or most expert leader present. Conclusions take into account what has been said in interventions, but they almost inevitably reiterate the main points of the introduction. This format serves a number of useful functions which favor the upper reaches of the party: it sets the agenda, communicates official interpretations, and gives the last word to headquarters.

These practices also filter inputs from the lower levels of the party in two important ways. When the top leadership (of the federation or the national party, depending on the type of assembly or congress involved) is not present, reports back to the center are written by the presiding functionaries. But even when top leaders are present, they are rarely exposed to a representative sample of rank-and-file activists. Delegates to congresses or conferences are indirectly elected, often through a series of lower-level meetings (occasionally cell, then section, then federation, then national). The few who actually end up in attendance, not to mention the far smaller number who get a chance to speak, are unlikely to be boat rockers. Moreover, particularly in such things as congresses, the ritual and solemnity of the occasion also tend to generate self-imposed restraint on most of those who intervene.

Thus, while inhibitions have lessened over time, it was still very rare, in the 1970s, to hear open criticism of party policy. My fieldwork coincided with a period when the *compromesso storico* and the national unity policy were known to be unacceptable to a large part of the PCI. Yet in scores of assemblies I attended, very few of the hundreds of interventions I heard directly attacked the strategy. Criticisms were deflected to specific proposals, and these criticisms were then reported back to headquarters in similarly oblique fashion, such as, "Many comrades still do not fully accept our analysis. . . ."

The broader implications of these points emerge when we recall that twice during the period of greatest disruption and uncertainty for the party, collective "consultations" of the entire PCI took place. In spite of the extreme difficulties besetting the party at the time—indeed, because of these difficulties—the encounters resulted in a facade of unity that in no way accurately mirrored the real situation.

Early in 1977, regional and provincial congresses took place in the country. This was already a highly problematic period, with dissatisfaction over the PCI's behavior in Parliament and toward the DC reflected in intense debates that reached the Central Committee.[54] Yet reports from Turin were that the federal and regional congresses had been exceptionally flat and filtered and, all things considered, quite boring. Evidence from the rest of the country also revealed little real debate above the section level—to such a degree that the national head of organization was asked in the party press why so little criticism had been heard when everyone knew it existed within the party![55]

Then, early in 1978, the PCI began its rank-and-file factory conferences, which led up to the party's Seventh National Conference of Communist Workers in Naples. Here again, there could be no doubt concerning the unhappiness of working-class cadres with both the PCI's and the unions' policies. The December 1977 metalworkers' strike had in fact brought down a government the Communists supported. And in Turin, even the FLM leadership opposed austerity, and everyone knew it.[56] But while individual factory conferences revealed deep dissention in the ranks, both the Turinese provincial conference and the national one came nowhere near indicating the true lack of general support for official policies. At most, it was admitted that not all workers (N.B.: not *Communists*) appreciated the seriousness of Italy's crisis, and hence the correctness of the party's and unions' austerity proposals.[57] An observer not privy to inside information, viewing only these large gatherings, would never have concluded that very deep divisions existed (and would soon erupt) at the grass roots and among the leadership of the unions.

4. These considerations lead to yet another reason why centralism would be reinforced in this period: it not only makes operations smoother for the leadership, but it also has traditionally served as a mechanism of unification and persuasion. When leaders are committed to a line, and it is clear that strong resistance exists at the grass roots, centralism has proven highly effective in bringing the base around. This, at any rate, is what leaders believe, and there is enough evidence from PCI history (e.g., de-Stalinization or the leaders' condemnation of the 1968 invasion of Czechoslovakia) to

offer a good deal of support to this view. With time, in sum, it proved possible in the past to force the base to go along with what turned out to be the leaders' more far-reaching and courageous analysis.

But even though Enrico Berlinguer obviously tried to use centralism in this fashion, persuasion did not pay off on this occasion. In spite of leaders' best efforts to convince the base that the PCI was achieving significant results, the rank and file appears, at most, to have only been partially persuaded that reforms really were in the offing or that the DC was a reliable partner. Doubts were widespread even before the PCI moved into the opposition in 1979,[58] and that move, of course, doomed any policy of collaboration to failure. Even the previously convinced cadres' support for party policy fell off rapidly when the Communists ceased supporting DC-led governments.[59]

We saw in Chapter 4 that those who strongly believed in the party's strategy and tactics were not so easily dissuaded in this period. In Turin, moreover, some leaders in headquarters felt that not even the entire apparatus supported the policies of austerity and national unity. Less experienced functionaries in the periphery were especially suspect in view of the intense pressure they were experiencing in the trenches. Several leaders told me that they often found it counterproductive to send newcomers to the apparatus into rank-and-file meetings to perform the traditional opening or summing-up functions. They did not accuse the zonal functionaries of opposing the party line, but they did feel that their ambivalence was so transparent that they made poor advocates for party policies.

Whether or not some peripheral members of the apparatus actually were as unreliable as is claimed is an empirical question that we can address, at least in part, in Chapter 8. What is important to underline here is that the perception in headquarters of their assumed unreliability was definitely another powerful contributor to centralization in Turin. The existence of this view also helps explain the frequently heavy-handed style, bordering on intolerance, that emanated from the center in this period.

5. Finally, Sidney Tarrow long ago suggested that democratic centralism was not only a holdover in the PCI but that it had also become a necessity to hold together the party's increasingly composite interests and constituencies.[60] Formulated even before the party's growth in the mid-1970s, this argument has certainly had its explanatory power enhanced since then. Here we have a truly deep source of tension for the Italian Communists, for the same new strata and expectations that have come to the party and threaten its older forms of unity also carry with them a very strong set of assumptions about the nature of what intraparty democracy ought to be. They are, objectively and subjectively, centrifugal forces that contribute to the fragmentation of the PCI. It is to this complex and important issue that we now turn.

## Centrifugal Forces in Turinese Communism

The ultimate justification for the presence of the *partito nuovo* in every crease and fold of Italian society is the assumption that the forces organized and the institutions occupied by the PCI can be molded into a bloc that can act in concerted fashion to realize the party's goals. This, at least, is the ideal that guided the party since the end of World War II. It was always a problematic ideal, but it made some sense as long as a guiding doctrine (Marxism) and a single social category (class) were the pillars on which the party organization rested. As we know, by the 1970s, these pillars were in doubt. Without them—especially in a locale with such a weak organization as Turin—

the party faced very serious problems. Many leaders openly feared that it ran the risk of degenerating into a federation of interests that reflected the PCI's local strengths and weaknesses but was unable to change the reality around it.

By the end of 1980, the federation summarized the situation in the following terms:

> Various councilors' groups are in practice the elaborators and defenders of relevant political decisions which either bypass the Party altogether or else commit it to certain policies without having involved it in the decision-making process. Comrades who operate in the unions are frequently the carriers of autonomous political proposals, the fruits of debates within the union movement which often are not exposed to discussion or verification in the Party. Communists involved in [professional or political] mass organizations are involved in the articulation of views which are not only autonomous but "corporative." [61]

And all this gives rise to "incomprehension" and "tension" among various levels of the party [62] — strong terms indeed in the PCI vocabulary, where "perplexity" has very negative connotations.

It also creates considerable ill will in headquarters, as I have often observed. Those in the center frequently complained publicly that comrades from the unions, the mass organizations, and especially public office regularly failed to attend meetings whose topics directly concerned them. There were even times when meetings called by sectoral commissions had to be postponed because Communists invited from outside the party proper (e.g., the unions) never showed up. In similar situations involving public officers, such behavior reinforced already strong beliefs that those who were absent considered themselves a privileged stratum within the party. When the absentees were unionists, I often heard outright hostility expressed toward "people who only care about the interests of their own category."

But the fragmentation of the party and the corporative and centrifugal drives within it go far beyond dual militance and the PCI's links to outside institutions and organizations. Sectoralism exists *inside* the party organization. This, in fact, may prove to be the most complicated problem of all to resolve in the long run; it is certainly one of the most interesting dilemmas for present purposes.

The dilemma is felt most acutely in the way the commissions in Turin operate, especially those outside the party's traditional areas of activity (organization, factories, propaganda). Here is where the legacy of workerism in Turin was felt most strongly in the 1970s, as a proletarian stronghold finally—and hurriedly—had to address its historic blind spots. This naturally led to the tendency to fall back on the available expertise in the party in Turin at the time when a commission had to be built (or resurrected). The practical result of this approach is for each sector, as one functionary put it, "to gravitate into the hands of the specialists in that area who have put themselves at the disposal of the Party—often for very selfish reasons."[63] The party further aggravates the situation by openly recruiting well-known figures in each field (evidence of its inferiority complex and zeal for legitimation). This kind of practice provides what Italians often sarcastically refer to as "flowers in the buttonhole" of the PCI. It also guarantees that many people who represent the most vested interests of a given sector will be put into strategically crucial as well as highly visible posts.

This appears to have happened, to cite one significant case, in the university. As one involved observer noted, the negative consequences for the PCI were twofold. The interests of some of the most notorious faculty "barons" were now part of the

Communists' own proposals, with the predictable result that ever larger segments of the student population were alienated from the PCI because of these actions.[64] This phenomenon was by no means limited to Turin, as criticisms of various national reforms and reform proposals to which the PCI contributed have shown.[65] And while the workerist traditions of the PCI in Turin make it especially vulnerable to takeovers in areas whose intellectual or cultural content is high, the phenomenon is, in fact, even more widespread. Testimony from activists and functionaries involved with social security, small business, and urban planning confirm that it might be more the rule than the exception. Even where the PCI has relatively well-developed proposals to start with, it is easy to see how a commission could become the depository of the special interests of very limited groups. It is equally obvious how functionaries, whose own expertise comes mainly from on-the-job training, could, when assigned to new areas, easily become the unwitting spokesmen for entrenched interests. The commissions, in short, themselves contribute to fragmentation within the party organization. And because they are so top-heavy and relate only to limited segments of many social groups, the party risks further distortions in its relationship to society:

> In this regard, we are handicapped in comparison with the DC. *It* mediates particu-larisms and corporate interests which exist within various categories and in the society at large. *We* govern (but for how much longer?) particular and sectoral interests which risk becoming exclusively those of an apparatus![66]

It is easy to understand why commissions that encompass interests of this nature often find it hard to collaborate with other commissions within the federation. A small number of leaders may even agree among themselves but then find it hard to get sectoral activists to accept specific initiatives that threaten their own vision of their category's interests. A few forays into individual commissions soon convince the leaders that there would be little fruitful discussion if efforts were made to bring several groups together. To this can be added the problem of an overworked apparatus in a situation of perpetual crisis. As we saw in the case of the *Commissione Formazione Quadri*, high priorities can remain unimplemented when no one really has the time to pursue them. To many leaders, having at least some activity in a sector (one they may understand poorly and have little interest in in any event) is presumably better than being completely "uncovered."

## Turinese Responses to Organizational Crisis

What did the federation actually do to alleviate the multifaceted crisis that plagued its organization? Let us restrict ourselves (at least initially) to the period during which the bulk of the fieldwork for this study took place, from late 1977 to mid-1979.[67] Let us then recall that during this period the party in Turin was involved in a general election, partial local elections, a national referendum, school district elections, and elections to the European Parliament. In addition, the PCI held its Conference of Communist Workers (1978) and its Fifteenth National Party Congress (1979), both of which required hundreds of smaller conferences and congresses, from the sections up, culminating in federation-level gatherings in both instances. This same period saw two drawn-out governmental crises, and each required exceptional activism from the PCI because of its close relationship to the governments of the time. It was also a period, particularly between November 1977 and May 1978, of constant mobilization around the terrorism issue. Finally, the local party organization also somehow found the time to carry on with its routine operations, most notably a membership drive that takes up much of each autumn and a round of *l'Unità* festivals that consumes most of each summer and tens of thousands of volunteer workdays.[68]

When we consider the total impact of this avalanche of tasks on a federation such as the one in Turin, the first question to come to mind is not what corrective measures the party took but how it managed to survive at all. A second important qualification is to remember that the transitional crisis is an ongoing phenomenon: as the federation found some breathing space, it began to address some of the issues that invest almost every aspect of its structure and operations. Many efforts were frankly experimental; some "solutions" raise at least as many questions as they answer.

Why, then, examine what the party did at all, especially when some of these efforts came to naught? Primarily, I would argue, to indicate the priorities the federation set for itself under pressure, and in this way to gain a fuller sense of how the PCI operates. Three initiatives are especially interesting, both for the problems they identify and for the reception they encountered within the party.

## The Comitato Cittadino: Centralization or Decentralization?

We have seen throughout this study that the party's condition in the capital is the weakest link in an organizational chain that is by no means sturdy. The disintegration of traditional proletarian and "popular" neighborhoods, the growth of intermediate strata less susceptible to the established techniques of mass parties, the encroachment of the means of mass communication, and the general atomization of metropolitan areas reach their acme in places like Turin.

The extreme difficulties encountered by the PCI in large urban centers account for the acute—and early—awareness of the shortcomings of established party practices in these locales in the 1970s. In fact, from the end of that decade onward, the federations with the largest urban populations were the ones that pressed Rome most forcefully for a special organizational conference of the PCI, in effect an extraordinary congress on organizational questions. The request was unsuccessful.[69]

The PCI, for various reasons including an awareness of the special problems faced in cities, has long permitted intermediate aggregations in towns and cities of all sizes. Bringing together Communists from the party, mass organizations, and public institutions, these *comitati cittadini* or (in smaller centers) *comitati comunali* enable the PCI in a given territory to speak with something like a single voice on issues that affect the town or city.

In light of the party's problems in Turin, I was surprised to find that the federation had no *comitato cittadino* in the capital. I raised this point with the functionary, the member of the federal Secretariat charged with liaison between the party organization and elected officials.[70] Noting that his job often made him sensitive to the lack of such a committee, he explained why the federation had considered but rejected the idea: indeed, in the past, it had twice put an end to committees that did exist.

The main argument against a *comitato cittadino* is Turin's distinctive urban-industrial profile. Dominated by a single industry and identical social problems, the capital and its industrial belt can only be separated arbitrarily. The populations of these two areas are nearly impossible to distinguish even in the simplest physical sense, for half the industrial workers who live in the capital are employed outside it, and vice versa.[71] Hence the basic question—what would the boundaries of a Turinese committee be?—poses a profound dilemma. To exclude the industrial belt would be absurd, but to include it would be to create a de facto "real federation" and a wildly heterogeneous and geographically scattered peripheral rump.

Moreover, he continued, the establishment of a separate structure for an urban area that is already so dominant opens the door to serious political problems inside a Communist federation. Confirming what other research has shown, he referred to the risk of a potential "parallel power" or a "federation within the federation" where an already dominant city's status is institutionalized by the party.[72] This certainly is not the way to achieve the political unity that is the justification for such a committee in the first place!

These were compelling arguments, and, given their source, they appeared definitive—especially since, in 1976, the leadership of the federation had mooted the idea of a *comitato cittadino* as the first serious postelectoral coordination problems were encountered. The 1976 proposal had been extremely cautious: "merely in order to open a discussion," is how it was framed.[73] In fact, as several sources attested, the idea was quickly dropped in the face of hostile reactions from all levels of the party.

It was thus a great surprise to me, as well as an indicator of the party's desperation by 1978, that the leadership of the federation proposed a *comitato cittadino* for Turin in July, just four months after the discussion reported above. At this time, the proposal was not offered for the sake of debate but was presented as a firm decision. Furthermore, the coordinator of the *comitato* was to be none other than my very informant from the Secretariat who had argued so persuasively against the idea!

The many drawbacks of such a structure had not been forgotten. The federation secretary went to some length, in explaining the decision to the apparatus, to assure everyone that this was meant to improve intraparty coordination; it was not, in other words, intended as yet another level of structures between base and summit.[74] But since the feeling was widespread that the party in the capital had become "just a collection of sectoral organizations,"[75] corrective measures were sorely needed. The committee was established shortly thereafter, with quite a wide range of groups and institutions represented on it. And the federation's commitment to the idea was further formalized when the Organization Commission was divided—as it had been years earlier—into capital-city and provincial subsections a few months later.

From the start, the proposal was received coolly by the cadres in the capital, whether functionaries or volunteers. Some of the former complained privately that the way the decision had been imposed on the rest of the party hardly represented a break with past practices. But they also strongly opposed the *content* of the proposal—and they did this openly.[76] Leaders might think a lot of the idea, they said, but the only sentiment one tended to hear in the zones was negative. There was the quite appropriate concern that a *comitato cittadino* would only aggravate the systematic understaffing and bypassing to which the urban zones were already subject. Regardless of the need for the committee, it was immediately viewed as a threat to the reinforcement of intermediate and grass-roots party organizations. Whatever headquarters might sincerely believe, initiatives would inevitably gravitate to the citywide organization and thus further perpetuate the second-class status of the peripheral structures of the party.

Such strong resistance would have blocked the smooth implementation of the committee even under ideal conditions, and the frantic pace of events from 1978 on created further obstacles to its full adoption. In fact, by the end of 1980, it was accepted that the *comitato cittadino* was not functioning as intended. One leader's explanation for the difficulties was quite blunt. It was, he said, "an absurd committee established according to absurd criteria."[77] By the mid-1980s, the committee was an acknowledged failure and had been reduced to a gathering of the section secretaries of the capital; it had become precisely what the leadership had claimed they wanted to avoid: an additional bureaucratic level between headquarters and the grass roots.

## Personnel Shifts and the Reinforcement of the Zones

The end of the 1970s and the early 1980s saw a continuation of the extensive shifting of full-time functionaries within headquarters and between headquarters and the zones. But while earlier activities had a distinctly improvised air (except where the very top leadership was concerned), this was less true of later changes. Nevertheless, these, too, were often governed by forces that were far more haphazard and unforeseen than might first appear to be the case.

From the extent of the turnover that took place between 1979 and the end of 1980, we can view this period as the shaking out that followed the massive disruptions in the wake of the victories of 1975. The federation finally took purposive steps to improve the situation in the zones: the apparatus was consciously reorganized "to put experienced and absolutely top-flight cadres" in the periphery.[78] In fact, six veterans were moved into the zones from the Palazzo, while eight zonal functionaries left full-time party work and another seven were recruited into the apparatus for the first time. Thirteen full-timers from the late 1970s remained in the zones, but only seven of these held their previous positions.

In headquarters, the shifts were even greater, although only one functionary actually left all forms of work for the party; he "reentered production," as the communist euphemism puts it. But by 1980, a total of ten members of the apparatus were moved either into the zones or into public office or flanking mass organizations, and another five were shuffled into different jobs in the central apparatus, leaving only four *responsabili* holding the same posts they had occupied two years earlier.

As we have seen, dramatic changes in personnel can create problems of discontinuity. But when highly experienced and well-known cadres are moved from center to periphery—as was extensively the case this time—grass-roots militants are not confronted with a largely unknown and inexperienced quantity. On the contrary, they find themselves working closely with people they have known a long time. Nor do those who "reenter production" face the trauma that this move used to imply. In the past, former PCI functionaries faced the likelihood of a blacklist from potential employers, at the same time as they were viewed within their own party as having abandoned a sacred commitment.[79] Today, legal guarantees protect most forms of political activism, and the PCI is no longer treated as a pariah. At the same time, the eclipse of Marxism-Leninism and of the idea of the functionary as a professional revolutionary greatly eases pressures on former members of the apparatus. On the whole, they do not appear to face extreme readjustment problems when they stop full-time work for the party.

Finally, the PCI has itself consistently tried to downplay the importance of a permanent apparatus, and this notion has always had special resonance in Turin, as one would expect of an area with strong workerist and "movementist" traditions. If anything, the rank and file have historically been a bit too quick to blame functionaries or an even more generic party bureaucracy when things have not gone well for the Communists—

although the post-1975 period, which saw so many problematic decisions taken on high, gave this charge a truthful ring.

This abstract commitment was given a strong boost at the beginning of the 1980s by a combination of developments already mentioned in other contexts of this study. The general drop in PCI membership that began in the late 1970s was even more marked in Turin than in most of the rest of the party: the federation fell from forty-seven thousand in 1976–77 to forty-one thousand in 1982 and thirty-nine thousand in 1983. This, of course, means that in a general climate of financial difficulty for the PCI, the Turinese federation has less of its own funds, and less claim to help from Rome, than other, chronically weak areas such as the South. Simultaneously—and indeed a key reason for the precipitous drop in membership—the economic crisis came to Turin with a vengeance in the 1980s, as we saw in the case of the thirty-five days in 1980. Tens of thousands of workers lost their jobs, and the depression that struck the auto industry froze young workers (always a prime source of new recruits to the party) out of the work force.

Hence, what was ideologically desirable also became financially necessary, and the federation proceeded in the early 1980s to trim its apparatus notably. This was facilitated by the sudden appearance of many laid-off or part-time workers among the ranks of the party faithful; with a lot of time at their disposal, they could, if they proved effective, move into positions vacated by former functionaries. By the mid-1980s, they represented a notable proportion of the zonal leadership of the Turinese PCI. In fact, six of the two dozen posts occupied by full-timers in the late 1970s were held by volunteers, or at most part-timers, by the middle of the 1980s. The situation in headquarters was not quite so dramatically altered, although the party did successfully hold down the number of full-timers there as well: from a high point of twenty in the 1977–78 period, the number fell to fifteen following the shakeout of 1980. With the judicious use of volunteers and *cassintegrati* through the early 1980s, this figure was maintained through the latter half of the decade.

The one factor that makes it difficult to predict with any certainty what the future holds for the federation is the party's fall from local power in 1985. Following the complete breakdown of collaboration with the Socialists, the PCI lost its hold on both the capital city and the region of Piedmont in the 1985 local elections. This, of course, means that not only many veterans of party work but also many of the "best and brightest" of the generation of the 1970s are now without full-time employment—for an opposition councilor in the PCI ranks is only a part-time occupation. Many of these people, because of their loyal service to the party but also because of their unquestioned abilities, will have to be reintegrated into whatever activities are available. Numerous public offices remain in PCI hands (especially in the industrial belt), but some militants may well have to be placed in either the regional or the federal party apparatus for lack of alternatives. Should that prove to be the case, the unpredictable events which made the trimming of the apparatus possible will be offset by an equally unforeseen set of circumstances. All one can say in this regard is that it will be no means be the first time that Turinese communism has had to improvise in the face of adversity.

## Efforts to Streamline Federation Practices

By the mid-1980s, there had also been two major initiatives to address what everyone recognized as some of the most counterproductive practices in the federation. At the end of 1980, a number of serious decentralization measures were undertaken in response to complaints from both the apparatus and the rank and file.[80] The major goals were twofold: to lessen overcentralization in headquarters, and to correct some of the worst aspects of frantic activism that led to the premature burnout of volunteers and full-timers alike. In the next few years, as these efforts met with only limited success, a series of potentially much more radical changes began to be entertained. These remain in their earliest stages and take us far from the 1975–1980 period. They will only be mentioned in passing as indicators of how the terms of debate within the party have left few sacred cows of organization untouched in the face of full-fledged crisis.[81]

The federation attempted to lessen the worst effects of overcentralization by broadening the composition of the working commissions in headquarters. More rank-and-file activists from the periphery were put on these commissions, in an effort to dilute the presence of sectoral specialists and insiders. At the same time, Communists in public office or mass organizations with a direct interest in given commissions were drawn more directly into their work, improving direct contact with the party organization and coordinating the work done on specific topics. This would at least ensure that local government did not treat the party organization as its handmaiden, and that trade unionists could no longer act as if they knew nothing of the local party's position on a given topic—practices that had become all too common by the late 1970s.

These proposals met with widespread support from within the party structures. That was less true of some of the federation's efforts to streamline routine operations. Some elimination of duplication was welcomed gratefully, such as cutting the number of utterly repetitious meetings, where precisely the same things were heard over and over and at which, as we have seen, functionaries and zonal leaders were always expected to preside. As many of these gatherings are replications of national-level meetings—with the Federal Committee reiterating the agenda of the Central Committee, and then zonal and section assemblies essentially repeating what the Federal Committee does—there was a strong feeling that most of the party's active cadres would be well informed without the endless duplication. But some peripheral leaders noted that many of the proposals to broaden participation on the commissions in headquarters, while ostensibly also measures taken to eliminate duplication and increase lower-level participation, in fact could easily lead to even more extensive centralization. After all, if zonal activists, public officeholders, trade unionists, and all the specialists now met in headquarters, and the commissions were not really reinforced in the zones, there might well be more coordination and efficiency, and there might even be less fragmentation of party initiatives, but there certainly would not be more decentralization and effective rank-and-file participation.[82] This appeared to be—and experience confirmed the skepticism—an effort to solve too many problems with a single remedy.

What was only implicit at the beginning of the 1980s was more bluntly acknowledged by the middle of the decade: the very structures of the *partito nuovo* were often impediments to the sort of presence in and communication with society that the PCI strived to achieve. Many of the streamlining efforts outlined above recognized that the sections, as they existed, diffused the party's energies and contributed to duplication while providing very limited benefits. And, as we have seen on several occasions, there is an inherent tension between maximizing the number of sections and extending the party's reach in society. By the mid-1980s, this contradiction was more openly recognized within the PCI itself. The sections—especially the urban sections—were seen as inadequate instruments of *social* intervention, however much they might serve to renew membership and replicate traditional activism.[83] And a least some of the leaders of the party were now willing to act to resolve this tension in favor of the social rather than the organizational functions of the party structure.

For the bolder spirits in the federation, this meant a redefinition of the roles of the sections and zones. The PCI's fundamental unit at the grass roots ought no longer to be the inward-looking section but the much larger zone, augmented by a more genuinely social institution such as a *circolo* or a *casa del popolo*, structures that did not have party membership as their major criterion of belonging. For this group, the urban section needed to be fundamentally restructured: it should have far more members, and it should cover a much broader territory. A zone might have only two or three sections, while the section, in deference to the organizational functions it could still perform, would carry on but without exercising such a drain on personal energies within the party. The section would become a sort of large cell and no longer even pretend to do what it had manifestly proven itself incapable of in any event: serve as the assumed base-level unit of participation in the party.

The more cautious or traditionalist spirits in the federation were less willing to take such radical steps, but even they were aware of the sections' shortcomings. In their view—which the more radically reform-minded leaders admitted had far more support in Turin—there ought to be some rationalization of the sections but not a total redefinition of the party's rank-and-file and intermediate organizational levels. While the reformers might ultimately be happy to see the one hundred sections of the capital reduced to forty—or even fewer—the "traditionalists" would be more comfortable eliminating the ten or fifteen most problematic sections, essentially leaving the overall structure of the federation unaltered. Ultimately, the final shape of the party structure will not depend on which orientation prevails in Turin (although it is safe to say that the most radical proposals would take an extremely long time to be implemented). Because they represent such a dramatic departure from established practices, the only way the radical proposals will ever be implemented will be if substantial segments of the party come to the conclusion that the PCI must rethink its structures from top to bottom. This is not something that appears imminent, but it is no longer entirely unthinkable in light of the problems and apparent impasse faced by Italian communism.

# 7

# The Party Apparatus in Transition:
# The Changing Role and Profile
# of the PCI Functionary

If the organizational capacities of communist parties have often been exaggerated (even by serious observers), conjecture about what goes on in the very heart of the party machine tends to be shot through with particularly strong and frequently sinister assumptions. Terms such as "communist functionary," "apparatus," and "apparatchik" may conjure up diverse impressions, but it is a safe bet that none of them is flattering.

A strong and consistent cold war tradition in the West helps explain much of the bad press, while communist behavior itself, especially the cynical manipulations and flip-flops of the Stalinist period, did little to reassure even less prejudiced observers. The negative image persists in attenuated fashion for less dramatic but still compelling reasons. Communist parties remain strongly centralistic, and unity—even unanimity—is almost an obsession with them. Their innermost workings remain one of the most understudied phenomena of party politics. And it is often useful for adversaries to exaggerate, or mystify, the cohesion and efficiency of a party, especially when it is in fact considerably weaker than most people suspect.

The events recounted in earlier chapters have already cast considerable light on the full-time members of the PCI organization in Turin. Now that we have also examined the impact of the transitional crisis on the PCI's structures, this chapter provides the opportunity to pull together several important themes and examine the changing role and composition of the apparatus in more depth.

## The Apparatus and the *Partito Nuovo*

The structure and leadership of mass parties may well be influenced by "iron laws"—or at least tendencies—but they are far more profoundly shaped by historically specific factors.[1] Schorske's important study of German Social Democracy showed that it was not simply the creation of a party bureaucracy but the conditions under which the apparatus emerged that gave SPD bureaucrats their distinctively conservative cast in the period preceding World War I.[2] And Sidney Tarrow's comparison of the PCI and the PCF shows how the different constitutive periods of each contributed powerfully to their different evolutions in the postwar period.[3]

These observations are not intended to gloss over the powerful tools for molding structures and cadres that the PCI has at its disposal. But those tools were much more powerful in the past, and even then—with a united leadership and the fairly clear aims of the *partito nuovo* in mind—the party could still only work with the material, and under the circumstances, at hand. A review of the changes in the apparatus at the end of the 1950s, when almost everything worked in favor of Togliatti and the *rinnovatori*, makes this point very clearly. De-Stalinization's importance for the party's modern history has been so central that it is worth reexamining briefly.

De-Stalinization brought the tenets of the *partito nuovo* to the top of the party's agenda. In the words of a perceptive team of contemporary observers, it ensured—when the outcome was by no means clear—that the "Togliattian soul" of Italian communism prevailed over its "Leninist soul."[4] This was possible for several crucial reasons. First, the top leadership had an alternative vision of both a strategy to follow and the type of organization required to implement it. Second, they had the will to impose this vision on the rest of the party, often against fierce opposition. Finally, an intermediate-level cadre was waiting in the wings to replace the old guard of the exile and clandestine period, ensuring that the outlines of the *via italiana* and the *partito nuovo* were implemented in the federations. These "renovators" (*rinnovatori*) were well suited to their historic task, with life histories that straddled the two periods Togliatti was attempting to bridge. They were creatures of the mass politics of the postwar period, having matured politically during the Resistance and the Liberation or, at the latest, in the broad struggles of the late 1940s. But they had also been socialized into a highly disciplined (and Stalinist) PCI. They were, in short, made to order for the hybrid nature of the *partito nuovo*, with its mix of mass and cadre qualities.

Yet if their strengths were those of the *partito nuovo*, so were their weaknesses. The PCI's hybrid nature ideally suited an opposition party. The renovators' backgrounds had trained them to be mobilizers of mass dissent in a democratic setting while simultaneously enforcing strict internal discipline. When extensive social and political change brought the party face to face with masses of new supporters and members who were not simple extensions of old constituencies, established practices often revealed themselves as inadequate. This underscores the degree to which the PCI's Togliattian soul and its Leninist soul share many organizational assumptions.

The Togliattian party retained much of the dogma, symbols, and rituals of the past.[5] More importantly, in order to function in accordance with its own goals, the internal agenda of the *partito nuovo* continued to call for the discipline, self-sacrifice, and commitment of the "professional revolutionary"—a term widely in use in the PCI until the 1970s. The ritualistic and symbolic activities called for by an ideological, cadre-based party, combined with the politics of presence and projection into civil society required by the mass party, put an immense permanent strain on the organization. It is not surprising that the ethos of self-denying frenzied activism carried over almost unaltered from the Leninist model of militancy, and it is a good thing for the party that the *rinnovatori* were there to act as a living bridge. But, as we have seen, their triumph set the stage for future difficulties when they did not anticipate their own replacement once they were solidly in power in the federations. The lack of a buffer or replacement generation did more than leave the party organization short-handed during the transition that began in the wake of the 1960s. It also helped perpetuate the older model of militancy in nearly unaltered fashion until well into the 1970s.

The challenges confronting the party organization in the late 1970s and early 1980s may not be quite as dramatic and lacerating as those linked to de-Stalinization, but they are profound. Moreover, they have been made immensely more complex by the fluidity of both the political and the organizational contexts in which the PCI has been forced to function. The earlier transition at least saw two reasonably well-defined visions of the party in direct confrontation and two relatively cohesive sets of intermediate-level leaders contending for control. The present transition may not be wide open, but neither the new vision of the party nor the orientations of the nascent leadership has taken clear shape.

## Organizational Lag in the Midst of Change

Before we examine the Turinese functionaries in greater depth, let us take what we have learned from the previous two chapters as an aid to understanding what the present corps of functionaries faces in its actual work. What, in short, is unaltered and what is changing in the tasks the modern functionary is called on to perform in the PCI? What is it about this work, today, that has thrown the party apparatus into crisis?

There are many ways of stating the functionaries' problem, but the essential dilemma is easily summarized. The underlying models of organization and militancy in the PCI were challenged but not profoundly altered by the de-Stalinization of the late 1950s. Since then, almost all aspects of party strategy—as well as the social context in which the PCI operates—have evolved radically, often in directions not anticipated by the assumptions that gave birth to the *partito nuovo*. By the late 1970s, the accumulation of problems within the organization could no longer be ignored.

The point is not that PCI organization did not evolve over two decades but that it did so much more slowly than was necessary in order to keep up with the strategic evolution of the party and the sociopolitical evolution of the country.[6] With the late 1970s, a conjuncture had finally arrived where even the powerful obstacles to change within the party's structures could no longer effectively hold back the organization's response to internal and external pressures, as they had been doing for nearly a generation. Natural turnover, aggravated by the wholesale shift of experienced functionaries into public office, called for the replacement of an entire generation of leaders. At the same time, problems that had been ignored altogether or addressed in erratic, unsystematic fashion became more urgent.

Precisely because it was a conjuncture, it involved many overlapping events. But surely one of the most important of these, and certainly the one that most deserves attention in a chapter on the functionaries in the party organization, is the inherent limits in the *partito nuovo* that came to the fore as the *rinnovatori* gradually gave up their dominant positions in the federations in the 1970s.

## The Functionary's Job in the 1970s (and Beyond)

> In the old days, what you needed was a good memory and a strong pair of lungs. All that has changed now.
>
> PCI functionary (1969)

Although this quotation is more to the point than ever in the PCI of the 1980s, it would be a serious error to underestimate how much the job of the modern party functionary continues to consist of mundane and repetitive organization tasks and endless, exhausting rounds of meetings. Even the top leadership of the federation logs an inordinate number of hours, the bulk of them in the evening or on weekends, attending (usually introducing or concluding) party gatherings or simply being present in other assemblies. The PCI's own research showed in 1979 that 60 percent of all functionaries spent at least three evenings a week in party-related activities; the figure for Turin during the same period was even higher.[7] Nor is it surprising, with such a work load, that the same proportion of full-time party workers reported having little or no time available for personal or family matters.[8] Italian Communist "party bureaucrats," whatever else one may say about them, are not deskbound paper pushers. A shirker, or for that matter someone without the ability to survive a crushing schedule, could not last more than a few weeks in a federation apparatus.

The price paid and the dissatisfaction felt by the full-time cadre is a perfect illustration of the way the hybrid *partito nuovo* works in practice. As a mass-membership party which relies on significant amounts of volunteer work, it must tailor its activity to the militants' free time, after working hours or on weekends. But as a party that insists on "orienting" its militants, it imposes a traditional and highly controlling structure on meetings—with functionaries almost always present—all the way down to the grass roots. Rare indeed is the PCI gathering that does not begin with a "report" (*relazione*), usually presented by a ranking member of the unit that has been assembled, and end with a functionary's conclusion. Sandwiched between these are the rank and file's "interventions" (*interventi*). Speakers who want to be taken seriously by the leadership know they must tailor their remarks to fit the framework set out in the *relazione*. This makes nearly every *intervento* longer and more cumbersome than it needs to be. Such meetings—and they are the rule, not the exception—almost inevitably end late, with dwindling attendance, in an atmosphere of glazed-eyed exhaustion. But the party always gets the last word.

This model of activity produces a regular routine that is punishing enough. But the load becomes truly crushing at least several times a year. Membership drives traditionally take up most of the late autumn, while *l'Unità*'s annual festivals occupy much of the summer. One can usually count on one congress or conference per year; most of these start at the grass roots and are then held at the zonal and, finally, the federation level. These events tend to be scheduled over the winter months. Then, at least since the mid-1970s, the PCI has been confronted nearly once a year by a major electoral campaign (local or general elections or a referendum). These are especially intensive, as we saw in Chapter 3, and permit little other activity for five or six weeks, generally in late spring or early summer.

Then there are extraordinary domestic or international developments, which are frequent enough to guarantee the near paralysis and breakdown of the organization at least once or twice a year. For many reasons, the party leadership feels compelled to mobilize the PCI on occasions that can include a serious governmental crisis or a dramatic world event or in response to important domestic developments that range from major labor contracts to important legislation to terrorism. The most dramatic of these events generate a spate of public as well as internal party assemblies: functionaries, in addition to coordinating PCI gatherings of various types, must also make endless rounds of speeches in markets and *piazze* and in front of factory gates.

We have not yet even mentioned the routine tasks of the apparatus. Here, as we saw earlier, the difference between an assignment in headquarters and in the zones can be immense. Work in the zones tends much more toward grubby and routine organizational maintenance, with emphasis on monitoring and trying to ensure the operation of the sections. The pace of work is hectic in both settings, but people in headquarters exercise real power and also can develop a specialization, factors that can only increase a sense of job satisfaction. Functionaries in the outlying zones of the province spoke positively of the smaller scale of operations and the autonomy (because of the distance from headquarters) they enjoyed. But the peripheral apparatus pays a terrible price for its autonomy: its lot is physically most demanding, requiring constant travel between zone and headquarters, as well as the obligation to cover the often large zonal territory. For reasons already touched on, an assignment in one of the zones of the capital city is probably the most difficult of all. Party headquarters is too close for any genuine autonomy, urban zones have no rational administrative or political counterparts, and the environment is least hospitable of all to established organizational practices.

Each job has its own specific frustrations and rewards. Leaders in headquarters frequently confess to feeling overwhelmed by what their individual commission is expected to do. How can a single individual hope to keep up with the operations of a multinational colossus such as Fiat while simultaneously coordinating all PCI activities in that company's plants? Where do the tasks of a Cultural Commission end? Everyone in headquarters below the very highest echelon spends hours on the telephone or in face-to-face contact listening to mundane complaints or endlessly hashing over the composition of party lists for every conceivable type of office. And even some of the presumed advantages of working in the center of events are double-edged: I often heard people in headquarters complain that studies or position papers requested by the Secretariat got, at best, cursory attention from leaders who never find the time to deal with issues in depth.

All functionaries face unrealistic demands on their time, but those in the zones quite accurately see themselves as more exploited than others. Powerful resentments often erupt over seemingly banal cases, until one realizes how much general frustration lies just below the surface. The coordination of the *Festivali dell'Unità*, especially in the smallest and most understaffed zones, provides a revealing illustration. These tasks can easily become a full-time job for the entire summer; they involve an astounding amount of tedious but crucial attention to detail. This can cause the rest of the zone's activities to grind to a halt. That is bad enough, but when zonal functionaries who have been denied a decent summer vacation because of the *festivali* see leaders in headquarters departing for summer sojourns of a month or so, they can become understandably incensed.

I also heard many complaints about the peripheral functionaries' precarious financial plight, and especially how it is aggravated by the maintenance and replacement costs for the personal automobiles which are an essential tool of the trade in the outlying zones.[9] The federation reimburses operating expenses, but distances which easily reach twenty to twenty-five thousand miles per year (three times the Italian average) quickly reduce to scrap the flimsy cars that most functionaries are able to afford. As one who has ridden in many such cars, I can attest to their lack of comfort and safety, even by Italian standards.

No summary of the functionaries' work can ignore the considerable time members of the apparatus devote to public office. They are councilors for the PCI at every level, from regional assemblies down to local health units and CdQs. Some hold positions of importance in local governments of the left; many others have been assigned posts on the boards of agencies, institutes, or utilities when the PCI's governing status gives it the right to make appointments. Because the party puts performance in public office at the top of its agenda, many of these positions require a good deal of their incumbents' energy. But even where only a ritualistic presence is required, it can take a lot of time.[10] In all, excluding the most insignificant posts, nearly two-thirds (63 percent) of the entire apparatus in Turin held public positions in 1978. The figure topped 80 percent in headquarters, while in the zones it was around 50 percent—reflecting both the youth of the zonal leaders and the recruitment of so many after the 1975 elections. Putting trusted functionaries in elective or administrative office is commonplace in the PCI, but it reaches exceptionally high levels in Turin.[11]

This information ought to suggest the overwhelming volume of work a PCI functionary faces, but only firsthand observation can truly provide a sense of the frantic pace at which this work is pursued. Simply to accompany a functionary through a single normal workday (and night) is an exhausting experience. To fix an appointment is a major accomplishment; to have the appointment kept is rarer still. Interviews simply cannot be completed without major interruptions, and many interviews come to abrupt ends when unanticipated problems require immediate attention. For a researcher with time on his hands, these interruptions—to a certain point—can provide additional insights and a broader perspective on the party. But their cumulative impact on the full-time party worker is exhausting, physically and emotionally (they make it nearly impossible to complete even routine tasks).

## The Persistence of the Old Model of Militancy

Why the PCI should impose so many demands on its paid operatives is obvious. Above all, it cannot afford additional staff. Moreover, however defined, its interests are not served by functionaries who view their work as just another job. Even if we ignore for the moment the legacy of the professional revolutionary, the murderous work pace demanded by the party organization is in addition a solid guarantee against bureaucratization understood as a staff of time servers. But narrowly organizational explanations only tell us why the party finds it convenient to fall back on a more traditional model of militancy; they do not explain why the model persists. Every organization would be well served if it could wring eighty hours' work for forty hours' pay from its staff. Yet few succeed.

If the PCI has succeeded, this is largely because the entire party continues to be permeated by an ethic which holds that a good communist militant must be prepared to make great sacrifices for his or her party in the service of a great cause. Militancy, in this view, is not so much part of one's activity as the defining aspect of one's entire personal and social being; as Giorgio Amendola put it in his widely read memoir, it is a choice of and for an entire way of life.[12] Functionaries themselves often point out that it is hardly the apparatus alone that overworks itself and gives up most of its free time and private life; unpaid militants do so as well, and serious activists do so to a striking degree. The festivals of *l'Unità*, to cite a well-known case, work only because a very large number of activists give up most of their annual summer vacation, year after year. In the face of such dedication, obvious to the casual observer and documented by empirical research,[13] could a full-time party worker be less than totally committed?

The ethos has waned over time, and it rapidly dissipates as one moves outward from the apparatus and militant core of the party. But it persists in spite of the immense organizational expansion and change of the 1970s. Why this should be the case long after substantial changes occurred in party doctrine and strategy is evidently the result of a complex combination of factors. The ideological and psychological dimensions of politics are obviously relevant at this level of involvement, but political and cultural biases on all sides, not to mention profound operational problems, have kept most studies that try to apply these concepts from being developed fruitfully.[14] Interpretations based on rational as well as symbolic political incentives have begun to break free from the corporate context that spawned them and suggest promising avenues to be explored in this regard.[15]

Regardless of the possible deep underlying motives for the persistence of the older model of militancy, there is a sound organizational explanation for its initial reinforcement in the 1970s before the PCI began to succumb to pressures for change in the wake of the hot autumn. The Turinese federation absorbed two distinct waves of recruits following the upheavals of the late 1960s and early 1970s.[16] The earliest wave overlapped considerably with the major cycle of labor and social militance and did not initially bring many new subjects into the party. White-collar and intellectual groups did not increase as dramatically as they would after 1973, the federation's age profile hardly changed at all, and the proportion of women actually declined sharply. At the same time, many members of the "generation of 'sixty-eight" very quickly found their way into lower and intermediate levels of the party's leadership structures.[17]

Much of the ethos of that period was extremely radical, with movements, groups, and "parties" appearing and disappearing rapidly. The PCI and other historic organizations of the left were criticized from the left, initially from antiauthoritarian positions but then from ultra-Leninist (or Maoist) standpoints as well. This was a period which "put revolution back on the agenda" and saw the PCI assume positions that were more militant and radical than had been—and were to be in future—characteristic or comfortable. Since this was demonstrably the case, it is not far-fetched to argue that many of those who joined the party in this first wave, and especially those who were strongly enough motivated to become activists, shared the radical ethos of the period. They undoubtedly brought a variety of critical attitudes into the PCI, including many that would directly challenge the party. But the heady spirit of the time contained, for such militants, a very strong commitment to change society, as well as the idea that the dedicated militant is a tireless struggler.

It is certainly the case that these values had already penetrated the PCI apparatus by the late 1960s. The youngest functionaries at that time—those who rose to prominence in the federations by the late 1970s—shared many of the radical critiques of the party that were being expressed outside, but they also remained wedded to the traditional, sacrificial model of militancy.[18] In this regard, as in many others, the legacy of the hot autumn was, for the PCI, ambiguous.

## Challenges to the Old Model of Militancy

By the mid-1970s, the forces acting on and through the PCI had become strong enough to challenge seriously the party's entrenched hegemonic and "totalizing" ambitions and assumptions. These changes also severely undermined the traditional model of militancy, rooted as it is in a bolshevik and Jacobin conception of politics and the revolutionary process. The process is complex, but its impact on the party organization is not difficult to describe. When established practices began to break down, and the implications of the party's evolving strategy called into question the need to "be present in every crease and fold" of society, it obviously became increasingly difficult to sustain an operational code that had persisted in no small measure because of these earlier assumptions.

The erosion of traditional subcultures and the emergence of myriad new forces in society made it difficult to continue to ignore a growing complexity which could neither be channeled into old organizational forms nor maneuvered very effectively by traditional techniques. The *compromesso storico* may have misread many trends, but it posited a permanent pluralism of forces in the future, which made it necessary for Italian Communists to begin to project their party's future role and "hegemony" in a much more innocuous way than had been the case in the past. The PCI's mass presence in society might still be desirable, but it was no longer assumed that the party had to "cover," and be compulsively active in, every aspect of social life. Finally, the PCI's electoral successes moved it much closer to the centers of political power. We saw firsthand in Chapter 4 how this sowed confusion in an organization that was previously geared only to mobilizing dissent and acting as an oppositional force. At the same time, the party's governmental ambitions and responsibilities forced additional (long-delayed) clarifications of the future society the PCI envisioned for Italy—which even further undermined many of the foundations of the *partito nuovo*. These domestic constraints, along with international developments (the Polish case was most conspicuous), accelerated the PCI's seemingly definitive break with any external model. It was unable to define an elusive "third way" between Eastern communism and Western social democracy in satisfactory fashion, but the PCI's commitment to this path appeared to be increasingly solid.

Criticisms of the party's attempt to cover everything were expressed consistently during the *autocritiche* of the late 1970s. Functionaries and militants alike saw this as a major cause of the frenzied dashing about that was wearing down and demoralizing the party, especially since so much of the compulsive activism seemed channeled to no good purpose or clear set of objectives. As many people in the federation put it at the time, the PCI had to stop treating cadres as firemen to be sent running wherever smoke is spotted. In the long run, such practices were dissipating the organization's limited energies and preventing a calm assessment of priorities and goals.

This was probably the most important challenge to the dominant model of militancy to arise from within the PCI in the 1970s. At the same time, many post-1968 values began to percolate upward into the party from outside as they became increasingly diffused in the society at large, especially on the left.

The old model, for example, assumed that the private life of a good Communist was to be kept totally separate from, and subjugated to, political commitment. This view is consistent with several ideological and practical assumptions. In the traditional (and vulgar) Marxist view, the sphere of the personal is understood as individualistic and therefore secondary and even tainted in contrast to the higher calling of politics. On the more practical side, keeping personal concerns at arm's length shields the organization from the complexities of its militants' lives—and provides individual militants with a haven from their intense political involvement. Vestiges of bolshevik moralism could still be found in the PCI, for instance, in pressures on functionaries in outlying areas to marry the persons they lived with. Most of those who complained about the totalizing tendencies of party militance, however, focused on the lack of legitimacy and space accorded to one's existence outside the party.

One young national leader asked pointedly how a party with governing ambitions could continue to view normal citizens as "incomplete militants" when they were simply people driven by a variety of motivations which did not happen to fit the PCI's pigeonholes.[19] Others also derided the party's arguments that the demands of new subjects were irrational simply because they focused on private, rather than public, institutional concerns.[20] But perhaps nothing revealed the penetration of these themes into the very core of the party organization as much as discussions with the functionaries themselves. Many spoke of the way party work had broken up the marriages or relationships of their comrades. Several ruefully cited what is apparently an old slogan in the PCI: "The Communist party unites the proletariat and divides families." One functionary tied the various issues together eloquently when she put it this way:

> We are constantly told that this is a different type of party from the old insurrectionary, clandestine one. But the basic model is still one that takes over your entire life [*totalizzante*]. There is no room in it for personal development, which is, however, an absolute necessity. Your human development cannot be determined by your political life. I have effectively stopped reading literature, going to the theater, and having a personal life since I became a functionary.

These criticisms resonate with themes brought forward by feminists in Italy and elsewhere; the slogan "The personal *is* political" goes to the heart of the traditional model of militancy. It is worth recalling that the radical women's movement that arose in the late 1960s initially directed many of its most telling attacks against the hypocrisy of left-wing movements and organizations that preached but did not practice equality.[21] The PCI was extremely slow to respond to the feminist challenge, for it was both tradition-bound and intent on a rapprochement with Catholics.[22] Eventually, changes in society—and strong pressure from women in the party—forced the Communists to begin to come to terms with the issues raised by the women's movement.

In the course of systematic interviewing, 56 percent of the Turinese apparatus said that the aspect of party work they liked least was the pace of work inflicted on functionaries. This extraordinarily high distribution did not alter significantly between headquarters and the zones or between younger and older respondents. It was the case, however, that among the large minority (29 percent) who injected considerations concerning their personal lives into such complaints, almost all were under thirty-five, and most were located in the outlying areas of the federation.

These statistics confirmed for me the impression that while the job of a PCI functionary had not changed much in a decade, the kind of people who held jobs in the apparatus and the expectations they brought to their jobs had altered notably. In the late 1960s, and even during the early 1970s, personal concerns were not normally discussed by functionaries; when broached, they were framed fatalistically, as in "This is a terrible job from the viewpoint of family life; luckily, my wife is very understanding." One simply would not hear such resignation, especially from younger leaders, by the late 1970s. They were far more likely to speak of the anguished discussions they had with their spouses when the party asked them to work full-time.

Of course, other factors have also undermined the ethos of total commitment in the party's innermost structures. If the party has historically demanded a great deal from its cadres, it also gave them plenty in return. Full-time cadres of an earlier generation—most *rinnovatori* are a good case in point—were often hired by the PCI after being fired and blacklisted for political and union activities. They were underprivileged and poorly educated and "went to school in the party" in both a literal and figurative sense.[23] They were not simply exposed to the party at a different historical stage, but the nature of this exposure was much more intense. It is altogether understandable why they often found the views expressed by their younger and more recently recruited comrades to be threatening, incomprehensible, or both. The Turinese federation in the late 1970s was the site of a true gap between generations and life-styles. And while the gap might have been greater in the Piedmontese capital, all the evidence suggests that it was rampant throughout the PCI.

These profound differences were almost never broached directly through the 1970s (or even well into the 1980s). But the very fact that they were not testifies to how well entrenched the traditional operational codes remained throughout that period. At the same time, the implications of the differences were never far from the surface in the federation, as two examples will indicate.

The first is the persistence of the frenetic and highly personalistic work style that prevails in Turin. Veteran leaders acknowledge that they are responsible for setting the tone for the apparatus, and everyone agrees that this includes subjecting functionaries to an impossible barrage of demands. It is also understood—but less candidly acknowledged by most veterans—that those who cope best with this barrage, ignoring the personal costs, are viewed with most favor. These biases in promotional criteria are not lost on younger leaders, a number of whom echoed the thoughtful comments of a comrade who spoke of the top leadership's identification with newcomers whose traits were most similar to their own:

> We are after all only a party of human beings, so this is natural. But there is a very strong feeling that these [promotional] criteria are highly subjective, and that it is usually those who are most compulsively active, and not those with the best abilities, who advance most rapidly in the Party.

The second example may be most telling of all. In the autumn of 1977, an apparatus meeting unexpectedly turned into a general discussion of the pressures felt by many functionaries. A good number of the issues discussed above were aired.[24] The functionaries who spoke of this meeting felt that they were heard out very politely (and with some embarrassment) but with very little real comprehension. And the matter was not brought up again after that encounter. At most, one could view the proposals late in 1980 that included lessening the number of meetings on the apparatus' schedule as a belated, halting effort to address a part of the broader problem. But it is clear that the party continues to avoid the underlying issues.

This is not the sort of problem that can be swept under the rug indefinitely. Here, as elsewhere, the contradictions in the *partito nuovo* have reached an impasse. The PCI's very success as a mass party has resulted in the penetration of the organization by a series of issues that existing structures and practices were not designed to handle. If these structures and practices—reflective of a cadre party—do not adapt to the new stimuli, the party will fall increasingly out of step with some of the most important changes that have affected Italian society. Yet if they do adapt, the pain and dislocation within the organization will be extensive. In the meantime, as with all such issues, it is the special dilemma of the functionaries that they are most directly exposed to these cross-pressures.

## The Apparatus: The Functionaries' Backgrounds

Because the apparatus is the heart of the party organization, and because the PCI's organization continues to be absolutely central to so many of the party's goals, we have already had ample opportunity to observe how important the recruitment, composition, and outlook of functionaries has been to the party at different junctures in its history. At this point, thanks to the opportunity I had to interview the entire apparatus in Turin during the course of fieldwork for this study, we can develop a profile of an apparatus in transition.[25]

Aside from furnishing a snapshot of the party apparatus at a critical historical moment, this profile provides the opportunity to illuminate, in considerably more depth than is usually the case, some of the broader implications of the PCI's transitional crisis. For instance, a recurring theme in the 1970s was the erosion of the PCI's class character, especially among newly recruited cadres. Has this been the case in Turin, and, if changes are evident, what do they signify? Or to take just one more important issue: we have just seen how many Leninist values and practices remain entrenched in the PCI's structures and selection mechanisms. How effective will these be in shaping a new cadre in an area whose social setting was among the most turbulent in the country, where turnover was unprecedented, and where the preexisting party structures were notoriously weak?

An obvious starting point is the apparatus's class composition. Chapter 2 documented the continuing strength of the federation's working-class roots; there was, however, a sharp rise in the representation of white-collar groups as one moved up the organizational ladder. When we examine the functionaries' jobs at the time they entered full-time party work, two findings stand out. One is that the working class, more narrowly defined in blue-collar terms, is represented in the apparatus in proportions almost identical to the general membership (56 percent); white-collar groups account for another 15 percent. The Turinese PCI thus shows some evidence of *terziarizzazione* in its apparatus — especially when we add the former teachers (7 percent) and professionals (5 percent) — but it can in no sense be considered rampant.[26]

The second finding does suggest a deviation from historic norms, although not to the extent that this has occurred in the rest of the party: 17 percent of the apparatus consists of former students who were not otherwise employed when they took up full-time party work.[27] This is a trend that makes many people in the party worry about the PCI losing its mass, "popular" nature. The development of a stratum of functionaries with strong intellectual predispositions and who furthermore have never worked elsewhere does in fact threaten some of the pillars of the *partito nuovo*. As we saw in our discussion of the PCI's political difficulties and *autocritica*, some critics were more than ready to attribute all the party's ills to the new cadres' shortcomings. As exaggerated as their accusations might have been, they resonated inside the party precisely because there is such widespread agreement that cadres and leaders "be the expression of *some* social reality." This phenomenon is not likely to affect Turin as profoundly as other areas of the country (particularly the South), but it is notable that it had become an issue even in Turin by the end of the 1970s.

How can we characterize the functionaries' family backgrounds? Three-fifths of the apparatus come from working-class families, which is nearly identical to the two-thirds of fifteen years earlier.[28] With respect to family political traditions, 42 percent of respondents reported that their fathers were PCI members. This is slightly lower than but not a dramatic departure from general PCI figures.[29] When we add the 15 percent who said their families were generically leftist in orientation (without any party members) and 12 percent whose families were socialist, we have a large majority (69 percent) recruited out of a family environment that is not hostile to the PCI. There is thus little evidence in the apparatus of the party's inroads into areas or subcultures that are hostile, which is not surprising since the strongest advances in this direction took place in the mid-1970s, by which time nearly all our functionaries were already in the party. Only 7 percent described their families as right-wing and anticommunist; the remaining quarter characterized their home environment as apolitical.

These data provide no real surprises, though they do underscore some of the observations and earlier findings of this study. A historically weak Communist organization in a highly industrialized area appears to have generated an organizational cadre which is somewhat more working-class but less historically Communist than the national norm. In light of the incredibly rapid turnover that has taken place in the apparatus, its ability to reproduce itself as well as it has along these dimensions is impressive.

When we turn to the functionaries' formal educational achievements, we can see more clearly how high turnover in Turin has exaggerated national trends. In the entire PCI, 32 percent of all functionaries had at least attended university in 1979, and 12 percent had completed their degrees. In Turin, 44 percent had attended university, and 17 percent had earned the *laurea*. Moreover, while nationally nearly half the functionaries had not gone beyond a junior high school level, this figure was only 25 percent in Turin. The crucial factor here was the age of the apparatus member: nationally, the great majority of those above thirty-five had not obtained a high school diploma; those who were younger had gone at least that far and even beyond.[30] In Turin, less than a third of the apparatus was thirty-five or older, and even they were relatively well educated, as Table 7.1 shows.

This is clearly a well-educated group. They appear to be the products of an increasingly highly educated society, but they also seem to be highly mobile. Two-thirds of their fathers, for example, never got beyond elementary school. There is, of course, a strong relationship between the functionaries' education and their class of origin, but it is not perfect. All those with less education were workers when they joined the party, but more than half the workers still managed to complete and in some cases go beyond high school. This suggests that the party's own mechanisms of recruitment are strongly attuned to the more educated, skilled, and articulate members of the PCI's traditional constituencies.

I have mentioned party schools in passing (note 23, above), but they deserve a further comment in this context. In 1964, Bonazzi found that just over three-fourths of the Turinese apparatus had attended courses of at least a month's duration.[31] In 1978, the total was a relatively low 37 percent, and it was lower still for the younger leaders. The notable rise in formal education and the concomitantly sharp drop in the role played by party schools in the functionaries' formation could be seen as a simple reflection of a changed society. They are indeed that, but behind them lurks a profound generational difference and at least a partial insight into the way the PCI has altered over the years.

*Table 7.1.* Educational Level of the Turinese Apparatus by Age Group, 1978

|  | Born 1943 or Earlier | Born 1944 or Later | Total | |
|---|---|---|---|---|
| Jr. high school or less | 6  (46%) | 4  (14%) | 10  (24%) | |
| High school or beyond | 7  (54%) | 24  (86%) | 31  (76%) | |
| Totals | 13 | 28 | 41 | |

Until the relatively recent past, militants moving into the apparatus needed additional training because of the deficiencies in their own backgrounds. When it had an official doctrine, the PCI felt it had to provide promising but underprivileged militants with both a broad theoretical background and at least the rudiments of the applied knowledge required through its party schools. (The bulk of the practical training was, of course, acquired on the job.) As we know, the weight of doctrine in the party faded at the same time as education was becoming more diffused in Italy; the two factors are clearly related. As we have seen, these parallel changes have emphasized the gap between the older and younger functionaries; one of the main reinforcements of the old militancy was the certain knowledge of the professional cadre that he literally owed everything to the party. But he also knew, given the investment in him and his accumulation of experience, that he was all but irreplaceable. As several acute observers have noted, the modern PCI's need for more sophisticated skills and the ready availability of those skills in society dramatically alter the nature of the party organization in a more "professional" direction.[32] Needless to say, such a radical change also profoundly undermines the role of the functionary. Ironically, the new generation threatens the old, but insofar as it really represents the new, its own situation is insecure.

As important as this trend toward professionalism is likely to become in the future, it coexists with more traditional practices in the present. But the current crop of young leaders is not, as I have stressed, as dependent on the party as once was the case. The poignant case of a promising zonal functionary illustrates most of the trends and dilemmas I have been discussing.

When first asked to become a functionary, he took six months to agree and did so only after extensive and agonized discussions with his wife. He resolved then, in 1975, to remain in the apparatus for only five years. In 1978, after three years on the job ("and, believe me, they feel like ten") he was approached by the party, which proposed that he go to the PCI's national school in Rome for a four- or six-month course. He knew that if he accepted, his previous plans would have to change, for the federation leadership obviously had a much longer career in mind for him. He also knew that his sense of responsibility would oblige him to stay on much longer, perhaps permanently, if he took up the offer. He was flattered at the vote of confidence in his future, but upset at the price he would have to pay. He was especially dismayed at the long-run prospects:

> I'm only thirty, and I don't want to end up getting sent off like some of the older comrade functionaries they don't know what to do with, to administer some waste of time [*cazzate*]. Or end up in Parliament with nothing to do except troop in and out and vote how they tell you.

In fact, he left the apparatus and returned to his job as a technical worker six months after our conversation.

A background characteristic of special interest in Turin because of the impact of immigration is where a leader was born or, better still, grew up. Delving into this issue has, at times, proved embarrassing to the federation. For example, in the 1960s, only one functionary was a Southerner—and he had been brought north as a small child. This no doubt reflects the weight of the "heroic generation" of the Piedmontese proletariat in the apparatus at that time, but it also is a clear indicator of the PCI's inability to penetrate the new, immigrant working class. Local traditions die hard in Italy, and Turin is no exception. One still hears conversations in Piedmontese dialect among party leaders in headquarters, and this is even more common in the sections as one moves farther from the capital.

At the end of the 1970s, the apparatus was still strongly Piedmontese, but it had changed considerably since the mid-1960s, when four out of five functionaries were natives of the region.[33] In 1978, just over half were from Piedmont, and 12 percent were from the South. If we use the more refined measure of where people actually grew up, just over a quarter of the apparatus can be considered non-Piedmontese. Five of these eleven are Southerners.

Finally, and highly significantly, the Turinese federation is very much like the rest of the PCI in the extent to which women are underrepresented in the apparatus, as in the higher echelons generally. Only three full-time workers were women in the period of 1978 to 1980, a proportion lower than the already low national average of 9.5 percent. Until 1970, the federation had no female functionaries at all, and through most of the 1970s, those it had occupied "women's posts": the Women's Commission and the Social Security Commission. At the end of the 1970s, following the national lead, the Youth Federation chose a woman as its head in Turin; in 1980, a "regular" Commission (Culture) got a woman as *responsabile*.

## Differences in Location and Recruitment

Aggregates like these are important in providing a very general outline of the apparatus. But as soon as we probe more deeply into the functionaries' backgrounds, it becomes impossible not to emphasize important differences *within* the apparatus that go beyond a rough dichotomy between younger and older leaders. In view of previous discussions, it will come as no surprise to learn that the headquarters-zone distinction emerges as especially important. It embraces age and party seniority, and reveals unexpected insights into the recruitment process in the federation. It also represents a boundary between differing political experiences, as well as organizational tasks in the functionaries' daily lives. All these elements taken together can be expected to have a profound effect on the apparatus's attitudes (which will be examined in the next chapter), and for this reason alone the sociological dimensions of the distinction deserve closer scrutiny.

Given the division of labor in the federation, a number of the most obvious differences between headquarters and the zones are very predictable. In 1978, the zonal leaders were younger, less experienced by far, more working-class, and less educated than their comrades in headquarters.[34] These differences, which are often dramatic, do not reflect significant class or educational distinctions, with one limited exception.[35] Moreover, most of the immigrants to Piedmont, and *all* the Southerners, were located in the zones. Strangely for such an urbanized area, a third of all the functionaries, and half of those in the zones, grew up in small villages (less than five thousand inhabitants). A majority of the headquarters apparatus (60 percent) spent their childhood in cities of fifty thousand or larger.

This summary makes clear that the way the apparatus took shape at the end of the 1970s, at least in Turin, was not quite the random or spontaneous process so loudly and universally decried throughout the PCI at the time. The zones turn out, on closer inspection, to be far more than a training ground (or parking lot) for younger functionaries. They served this purpose for some new recruits, but these also happened to be more working-class and immigrant in origin, and less educated. The younger neofunctionaries with the skills and background required for the federation's command positions moved into headquarters quite swiftly. The opposite side of the same coin is that the young zonal leaders have backgrounds that conform quite closely to the rank and file with whom they are in daily contact.

What we see here is thus a strong tendency of the Turinese party organization to reproduce established patterns. But the dominant pattern of veterans in headquarters at a time of confusion and crisis for the party proved to be highly problematic, as we saw in earlier chapters. Among other things, it threw those with least experience into the trenches at a time when experience might have made a real difference—and the personnel shifts early in the 1980s tacitly acknowledged the error.

The most dramatic difference of all to emerge with reference to the recruitment of the apparatus is political. Reflecting the immense changes that have taken place in Italian society since the 1960s, the functionaries' political itineraries before joining the PCI vary radically according to generation. Moreover, the newer recruits into the apparatus have personal histories that are complete departures from the assumptions that have historically guided the party's recruitment and socialization of leaders.

Specifically, what the 1960s brought was a massive influx of cadres (many of whom eventually became functionaries) with intense initial involvement and extensive political experience outside of and often in opposition to the PCI. The PCI had always attracted some cadres and leaders from other groups or parties, but the pattern through the mid-1960s was overwhelmingly one whereby the party "formed" its own activists, often from late adolescence (see the figures on FGCI membership in Table 1.2). By the end of the 1970s, 28 percent of the most active cadres had been in a group, party, or movement before joining the Communist party. This figure embraces all political generations in the PCI; it was, naturally, much higher for those who joined the PCI after 1968 and peaked at over 40 percent of all cadres in the mid-1970s.[36] And functionaries had "extra-Communist" experiences even more frequently than activists.[37]

As striking as these findings are for all PCI functionaries, they are even more pronounced for the Turinese apparatus. Fifteen percent of the Turinese (vs. 11 percent for the party as a whole) had been members of other political parties;[38] 32 percent (vs. 25 percent) had been active in the student movement or in extraparliamentary groups. Hence, barely half the apparatus in Turin joined the party or its Youth Federation directly without passing through some other form of political militancy.

The extent to which recruitment patterns differ by generation is dramatically evident in Table 7.2. Since most veterans were located in headquarters, and all of the most

*Table 7.2.* Route of Turinese Functionaries into the PCI, by Party Seniority (1978)

| | Period in Which Functionary Joined PCI or FGCI | | | | | |
|---|---|---|---|---|---|---|
| | 1945–1966 | | 1967–1972 | | 1973 or Later | |
| Militance in student movement or extraparliamentary group | — | | 8 | (36%) | 5 | (83%) |
| Membership in another party or formation | 2 | (15%) | 3 | (14%) | 1 | (17%) |
| Joined PCI or FGCI directly | 11 | (85%) | 11 | (50%) | 1 | (17%) |
| Totals | 13 | (100%) | 22 | (100%) | 7[a] | (117%) |

a. Includes one double response: one functionary was a member of both another party and a group.

recent recruits were in the zones in 1978, the differences were, if anything, even more accentuated. Nearly three-fourths of the leaders in headquarters entered the PCI or FGCI directly; those with an unmediated, "pure Communist" background outnumbered comrades with some other experience by more than four to one. In the zones, only 43 percent came directly to the party—a figure identical to the proportion of ex-militants of movements, groups, or other parties.

The table leaves no doubt about the impact of the period of student and then worker militance of 1967 to 1972 on the top cadres of the federation, especially on those who were reaching political maturity at the time. But the generational explanation is far more complicated than a first glance at the table indicates. The situation appears clear enough for the extreme cases, yet we can see that the middle (and largest) group, the broadly defined "generation of 'sixty-eight," is evenly divided between those who came to the PCI or the FGCI directly and those whose political apprenticeship was mediated by other experiences. Are there more revealing dimensions along which those who became Communists in the hot period can be divided?

There are indeed, and the headquarters-zone distinction is perhaps the most significant. The "generation of 'sixty-eight" is proportionately divided between head-quarters and the zones, but individual paths into the party differ dramatically according to location. Only 30 percent of those in headquarters reported any significant political activity prior to joining the party, and all of them were active in the student movement, broadly defined. Twice as many zonal functionaries had an earlier political experience, and of these, only one named the student movement as his locus of activity. The others were active in a party or in specific, organized extraparliamentary groups (e.g., the *Collettivo Lenin* or the nationally known *Lotta Continua*).

The headquarters-zone differentiation is also significant when we analyze the impact of a related but broader background phenomenon: the zonal functionaries were far more likely to have had Roman Catholicism play an important role in their political development. Nearly a third (29 percent) of the entire apparatus reported that religion had weighed heavily in their backgrounds, and they were equally divided between the center and the periphery of the federation. Yet only one of the five in headquarters had ever militated anywhere other than in the PCI, and this was in a postwar Catholic organization openly allied with the PCI. In the zones, six of the seven ex-Catholics had been active in other parties or groups, and most mentioned that this was a result of originally strong anticommunist sentiments. Some of the ex-Catholics in headquarters reported "reservations" about the PCI, but this never led them to choose antagonistic alternative organizations.

Even for such small numbers, these are impressive differences.[39] They conform to any number of explanations. The most plausible is simply that a "purely Communist" political background immensely increases the likelihood of being promoted into the federation hierarchy. This need not imply a felt need to quarantine people with a different background out of suspicion or hostility—which is another hypothesis but not a very plausible one (recruitment of "suspects" into the apparatus would be most unlikely). If we recall the extent and rapidity of the turnover from the mid-1970s onward, it is only logical that the leaders in headquarters, perhaps unconsciously, would co-opt those who had internalized many of the unspoken rules of the game of the PCI and probably had a more nuanced sense of the party's language and practices. Here, then, is additional evidence that the formation of new leaders in the 1970s was not really left to chance, in spite of many complaints to that effect at the time.

These findings also raise interesting questions about the sort of attitudes one might expect to find among functionaries in headquarters versus the zones, questions we can answer in the next chapter. For a good part of the 1970s, common wisdom in the PCI echoed a top party leader: he claimed that new cadres who had been militants in other groups before joining the PCI tended to be rather orthodox in their views. They were especially seen as less tolerant of extremism, for, having had their own firsthand experience of the phenomenon, they were "inoculated."[40] In fact, this conclusion turned out to be wrong: cadres with non-PCI experiences turned out to be far more tolerant than their comrades of many "deviant" forms of militant behavior such as housing occupations and obstructive actions during strikes.[41]

A final consideration in the background and recruitment of the apparatus is to go beyond the functionaries' experiences before joining the PCI and ask what they did once they became Communists. Their activities within the party surely represent important factors in the socialization of these leaders. At a time of rapid turnover and the breaking of long-established habits, such activities and any differential patterns that might emerge can be very revealing. To take some obvious questions: How long was the functionary in the party before becoming a full-time worker? Where did militancy first take place? Was the functionary ever a rank-and-file militant?

The personal histories of the apparatus in Turin conform quite closely to the rest of the party along one important dimension: those who joined the PCI before 1969 spent an average of just under five years before becoming functionaries. At the same time, the Turinese apparatus does not show the sharp drop that seems to occur in the 1970s in the whole party.[42] In Turin, the gap closes, but only from five to four years.

Much more notable distinctions emerge when we inquire into the site of the functionary's first activism as a member of the PCI. Initial experiences in the party need not stamp one forever, though they frequently do. And they surely do not preclude other experiences at a later date. There is, however, an important difference between the leader who began as a shopfloor militant and one who was assigned to factory work in the federation (or in a zone) after rising into the apparatus via the student movement. The former has actually lived the experience of a rank-and-file militant, and the latter has not. In Turin, one would expect an initial experience at the base of the party to be quite high, particularly in view of the high percentage of working-class cadres who have been drawn into the apparatus. At the same time, it is likely, considering the other differences we have found, that the headquarters-zone distinction will be significant in this aspect of the functionaries' experiences. Table 7.3 examines the evidence and confirms both suspicions.

*Table 7.3.* Site of First Activism as a Communist, Turinese Apparatus (1978)

| | Headquarters | | Zones | | Whole Federation | |
|---|---|---|---|---|---|---|
| Factory, union | 22% | } 44% | 39% | } 78% | 32% | } 64% |
| Cell or section | 22 | | 39 | | 32 | |
| Teachers' union | 6 | (1) | — | | 2 | |
| School, FGCI | 39 | | 22 | | 29 | |
| Federation HQ or higher | 11 | | — | | 5 | |
| Totals  (N) | 100 | (18) | 100 | (23) | 100 | (41) |

The grass-roots experience of the zonal functionaries is impressive. Equally impressive is the initial grass-roots experience of less than half the top leaders of the Turinese party organization. Moreover, most of the top leadership with a grass-roots experience had it in the late 1950s and early 1960s—long ago and when the party and society were quite different from what they became fifteen and more years later. When we consider that many organizational problems in the late 1970s were experienced as a flood of directives from above, frequently with little selectivity and sensitivity to the base's ability to translate them into concrete initiatives, the implications of these data are evident.

An equally impressive, related figure was provided by the new organizational *responsabile* at the end of 1980: out of a total political apparatus of forty-four members at the time, "no more than thirty" could be said to have any meaningful contact with the base of the party.[43] Those with the least contact were, of course, most headquarters functionaries—with the exception, one would assume, of the Organization and Factory commissions. Here the importance of the personnel rotation summarized in the last chapter cannot be overstated. Even though the amount of truly new blood brought into headquarters was limited, the shifts would put at least some top leaders into more sustained, direct contact with regular militants than had been the case for years, while bringing into headquarters a number of respected and skilled zonal leaders with recent experience among the rank and file. Hardly a panacea for the many problems of the party organization, this rotation at least increases the exposure of the upper reaches of the federation to the reality of the 1980s.

The rotation shows yet again how important the conscious intervention of leadership has been in shaping the PCI organization over the years: recruitment patterns in the wake of 1968 were "spontaneous" outgrowths of ingrained habits and the press of a nonstop crisis situation. By the beginning of the 1980s, the leadership of the federation read these patterns and decided that the party's mass capacities could be at least in part resuscitated by more calculated leadership changes than had taken place earlier. This might have been too little, too late, but it does show how intervention from above remains an immensely powerful tool within the party.

A subsidiary theme of this chapter has been, however, that the powerful tools in the hands of party leaders are limited by the raw material with which they can work. Now that we have had a closer look at this raw material, we have a clearer appreciation of the PCI's dilemma. On one level, the party has tapped some of the most dynamic forces in recent Italian history and brought them directly into the inner sanctum of the organization. The "generation of 'sixty-eight" was present everywhere in the party, and it even dominated the apparatus numerically by the beginning of the 1980s. But, very much like the same generation outside the party, this was not a group with a common history or series of life experiences. And it certainly was not a group, from the party organization's point of view, that would be able to serve the same functions that the *rinnovatori* had served twenty years earlier. This may be healthy for the party's eventual adaptation to the changes that have been going on around it, but it is certain to be painful and disruptive as well.

# 8

# The Turinese Functionaries'
# Attitudes on the Party,
# Tactics, and Strategy

By the late 1970s, confusion, and even contradictory claims, abounded in references to the PCI. As we have seen, within the party itself, a high degree of heterogeneity was assumed to exist at all levels of the party, up to and including its middle-level leadership. But more recent and systematic studies have indicated a party cadre far more homogeneous in its views than many of the most commonly accepted generalizations of the past decade would lead us to expect.[1] At the very least, these contrasting claims require clarification. This chapter looks in depth at the small but crucial full-time cadre of the Turinese Federation of the PCI to begin to provide some of the detailed information that studies pitched at high levels of generalization are unable to furnish.

How heterogeneous is the federation apparatus? Do diverse background and recruitment patterns translate into different attitudes on organizational questions or on key matters of party tactics and strategy? Or, given the small number and selective recruitment of full-time party workers, do traditional mechanisms of socialization within the party create cadres who share many more attributes than one might otherwise expect?

This is no small distinction. A relatively homogeneous corps of functionaries would suggest a durable model of party organization, still able to generate operatives in its own image in spite of the troubles chronicled in this study. A more differentiated group, on the other hand, would further reinforce the notion that the underlying organizational model of the PCI is in profound crisis. After all, a party unable to hammer out a notable measure of consistency, even among its full-time functionaries, obviously will find its efficiency hampered in the outlying reaches of the organization, not to mention society at large.

## The Major Groupings in the Turinese Apparatus

To anticipate our findings, the attitudes of Turinese Communist functionaries, with a number of extremely important exceptions, do indeed show a good deal of diversity. We can easily speak of several distinct groupings within a relatively small apparatus of forty-odd members. To anticipate our findings even further, Chapter 7 has already pointed to three important variables, and systematic interviewing confirms that these are most often associated with marked differences in the functionaries' responses. The variables are the functionaries' class origins, the year they joined the PCI (i.e., political generation), and their location in the federation structure (zones vs. headquarters). We should avoid overstating our findings, and we certainly must be cautious about generalizing from Turin to the entire PCI.

Nonetheless, with the necessary caveats, it is possible to distinguish four distinct groups among the leadership:[2]

1. "Veteran" workers, especially in headquarters.
2. "The generation of 1968" in headquarters.
3. "The generation of 1968," mainly working class, in the zones.
4. "The non-working-class *compromesso* generation" in the zones.

*"Veteran" workers* were primarily found at the core of the top leadership of the federation at the end of the 1970s. They joined the PCI at the end of the 1950s or, at the very latest, in the early 1960s. Those in headquarters were full-time party workers by the mid-1960s, whereas those in the zones did not leave their jobs for full-time party work until the beginning of the 1970s. But they share strongly similar backgrounds, which are markedly different from all other groups in the federation.

In 1978, most of these veterans were in their late thirties (average age thirty-seven) and had gone only as far as junior high school, if that far. They were predominantly Piedmontese, and Catholic influences in their lives through adolescence were negligible. Nor did they report being drawn to the PCI primarily for intellectual or idealistic reasons, even though this was the most common reason cited by the entire apparatus.[3] In fact, all veterans except one said they had joined the party either as a result of strong family influence or as an "instinctive" reaction that grew out of labor or political conflict. These ex-workers, all men, had been to party schools more often, and they also had attended more lengthy courses in these schools than had their younger comrades. This reflects their lower formal educational achievement and also the PCI's historical recruitment practices. In the past, as we have seen, cadres were consciously chosen from those of more humble origin, which tended simultaneously to reinforce the party's class image and its ability to indoctrinate its new leaders more systematically. None of the working-class veterans in Turin had any political experience before joining the PCI, making this the only group in the federation with a completely unmediated political history.

Reflecting their greater age and party seniority, the veterans were not collectively marked by the struggles of 1968 to 1972. But two (of nine) respondents did mention that these events had played an important role in their political maturation and development (*formazione politica*).[4] Regardless of the content of the decisive events in their socialization, the veterans discussed these events in strongly personalized terms more than half the time. The following remark was typical: "A crucial moment for me came when I was made a functionary and had to face up to my own ignorance. It was a real trauma, and I was not sure I was capable of doing the job."

If the veterans have similar backgrounds, they frequently differ in their emphases with respect to what they like most about party work and what they feel are the most important qualities for leadership. Here, in many important respects, the veteran ex-workers in the zones resemble ex-workers in the zones more than they resemble veterans in headquarters. The zonal veteran leaders prefer the concrete aspects of party work, they stress the importance of face-to-face leadership skills, and they do not mention the ability to set priorities or achieve concrete results among the leadership qualities they cite most frequently. In contrast, the veterans in headquarters place more emphasis on results and less on interpersonal skills than any other group in the entire federation.[5] Here the conditioning effect of one's position in the organizational hierarchy on one's views is evident, although the relationship is by no means simple or mechanical. Veterans with an exceptional "common touch" may be consciously assigned to the zones; I heard of a few cases in which some veterans demanded a job in the zones after effectively languishing in headquarters.

*The "generation of 1968" in headquarters* includes all three women in the Turinese apparatus in the late 1970s. It differs notably from the veteran ex-workers both in terms of when the PCI was joined and in its much more privileged social background. Only two of the nine former workers of this generation were located in headquarters in 1978; only four of twelve nonworkers were in the zones. We could almost as easily divide the generation of 1968 by class as by location in the party apparatus.

A few factors make the functional division more interesting than the sociological one; perhaps most striking is the direct route the headquarters group followed into the Communist party (see Chapter 7). Only three of its ten members were involved in any political activity before joining the PCI or its Youth Federation (the FGCI), and none belonged to another party or to an extraparliamentary group; all were in the student movement exclusively. Direct entry into the PCI in turbulent times may account for the rapid rise of this cohort in the 1970s, for more than half of those in headquarters— compared to only a third in the zones—were already in the party by 1969. By gaining experience inside the party before the PCI's phase of maximum expansion (and need), they were ideally situated for rapid promotion a few years later. And while everyone who joined the party after the late 1960s mentioned ideological motives more often, this specific group easily had the highest frequency of all (70 percent). Catholicism, which figures in the backgrounds of more than half the generation of 1968 in the zones, is present in headquarters but to a notably lesser extent (three of ten cases).

A whopping four-fifths of these leaders mentioned the struggles of the late 1960s when they discussed why they joined the Communist party. But, like all leaders located in headquarters, when discussing political maturation, the discourse was framed in personalized terms: 54 percent of the veterans and 60 percent of the generation of 1968 in headquarters expressed themselves in this fashion. In contrast, only 27 percent of the zonal generation of 1968 fell into the same category.

Thus, while there are many broadly sociological factors that differentiate the headquarters group from the same cohort in the zones (80 percent of those in headquarters went beyond high school, for example), organizational considerations seemingly have the upper hand in shaping attitudes toward militance and party work. Emphasis on "face-to-face" skills was lower in this group than in the same generation in the zones (40 percent vs. 55 percent), and the generation of 1968 in headquarters was also the group that most stressed the importance of experience and specialization in one or more fields as a crucial requisite of leadership in the PCI (60 percent).

*The (mainly working-class) "generation of 1968" in the zones* is the "cleanest" of all our groups. Only two of the ex-workers in the apparatus who joined the PCI after 1968 were in headquarters at the time of this study. Some of those in the zones (four) joined the party at a relatively late date (between 1973 and 1975) for inclusion in the generation of 1968, but this reflects the richer political experience of the zonal cohort. In strictly chronological terms, the generation of 1968 averaged twenty-nine years of age regardless of location in the zones or headquarters.

As its working-class origins lead us to expect, this group's education is considerably below that of all others except the veteran ex-workers. Just over half ended their studies with a high school or equivalent diploma, and just over a quarter went beyond high school. Two respondents had a junior high school certificate or less. This is also by far the least "native" group in the federal apparatus: of eleven functionaries, only one was born in Turin, while three are native Piedmontese. Seven spent their first ten (or more) years outside Turin. Four are Southerners.

Other background factors also stand out, especially when compared to the same generation in headquarters. Catholicism figured in more than half these leaders' personal histories, making its incidence twice as great as among the same cohort in headquarters. Also twice as frequent were family-related or instinctive reasons for joining the PCI.[6] The 1968–1972 events figured prominently in the zonal group's political maturation, with nearly three-quarters mentioning that key period. However—in contrast to the same generation in headquarters—the hot period did not figure prominently in the motivations of the zonal group for joining the PCI. Finally, recall that a majority of both groups in headquarters tended to discuss their political maturation in personalized terms. For the ex-workers in the zones, this tendency was negligible, with less than one functionary in five personalizing his political development.

Perhaps the most interesting contrasts between the two parts of the generation of 1968 involve multiple experiences in their respective political backgrounds. Those in headquarters had a restricted political experience before joining the PCI; a minority of the group (30 percent) was limited exclusively to the student movement. In contrast, almost three-fourths of the zonal ex-workers had not only a pre-PCI experience, but they did so overwhelmingly in extraparliamentary groups. In fact, every ex-worker in the zones claimed either that the struggles of 1968 to 1972 represented decisive moments in their maturation or that they had been members of a group or party before joining the PCI; just under half could register both in their personal histories. In headquarters, 40 percent had experienced neither, and no one had done both.

This clustering effect becomes even more marked when we add yet another background factor—Catholicism—to the discussion. Previous militance, Catholicism, and the impact of the 1968–1972 struggles cluster dramatically among ex-workers in the zones, while they are broadly diffused, regardless of previous employment, in headquarters. In other words, in headquarters, one's background included either Catholicism or prior militance in the student movement or the struggles of the hot period as a decisive formative moment. In no case do even two of these factors join together. In the zones, all three factors figure in the past of four of eleven respondents, and another three reported at least two of them. Two-thirds of the workers of the generation of 1968 in the zones would appear to be strongly marked by several of the most important background factors associated with that period.[7] Figure 8.1 summarizes these differences.

What are the implications of these highly distinctive and interesting patterns? At the very least, they demonstrate the ways in which personal histories and party structures can interact and reinforce certain organizational tendencies. For instance, we have seen that 1968 to 1972 was not irrelevant in the experience of those in headquarters: 80 percent joined the party as a result of the events of this period. The period did, however, tend to wash out as a decisive formative experience because of later developments in the functionaries' careers. Secondly, although the two groups are of the same age and political generation, the unmediated political experiences of the functionaries in

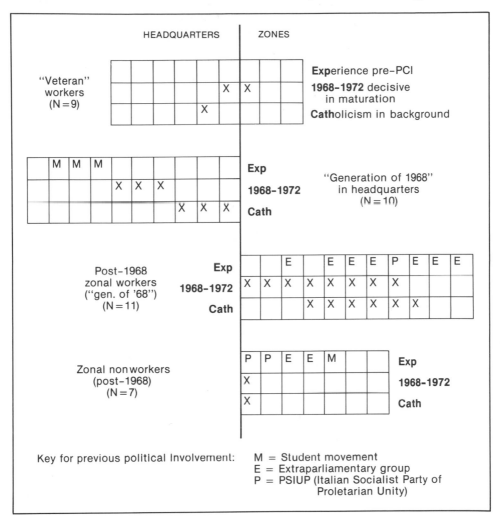

*Figure 8.1.* Clustering of Three Key Background Factors in the Turinese Apparatus (*Vertical Sections Represent Individuals*)

headquarters gave them several years' additional seniority in the PCI over their cohorts in the zones. Thus, the bulk of the zonal functionaries, precisely because of their previous political involvement, were late arrivals to the party. This relative lack of seniority as Communists would therefore place them on the lower rungs of the party hierarchy, in the zones rather than in headquarters.[8]

Do these distinctive experiential differences translate into attitudinal differences as well? Indeed they do. The ex-workers in the zones very rarely expressed themselves in highly personalized terms when discussing their own political development; only two of eleven did so, compared to 60 percent of their cohorts in headquarters. And an identically sharp difference marked the emphasis on specialization as a vital leadership quality. At the same time, nearly three-quarters of the zonal generation of 1968 stressed the importance of human warmth for good leadership, versus 40 percent in headquarters. A majority of each group liked "contact with the masses" most of all aspects of party work, but while nearly half of those in the zones also stressed how pleasurable they found the concrete side of party work, no one in headquarters mentioned this. Neither group mentioned "the ability to get results" as a leadership quality with anything like the two-of-three frequency of the veterans in headquarters. Finally, both groups put heavy emphasis on the purely personal costs of being a full-time party worker. For the generation of 1968 as a whole, more than half the functionaries voiced this complaint; 40 percent of those in headquarters and nearly 75 percent in the zones lamented the inroads their work made into their private lives. This is a notable difference within the generation, but the contrast is even greater when compared to the veterans, who scarcely voiced the personal complaint at all—or who did so with an attitude of resignation, not resentment.

The non-working-class *"compromesso generation"* in the zones represents the final distinctive grouping in the apparatus. Somewhat more heterogeneous than the other groups, this one can still be viewed collectively without doing excessive violence to the data. As Figure 8.1 shows, these functionaries had both extensive and varied political involvement before joining the PCI. Five of seven belonged to another party, an extraparliamentary group, or were at least active in the student movement. On the other hand, Catholicism and the 1968–1972 period were important factors in the background of only one person, and this sets the group off from the generation of 1968.

In large part, these differences may simply reflect the slightly lower age of this group, which averaged just under twenty-six years in 1978 versus twenty-nine for the generation of 1968. The youngest would have been too young to be much affected by either the peak period of the student movement or the slightly later hot autumn of 1969. And, in fact, five of seven pointed to decisive formative experiences in the mid-1970s: the 1973 Chilean coup, Berlinguer's enunciation of the historic compromise later that year, or the 1975–76 elections. This is why I think it appropriate to attach the *compromesso storico* label on this group, for these events are all inseparable from the emergence of the strategy. (The negligible impact of Catholicism, which we would expect to be much higher, may be nothing more than an artifact of a tiny subsample.)

Where these more recent arrivals do resemble the generation of 1968 in the zones is in the emphasis they put on face-to-face or interpersonal leadership qualities. They are similar to the entire generation of 1968 in the resentment they feel against the encroachment of party work into their private lives. A clear majority of the generation of the *compromesso storico* mentioned both elements.

Like all other groups with political experience before joining the PCI, this one also reported low family-linked or "instinctive" reasons for joining the party. Perhaps reflecting class origins as well, these factors were present with the lowest frequency in the entire federation (one respondent). Equally low was a personalized accounting of political maturation, which made these functionaries similar to others in the zones. Much more surprising was the very low—29 percent—ideological or idealistic set of reasons given for joining the party. This figure is especially striking given the high level of education; everyone in the compromise generation completed high school, and most went beyond secondary training. As a general rule, high education and idealistic motivations go hand in hand in the federation.[9] Yet for the generation of the *compromesso storico*, the primary motivation for joining was related as contact with and pressure from friends.

## The Functionaries' Vision of the Nature of the PCI

Most of this section will examine the functionaries' responses to open-ended questions that bear directly on the structure and operations of the PCI as an organization. The bulk of these questions were highly topical during the period of field research. They were the source of open and often lively debate within the party. None had been definitively resolved at the time. How the apparatus as a whole reacts to these questions will inform us of the extent to which a consensus exists on the nature of the party and some of its most hotly contested organizational dilemmas. But we will also be concerned with the variation within responses, and especially with whether we can find patterns that characterize the views of the various groups in the apparatus.

### *The PCI's Class Identity*

A party organization with working-class traditions as strong as those in Turin would undoubtedly be sensitive to the degree of sociological fit between cadres and the mass membership in the best of times. But with a lengthy debate in the national party press on the subject stimulated by no less a figure than the brother of the secretary general, the topic had become central by the end of 1977. It was discussed in meetings at all levels of the federation; some of the top Turinese leaders contributed to the national debate.[10] I asked each functionary whether *terziarizzazione*, the shorthand expression for the displacement of working-class cadres by those of white-collar or middle-class origin, represented a threat to the PCI's identity. I also asked what they thought accounted for the phenomenon.

Two-thirds of the apparatus did see *terziarizzazione* as a problem, but most immediately qualified their remarks with respect to their own federation. Given the extensively proletarian nature of the membership in Turin, most functionaries were far more worried about the national party or the very highest reaches of the federation; they did not feel that the local organization was seriously threatened.

Among those who did see a problem for the PCI as a whole, what were perceived as the major underlying causes of the decline of working-class cadres? The most common explanation offered dwelled on social and political factors. Just over a third of the functionaries attributed the drop to changes in society such as the diminished weight of the traditional proletariat and the increase of nonworkers with high levels of skill and education who were willing to be Communist militants. Many of these respondents mentioned that the PCI's strategy and policies were more broadly focused and complex than in the past, which also accounted for the party's increased attractiveness to nonworkers. The total rises to just over half the entire apparatus when we add another half-dozen functionaries—all from the zones—whose responses, less "sociological," underlined the benefits that the party now enjoyed because of a more heterogeneous cadre.

In many instances, functionaries used their responses to this question to address numerous problems related to broader PCI policies rather than the details of *terziarizzazione*. To take one example raised earlier in this study, less than a third of the apparatus brought up the issue of courses to train working-class, or any other, cadres. If we recall the emphasis formal training was receiving everywhere at the time, this is a very low rate indeed.[11] Moreover, the limited number of leaders who spoke positively about party courses tended to be located almost exclusively in headquarters (six of eight). Zonal functionaries were much more skeptical of the rather formalistic proposals that enjoyed a measure of support in headquarters. This may help explain why, as we found in Chapter 6, the courses encountered very limited success in the periphery of the federation.

Another emphasis that failed to materialize in the functionaries' responses was workerism. In light of Turin's traditions, one might have expected especially those functionaries with working-class backgrounds to lament the loss of the party's class character, perhaps nostalgically. But precisely the opposite was the case. A quarter of the respondents, all but one of whom were themselves former workers, actually put the primary blame for fewer working-class cadres on workerism and double militancy. As documented in Chapter 6, these related phenomena tend to limit drastically the number of cadres available to the party in the factories. A number of other functionaries also went out of their way to stress that in any discussion of the party's class character, *operaismo* and the mythologization of the working class were to be avoided at all costs, since this often generated simplistic analyses and "solutions" to complex problems.

If the above suggests a tendency for ex-workers, especially in the zones, to frame their analysis in party-organizational terms, the impression is reinforced by another point made by many leaders. A quarter of the apparatus, but fully half the veteran component, framed the issue of diminished working-class cadres in terms of low rank-and-file participation in the PCI. That is, cadres, or active members, are seen as the products of positive experiences at the grass roots of the party. In this view, it is the PCI's lack of openness and its centralization of decision making in headquarters that has effectively degraded the lower levels of the party organization. And this, in turn, undercuts its own expressed goal of recruiting and promoting activists from the working class. Where, if not in the lived experience of the rank and file, would one expect workers to obtain the experience and skills necessary to become cadres? This response is interesting not only because it is strongly associated with the most experienced part of the apparatus but also because it anticipates by two years the federation's commitment to reinforce the zones and sections in 1980.

A special category of response also deserves our attention. It was not expressed by many functionaries (six in all), but in this instance respondents used a question on the party's class composition to raise more general criticisms of the PCI's policies in the late 1970s. One ranking leader began with a reference to grass-roots participation but rapidly turned to the general tendency—"in existence far too long"—for the party line to be dictated from on high with no real consultation of the lower levels of the party. Especially aggravating was the claim that accompanied these *diktats:* nothing else is possible under present circumstances. "That is not true!" she fumed. Clearly, the point here was no longer the PCI's composition or class identification, or even its centralism.

Others made the same point in strikingly similar fashion. When queried about the implications of the composition of cadres for the party's identity, they responded that an identity problem indeed existed, but it had nothing to do with sociology. For them, the PCI's failure to clarify what it stood for and where it was going was seen as the real problem; a vague line and the lack of an overall project or proposal was the real source of the identity crisis. These people were scattered widely in the federation, although three of six were veteran workers.

## The PCI and Young People

> My generation had Vietnam and that really counted for a lot. Today, what do you have? Eritrea? The Horn of Africa?
>
> A zonal functionary

The PCI has had a tumultuous relationship with at least the most politicized young people in Italy since the late 1960s. By the mid-1970s, the situation had improved considerably, and all authoritative observers agree that the great jumps in the Communist vote in 1975 and 1976 can be explained in large measure by the disproportionately high youth vote. [12] But problems arose almost as soon as the PCI gave its support to DC-led governments; by early 1977, as we saw in Chapter 3, bloody clashes with the police had occurred on the campuses and in the city streets of Rome and Bologna.

While signs of mass disaffection would not be registered until the Radicals' triumph in the 1979 general elections, there were indications of deep trouble during the main period of interviewing in 1978. Many functionaries were upset by these developments. Their responses to the open-ended question asking why the PCI had so much trouble attracting young people fell into four major categories with very different emphases. The functionaries' responses are found in Table 8.1.

The difference between responses 1 and 2 ought to be clear. Both are critical of the PCI, and some functionaries voiced both complaints. But the first focuses on the party's organizational shortcomings, while the second addresses its goals, strategies, or ideals. And these two responses, in turn, are distinct from the others in the assignment of primary responsibility to the party, as opposed to external social and political forces. This example of a young functionary's summary of his analysis illustrates why his answer was classified under response 2, although his commentary contained numerous references to a general societal crisis: "They don't see a broader set of references in our appeal because, in truth, we don't have any. In the name of what ideals can I call young people to struggle alongside us?" In contrast, other references would frequently be phrased more passively, in terms such as, "they see us as too bureaucratic." Those references avoided almost entirely any penetrating critique of the PCI.

Emphases among the functionaries varied a good deal across the different response

*Table 8.1.* Turinese Functionaries' Evaluation of Why the PCI Has Difficulties with Younger People, 1978

| | |
|---|---|
| 1. The PCI (or FGCI) is too closed, moralistic, and bureaucratic toward youth, and the world outside the party in general. | (45%) |
| 2. The PCI has no truly alternative proposal to make to young people; its ideals are unclear. | (32%) |
| 3. Today's young people are different; the party's line and/or goals are hard for them to accept. Moreover, little has been obtained to date by the party that would impress them. | (29%) |
| 4. There is a general crisis in society that has marginalized youth and left the PCI unprepared. | (24%) |
| 5. Although this is a serious problem, one cannot expect the PCI to "cover" all issues in society. | (5%) |

N = 38. Total is greater than 100% because of multiple answers.

patterns. The party's lack of ideals or a project was mentioned by just under half of all nonworkers but by only a quarter of the ex-workers in the apparatus. The critique of bureaucratism, on the other hand, was voiced by more than half the generation of 1968 in headquarters but less than a third of all others. The youngest former workers put the party's organizational forms and mentality at the center of their explanations in overwhelming (two-thirds) proportions. In each of these distributions, we can readily see how earlier experiences, as well as the antibureaucratic and idealistic themes of the late 1960s and early 1970s, carried into the apparatus.

We can also see something of the opposite tendency among the veterans of the federation, and especially among those in headquarters. Only one of the latter explicitly criticized the party's closedness to youth, for instance. Since all but one of the veterans were formerly workers, this tendency to be less critical of the party deserves further exploration—since we have just seen how likely veterans are to strongly criticize the PCI on the issue of working-class cadres. These differences suggest that the veterans are not simply more "patriotic" than their juniors. Instead, they appear to be more reticent to criticize the party as the subject falls outside the PCI's traditional constituencies. This would also explain why the younger leaders—especially those who took part in struggles in which young people were protagonists—are so different from their older comrades on this issue. A deeply critical attitude toward the party seems to be born out of frustration: apparently, the party first must be identified as having muffed its opportunities with a "natural" constituency. The degree of frustration and anger will then vary considerably depending on the respondents' backgrounds and experiences.

## Party Doctrine, Democratic Centralism, and Internal Democracy

By the late 1970s, the long-postponed issue of the PCI's official commitment to Marxism-Leninism had to be confronted directly. The party had gradually abandoned rigid dogmatic formulations through the 1960s. But once it put in a serious claim to govern Italy, even in coalition, it obviously would have to respond less evasively than in the past to questions concerning precisely what it meant by democracy and pluralism. And this challenge was not long in coming.[13]

The contingent nature of the debate on Marxism-Leninism is clear from even a cursory review of the way the issue eventually was posed. For decades, two inconsistent articles had coexisted in various versions of the PCI Statute. One (article 2) opened party membership to all who accepted the PCI's political program, stating that philosophical convictions or religious beliefs were irrelevant. But the other (article 5), which spelled out militants' duties, included a reference to learning and promulgating Marxism-Leninism as the doctrine of the entire party. In the late 1970s, finally, Lucio Lombardo Radice, a well-known maverick Communist intellectual, suggested that references to Marxism-Leninism simply be eliminated, since the term had in any case long since ceased to figure in official documents or acts.[14]

Initially, the proposal was received in chilly fashion by the top party leadership. At a national Festival of *l'Unità*, Enrico Berlinguer essentially ridiculed the idea of abandoning the PCI's ideological patrimony. Yet a month later, Berlinguer emphasized the party's laical and agnostic character in an open letter to the bishop of Ivrea. The content of the letter differed little from Lombardo Radice's proposal.[15] Whatever the motives for this abrupt turnaround, the matter was left temporarily unclear. It subsequently became apparent that the 1979 Fifteenth Congress would in fact amend article 5 and replace all references to a fixed party doctrine with a more generic reference to the very broad philosophical influences that inspired the PCI.[16]

The situation was, then, fluid in 1977–78. In the interviewing, I attempted to determine how attached the functionaries were to Leninism. But I was even more interested to see if they saw the need for *any* underlying theory or analysis to guide the PCI. The proposed (and later realized) changes in the Statute left open the possibility of a party so "agnostic" that any common set of ideas on which a program could rest might be obscured. At the same time, to probe further the functionaries' views of the party and to discover their feelings about democratic centralism, I decided to raise the latter as a follow-up. Since the PCI continued to hold very strongly to democratic centralism through the 1970s, I felt it important to determine on what grounds my interviewees thought strict obedience to orders and the banning of organized factions could be justified.[17]

Finally, in a lengthy questionnaire that followed the open-ended interviews, the functionaries were presented with a series of forced-choice items. Those most relevant to this discussion deal with attitudes on collective and individual tolerance and behavior. I introduced these items to complement the discussion on democratic centralism. To most of us, the term has deeply antidemocratic connotations, but it has, in fact, a wide variety of meanings within the party, as the PCI's lively internal debates attest. Rather than jump to hasty conclusions about how open or closed a respondent's attitudes are on the basis of a reaction to this single, charged term, it is much more sensible to examine at least a range of responses.

The functionaries' answers to the question about article 5 were among the richest encountered in the course of all the interviewing carried out for this study.

Eight respondents went out of their way to mention Lenin or Leninism in a highly positive way, leaving no doubt that they wanted the party to retain its tradition. But only four of the eight spoke positively or forcefully with regard to Marxism-Leninism, with all its resonances of the Third International. Here is the most critical reaction, but it is quite representative in content:

> I am not at all in agreement with certain things being discussed in the party right now. You should go ask Lombardo Radice about this. Of course, Marxism-Leninism is not a rigid and dogmatic thing. . . . It is a way of analyzing reality, and you don't do that with a manual. But to say the party should not have an ideology, a vision of the world, a *Weltanschauung*, does not convince me at all. What will we be, eclectics?

Only two of the eight who felt strongly about Leninism were veterans; both also wanted to maintain Marxism-Leninism. The other six were spread throughout the federation.

At the other extreme were six leaders who could not be shaken from their insistence on the PCI becoming truly laical and open. Not surprisingly, they were the group most willing to acknowledge inconsistencies in the very notion of democratic centralism. As an ex-worker in the zones put it, "This is a real problem, for [democratic centralism] works, but it is tied to the kind of party we want to leave behind us." A veteran in headquarters was even more blunt. He dismissed terminological disputes as irrelevant and said the real issue was the PCI's "profound inability, as it is currently structured and confronts problems, to understand far too many real processes." For *this* reason, change was essential. He then continued:

> The party must be able to open itself up and have a true debate [*contradditorio*] internally. This is where the real issue lies. If we are going to reach the masses without

clichés which have clichés as responses, it means we have to have a truly qualitative change in the nature of our internal discussion and democracy. . . . Democratic
centralism has to change, it has to move away from being a forced, phony unity,
which of course is no unity at all. We have very broad disagreement on many central
problems, and we need to resolve them. The question is, how?

Three other leaders—all members of the generation of 1968 in headquarters—put equal
stress on the need for the party to be open and laical but held very strongly to democratic
centralism at the same time. They saw no contradiction in their position, for they defined
democratic centralism, which they acknowledged must be made more democratic, strictly
as a method. They were not alone in defining the practice in more or less pragmatic
terms (three others joined them on this point), but they were the only ones to do so from
this apparently contradictory stance. It is probably accurate to define such a position
as "pragmatically centralist," while the more rigorous attitude discussed above is best
summarized as "consistently laical."

The cases analyzed thus far account for just under half the apparatus. How does the
majority view the same issue? The answer is, with near uniformity. On the central point
of the PCI's basic identity and underlying theory, most attitudes were quite similar to
that of a young ex-worker, who said:

I think we have to be ready to reconsider *everything* [e.g., Leninism included], but at
the same time I strongly believe that we *must* retain the principle of social conflict,
of class conflict. I am not prepared to put this aside, for otherwise you lose your
class analysis and those qualities that makes you a working-class and Marxist party.
That would blunt us and lead to a situation where all sorts of other tendencies would
prevail in the party. . . . If we lack this quality, we lose our whole political project
[*proposta*] and end up with positivism or determinism.

It is apparent that this position is much closer to that which stresses Leninism (even
Marxism-Leninism) than it is to the more laical conception of the party. Belief that
the PCI needs a guiding theory—many functionaries used the term *rigore ideale*—
therefore binds together three-quarters of the Turinese apparatus.[18] What divides them
in the theoretical or ideological sense is whether they want to maintain, ignore, or even
abandon Leninism altogether.

A similar spread is found in attitudes on democratic centralism. Half a dozen "consistently laical" respondents have very strong doubts about the adequacy of the concept.
Another six (including the remaining three "laical" functionaries) defend democratic
centralism on pragmatic grounds alone. This leaves two-thirds of the apparatus who
defend the concept as integral to the PCI's nature—but five of these leaders are as
blistering in their attacks on ritualism and stultifying practices as are the severest laical
critics.

How do the patterns break down with reference to the major groups in the federation?
The veterans, not surprisingly, include the fewest laical attitudes on the party and are
least pragmatic on the issue of centralism. The generation of 1968 is impressive for the
very high incidence of laical views of the party. Roughly a third of the generation can
be called laical. Perhaps even more striking is the fact that five of the six consistently
laical leaders of the federation are found among the generation of 1968 in the zones.
That is, nearly half the younger ex-workers in the zones, and only one other person
in the entire federation, can be classified as consistently laical. This is, at least on the

surface, unexpected, for the young workers' responses on the issue of *terziarizzazione* and related matters had a strong class content.

The highly critical attitude toward democratic centralism expressed by former workers in the zones (40 percent) and by all younger zonal functionaries regardless of previous employment (41 percent) makes that particular view less astonishing, especially in light of the extensive resentment against headquarters' high-handed practices that we have found throughout this study. The desire to see the PCI maintain a strong sense of class identification obviously does not require that this identification go hand-in-hand with an official party doctrine.

What are the likely causes of this undoubtedly complex vision of the party? One highly interesting finding, all the more suggestive because it confirms more recent work based on a very large sample of PCI militants, shows a strong relationship between laicism and previous militance in a party or group other than the PCI.[19] In fact, five of the six "consistently laical" functionaries in the federation had this previous experience. At the very least, this suggests that one cannot easily generalize, as party leaders did in the 1970s, about cadres with previous experience "arriving already inoculated" against what the PCI considered to be extremist views.[20] Here the assumption was that (unpleasant) prior experiences with other groups would make such cadres less critical of—and even apologetic toward—the Communist party. Matters are clearly not so straightforward or so intrinsically favorable to the PCI. Table 8.2 summarizes the distribution of the apparatus into the categories we have been discussing.

The relatively small number (only six functionaries, just under a fifth of the total) of "pragmatic" defenders of democratic centralism should not be misinterpreted. Nearly everyone in the apparatus defended the efficacy of centralism, as we have seen. Many brought up the negative example of the costs of organized factionalism in the Socialist and Christian Democrat parties. But since everyone else *also* mentioned that centralism requires an underlying ideology or theory, with many denouncing nonideological centralism as pragmatism or empiricism, I feel the "ideologically rigorous" classification is justified.

*Table 8.2.* Turinese Apparatus's Positions on Party Ideology and Democratic Centralism

| | Need a Core Ideology | | Laical Party |
|---|---|---|---|
| Democratic Centralism Theoretically necessary (N = 21) | Ideological rigor (N = 21) | | Inconsistent (N = 0) |
| Pragmatically, instrumentally necessary (N = 6) | Ideological "realist" (N = 2) | Borderline (N = 1) | Pragmatic centralist (N = 3) |
| Critical, wants "open" party (N = 11) | Ideological pluralist (N = 5) | | Consistently laical (N = 6) |
| Total = 38 | (N = 28) | (N = 1) | (N = 9) |

A number of interesting questions arise from these findings. How, for example, do such broad positions fare when the functionaries are asked to pronounce themselves on much more narrowly defined principles? As is well known, people can be generically in favor of openness but much less tolerant of specific positions with which they strongly disagree. While this group is considerably more sophisticated than the mass publics on whom most of the tolerance literature is focused, these are immensely complex issues, with deeply charged implications for Communists. It would be highly surprising if the functionaries' reactions fell neatly and cleanly into predictable categories.

Two forced-choice responses from the questionnaire bear on these questions. The assertions, with which functionaries were asked to agree or disagree, were as follows:

> A group that tolerates differences of opinion among its members that are too great cannot survive for very long.

> The worst possible behavior is to attack publicly those who believe in the same ideals as oneself.

These items are specifically focused; although neither mentions "the party," it is difficult to imagine a Communist pondering a response without thinking of the PCI. These are not, in sum, indices of tolerance in the abstract, which the Turinese apparatus supports with near unanimity.[21]

Both questions generated sharply divided responses among the functionaries. The question on group survival saw our respondents split neatly in half: 49 percent agreed that great differences of opinion spell disaster for a group, while 46 percent disagreed (the remaining two functionaries were unable to choose). As Table 8.3 reveals, those in headquarters were far more sanguine than their comrades in the zones; they were, in fact, twice as dubious about the harmful effects of differences of opinion. When broken down even further, the determining groups turn out to be the ex-workers. Of the veterans in headquarters, only one in six agreed with the assertion. Of the younger ex-workers in the zones, a very significant 69 percent agreed.

The issue of public attacks on comrades or like-minded people also divided the apparatus, but in this instance the level of tolerance was lower than for the first assertion. Here the breakdown was 65 percent who agreed that public attacks are a terrible thing and 35 percent who disagreed. There is a notable degree of consistency in the responses. Fifteen functionaries agreed with both assertions, and ten disagreed with both.[22] The consistent responses account for just over two-thirds of the apparatus, with 41 percent "closed" and 27 percent "open."

Who are these people? When we divide the apparatus by class, we find a fairly clear polarization. Ex-workers fall mainly into the most closed position: nearly half

*Table 8.3.* Responses of Turinese Apparatus to the Assertion "A Group Cannot Survive If It Tolerates Excessive Differences of Opinion Among Its Members"

|  | Federation | | Headquarters | | Zones | |
|---|---|---|---|---|---|---|
| Agree | 18 | (49%) | 5 | (31%) | 13 | (62%) |
| Disagree | 17 | (46) | 10 | (63) | 7 | (33) |
| Unable to choose | 2 | (5) | 1 | (6) | 1 | (5) |
| Totals | 37 | (100) | 16 | (100) | 21 | (100) |

(45 percent) are located there. The nonworkers emerge with the highest incidence of consistent responses—38 percent are consistently closed, and a very high 44 percent are open. The *only* workers (three) who are consistently open are veterans located in headquarters. No ex-worker who joined the PCI after 1968 was consistently open.

In view of these findings, and the fact that there were also strong class associations with the functionaries' general outlook on the PCI, we should expect rather surprising relationships between general conceptions of the party and tolerance as measured by these two items. In fact, only the very small (five people) group of ideological pluralists has a majority of members who are consistently open on both questions. Perhaps most surprisingly, the leaders who were most laical in their outlook are far from open or tolerant where specific issues are concerned: only two of nine are consistently open, while a third are consistently closed. The reason for this showing is the very high agreement among the "laical Communists" that it is a very bad thing to attack those who share one's ideals. In spite of their resistance to the idea of an official party theory or philosophy, seven of the nine agreed with that assertion. The "rigorous ideologues" divided in roughly the same proportions as the entire apparatus, with a quarter consistently open and 40 percent (including the bulk of the Leninists and Marxist-Leninists) closed.

## The Functionaries' Attitudes on PCI Strategy

### *The Historic Compromise and the Nature of the DC*

By the end of the 1970s, nowhere were the PCI's strategic problems more evident than with regard to the Christian Democratic party. Long after the national unity policy had ceased to bear fruit, rapprochement with the DC had nonetheless been pursued. This generated considerable tension within PCI organizations throughout Italy, although the steadfastness of Berlinguer's commitment apparently did serve to keep numerous middle-level leaders from seriously questioning the PCI's overall strategy.[23] As we will see, however, strong reservations and open doubts existed in the Turinese apparatus before the unity policy and the *compromesso* were abandoned late in 1980.

In fact, this part of the interviewing involved some of the strongest probing of the functionaries' attitudes in all of the research. When a respondent stressed the need for unity with the DC, every effort was made to see how firmly committed he or she was to this position. Was the DC *really* likely to change, or to allow the implementation of the reforms the PCI insisted upon? Did the respondent seriously believe that long-term collaboration with the Christian Democrats was possible or that it would profoundly alter Italian politics and society?

Just over a third of the Turinese apparatus strongly supported the policy of national unity with the DC;[24] a group of equal size was more cautious and qualified. A few of these "qualified supporters" found the PCI's analysis of the DC, and indeed of the entire political scene, to be utterly without merit, and said as much. The most typical qualified response expressed some doubt about the DC and emphasized that the PCI had to be far more aggressive toward the ruling party. Binding all these responses together, however, was the belief that long-term collaboration with the DC was necessary in view of the distribution of power in the country for the foreseeable future.

Of the remaining members of the apparatus, a fifth expressed no faith at all in the DC and went so far as to argue that the ruling party had to be split apart, or that another strategy (generally, unity of the left) had to be adopted by the PCI. This proportion rises to just under a third of the apparatus if we include three wavering leaders who could not quite bring themselves to call for abandoning the policy of national unity but who could also find nothing positive to say about the DC and its capacity for change.

These figures testify to the PCI's problems, while underscoring the party's strategic dilemma. Just over 30 percent of the apparatus disagreed with the very underpinnings of the *compromesso*, but (1) they remained a minority, albeit a large one, and, most importantly, (2) there was no widely shared alternative to the prevailing strategy. Most critics probably agreed with the view expressed by several leaders in headquarters: the historic compromise and the period of national unity had been *tactically* necessary to legitimize the PCI in the national political arena. But while many of these leaders were quite prepared to project a period when a (smaller) DC would be relegated to the opposition, some felt that truly radical change could never be brought about if Christian Democracy remained intact. As one leader put it, "You don't shift the DC [to the left]; you disintegrate it, you break its system of power and hence its social bloc." Still others were contemptuously dismissive of Italy's dominant party but did not seem overly concerned about the form eventual alternatives would take. "This is the party of the bosses, and of course we cannot really expect to make it into something different," was how one zonal leader put it.

The veterans in headquarters, along with the generation of the *compromesso*, were most positive in their assessment of the DC and in their projections for the future of the *compromesso storico*. The generation of 1968 in headquarters was polarized: nearly half (44 percent) were very negative, but a third were favorably inclined toward the DC.

## *Views on the Party's Mobilizational versus Institutional Role*

Earlier (Chapters 3 and 4), we saw how difficult life became in local party organizations when the PCI took over many local governments following its smashing success in 1975. With so much discussion about these problems in Turin, the issue called for further exploration. Thus, the functionaries were asked what the appropriate relationship should be between local party organizations and local governments in which the PCI played a generally dominant role. In light of Turin's traditions and the emphasis put on mass mobilization in intraparty debates, the functionaries were pressed to express an opinion on whether it was feasible—or desirable—to expect local Communist organizations to mobilize public opinion, if the need arose, against local governments in which the PCI was prominent. This extreme measure had been suggested in some debates as one way to "keep the PCI honest" and to mount pressure on its otherwise recalcitrant coalition partners, as well as to keep local party organizations from becoming totally subservient to red municipal governments.[25]

Most respondents, not surprisingly, indicated an acute awareness of the PCI's difficulties, especially in the city of Turin, where the party's identification as a mobilizer of dissent against sitting governments was strongest. In the rest of the federation, confirming what we saw in earlier chapters, the chief concerns involved efforts to revitalize local party sections, which had lost both personnel and the ability to adopt autonomous political initiatives when the PCI moved into the *giunte* of the province. In all responses, functionaries were acutely aware of the PCI's loss of identity as a mobilizing force and spokesman for mass participation.

Just under a third of the apparatus (31 percent) felt so strongly about the need for the

PCI to maintain—or regain—its identity as a party of mass mobilization that they were willing to countenance, "as a limiting case," Communist organizations protesting against local left-wing coalitions.[26] Some of the fiercest criticisms came from ex-workers in the zones, that is, the generation of 1968. The following will give some of the flavor of the more forceful critics, who had little patience for the "Do not disturb the driver" attitude they felt many Communist politicians adopted once they took over positions of power.

> You can't limit yourself to supporting our local governments and their mediations or else, god damn it, you become a social-democratic party. The *giunta has* to mediate because it has many different forces within it, but the party can't do that stuff. . . . Mediations at all levels are not socialism. And mobilization *helps*, it doesn't disturb, the driver.

Interestingly, and in spite of the stronger criticism in the zones, there was not a significant difference between headquarters and zonal functionaries in the degree to which they expressed an explicit willingness to criticize left-wing governments (25 percent vs. 33 percent).

On the other extreme, we find just under a quarter of the apparatus unwilling even to consider the idea of public conflict between local PCI organizations and *giunte*. A veteran in one of the zones in the capital expressed the most common view quite succinctly:

> You have to be joking: the entire Party is responsible for what the *giunta* does. Some people, even in the apparatus, want to protest against our *giunte*, but this is madness, not only for inside the Party but also for what the people outside, the citizens, will think.

Those who expressed similar views did not, as is evident, argue that "the administrative party" should dictate to the PCI rank and file. They, along with those whose responses fell into neither extreme category, felt that there had to be much closer collaboration and consultation between Communists in public office and their comrades at the grass roots. But, sensitive to the requirements of officeholding and coalition politics, these leaders drew the line at reverting to forms of behavior that had prevailed when the PCI was in the opposition. The more critical functionaries were not ignorant of these constraints, but they apparently put a much higher value on the party's traditional mobilizational identity.

It is hardly surprising that the functionaries' attitudes have not furnished convincing solutions to a dilemma that is rooted in the PCI's changing role in society. What is at least partially surprising is the negligible difference we find between attitudes in headquarters and the zones, and also between veterans and newcomers to the apparatus. And on this crucial issue we have found a division of opinion within the apparatus strong enough to dispel simplistic notions of salaried party bureaucrats keeping some sort of lid on a restive rank and file.

## A More General View of Institutions and Change

To conclude discussion of the functionaries' views on the political and institutional aspects of party strategy, it is worth reporting the responses registered to one of the forced-choice questionnaire items. The assertion was:

> If this country had a bureaucracy that carried out the laws that are already on the books, a large part of the necessary changes would come automatically.

This is a provocative statement for an Italian Communist to ponder. Someone committed to radical change—particularly a Marxist—would have at least an ambivalent attitude toward "bourgeois state institutions," especially the bureaucracy. But in the case of Italy, the PCI has held, since the founding of the postwar Republic, that the constitution provided much more than a simple bourgeois framework—thanks to the Communists' vital contribution in framing the basic law of the land in the late 1940s. Furthermore, the party has also taken considerable pride in the progressive legislation that has gotten onto the books in the postwar period, claiming, justifiably, that its contribution to the record has been decisive.[27] Thus, an assertion which in other countries might tap a straightforward radical-versus-reformist dimension becomes much more ambiguous in the Italian case. Still, this statement is the antithesis of any conception of change that relies on mass mobilization or extrainstitutional means.

It is notable that nearly a third of the Turinese apparatus (31 percent) agreed with the assertion. This figure is all the more interesting since we can compare the reactions of PCI functionaries to the same exact statement, but at an earlier date. In interviews in seven PCI federations carried out prior to the historic compromise's enunciation in 1973, only 11 percent of functionaries expressed agreement.[28] Moreover, there is no appreciable generational differentiation on this item: 27 percent of those who joined the PCI before 1969 agreed, as opposed to 33 percent of those who came to the party in 1969 or later.

It therefore appears that the party's strongly "institutional" line, dominant through the 1970s, helped implant this view in a sizable minority of the Turinese apparatus. But it is only a minority: two-thirds of the functionaries continued to believe that strictly institutional applications of existing legislation, however progressive, would *not* bring any significant number of necessary changes to Italian society. And since these responses were generated before the Communists' return to the opposition in 1979, one might expect even less support for such assertions in the future.

## Alliances: The Social Dimension

Additional evidence regarding the difficulties in the PCI's general strategy comes from responses to a pair of assertions relating to the party's social, as opposed to political, analysis. When queried about whether the petite bourgeoisie could be trusted in the event of a historical crisis, fully half the apparatus said no, while another 14 percent was unable to choose between a simple affirmative or negative answer. Put somewhat differently, just one-third of the Turinese apparatus felt that the petite bourgeoisie could be counted on in the crunch. When the same question was put to functionaries before the epoch of the historic compromise, roughly twice as many respondents gave affirmative answers.[29] Although we have seen that crude workerism is by no means a rampant attitude in the apparatus, it is likely that Turinese traditions, which include a historically weak and insignificant middle class, have made themselves felt on this particular item.

The next assertion found majoritarian support in the apparatus, but it was a skimpy majority indeed (53 percent), and it again found a relatively large number of functionaries (11 percent) unable to provide an unqualified answer. The item on the questionnaire appeared as follows:

> If tension arises between a given reform and the maintenance of the broadest possible alliance front, the alliance should be favored.

This statement is actually a direct citation from Enrico Berlinguer, made a number of years earlier.[30] Of course, anyone who closely observed the PCI's behavior in the post-1973 period, and particularly in the period of 1975 to 1978, would recognize that, regardless of official pronouncements, this was in fact a highly accurate summary of the party's actions. For these very reasons, the disagreement of over a third of the full-time functionaries with the assertion is another interesting reflection of the party's difficulties in the late 1970s. And few of its dilemmas can be captured so succinctly in a single statement. After all, if there was a single reason for the abandonment of the unity policy, it was precisely that the party had begun to see its own social bloc begin to crumble because it had failed to translate promises into practice. Favoring *political* alliances at the expense of reforms had undermined the PCI's own *social* alliances.

Who are the functionaries in Turin who were most skeptical of the party's policy before it was actually abandoned? Interestingly, the only group in the federal leadership that could not muster a clear majority in favor of maintaining alliances at all costs were the veteran workers; only 40 percent of them agreed with the statement. But importantly, it is the veterans in the zones who are highly negative. Those in headquarters favor alliances over reforms in the extreme hypothetical case. The generation of 1968 in headquarters, which has frequently figured among the most critical and skeptical where various aspects of the *compromesso storico* are concerned, turns out in this instance to be most supportive of the assertion (two-thirds favored alliances over reforms).

We also find, as Table 8.4 shows, a fairly diffuse division of attitudes on the individual items we have been discussing. One can, with some reason, define distrust of the petite bourgeoisie and the favoring of reforms over alliances as consistently critical of the prevailing PCI orthodoxy in 1978. And one can similarly define trust of the petite bourgeoisie and a proalliance position as more orthodox. The table shows that not even half the apparatus, even on these two relatively straightforward items, can be called consistent in either an orthodox or a critical sense. And when we attempt to search among those who are more consistently orthodox or critical (in this extremely limited sense), the numbers rapidly become so small as to make any effort at generalization appear quite forced. The only group with a notably consistent pattern is the younger ex-workers, the generation of 1968 in the zones, which tends to be less critical than any other grouping in the federation.

Once again, as was the case with the PCI's strategy of political alliances, widespread dissatisfaction could be seen even in the innermost reaches of the party organization, but neither the lines of cleavage nor the alternative proposals fell into neat categories. Most significantly of all, in terms of implications for internal party unity, there was a relatively low degree of overlap with regard to critical attitudes.

*Table 8.4.* Relationship between Trust of Petite Bourgeoisie and Favoring Alliances vs. Reforms: Turinese Apparatus, 1978

|  | Can Trust Petite Bourgeoisie | Cannot Trust Petite Bourgeoisie | Unsure |  |
|---|---|---|---|---|
| Favor alliances | 8 | 10 | 1 | (19) |
| Favor reforms | 5 | 7 | 1 | (13) |
| Unsure | — | 1 | 3 | (4) |
| Totals | 13 | 18 | 5 | (36) |

## *The International Dimension of PCI Strategy: Views on the USSR*

> The biggest international question for us is to find a way to distinguish ourselves from the traditional European social democracies. I find a lot to admire in what they have accomplished, and I find them a lot more *simpatici* than Catholics, to be sure. But they remain what they are, and Eurocommunism either distinguishes itself here, or it fails.
>
> Turinese functionary (1978)

The PCI has walked a tightrope in its attitude toward the Soviet Union since 1956. Following the 1968 invasion of Czechoslovakia, Italian Communists increasingly stepped up the frequency—and the profundity—of their criticism of the USSR. By the late 1970s, under pressure from others, but aware that their own credibility and consistency demanded no less, the top leadership's pronouncements on the nature of the USSR were marked by two consistent elements. The first was the articulation of a pluralistic, democratic socialism as more suited to the West, explicitly rejecting the repressive, party-centered model found in the East. The second was the increased tendency to speak of the deep flaws in Russian society as logical outcomes of the way the Soviets had conquered and consolidated power. In other words, the PCI gradually abandoned its tendency to explain (or explain away, according to some critics) problems in the East as historically contingent, acknowledging that these are *systemic* flaws.

In spite of this evolving position, even many of the PCI's well-wishers pressed the party to carry its analysis farther and break completely with the Soviets. If socialism and democracy were, as claimed, inseparable, and if the USSR was not, by the PCI's own admission, a democratic society, did it not follow that the USSR was not a socialist society? And did it not also follow that the PCI should draw this conclusion openly? But the PCI has always refused to burn this last bridge to the USSR, and that refusal has kept them on the tightrope.

In 1981, Enrico Berlinguer came very close to jumping off the rope when he denounced the imposition of martial law in Poland that was meant to crush the Solidarity movement, for the PCI's condemnation included the entire system of power that had evolved in the wake of the Russian Revolution.[31] But this move—long overdue in the eyes of some but highly courageous in my own opinion—was still several years in the future in terms of the research reported here.

I asked everyone in the apparatus how far they felt their party's critique of the USSR ought to be pushed. I explicitly brought up the question of the link between socialism and democracy and the argument that many felt it was time for the PCI to draw "certain conclusions" about the Soviet Union in order to show its own consistency on the issue. A summary of the apparatus's responses to this open-ended question follows.[32]

1. Thirteen respondents felt that the critique had not gone far enough and had to be pressed. But very few were willing to push the criticism radically, and most were quite explicit in stating that an open break similar to the one effected by the Spanish Communist Party had to be avoided. What really unifies this group, though, is the emphasis in responses on the importance of a critique and analysis for the PCI's own future.

2. Thirteen others also wanted more criticism and even added that PCI had to be more coherent and consistent in its analysis. Like the first group of respondents, these functionaries also tended to warn against an open break with the Soviet

Union. But this group, unlike those above, did not frame its answer in terms of the PCI or the need to distinguish between Italian Communism and social democracy.
3. Five functionaries gave extremely cautious and in some cases apologetic answers, making clear that in what was still for them primarily a bipolar world, they chose the socialist side as opposed to the capitalist/imperialist. But even among these respondents, often biting criticisms of the USSR were heard. Four members of the apparatus were about on the same position, with emphasis on the need for a "balanced" criticism and caution, but with the additional proviso of concern for respecting the sentiments of the rank and file. (One of this subgroup overlapped with the above, making the total here eight.)

With three-fourths of the apparatus calling for a more incisive—many used the term "courageous"—criticism, it is clear that the PCI's basic position on the Soviets was broadly supported in Turin. Several leaders made clear that they considered the USSR an imperialist power; some openly doubted that it merited the title "socialist," in view of the subordinate place of workers in the country's real decision-making structures. Most openly stated that they viewed their party's decision not to break with the USSR as strictly a contingent or tactical matter. Only in the third group, which accounts for roughly one functionary in five, was the PCI's identification with "the socialist camp" a more profound matter. But even here, what emerges in the responses is a concern for the PCI's general identity more than a blind allegiance to the Soviets. This view was most common among veteran workers, which is not surprising, but it was also found relatively frequently among the generation of the *compromesso storico*, the nonworkers in the zones. The strongest criticisms of the USSR, conversely, were found among the generation of 1968—in both headquarters and the zones.

As the breakdown above suggests, how the functionaries framed their responses was as interesting as the depth of the specific criticisms they voiced. Fully half of those who felt that a more sustained, consistently critical stance was required did so within the broader context of the need for the PCI to stake out an independent identity that was neither identified with the USSR nor simply that of the Western social-democratic parties. Like their more apologetic comrades, their party's identity crisis loomed large for them. Unlike their comrades, however, they were less willing to fall back on more traditional positions; they wanted to press forward with the critique *and* to try to maintain a distinctive profile for the PCI.

One tradition strongly rooted in Turin—*operaismo*, or workerism—revealed itself as a two-edged sword, at least among respondents as sophisticated as party functionaries. It may well be the case among the rank and file (and even, as we have seen, among older leaders sensitive to rank-and-file sentiments) that elements of the hard-line working-class membership are drawn by instinct to the Soviet "Workers' State." But many functionaries, mainly but not exclusively the younger ones, made clear that they could not forgive the USSR for trampling on the rights of its own working class. For every functionary who counseled caution, stressing the base's reflexive attachment to "the country of the October Revolution," there were others who echoed the young ex-worker in one of the city's zones. He commented bitterly that Stalin's greatest crime, "greater even than the camps, was to have torn the banner of freedom from the hands of the working class." By this, he meant not the hands of the Russian working class, but the working-class (i.e., communist) movement in general, which would ever afterward have to explain that it really stood for freedom and civil liberties, or contort itself in attempting to justify the situation that existed in the USSR.

## The Functionaries' Views of the PCI's Most Pressing Challenges

The final part of the open-ended interviewing of the apparatus consisted of a very general question: "What, in your view, will be the most serious challenges [*nodi da sciogliere*] the PCI will have to confront in the next several years?" Most of the functionaries saw the challenge as multifaceted, and thirty of them listed two or more central issues.[33] These responses ranged considerably, but they did cluster around three overriding issues. Taken collectively, they mirror a good many of the difficulties that we have seen afflicting the PCI in Turin and Italy at the end of the 1970s.

Confirming the crisis in the PCI is the fact that the problem mentioned most frequently as requiring a relatively rapid solution was the *compromesso* itself. Over half the apparatus (58 percent) brought this up, and most did so very directly. The following pair of quotations provides a sense of how some of the federation's top leaders responded.

> Not only our adversaries but part of the Party has understood [the strategy] as an embrace between us and the DC cutting out the Socialist comrades. Look, for instance, at these local experiments in "broad understandings": the whole atmosphere has compromised us in an extremely strong way without providing us with the real levers to change things. This has flattened out the struggles we can carry on. . . . This is a crucial knot because it also has theoretical implications, it ties into searching for the route by which we want to arrive at a pluralistic socialism.

> Our entire discussion since 1973 has maintained that given the specificity of Italy and the international situation, we could only overcome the crisis here by avoiding a head-on confrontation among the forces of the constitutional pact. This was supposed to give us a way around the Western European model of the alternation of parties in power, the international division of labor, and all the rest. Hence we pointed everything at *political unity*, with the consequent need to reach an agreement with the DC. Now we have to ask how our approach to the DC can dislocate it toward a programmatic agreement that truly will change certain things: this raises the question of alternation, along with a way of organizing society that is different from the DC's model.

It is also worth noting that just under a third of the apparatus emphasized, usually in reference to the weaknesses of the party's general strategy, that only some sort of project or explicit program would even begin to remedy the PCI's recent problems. Both the high frequency of the focus on the historic compromise and the explicit mention of the need for a project strongly echoed themes that were only beginning to be aired seriously within the PCI at the time. The strength of these attitudes confirms that the Turinese Federation of the PCI remained, even at the level of the apparatus, on the left within the context of the PCI of the late 1970s.

Almost as many respondents (53 percent) mentioned the need for a better analysis of Italy's political economy. The emphases in these responses ranged widely. Some people brought the economic issue up to illustrate the party's flawed or problematic general analysis (e.g., its assessment of the crisis in the country). Others simply raised the point as a genuine political priority which required quick remedial action if the party ever hoped to realize any of its more ambitious goals.

The final type of response that a significant portion of the apparatus mentioned related to the nature of the party itself. Just under a third of the functionaries felt that the PCI's immediate future required, if not the resolution of the problem, then at least that it be addressed much more directly and profoundly than in the past. Most frequently denounced were things like ritualism and what several functionaries called the party's sclerotic tendencies. Several informants simply referred to "our whole way of being" or "the way we relate to society and the world." The lack of true participation in internal decision making was also frequently noted.

A good many other issues, of course, were raised in these responses, but none was mentioned by more than three or four functionaries (the USSR, public morality, southern Italy, union-party relations, and youth were the most frequent). In view of the opportunity to discuss anything at all, the apparatus's concentration on these limited but absolutely central topics is striking. The fact that the party's general line was called either inadequate or badly in need of serious rethinking and revision by a clear majority of the apparatus provides further insights into the serious revision and eventual abandonment of the *compromesso storico* that eventually took place in the highest reaches of the PCI hierarchy. There may not have been the division among functionaries that there was in the rank and file on this score, but there was nothing like unanimous support for a strategy that obviously was bearing no appreciable fruit.[34]

These findings tie into the attitudes we saw concerning the nature of the USSR and how far the PCI ought to press its criticisms. As if confirming a younger leader's observation that the Soviet Union figured more as a nuisance than a focal point for the PCI, only a handful of respondents mentioned the USSR (or, more generically, "the East") as a discrete issue high on the party's agenda. As we have seen, however, many raised this as one element of a much broader picture involving the party's search for an autonomous path to socialism within a Western tradition. It is a measure of both the Italian Communists' evolution and the pressing nature of the crisis of the late 1970s that this historically burning question was able to be treated in such a way.

Some of the patterns in the responses recall those we found on the issue of support for the historic compromise and attitudes toward the DC. Leaders not inclined to call the entire line into question are also those who were most adamantly in favor of unity with the Christian Democrats: the veteran ex-workers in headquarters. More than half the federation felt the *compromesso storico* needed serious review and/or revision, but only one out of six of these veterans felt the same way. Conversely, the group most inclined to review the *compromesso* is the one that was most openly dubious about long-term accommodation with the DC: the generation of 1968. But whereas it was only the members of this group in headquarters that was highly hostile to the DC, the entire generation voiced its doubts in strongly majoritarian fashion (70 percent) about the party strategy. If we keep in mind that at the time of this study the key power positions in the federation were largely in the hands of the veteran ex-workers in headquarters, this evidence would tend to confirm the complaints of some of the disgruntled functionaries lower down in the hierarchy, who claimed that the federation's inner circle of leaders hewed to a line without much concern for what the bulk of the apparatus thought. To be sure, the relationship between attitudes and strategic location in the party organization was never perfect, but it was undeniably strong.

A similar but inverse relationship was found with regard to the issue mentioned with the second greatest frequency, Italy's political economy. Those most likely to mention this as a major problem to be confronted by the PCI in the near future were the veteran ex-workers (in headquarters and in the zones), followed very closely by the younger ex-workers. Overall, 75 percent of the former proletarians in the apparatus stressed the issue, while just over 30 percent of the former nonworkers did so. As these findings suggest, it is more likely the class origins, rather than the political views, of the functionaries that explains this very significant difference.[35]

## The Turinese Apparatus in Transition: A Summary

The attitudinal data provide a mixed portrait which illustrates the cross-pressures to which the party organization, and the functionaries who staff it, are subjected. There was no uniformity of views, but a strong consensus was found on several of the perennial problems that the PCI has had to face. This was most apparent in the respondents' attitudes toward democratic centralism, the need for the glue of either a core theory or a strong class-based identity, and an autonomous international stance—issues of considerable importance to the party at any time, but especially in a period when its identity was subject to so many challenges. And notable consistency was also found in responses to questions relating to work in the party organization. Judging from these answers, the organization of the Italian Communist Party remains, even with a model of militancy which is badly frayed around the edges, a relatively stable and formidable shaping force at its core.

But even the most powerful mold is limited by the raw material that is poured into it, and in this sense the PCI reflects the much broader forces at work in Italian society. Many attitudes in the apparatus reflect internal organizational problems, such as the PCI's inherent elitism and the functional division of labor that would plague any complex hierarchical organization. Yet even when we take these factors fully into account, a good number of variations remains that can only be traced to the differences—of social origin, political experience, or simply age—between and among the people in the apparatus. The influx into the apparatus of so many ex-militants of other parties and organizations and the startling increase of those who joined the PCI for idealistic or intellectual motives are two related, highly relevant illustrations of this point. Many findings confirm this on the strictly attitudinal level, but perhaps the most interesting cases concern the different ways functionaries found to voice strong criticisms of the PCI. Veterans tended to do so most forcefully when discussing the party's changing class composition; their criticisms were largely aimed at the lack of internal democracy and rank-and-file participation. More recent arrivals to the apparatus tended, in contrast, to be most critical when they addressed the party's inability to grasp new phenomena in society, groups with whom they themselves obviously identified.

It is fascinating that many of the most impressive differences to emerge in the functionaries' attitudes resist easy categorization. When we further consider that many of the topics that most resist convenient breakdown are central components of party strategy (the desirability of a specific project or program, the role of mobilization, the role of institutions, social alliances, and reform vs. alliance priorities), this point obviously becomes one of more than passing interest. Do the diverse attitudes we have found reflect the PCI's general crisis, or are they more appropriately to be seen within the Turinese context? Given the nature of our study, which has focused on only one party federation, it is impossible to answer the question with any definitive evidence, although I have tried, wherever possible, to suggest where the circumstantial evidence points. In many cases, there is abundant evidence for a strong Turinese component in the explanation, in view of the emphasis one finds on the working class, on strong social mobilization, and on other factors generally linked to leftism in the PCI. This in turn implies that although research of a similar kind in other federations might find equally significant variations in responses, it would be likely to find different emphases in various parts of Italy.

Finally, it is worth pointing out that the intensive type of research reported on the Turinese federation does provide us with a control that is very rarely encountered in studies that involve attitudinal research. Precisely because this study is restricted to one party organization, fieldwork was able to encompass extensive interviewing and a good deal of onsite observation. Functionaries spoke at length privately, but they were also observed in meetings and in actual political encounters. To be sure, observations could not be exhaustive, but they certainly provided the opportunity to establish whether there was congruence between what the respondents said in private and what they then did in more public forums.[36]

How similar were their public and private utterances? In general, they were extremely close, with numerous occasions on which they were identical. And I never encountered a situation where someone said one thing in a party meeting and its opposite in private conversation. More typical was the toning down of critical comments in the public utterances of most members of the apparatus. But the most powerful insight into the pressures of organizational conformity came on the numerous occasions when people with critical views simply remained silent when an issue on which they dissented was discussed in, say, a meeting of the entire apparatus. Not surprisingly, this phenomenon was most evident where the young peripheral functionaries were concerned, but it was by no means restricted to them. In these cases, the most common practice—if one spoke up at all—was to address one's own local situation in highly concrete terms with perhaps a passing "coded" reference to the broader issue of policy or strategy. This practice was openly acknowledged by many functionaries. It also helps account for the very strong resentment voiced against the ritualistic internal codes of the PCI by the youngest leaders. And these same leaders were the ones who also pointed out the unwillingness or inability of the older functionaries to take seriously their arguments against the murderous work pace and the unrealistic expectations to which all members of the apparatus were exposed.

We can easily see from this overview the intriguing ways in which the organization of a PCI federation acts in some ways as a buffer against external forces pressing on the party. This, most obviously, perpetuates the party, both in the narrow, structural sense and in the broader sense of ensuring that its operational code (or model of militancy) continues to operate. At the same time, the buffer is never impermeable—which, of course, is just as well in terms of the organization's long-term survival. In a particularly tumultuous period, such as the one that prevailed during the fieldwork for this study, it is especially porous: a problematic strategy combined with very rapid leadership turnover exposed it to much greater stress than would normally be the case. Finally, even though the self-perpetuating mechanisms of the party served it well on balance, the fact that many of the most entrenched internal codes clashed with the broad outlook on militancy that the newest leaders brought into the PCI in the 1970s meant that a new source of tension would be rooted inside the organization for the foreseeable future.

# 9

# Conclusions:
# The PCI in Transition

## The Past as Prologue: Turinese Communism
## from the 1970s to the 1980s

*Opposition without Involution*

If we recall the strength of the Turinese PCI's historical identity as a quintessential opposition party, it will come as no surprise to learn that many of the developments in the Piedmontese capital foreshadowed those of the entire party as it once again settled into an oppositional role in the 1980s. At this stage of our study, it is not necessary to dwell extensively on material that has already been covered, but a rapid review of the major points will illuminate some of the most critical questions the PCI faces in Turin and in Italy.

The strongest hint of future development for the entire party came, naturally enough, with regard to the working class and a general demand for a more militant, mobilizational posture from the party. The Turinese PCI began to register serious difficulties with the working class as early as 1977, by which time it also found its overall mobilizational capacities drastically undermined by national policies. Party activists and a good number of leaders in Turin, though by no means all of them, felt vindicated when the national party leadership finally shifted gears. In the aftermath of the 1979 general (and 1980 local) elections, especially when faced with an increasingly aggressive reedition of the Center-Left, the PCI openly began to appeal to the workers in a fashion that had not been seen for a decade. This grew out of two aims: to try to retain a solid base in the party's key constituency and, simultaneously, to attempt to show the DC—and, increasingly, the PSI—that the PCI remained an absolutely essential spokesman for the working class.

It is worth emphasizing yet again that this shift was not accompanied by a generally sectarian, workerist involution, even though the temptation to turn inward certainly existed in Turin and was in fact expected by some as a "natural" consequence of the PCI's return to the opposition. But the PCI does not have the suicidal inclinations of the PCF. In fact, in Turin, as throughout the party, the shift to a more militant stance was accompanied by a significant opening up of internal practices: not only was there extensive debate and plenty of public discussion of disagreements within the party, but this trend was formally sanctioned in congresses in the 1980s.[1] These developments represented responses to internal pressures that were not limited to the rank and file: we have seen strong evidence of the internalization of participatory values in the functionaries' attitudes. Even democratic centralism was vigorously criticized by a sizable minority of the apparatus, particularly by younger leaders.

There was also no sign in the apparatus, in spite of an acknowledged identity crisis, of any regression concerning the PCI's criticism of the USSR and the Soviet model of the party or society. On the contrary, most Turinese functionaries were highly critical of the Soviets and felt that the PCI could go even farther in its analysis of and dissociation from their system. The party's critique was reiterated and then escalated in the late 1970s over Afghanistan and, particularly in 1981, when the Solidarity movement was crushed in Poland. On the latter occasion, the PCI came very close to a complete break with the Russians but, characteristically, insisted on leaving the door slightly ajar.[2] In short, on some of the most fundamental issues, a mix of attitudes and behavior emerged both locally and nationally that is quite characteristic of the PCI but confounds notions of how "real" Communists are supposed to think and behave.

There were, of course, any number of areas in which Turin's leftist tradition set the federation off from mainstream thought in the party as a whole. This was evident in the functionaries' oft-expressed concerns about the perils of social democratization. In the very broadest sense, there is a view widely held in the PCI about the need for the party to maintain a distinct identity. This underlies the insistence that the PCI is a different type of party and needs to find "a third way" between the East and the social democracies. But after brief flirtations with terminology that suggests an exit from or transcendence of capitalism (*fuoruscita dal capitalismo*) during debates leading up to party congresses, such phrases have been discreetly dropped from general discussions. Similarly, the Turinese leaders' views about the party's need for a project or program had a far more radical and class-based thrust than have the national party's generally feeble and broad-based efforts to be programmatic. This difference is an even clearer illustration of the very specific social context in Turin. It also points to the serious constraints that limit a national party desperate to get the attention of other political and social forces in an effort to break out of the isolation to which it has been relegated since the beginning of the 1980s.

In a review of developments in Turin, the local governing experience also deserves at least a brief comment. The PCI remained the governing party locally long after the 1979 shift in the national line, but the dead-end nature of seeking broad alliances in spite of a clear left majority was apparent early and cost the Communists dearly. It also contributed to acute tensions within the party between leaders in administrative posts and most of the rest of the organization. Finally, owing to the party's unexpectedly strong showing in the capital in the 1980 local elections, the PCI continued to dominate the *giunte* of Turin and Piedmont until 1985, even though it had become clear years earlier that relations with the Socialists had degenerated beyond repair, making the demise of left-wing local governments only a matter of time wherever the mathematics made alternatives possible.

## Internal Organizational Questions

True to the PCI's hybrid nature, the evidence from this study points to a set of mixed and even somewhat contradictory conclusions with regard to the party as an organization. The PCI is in constant flux and endlessly juggles structures, personnel assignments, and the like. It has also begun, with excruciating slowness, to question some of its most entrenched and cherished practices. If the trends that were evident in the 1980s persist, there would appear to be even greater scope for experimentation on a local level than has been the case in the past. This is extremely important for party organizations in big cities, where none of the efforts to date has proved very successful. In this effort, the party is hampered by its established patterns and by a genuine confusion about the very purposes of the party's structures (what is the obligation to members vs. sympathizers or normal citizens, what is the role of the party in the workplace, etc.). The organization staggers along under so many conflicting demands that it would be extremely unrealistic to expect any dramatic successes on this front, particularly in light of the organizational problems that have come with the crisis of the 1980s.

Especially in light of the weakness of the Turinese federation, much evidence from this study helps us understand the contribution of its mass-party principles to the PCI's survival and durability. However flawed or limited, the basic tenets of the *partito nuovo* not only persist but are perpetuated in the ongoing commitment to social presence and activism that are rooted in all levels of the organization. It is easy to be critical of the frenetic pace of activity, so much of which appears to serve no function other than ritual, or "preaching to the converted." At the same time, to return to the point I made at the beginning of this chapter, the lure of sectarianism and crude workerism is great in a setting so inhospitable to traditional mass organizations. Although temptations in this direction have always existed in Turin, and certainly reemerged powerfully in the late 1970s, they were strongly and successfully resisted. A good portion of the credit for this achievement—and it is significant, even though negative—must go to the leadership of the federation and to the apparatus.

Much that we were able to discover about the apparatus also helps us understand the party's continued existence. On one level, there was a serious lack of substantive agreement on many crucial issues. If there is a transitional generation in the party, it is distinctive more in its heterogeneity than anything else. There also is clear and abundant evidence, often expressed in highly critical form, that many of the tensions and values of a very complex society have found their way into the deepest recesses of the party organization. This may lead to a crisis within the party, but is also undoubtedly a sign of the organization's vitality. Many of these views openly challenge the old style of militancy in the party, but, however disruptive they may be in the short or medium term, it would be far more damaging to the party's longer-term prospects of adaptation and survival if they were ignored or dogmatically brushed aside.

Yet at the same time, on a number of bedrock attitudes that define the specificity of the PCI, the consistency among the functionaries was impressive. These included a very strong belief in a guiding theory (not a dogma, however) based on the centrality of the working class, as well as a specific commitment to avoid the pitfalls of pure pragmatism or social-democratization. There were also strikingly few laical attitudes expressed with regard to the party's nature, with a very large proportion of the apparatus quite favorably inclined toward some version of democratic centralism. As I have already noted, this may well be a distinctively Turinese profile. But the point is not that the same values must exist inside the party everywhere in the country. It is rather that to function even reasonably well, an apparatus needs a degree of attitudinal and ideological cohesion, and this existed in Turin in spite of many important differences.

## *The PCI's Reaction to the Crisis in Turin*

During the main period covered by this study, the situation in Turin differed from most of the rest of Italy in terms of the state of the economy. There were signs of crisis in Piedmont throughout the 1970s, but they were not sufficient to convince the most militant sectors of the labor movement that drastic measures were required of them. The party's (and the unions') emphasis on the need for austerity to cope with the crisis met with little sympathy through most of the late 1970s, and not only because militant cadres rejected the idea of sacrifices on ideological grounds. The fact is that during most of this period, the militants' own experience did not square with what their leaders were saying.

The figures are telling: in 1981, industrial employment in Italy had increased by 11 percent over the previous census, while the number of industrial plants rose by 33 percent. These increases reflected a trend that has become familiar throughout the capitalist world since the 1970s. Larger firms modernize and often drastically cut back their work forces. Smaller firms (which represent a far more unfriendly environment for organized labor), frequently equipped with the most modern equipment, show rapid growth in response both to new market opportunities and to a rise in the amount of work subcontracted out to them by the larger enterprises. The smaller firms may even absorb the workers expelled from the larger factories, keeping employment relatively stable — at least for a time.

The national trend was grossly magnified in Turin, home of so many large (and in many cases obsolete) factories. Industrial employment actually declined by 12 percent between 1971 and 1981, while the number of factories increased by an astonishing 50 percent.[3] Industrial fragmentation and decentralization had been under way through the 1970s and was in fact much commented upon. But the employment crisis, in spite of the decline noted above, was not strongly felt in Turin until 1980. At that point, the thirty-five days at Fiat jolted the Turinese workers' movement out of its lethargy.

The thirty-five days had more than symbolic significance. This episode was a critical turning point in Italian labor relations, for it showed management that the labor movement was no longer able to defend the victories of the previous decade. With Fiat in the vanguard, Italian capitalism's largest firm made the restructuring of industry a far more brutal affair than it had been through 1980. Between 1981 and 1986, industrial employment in the country fell by 15 percent, which means eight hundred sixty thousand jobs, even though both investment and productivity rose in the same period.[4]

It would be grossly unfair to hold the PCI responsible for trends in world or even Italian capitalism, but I have argued repeatedly that its tendency to avoid careful analysis certainly contributes to its confusion and inability to propose anything other than generic slogans or formulas. Party leaders are themselves aware of the PCI's sloppiness in this regard, as is evident in the highly critical remarks in 1982 of the man who would shortly become the new secretary of the Turinese federation:

> Today we are *a posteriori* forced to face the fact that we have abused the term "crisis," in the sense that only today are we really in a crisis, in a recession, in a phase in which employment and capital accumulation have crumbled. *This* is a crisis. I can't remember, from the time I became active in the PCI, when one of our documents has not said, "The country is in a crisis." That wasn't true: the country was in a phase of chaotic, distorted, unbalanced development that generated serious contradictions in the use and distribution of resources, etc., but there was a developmental trend . . .[5]

Italian capitalism has, in fact, emerged from this major restructuring phase in impressive shape. But the costs have been especially devastating in Turin. The Turin of the late 1980s remains a vital industrial center, but it is no longer the proletarian citadel of heroic struggles. The collapse of the 1980 strike at Fiat is a crucial symbol in this regard, for it represented a breakdown of class unity on the classic trade unionist issue of job protection.

Yet in many ways, the most devastating sign of all came nearly five years later, with the 1985 referendum to give back to the workers what a government decree had lopped off their cost-of-living escalator.[6] The PCI insisted that the referendum be held. Its pressure provided the final break in the already disintegrating unity of the unions, for it essentially constrained the CGIL to support the referendum. (Socialists in the CGIL, plus the entire CISL and UIL, did not support the referendum.) Whatever one thinks of the judgment exercised by the Communists in this matter, a relatively good showing for such an undertaking would normally be expected in a place like Turin. But the referendum could not muster a simple majority either in the capital, where the margin was a razor-thin 49-to-51 percent, or in the province, where it was 48-to-52 percent. The nationwide result was a 46-to-54 vote, and the cut in the escalator was sustained. The demoralization that accompanied this defeat can only be imagined, as the party and the labor movement were provided with powerful evidence of the diminished weight of the working class in what had always been a proletarian bastion.

Obviously, the weight of these development has made itself felt both organizationally and electorally, as we have already had some occasion to see in Chapters 2 and 4. But the downward spiral accelerated dramatically in the 1980s. Although in terms of members the Turinese PCI remains better off at the end of the 1980s than it was at the end of the 1960s, the drubbing it took in the 1987 general election actually dropped the party below its 1968 vote and put it a full 11 percent below its peak. Figure 9.1 demonstrates this trajectory graphically. These are by no means indicators that the PCI in Turin has been reduced to marginal status, although the figures do indicate an extremely serious decline. Membership has fallen by more than eleven thousand since the peak period, as thousands of cadres have been laid off and as recruitment has plummeted because of the effective disappearance of young workers that has accompanied industrial restructuring. Table 2.4 shows that the rate of recruitment in the 1980s has fallen well below half the overall rate from 1968 to 1980.

These trends have had a devastating effect on the federation's membership profile. The evidence concerning recruitment would lead us to expect the party to have aged significantly, and this is in fact the case. Official statistics for 1985 showed that just over a fifth of the members in Turin were pensioners, whereas only 12 percent were in that category in 1977. But the truly dramatic decline is found in the class composition of the Turinese PCI. By 1985, the working-class membership had fallen to 44.5 percent of the total—down from nearly 59 percent at the peak of the party's fortunes only eight years earlier and a mere 7 percent more than the PCI's national average.[7] These figures suggest that the most serious aspects of an identity crisis in Turin probably lie in the party's future, which looks quite bleak. At least for the present, the figures tell the story of an organization that is no longer in a position to set the politial agenda, or even to catalyze dissent and carry forward a broad movement for change.

## The PCI in the 1980s and Beyond: Transition to What?

God is dead, Marx is dead, and I'm not feeling too well myself.
                                                            Graffito (Bologna, 1984)

Our brief discussion of the situation in Turin underscores the PCI's difficulties. If the party has not crumbled before the onslaught of its combined problems, it has barely

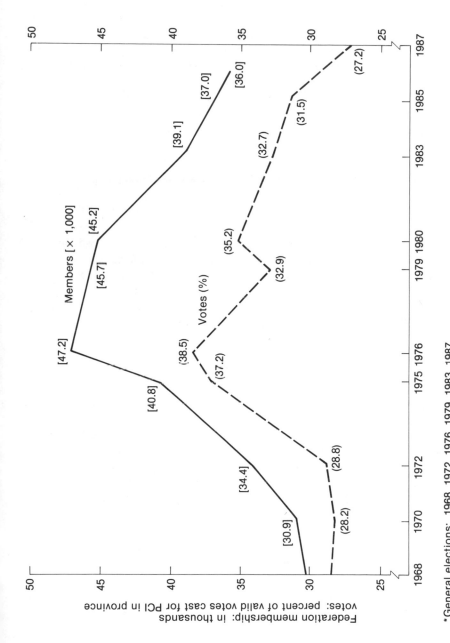

Figure 9.1. The Turinese PCI's Votes and Members in Selected Election Years*

*General elections: 1968, 1972, 1976, 1979, 1983, 1987.
Regional elections: 1970, 1975, 1980, 1985.

215

managed to hold on, in organizational and electoral terms. Its continuing evolution in what used to be called a Eurocommunist direction has undoubtedly prevented catastrophic damage, but it has not been able to reverse the stagnation and decline that began in the late 1970s. It finds itself surviving, but in the role of an opposition party that is in danger of becoming even more marginalized. And since marginalization is likely to weaken it further, the PCI must do more than simply hold on and wait for conditions to change to its advantage.

Here, of course, is the nub of the problem. What is it exactly that the PCI must do? How much of its fate is in its own hands, and how much depends on other political actors and broader sociostructural forces? The party's difficulties are apparent, but there is little agreement on these larger questions because they involve different interpretations of probable Italian political developments and the closely related puzzle of the trajectory of current socioeconomic trends. To render full justice to all the alternative interpretations would take us far beyond the constraints of this study. At the same time, it is impossible to discuss the PCI's future intelligently without at least brief reference to the broader context and some of the issues that various debates have raised.

In the remainder of these conclusions, I will address the PCI's future in two segments. I first spell out, under a series of broad headings, the principal problems the party faces. These are widely recognized as critical issues, and many have been amply documented in this study. Documentation will therefore be kept to a minimum except where quite recent developments need to be included. In the second and final segment, I will explore the major possibilities or options that appear to lie ahead for the PCI.

## Open Questions, Unresolved Problems

*A Badly Divided Left and Labor Movement.* Even in the narrowest sense of simple political arithmetic, the intentions and actions of the Socialist party have had a decisive influence on the PCI. And the brutal fact is that the PSI under Bettino Craxi has made quite clear that it is not even interested in a dialogue with the PCI (except when this serves the PSI in power struggles with the DC). The Socialists' maneuvers and reversals are legendary, but they do have a long-range plan for expansion in what they and most observers perceive as the growing laical center of new middle-class voters in Italy. Given that their main base in the union movement is among the skilled and white-collar sectors, their strategy is not as one-sided as might at first appear to be the case. But this strategy, and Socialist behavior in government, plays on sociological as well as political divisions in the working-class and labor movement.

These divisions have become far more serious since the PCI moved back into the opposition. Union unity, tenuous at best, could hardly have been expected to survive the political break of 1979. More importantly, the economic crisis eventually undermined the unions' leverage throughout the system—and this had been the Communists' trump card since the late 1960s. Even a bid for power based on austerity and restraining the labor movement becomes unattractive once the movement is perceived as weak and divided.

These circumstances put the PCI in a terrible bind. Appeals to the working class over the heads of union leaders—and the party has had to bypass Communist unionists on occasion—obviously exacerbate already serious political divisions in the labor movement. At the same time, because such class appeals inevitably take a militant tone, when it adopts this approach the party tends to alienate some blue-collar and many important white-collar groups. The 1985 referendum (and the thirty-five days) poignantly underscored the dilemma. By carrying the contractual concerns of the workers into the public arena and making them a partisan political issue, the PCI undercut its broader appeal.

Although the political situation in Italy remains uncertain because of feuding between the DC and the PSI, none of the most likely scenarios can be cheering to the PCI. Political stagnation had become so widely recognized as a serious problem by the 1980s that the Italian Parliament actually gave serious consideration to a number of far-reaching institutional reforms. These reforms died in parliamentary committees, although the Communists continue to press for changes in the electoral system and local government. Some of the more acute observers of the Italian scene have noted that the question at the end of the 1980s appears to be whether Italy will be embarking on a reedition of the centrism and labor exclusion of the 1950s or the more ambitious, but still limited, Center-Left reformism of the 1960s.[8]

*The General—and Specific—Crises of the Left.* To a great extent, the problems discussed are simply the institutional manifestation in Italy of the general crisis faced by the left all over Europe. But it is extremely important to go beyond a discussion of the current political conjuncture and not reduce everything to questions of political formulas and institutional maneuvers (a practice all too prevalent among the parties and many observers).

This is hardly the place to elaborate on the immense number of explanations that have been offered for what is really a series of phenomena that have either arisen or matured in advanced capitalist democracies. Depending on one's discipline, interests, or politics, the emphasis tends to fall on long waves or cycles of capitalism, changing class structures, value shifts in a "postmaterialist" epoch, new forms of politics, new social actors or movements, rising social complexity and fragmentation, bankrupt economic doctrines, outmoded governmental structures, obsolete ideologies and organizations, and a host of other factors as well. For our purposes, the issue is not to decide which of these varied (and often contradictory) analyses is most convincing but to emphasize that almost all of them ultimately point to serious difficulties for the historic organizations of the left.

Especially because it opted for a mass-party structure, the PCI is very much part of the tradition that has suffered from the left's general crisis. But the PCI also faces, as we have seen repeatedly, a number of problems that derive from its distinctive communist lineage. The PCI's strategic and organizational choices have spared it from the worst consequences of an inability to adapt to changing conditions, but even the *partito nuovo* of the 1980s continues to carry Third International birthmarks. They are most notable in the persistence of hierarchical and centralized organizational practices and in an enduring model of militancy, both of which seriously condition the way the party relates to the social sphere. These rooted remnants from another period have proven to be serious impediments to the PCI's ability to respond to—and indeed at times even to understand—many of the developments taking place around it.

The party's ideological heritage also figures prominently in another shortcoming that has been much discussed since its failure to capitalize on the great advances of the mid-1970s. That flaw is summed up in Italian political shorthand by the term *cultura di governo* and the fact that this quality is missing in the PCI. The absence of a "culture of government" can, of course, be attributed to permanent residence in the opposition since

1947, but it is hard to separate its nature as a communist party from its relegation to a place on the sidelines of Italian politics. Moreover, without an interpretive framework that views ideology as a potent contributing factor, it is difficult to comprehend some of the PCI's actions vis-à-vis Italy's political institutions and legal system (one need only recall the question of terrorism, the *Legge Reale*, etc.), as well as its inability to abandon typically didactic mobilizational techniques when they are inappropriate.

Finally, and ironically, one of the most damaging legacies of the *compromesso storico* was the way it reinforced some of the PCI's most entrenched and outmoded assumptions about society at a time when the party badly needed to adopt new interpretive tools. As noted in Chapter 1, the "strong" interpretation of the strategy viewed it as a consociational arrangement that would not challenge the major parties and the subcultures and constituencies they controlled. The content of the party strategy in this sense not only failed to sensitize the Communists to a dramatically changing set of social structures and values; it often acted as an impediment. In the 1970s, the Communists looked on various actions and manifestations of autonomy emanating from the social sphere—from students, young people in general, feminists, ecologists, civil libertarians—with incomprehension and even open hostility. There was much impatience in this reaction: precisely because these "new movements" and "new social subjects" *were* new and did not fit neatly into traditional pigeonholes, they threatened to complicate an already complex set of political mediations. But behind the PCI's hostility was also a deeply negative reaction to what it considered episodes of degeneration and social breakdown, which the *compromesso* would remedy by recomposing a system in crisis. This helps explain why it took so long for the party to appreciate that these phenomena were legitimate manifestations of a society in flux.

The leadership's obsession to establish the PCI's full democratic legitimacy in this period also disastrously undermined the party's long-term credibility as a serious force for change. The PCI's zeal in defense of the existing institutional order, including smear tactics against many who did not share its official convictions, persuaded many—especially intellectuals who had previously been favorably disposed toward Italian Communism—that this organization was hopelessly out of step with the times. Its continual insistence on the "popular" base of the DC, combined with the tolerance it showed toward a do-nothing government, undermined definitively one of the PCI's strongest previous sources of legitimacy: its claim to be different from other parties.

In turning the party away from much of what was new, and in making it identify with much of the worst that was old, the strategy ensured that the subsequent impasse would be even more paralyzing than might otherwise have been the case. It would be silly to argue that the PCI would by now have found more satisfactory answers to all the problems plaguing it and Italian society had it begun to examine these more systematically in the early 1970s. In no country has the left come up with persuasive solutions to these issues. At the same time, it would be ridiculous to deny that the PCI, at the height of its credibility and powers, would have evolved in a more open, flexible, and intelligent direction by now if it had not embraced a set of assumptions in the early 1970s that were so demonstrably wrong. In this sense, the *compromesso* caused the party to miss a crucial opportunity that will never come again. Instead of riding the wave of the 1970s, the PCI was flattened by it.

*Organizational and Electoral Trends.* From a strictly organizational viewpoint, membership and recruitment trends in the 1980s have exacerbated the grim situation that already existed at the end of the 1970s (see Table 1.2). Total membership has fallen to the level of the late 1960s. Recruitment figures show an even more disturbing trend, for they have dropped to and remain at all-time low levels. Moreover, the average age of new recruits in 1985 was thirty-six years. Clearly, without the membership renovation and organizational revitalization of the 1970s, the PCI's situation would be desperate by now. If the average age of PCI members in 1985 was fifty and a half years, and if members had a mean seniority in the party of twenty-one years, it does not take too much imagination to appreciate how glum the situation would be without the influx of the 1970s; in fact, even in the mid-1980s, a third of all members had joined the party in the 1970s, and half had joined since 1969.[9] In addition, the class composition of the Turinese party's membership may have changed notably in the 1980s, but the party as a whole has stagnated in this regard since the 1960s. Yet, while the party's class profile remains fixed, that of Italian society does not, and the increasing gap has caused considerable alarm among party leaders. The strata that are expanding most among the employed population—technical and clerical white-collar categories—continue to be seriously underrepresented in the PCI's ranks.[10]

The PCI's electoral fortunes will naturally depend a good deal on the vagaries of Italian party politics, but there can be no doubt that these fortunes took a sharp downturn in the 1980s. Although the party lost in the general elections of 1979 and 1983, it appeared to have stabilized at around 30 percent. Indeed, in the 1984 European Elections, the PCI equaled its all-time high of 34 percent and actually exceeded the vote of the DC. It soon became clear that the European vote, in which nothing was really at stake, reflected an immense outpouring of sympathy for Enrico Berlinguer, who had died during the campaign. The local elections of 1985, and especially the general elections of 1987, reintroduced the reality factor in Communist calculations. The latter vote not only shattered the 30 percent barrier but put the party (at 26.6 percent) a shade below its 1968 level. The Communists' decline continued in the urban center, and, for the first time, there was even a sharp drop in many of the red regions. The party had suffered three straight losses, and, as many people noted, electorally it was as if the hot autumn had never taken place.

Until Italy's sociostructural changes and the party's political blunders began to take their toll in the 1980s, most informed opinion saw a fairly rosy, or at least solid, future in store for the PCI. A number of elements now make this future much less certain. First, the industrial working class is shrinking rapidly, and the Communists are much less successful in attracting broad support from the expanding white-collar categories. Second, the PCI's appeal to young people has clearly waned. The Communists have not been able to count on a high youth vote since the mid-1970s, and it was widely acknowledged within the party that in 1987 the PCI's support among the youngest voters was actually far below its national average. (Leaders of the Youth Federation estimated that the party only received 20 percent support from this group.) Finally, recent research suggests that secularization may have stabilized, at least temporarily. For the first time, the very youngest Italian voters appear to be no less religious than their immediate elders. Partly for this reason, Italy's political subcultures are proving more durable than was once supposed: fully half the electorate remains evenly divided between a leftist and a Catholic subculture.[11] This may help the PCI maintain a reasonably solid underpinning, but it also suggests even less potential area for electoral expansion than was previously supposed.

Of course, in the final analysis, such trends are never the simple result of blind forces. If young people no longer vote for the PCI in such large numbers, or if clerks or technicians prefer the Socialists or the lay parties of the center, they are also reacting to what the Communists have to offer. And the brutal fact of the matter is that, for nearly a decade, the party has been unable to maintain the support of those who once flocked to its colors, let alone increase its appeal among any social groups or strata.

## A Landscape of Limited Options

What has the PCI done under these daunting conditions? Even more to the point, what *can* it do? The political situation it has faced since the Socialists entered the government in 1979 has left it very little maneuvering room. Thus far, the government's efforts to isolate the Communists while dividing a weakened working class in order to strip away once impressive gains have proven largely successful. Precisely because it has been isolated and weakened, the PCI's responses have been defensive and feeble. It has struck a more militant posture in defense of the working class and the lower strata, but it has remained incapable of articulating a program or platform with broad or fresh appeal. Its late, halting embrace of antinuclear, ecological, and other "postindustrial" causes has seen it follow the lead of others rather than set out any new or interesting proposals or syntheses.

Because of its extremely cautious nature, the PCI has proven even more leery than usual of spelling out a concrete program. This caution is born of experience: the Communists have consistently been thwarted in their efforts to open up a dialogue with other parties (especially the Socialists). In this waltz without a partner, they have learned that whatever they attempt to set out usually serves as little more than a handy target for others to shoot down. And as long as the PSI continues to thrive, this situation is likely to persist.

The regrettable result is that almost all the PCI's alleged proposals are little more than contingent political calculations that seem geared to playing on, and counting on, divisions between the PSI and DC. This was painfully evident through the mid-1980s, when, having failed to engage the attention of other parties, the PCI abandoned the idea of the "democratic alternative." In its stead, the party leadership came up with a plan for a "programmatic government" which spelled out neither the political forces nor the content of the package of reforms this government would agree to implement. [12] The idea is that forces interested in reform should come to an agreement strictly on the merits of the most needed changes—without any prejudgment of coalition partners or favored legislative shopping lists. The proposal represented the institutionalization of the PCI's vacillation and fear of isolation, and it has a desperate air to it. The party's fears are understandable and real enough, but this is not a very promising or innovative course of action.

In a similar vein, the PCI's current dilemma provides a stimulus to debate organizational questions, but here even more than in other areas the party's options are severely limited. Even if we leave aside the various forces within the party that will resist change, any hope of significant initiatives with regard to the party structure must remain extremely slim.

First, the party is committed to a policy of expanding internal democracy and the input of common militants. This may turn out to be more promise than performance, but it has generated lively debate and widespread support throughout the PCI. To turn around and suggest that sections ought to be amalgamated, or that militants' concerns must be balanced against voters', or that traditional grass-roots activities should be curbed, would be to go against most of the major impulses generated within the party since the late 1970s.

Second, the party's present isolation and oppositional role pushes it toward more traditional organizational reinforcement, since its activities—by definition—are of a more mobilizational and oppositional nature and rely on internal structures that are as robust as possible. (The referendum on wage indexation is a good, if extreme, example.) Under these conditions, it is only natural to avoid too much experimentation.

Third, the loss of the last bastions of important local political power outside the red belt in 1985 deprived the PCI of a significant counterweight to strictly organizational concerns in two different respects. The party lost many important forums from which to launch social and political initiatives, while it simultaneously lost the institutional resources that went with local power. But these electoral setbacks also deprived the party, internally, of a very important counterweight to cadres with strictly organizational interests. On the basis of the evidence from Turin, "the party of administrators" will probably not be missed much by organizational cadres. But regardless of the merits of the respective viewpoints, the weight of the administrators has been greatly diminished in most areas of Italy. Many have returned to organizational work, but they have done so without the leverage that public office provides.

Thus, we have, by default, the diminution of "external factors" and the growth of the relative importance and weight of the party organization. This is quite a common phenomenon in all mass parties when they pass into the opposition, and the Italian Communists are no exception to the general rule.

Barring a truly unexpected turn of events, it would therefore appear that the PCI remains locked onto a course that promises more of the same for the foreseeable future, with all the risks involved. Changes will undoubtedly occur, but as a result of *force majeure* rather than conscious design. In spite of the immense difficulties it now faces, this does not mean the PCI is on the brink of catastrophe. A worst-case scenario would probably conform to the prediction of one of the party's most persistent critics:

> When I speak of "decline," I am thinking of a long period of time, for I am well aware that the PCI in 40 years has constructed an infinite set of relationships with society, naturally different from place to place. This being present in an active fashion at least to some degree throughout the entire society means that if you talk about decline you have to understand that it will take place very gradually. I don't foresee a collapse of the PCI, but rather a slow and continuous loss, at least as long as this ideology and organization persist.[13]

A more optimistic prognosis would emphasize the proven cravenness and ineptitude of Italy's governing parties and predict that before long a conjuncture more favorable to the Communists is bound to arise. Such a view appears rather mechanical and deterministic, for it underplays the deeper changes that have occurred since the late 1960s. But this view is held by many who cannot quite believe that the PSI and DC's run of luck will continue unabated. Although not explicitly expressed, the notion that the tide will have to turn sooner or later is implicit in much of what the Communists have done—by default and often out of desperation. But not everyone in the PCI is so sanguine about the party's future.

More time has now passed since the historic compromise was abandoned than it lasted as official party doctrine. Yet serious discussions of the party in the mid-1980s were still taking the *compromesso storico* as their point of departure.[14] However ambiguous and flawed it might have been, the strategy had an underlying coherence that has been missing in the PCI since it was dropped. The PCI may be the only surviving Eurocommunist party, but it is a rather dazed survivor.

Fate has conspired to make the post-*compromesso* period more difficult for the Communists. It is characteristic of the PCI's emphasis on continuity that Enrico Berlinguer was leading the party in a new direction, even though he was not fully committed to the abandonment of the old strategy. This continuity ended abruptly with Berlinguer's death in 1984. The loss of a leader of unquestioned stature at such a critical moment complicated the party's already difficult situation. Berlinguer's successor, Alessandro Natta, was chosen more for his skills at mediation and administration than for any particular vision of the party's future. Many observers quickly predicted that his stewardship would ultimately serve as a sort of stabilizing interregnum (much as Luigi Longo served as a bridge between Togliatti and Berlinguer).

The Communists' defeat in the 1987 elections seemed at first to signal an end to the stable but immobile internal dynamic that had evolved after Berlinguer's death. The sense of shock and urgency led many people at all levels of the party to call for the resignation of the top leadership. Some of the protagonists in these events explained that this was not a condemnation of Natta or any other individuals as much as a demand for a change of outlook at the summit of the PCI. The established leaders were simply too preoccupied with issues like constantly establishing the party's democratic credentials, which a younger generation of leaders took for granted. The older group had also demonstrably run out of ideas and seemed locked into a mentality of infinite parliamentary maneuvering. While many of the younger leaders admit that they do not have ready-made answers, they reason that even the possibility of a fresh approach requires a new group at the helm of the party.[15]

These factors help explain why, just a few weeks following the elections, Achille Occhetto was named vice-secretary general of the PCI, and thus heir apparent to Natta. The question of both the interregnum and generational change had been quite dramatically resolved.[16] And the drama was high indeed, for in voting on Occhetto's promotion, the Central Committee split quite publicly: the vote was 194 in favor and 41 opposed, with 22 abstentions.[17] Most of those who opposed Occhetto were leaders from the party's right wing. They raised (warranted) objections to the hasty way the nomination was engineered, but they were also expressing a clear political dissent. Occhetto had reacted very quickly to the defeat at the polls with criticisms of the party's caution and indecisiveness and the suggestion that the Communists had lost significantly to their left because they had ignored numerous protest movements. The analysis was not altogether accurate, but it brilliantly succeeded in putting the right on the defensive while identifying Occhetto as action-oriented. Following his selection, some of the most prominent right-wing Communists announced that they were resigning from the Secretariat. This turn of events was by no stretch of the imagination a victory for the party's left wing, but it was the first time the right had been so totally isolated.[18]

But any hope that the party would signal bold departures for the PCI appears likely to be disappointed. By the end of 1987, less than six months after the dramatic postelectoral struggle over Occhetto's promotion, leading exponents of the party's right wing resolved their differences with the majority in the Central Committee and Secretariat. This strongly suggests that, with minor adjustment, the leadership is likely to continue as it always has done (except in the early days of the *compromesso*): that is, to plot out a centrist course that does not grossly offend anyone in the party—but which also avoids making sharp and clear choices among the conflicting perspectives that coexist within its ranks. Amidst a consensus that the PCI needs to become a "modern party of reform," there is actually little agreement about what this phrase really means or how it can be translated into reality.

For the moment, a middle-of-the-road course may be the only viable option. Of the contrasting visions within the PCI, each has serious limitations. Those Communists who wish the party to remain closer to the original conception of the *partito nuovo* have an appreciation of mass politics and grass-roots participation but seem unable to acknowledge or cope with the inherent contradictions of a large mass organization. They *assert* the importance of new structures, projects, and social activism. However, they have been incapable of answering the key challenges to their basic assumptions.

Meanwhile, the continuing erosion of the party organization may settle these issues by default. How can a mass-party structure be reformed to make it function successfully under current conditions? What would a transformative project look like? How can the so-called new strata and the traditional working class be brought together in a fashion that would build a genuine coalition for change? It is stirring to invoke social mobilization and new forms of participation, but in the absence of results, these invocations sound increasingly ritualistic.

On the opposite extreme are the right-wingers who form a "realist" or *migliorista* (roughly, "improvement") tendency that openly represents little more than classical social democracy. Indeed, exponents of this view are in fact widely known as *laburisti* inside and outside the party. They have been the strongest proponents of rapprochement at practically any cost with the PSI. These people recognize the shopworn character of old slogans and styles of militancy, as well as the complexity of advanced capitalist society, but they appear to throw their hands up in the face of that complexity. For most "realists," neither a transformative project nor a mass-party structure is seen as a suitable political tool for the conditions that prevail at the end of the twentieth century. They view these largely as impediments to the party's freedom to maneuver both socially and within established institutions. Given the crises that confront the traditional social-democratic parties they hope to emulate, the "realists" can hardly inspire much confidence or enthusiasm. And given the Socialists' interest is even further eroding and marginalizing the PCI, the practical politics of the *laburisti* seem to point to a dead end.

Although the Communist leadership is likely to attempt to steer a middle course between these (and less extreme) views within the party, a fundamental dilemma remains. These are irreconcilable views, not emphases that can somehow be blended together in a grand synthesis that will—finally—represent the elusive "third way" between Western social democracy and Eastern state socialism. The *partito nuovo* is obviously in need of drastic changes. But it would quite sad for the PCI, and for the left in general, if it "resolved" its crisis by aimless drift while abandoning altogether any broader vision of the radical transformation of society. Indeed, if it follows such a course, it may hasten its reduction to permanent irrelevancy.

# NOTES

## Introduction

1. For an interesting review of trends on the left that is sober but not pessimistic, see Goran Therborn, "The Prospects of Labour and the Transformation of Advanced Capitalism," *New Left Review* 145 (May–June 1984), pp. 5–38.

2. In the European elections of 1984, the PCI approached its high point again, but the circumstances surrounding these elections (they came immediately after the death of PCI General Secretary Enrico Berlinguer, as well as a very unpopular governmental assault on the cost-of-living index, and had no bearing whatever on the internal balance of political power in Italy) made them extraordinary. The 1985 local elections saw the PCI descend once more to around 30 percent.

3. Ernest Mandel, *From Stalinism to Eurocommunism* (London: New Left Books, 1978), draws some of the more systematic and convincing parallels between the PCI's strategy and that of Karl Kautsky and the German Social Democrats in the period around World War I.

4. For scholarly examples of this position, see most contributions to Austin Ranney and Giovanni Sartori, eds., *Eurocommunism: The Italian Case* (Washington, D.C.: American Enterprise Institute, 1978).

5. For a very recent illustration, see Jane Jenson and George Ross, *The View from Inside: A French Communist Cell in Crisis* (Berkeley, Calif.: University of California Press, 1984), pp. 9–10.

6. A good synthetic summary of the labor movements in less and more conflictual European societies can be found in Stephen Bornstein, "States and Unions: From Postwar Settlements to Contemporary Stalemate," in Stephen Bornstein, David Held, and Joel Krieger, eds., *The State in Capitalist Europe: A Casebook* (Winchester, Mass.: George Allen & Unwin, 1984), esp. pp. 56–60. For an extended discussion of the French and Italian labor movements, see Peter Lange and George Ross, "Conclusions," in Peter Lange, George Ross, and Maurizio Vannicelli, *Unions Change and Crisis: French and Italian Union Strategy and the Political Economy, 1945–1980* (London: Allen & Unwin, 1982), pp. 207–91.

7. Italian fascism's twenty-year dictatorship; the Spanish Civil War and the subsequent Franco dictatorship from 1939 until 1975; the German invasion and conquest of France in 1939 at a time when the Soviet Union and the Nazis were bound by a nonaggression pact.

8. This important point is stressed in Sidney Tarrow, "Communism in Italy and France: Adaptation and Change," in Donald L. M. Blackmer and Sidney Tarrow, eds., *Communism in Italy and France* (Princeton, N.J.: Princeton University Press, 1975), esp. pp. 585–86.

9. There *were* local elections, and the PCI lost votes everywhere.

10. For an excellent summary of the tensions in the PCF on the eve of the left's victory, see Jenson and Ross, *The View from Inside*. See also the conclusions in George Ross, *Workers and Communists in France* (Berkeley, Calif.: University of California Press, 1982).

11. For one of the most lucid presentations of this position, see Marcello Fedele, *Classi e partiti negli anni '70* (Rome: Editori Riuniti, 1979). For a synthetic and very forceful statement, see Angelo Bolaffi, "Nuovi soggetti e progetto operaio: la 'forma' partito nella crisi di governabilità," in Pietro Ingrao et al., *Il partito politico e la crisi dello Stato sociale: Ipotesi di ricerca* (Bari: De Donato, 1981), pp. 147–62.

12. The research involved several field trips: in 1977–78 for fifteen months, and then for three and a half months in 1979 and two months in 1980 (with a shorter follow-up visit in 1984).

13. For strong methodological justifications for extreme or exceptional case studies, consult Harry Eckstein, "Case Study and Theory in Political Science," in Fred I. Greenstein and Nelson W. Polsby, eds., *Handbook of Political Science, Vol. 7: Strategies of Inquiry* (Reading, Mass.: Addison-Wesley, 1975), pp. 79–137.

## Chapter 1

1. There is an enormous bibliography available on every aspect of this phase of the PCI's history. For a thorough analysis in a single volume, see Paolo Spriano, *Storia del PCI, Vol. V: La Resistenza, Togliatti e il partito nuovo* (Turin: Einaudi, 1975). A good brief discussion of the implementation of the mass party in the postwar period is Marcello Flores, "Dibattito interno sul mutamento della struttura organizzativa 1946/1948," in Massimo Ilardi and Aris Accornero, eds., *Il Partito comunista italiano: Struttura e storia dell'organizzazione 1921–1971* (Milan: Feltrinelli, 1982), pp. 35–61. In English, a well-documented discussion can be found in Donald Sassoon, *The Strategy of the Italian Communist Party* (London: Frances Pinter, 1981), esp. chaps. 1–3.

2. He did this even before the war's end; see Palmiro Togliatti, *Lectures on Fascism* (New York: International Publishers, 1976). His postwar pronouncements are replete with references to the earlier errors of the left. In English, see esp. Palmiro Togliatti, *On Gramsci and Other Writings*, ed. Donald Sassoon (London: Lawrence and Wishart, 1982), esp. chaps. 2 and 3 and chap. 9, pp. 233–39.

3. Quoted in Leonardo Paggi, "Paradigmi di analisi della crisi dei partiti," in Pietro Ingrao et al., *Il partito politico e la crisi dello Stato sociale: Ipotesi di ricerca* (Bari: De Donato, 1981), p. 61.

4. The most stable areas were the "red" Center and the "white" Northeast, whereas the South was most volatile (and arguably remains so). The industrial Northwest has always had both red and white pockets, with most of its major urban areas having a strong left but not a profound subcultural network. For a discussion of partisan stability in the postwar period, see Samuel H. Barnes, *Representation in Italy* (Chicago: University of Chicago Press, 1977), chaps. 4 and 5.

5. The term is Ernesto Galli della Loggia's. See his "La crisi del togliattismo," *Mondoperaio* 31 (June 1978), pp. 53–58. A similar argument is developed at much greater length and in more detail in Marcello Fedele, *Classi e partiti negli anni '70* (Rome: Editori Riuniti, 1979).

6. This is not to argue that militants are only motivated by symbolic or ideological incentives; I am arguing, however, that the levels of activism in the PCI, particularly among tens of thousands of rank-and-file volunteers, are incomprehensible without this as a primary explanation.

7. Lucio Magri, "Problems of the Marxist Theory of the Revolutionary Party," *New Left Review* 60 (March–April 1970), p. 122.

8. The internal debate of this period is covered in detail in S. Hellman, "PCI Strategy and the Problem of Revolution in the West," in Shlomo Avineri, ed., *Varieties of Marxism* (The Hague: M. Nijhoff, 1977), pp. 205–15. See also Grant Amyot, *The Italian Communist Party: The Crisis of the Popular Front Strategy* (London: Croom Helm, 1981), esp. chaps. 2, 3, and 10.

9. Berlinguer's opening address and conclusions at the PCI's Thirteenth Congress in 1972 contained most of the contours of the *compromesso storico*; see PCI, *XIII Congresso del PCI: Atti e risoluzioni* (Rome: Editori Riuniti, 1972), pp. 54–59, 475–89. The term itself, along with specific overtures to the DC, appeared in a series of three articles published in the party's weekly, *Rinascita*, in the autumn of 1973; see the issues of September 28 and October 5 and 12.

10. The PCI employs this term to refer to all political parties except those of the extreme right and left.

11. For a good sample of his views, see Franco Rodano, *Questione democristiana e compromesso storico* (Rome: Editori Riuniti, 1977).

12. For a fuller discussion and more thorough documentation, see S. Hellman, "The Longest Campaign: PCI Strategy and the Elections of 1976," in Howard Penniman, ed., *Italy at the Polls:*

*The Parliamentary Elections of 1976* (Washington, D.C.: American Enterprise Institute, 1977), pp. 162–70.

13. "Hot autumn" technically refers to the fall of 1969, when labor mobilization peaked, but the term is also used in a broader sense as shorthand for the 1968–1972 cycle of labor struggles and broad societal agitation.

14. On traditional left and right views within the framework of the *via italiana*, see Hellman, "PCI Strategy and the Problem of Revolution," and Amyot, *The Italian Communist Party*.

15. See especially Togliatti's opening addresses to the Eighth and Ninth Congresses of the PCI in Palmiro Togliatti, *Nella democrazia e nella pace verso il socialismo* (Rome: Editori Riuniti, 1963), pp. 52 and 146–48. A good synthetic statement is "Capitalismo e riforme di struttura," in Palmiro Togliatti, *La via italiana al socialismo* (Rome: Editori Riuniti, 1964), pp. 263–68.

16. Eloquent testimony to this concern is a special supplement of 400 pages to the PCI's official theoretical journal, brought out in 1972 to commemorate the party's fiftieth anniversary. See *Critica marxista, Quaderno n. 5: Storia politica organizzazione nella lotta dei comunisti italiani per un nuovo blocco storico.*

17. With considerable justification, Italian Communists could point to the writings of Antonio Gramsci, martyred party leader and theoretical source of at least the outlines of many of Togliatti's more original ideas, for their sensitivity to the problems the PCI would face because of the "Roman question." References abound to the moral, ideological, and political role of the church in Antonio Gramsci, *Selections from the Prison Notebooks*, Quintin Hoare and Geoffrey Nowell-Smith, eds. (New York: International Publishers, 1971). Of course, whether PCI behavior toward the DC has anything to do with Gramsci is a much more dubious proposition.

18. For an analysis of the place of the midddle classes in PCI strategy, see S. Hellman, "PCI Strategy and the Case of the Middle Classes," in Donald L. M. Blackmer and Sidney Tarrow, eds., *Communism in Italy and France* (Princeton, N.J.: Princeton University Press, 1975), pp. 373–403.

19. His initial sortie at the Thirteenth Congress was a more traditionally framed option: he spoke in terms of long-term collaboration between "the three great popular currents in Italian history" (Communists, Socialists, and Catholics). PCI, *XIII Congresso*.

20. For the earliest statement of this position, see Gerardo Chiaromonte, "I conti con la DC," *Rinascita* (May 25, 1973): 14. Note that this was formulated several months before the coup in Chile.

21. See, e.g., his speech to the Chamber of Deputies on July 5, 1972, as well as a meeting with workers in Ravenna on November 8, 1973. Both speeches are reprinted in Enrico Berlinguer, *La "questione comunista" 1969–1975* (Rome: Editori Riuniti, 1975), Vol. I, p. 469, and Vol. II, p. 657. An extended discussion of the fate of the lesser left-wing lists in the 1972 elections can be found in Mario Caciagli, "L'insuccesso delle liste minori di sinistra," in Mario Caciagli and Alberto Spreafico, eds., *Un sistema politico alla prova* (Bologna: Il Mulino, 1975), pp. 179–250. A more specific analysis of the Catholic lists' fate is in Luigi Covatta, "L'itinerario della sinistra cattolica," *Giovane Critica* (Winter 1973): 17–33.

22. Thus avoiding the entanglements characteristic of social-democratic parties, against which Togliatti often warned. See note 15, above.

23. The classic document in this regard is V. I. Lenin, *The State and Revolution*, in *Selected Works* (New York: International Publishers, 1967), Vol. II, pp. 263–361.

24. There is a massive literature on this topic. Some of the best analyses include Ruggero Orfei, *L'occupazione di potere* (Milan: Longanesi & Co., 1976); Giorgio Galli and Alessandra Nannei, *Il capitalismo assistenziale* (Milan: SugarCo, 1976); Antonio Mutti and Paolo Segatti, *La borghesia di Stato* (Milan: Mazzotta, 1977); and Eugenio Scalfari and Giuseppe Turani, *Razza padrona* (Milan: Feltrinelli, 1974). In English, see esp. Giuseppe Di Palma, "The Available State: Problems of Reform," in Peter Lange and Sidney Tarrow, eds., *Italy in Transition* (London: Frank Cass, 1980), pp. 149–65.

25. In addition to "normal abuses" such as extensive political surveillance, wiretapping, and

excessive force in dealing with demonstrators, the early 1970s witnessed widespread sabotage of investigations of rightist terrorism and rumors and partial evidence of coups plotted high in the military and security service hierarchies.

26. Most notably by the case of *Il Manifesto*, the name of both a group of many of the party's best-known leftists and the journal they published. They were ejected from the party in 1969, taking with them some of the most articulate representatives of the radical tendency in Italian communism. This episode chilled discussion inside the PCI, as might be expected. The one outcome which might have helped left-wing tendencies inside the PCI—a good showing in 1972 by the numerous groups and parties to the left of the PCI—failed to materialize. In fact, these groups so badly split the vote that none elected a single candidate, and more than a million votes on the left were "wasted." For a discussion of the Manifesto, see Hellman, "PCI Strategy and the Problem of Revolution," pp. 215–19. For a discussion of the travails of this group and the others to the left of the PCI through the mid-1970s, see S. Hellman, "The New Left in Italy," in Martin Kolinsky and William Paterson, eds., *Social and Political Movements in Western Europe* (London: Croom Helm, 1976), pp. 243–73.

27. Luciano Gruppi, *Togliatti e la via italiana al socialismo* (Rome: Editori Riuniti, 1976), esp. chap. 8. Although the publication date of this work is 1976, the text consists of a course given by the author, the head of the national party school, in 1974.

28. See note 11, above.

29. Berlinguer spoke for the first time of a "possible alternation" of governments without catastrophic results in a speech to provincial and regional leaders of the PCI; the text appears in *l'Unità*, May 26, 1978. He elaborated on this point in the July 1978 Central Committee meeting, which is reported in *l'Unità*, July 25, 1978.

30. Bulletin of the Executive (*Direzione*) of the PCI, *l'Unità*, November 27, 1980.

31. It is quite clear that Togliatti himself strongly believed that the tripartite collaboration would be long-term, and accounts of the period usually portray him as deeply shocked when the PCI and PSI were ejected from the government in 1947. Good summaries and analyses of his expectations can be found in Spriano, *Storia del Partito comunista*, Vol. V, chap. 15; Giuseppe Mammarella, *Il Partito comunista italiano 1945/1975: Dalla Liberazione al compromesso storico* (Florence: Vallecchi, 1976), pp. 27–55; and Alessandro Natta, "La Resistenza e la formazione del 'partito nuovo,' " in Paolo Spriano et al., *Problemi di storia del Partito comunista italiano* (Rome: Editori Riuniti, 1971); esp. pp. 57–73. An excellent, well-documented synthesis that analyzes the PCI leadership's postwar expectations in depth can be found in Severino Galante, "Sulle 'condizioni' della democrazia progressiva nella linea politica del PCI (1943–1948)," *Il Politico* (September 1975): 455–74. In English, see Sassoon, *The Strategy of the Italian Communist Party*, chaps. 3–5.

32. The Communists' electoral gains were primarily achieved in the South. In their central strongholds, they advanced at a much more modest rate. In the North—both the Catholic Northeast and the industrial Northwest—the PCI lost votes and members.

33. The definitive study of the PCI's relationship with the USSR in this period remains Donald L. M. Blackmer, *Unity in Diversity: Italian Communism and the Communist World* (Cambridge, Mass.: MIT Press, 1968). For a recent and excellent study of PCI–CPSU relations, see Joan Barth Urban, *Moscow and the Italian Communist Party* (Ithaca, N.Y.: Cornell University Press, 1986).

34. The number of PCI–PSI coalitions dropped from 1,119 to 708 following the creation of local Center-Left governments, although the PCI never suffered quite the degree of isolation its adversaries hoped for because it was able to reconstruct numerous leftist coalitions with breakaway factions of the PSI. For more details, see Martha H. Good, "The Italian Communist Party and Local Government Coalitions," *Studies in Comparative Communism* 13 (August 1980): esp. 206–19.

35. The most important contribution is that of Marzio Barbagli et al., *Fluidità elettorale e classi sociali in Italia: 1968–1976* (Bologna: Il Mulino, 1979), esp. part III. For an earlier but identical argument based on interviews with communist leaders, see Hellman, "The Longest Campaign," 165–70.

36. The referendum can only be used to repeal a specific law or designated articles of a specific law; the number of the law, along with its date of promulgation, must be stated on the petitions calling for abrogation. To rewrite a law would therefore nullify the petitions, which must contain a half-million valid signatures of Italian voters. To repeal a *new* law, then, would compel the abrogationists to begin the entire process from scratch, with new petitions specifying the new law (or its offending articles) by number.

37. See Berlinguer's addresses to the June and December 1974 Central Committee Meetings in Berlinguer, *La "questione comunista,"* Vol. II, pp. 758–59, 965.

38. For an explicitly blunt refusal to countenance deep criticism of the strategy, see Berlinguer's conclusions, PCI, *XIV Congresso del PCI: Atti e risoluzioni* (Rome: Editori Riuniti, 1975): 634–35. For a sampling of the criticism of the DC's leaders, see Gerardo Chiaromonte, "I conti con la DC," *Rinascita*, May 25, 1973, p. 15; Luciano Barca, "L'intreccio politico con l'industria di Stato," ibid., pp. 14–15. On DC support, see Romano Ledda, "Il volto laico dell'Italia," *Rinascita*, July 2, 1976, pp. 1–2; and Gerardo Chiaromonte's address to the July 1976 Central Committee Meeting, *l'Unità*, July 3, 1976, p. 10.

39. The strongly procompromise leaders refused to abandon the basic contours of the *compromesso* even after the revisions at the end of the 1970s. Exemplary in this regard is Gerardo Chiaromonte's insistence, in 1980, that left unity was intended not as an alternative to the DC but as a means to achieve an even broader unity; see his contribution to "Tre domande sulla strategia della sinistra," *Critica marxista* 18 (July–August 1980), p. 47.

40. Out of nearly thirty-seven million votes cast. The immensity of the gain is a result of the fact that the voting age for the Chamber of Deputies was lowered, between 1972 and 1976, from twenty-one to eighteen years of age. The electorate increased by just over 9 percent between these two elections. See Giacomo Sani, "Le elezioni degli anni settanta: terremoto o evoluzione?" *Rivista italiana di scienza politica* 6 (March–April 1976), pp. 261–88.

41. This argument is developed at greater length in S. Hellman, "Il Pci e l'ambigua eredità dell'autunno caldo a Torino," *Il Mulino* 268 (March–April 1980), pp. 249–50.

42. The earliest and, in my view, still the best discussion of the different motivations to emerge in the Italian electorate in the 1970s is Arturo Parisi and Gianfranco Pasquino, "Relazioni partiti elettori e tipi di voto," in Parisi and Pasquino, eds., *Continuità e mutamento elettorale in Italia* (Bologna: Il Mulino, 1977), pp. 67–102. For a summary of their argument in English, see their "Changes in Italian Electoral Behaviour," in Lange and Tarrow, *Italy in Transition*, pp. 6–30.

43. Table 1.1 shows that although the DC managed to maintain its vote in 1976, it did so primarily at the expense of its minor partners among the laical parties. Thus, precisely when the PCI was arguing that many progressive Catholics supported the DC, the ruling party had obtained an unprecedented degree of support from moderate and conservative but secular urban middle strata. And these groups flocked to the DC because they saw it as the most effective bulwark against the PCI, which, in 1976, appeared to have a chance to overtake the DC as the country's largest party. For contemporary efforts by the Communists to discount the importance of this polarization—or to deny that it even occurred—see Ledda, "Il volto laico"; and Vasco Calonaci and Ugo Pasqualetti, "Una logica de rifiutare," *l'Unità*, July 15, 1976, p. 3.

44. Enrico Berlinguer, address to provincial and regional leaders, reported in *l'Unità*, May 26, 1978.

45. Ibid.; see also Berlinguer's address to the July Central Committee Meeting, *l'Unità*, July 25, 1978.

46. There was a particularly agitated Central Committee Meeting in October 1976, at which numerous speakers pointed out the dangers of not spelling out a clear set of priorities, both to provide an agenda for militants and as a platform from which to force the DC into action. For extensive coverage, see *l'Unità*, October 19-22, 1976.

47. Most notably in a campaign to link the idea of austerity to a transformative vision for Italy, and in a "Medium-Term Project." Both initiatives date from early 1977, although the project was not finally produced until the summer of that year, an indication of the difficulties among top

leaders in thrashing out an agreement. See Enrico Berlinguer, *Austerità occasione per trasformare l'Italia* (Rome: Editori Riuniti, 1977); and Giorgio Napolitano, ed., *Proposta di progetto a medio termine* (Rome: Editori Riuniti, 1977).

48. Gianni Cervetti, *Partito di governo e di lotta* (Rome: Editori Riuniti, 1977). Cervetti was the head of the party's Organization Section at the time, and this text was his address to the Central Committee Meeting of December 1976.

49. A good analysis of these activities and the problems they created for local activists in Naples can be found in Judith Chubb, "Naples under the Left: The Limits of Local Change," *Comparative Politics* 13 (October 1980), pp. 70–71. For probing insights into the phenomenon in a generally superb overview, see also Gianfranco Pasquino, "Il Pci nel sistema politico italiano degli anni settanta," *Il Mulino* 284 (November–December 1982), pp. 875–76. Pasquino points out that Communist efforts to enforce a homogeneity of governments at all levels of the country raised serious questions about the PCI's understanding of democracy.

50. The speaker was Maurizio Valenzi, the mayor of Naples, as cited in Chubb, "Naples under the Left," p. 78, n. 25.

51. For a more extended discussion of what follows, see S. Hellman, "The Italian CP: Stumbling at the Threshold?" *Problems of Communism* 27 (November–December 1978), pp. 33–35.

52. The Communists eventually signaled that they would accept the inclusion of nonparty "technicians" acceptable to the left in the cabinet. The Christian Democrats encouraged the PCI to believe such a cabinet would be presented, as the early edition of *l'Unità* of March 15, 1978, makes clear. When the cabinet's composition was announced later the same morning, the edition was quickly yanked from the stands.

53. Federico Stame, *Società civile e critica delle istituzioni* (Milan: Feltrinelli, 1977), makes this point in a variety of contexts. A lucid summary is presented in Marco Cammelli, "Politica istituzionale e modello emiliano: ipotesi per una ricerca," *Il Mulino* 259 (September–October 1978), pp. 763–65. For a similar argument from within the PCI, see Giuseppe Vacca, "Figure della crisi: Le sinistre e il caso italiano negli anni Settanta," in Ingrao et al., *Il partito politico*, pp. 120–26.

54. Nino Magna, "Dirigenza e base," in Aris Accornero, Renato Mannheimer, and Chiara Sebastiani, eds., *L'identità comunista: I militanti, le strutture, la cultura del Pci* (Rome: Editori Riuniti, 1983), p. 189.

55. In the first month following the 1975 voting, communist participation in municipal governments alone rose from 1,600 to 2,500 (out of approximately 8,000 municipalities in Italy); *L'Espresso*, July 20, 1975, p. 9. This figure does not include equally significant gains in Italy's twenty regional and ninety-four provincial assemblies. For a summary, see Good, "The Italian Communist Party," pp. 208–14, esp. Table 2, p. 210.

56. See especially Magna, "Dirigenza e base," as well as his "Eletti e amministratori," also in Accornero, Mannheimer, and Sebastiani, *L'identità comunista*, pp. 223–56.

57. PCI, Sezione scuole di partito, *Formazione dei quadri e sviluppo del Partito: Atti del V Convegno nazionale della sezione centrale scuole di partito* (Rome: Editori Riuniti, 1978).

58. The debate in the pages of *Rinascita* was kicked off by the brother of the secretary general, himself an important figure in the PCI. See Giovanni Berlinguer, "Perchè meno quadri operai e contadini?" *Rinascita*, June 10, 1977, pp. 7–8. This was followed by more than a dozen articles and several dozen letters in the PCI's weekly; the debate lasted into the summer of 1978.

59. This would include the Northwest and the South. In the Center, the PCI had been a dominant local political force since the end of the war, while in the "white" Northeast, it remained, by and large, below the level where it could become a governing party even though it had made substantial gains in 1975.

60. The impact of de-Stalinization on local party organizations is discussed in S. Hellman, "Generational Differences in the Bureaucratic Elite of Italian Communist Party Provincial Federations," *Canadian Journal of Political Science* 8 (March 1975), esp. pp. 97–106.

**Chapter 2**

1. The PCI Federation of Turin embraces the entire Province of Turin (population 2.4 million). The city of the same name (population 1.2 million) dominates the province, as well as the region of Piedmont; it is the capital of both. It is to the capital that "Turin" in the text will generally refer. The context will make clear when the province or the federation is the subject of discussion.

2. A good, if somewhat dated, synthesis in English of the basic outlines of Italian political geography is Giorgio Galli and Alfonso Prandi, *Patterns of Political Participation in Italy* (New Haven, Conn.: Yale University Press, 1971). More recently, Arnaldo Bagnasco has refined the older conceptions even further. See his *Tre Italie: La problematica territoriale dello sviluppo italiano* (Bologna: Il Mulino, 1977).

3. See in particular Harry Eckstein's provocative arguments in "Case Study and Theory in Political Science," in Greenstein and Polsby, eds., *Handbook of Political Science, Vol. 7*.

4. Antonio Gramsci, *L'Ordine Nuovo 1919–1920* (Turin: Einaudi, 1955), p. 320.

5. Out of the vast bibliography on this topic, I have primarily relied on two recent studies for my very restricted summary: Gianfranco Zunino, "Struttura industriale, sviluppo tecnologico, e movimento operaio a Torino nel secondo dopoguerra," in Ettore Passerin d'Entreves et al., *Movimento operaio e sviluppo economico in Piemonte negli ultimi cinquant'anni* (Torino: Cassa di Risparmio, 1978), pp. 61–128; Valerio Castronovo, *Il Piemonte*, Vol. I of *Storia delle regioni dall'Unità ad oggi* (Torino: Einaudi, 1977), pp. 613–726.

6. Castronovo, *Il Piemonte*, 639–43.

7. Ibid., p. 690. Figures for the industrial belt were adapted from 1971 census data reported in Associazione Piemonte Italia, *I Comuni del Piemonte 1974* (Turin: Stamperia Artistica Nazionale, 1974), pp. 23–29, 38–52.

8. Anna Anfossi, "L'immigrazione meridionale a Torino," in Centro di Ricerche Industriali e Sociali di Torino (CRIS), *Immigrazione e industria* (Milan: Comunità, 1962), p. 169. In this period, 155,000 of the 464,000 newcomers to Turin were Southerners.

9. Filippo Barbano and Franco Garelli, "Struttura e cultura nell'immigrazione: Il caso di Torino," in F. Barbano et al., *Strutture della transformazione* (Turin: Cassa di Risparmio, 1980), pp. 193, 130. See also pp. 249–54 for an extensive bibliography on Turinese immigration since World War II.

10. Renata Yedid Jodice, "L'organizzazione del 'partito nuovo': Il Pci torinese nel 1945–46," in Aldo Agosti and Gian Mario Bravo, eds., *Storia del movimento operaio, del socialismo, e delle lotte sociali in Piemonte* (Bari: De Donato, 1981), Vol. IV, pp. 72–85. See also Renzo Gianotti, *Trent'anni di lotte alla Fiat (1948–1978)* (Bari: De Donato, 1979), pp. 7–29, esp. pp. 19–20.

11. There is an extensive literature on all aspects of the policies of this period. For good syntheses, see Eugenio Scalfari, *L'autunno della Repubblica* (Milan: Etas Kompass, 1969), chaps. 2 and 3; Gianotti, *Trent'anni di lotte*, pp. 47–70. For superb firsthand accounts which include excellent broader insights as well, see Aris Accornero, *Gli anni '50 in fabbrica* (Bari: De Donato, 1973); Aris Accornero and Vittorio Reiser, *Il mestiere dell'avanguardia* (Bari: De Donato, 1981); and Emilio Pugno and Sergio Garavini, *Gli anni duri alla Fiat* (Turin: Einaudi, 1974).

12. One experience, recounted to me by a veteran of the period, involved the sorting of various nuts, bolts, and screws of different sizes from a large drum into smaller bins. When the task was completed, a foreman would arrive and dump the bins' contents back into the original drum, instructing the worker to start all over.

13. Paolo Spriano, *Storia del PCI, Vol. V: La Resistenza, Togliatti e il partito nuovo* (Turin: Einaudi, 1975), pp. 412–13. See also Direzione del PCI, "Informazioni riassuntive sull'attività delle Commissioni centrali di lavoro per l'anno 1946," *Conferenza Nazionale d'Organizzazione* (Florence, January 1947), esp. pp. 17 and 18, where 98 percent of federation secretaries and 70 percent of all members of Federal Committees are reported as pre-Resistance veterans. More than

four-fifths of the secretaries were over thirty-five years of age, and this distribution was described as "good" (p. 13).

14. The quotation is from Luciano Barca, "Per una storia della Fiat dalla Liberazione alla situazione de oggi," *Rinascita* (July–August 1957), pp. 81–82. For testimony on the intervention from party headquarters in Rome, see Giorgio Amendola, *Lettere a Milano*, 2nd ed. (Rome: Editori Riuniti, 1976), pp. 503–4. A detailed discussion of the problems can be found in Yedid Jodice, "L'organizzazione," pp. 74–97.

15. Luciano Lama (interviewed by Massimo Riva), *Intervista sul sindacato* (Bari: Laterza, 1976), pp. 33–34.

16. For succinct illustrations, see Gianotti, *Trent'anni di lotte*, pp. 33–37; and Accornero, *Gli anni '50*, pp. 65–77.

17. Pietro Ingrao, "Il XX Congresso del PCUS e l'VIII Congresso del PCI," in Paolo Spriano et al., *Problemi di storia del Partito comunista italiano* (Rome: Editori Riuniti, 1971), p. 142.

18. See Giuseppe Berta's superb analysis in "Il neocapitalismo e la crisi delle organizzazioni di classe," in Agosti and Bravo, *Storia del movimento operaio*, esp. pp. 123–34.

19. Roberto Gabetti, *Architettura industria Piemonte negli ultimi cinquant'anni* (Turin: Cassa di Risparmio, 1977), p. 187.

20. Gian Primo Cella, "Stabilità e crisi del centralismo nell'organizzatione sindacale," in Fondazione Giangiacomo Feltrinelli, *Annali (1974–75)* (Milan: Feltrinelli, 1976), Vol. XVI, pp. 645–47.

21. Berta, "Il neocapitalismo," p. 123.

22. Castronovo, *Il Piemonte*, pp. 724–25.

23. On these changes, see S. Hellman, "Generational Differences in the Bureaucratic Elite of Italian Communist Party Provincial Federations," *Canadian Journal of Political Science* 8 (March 1975): 99–106. On the situation in Turin at the same time, see Giuseppe Bonazzi, "Problemi politici e condizione umana dei funzionari del PCI: Una indagine sulla federazione comunista di Torino," *Tempi Moderni* 8 (July–September 1965): 51–54.

24. Berta discusses the party's general slowness to come to terms with the full implications of the change in "Il neocapitalismo," pp. 155–68. On Turin, see Grant Amyot, *The Italian Communist Party: The Crisis of the Popular Front Strategy* (London: Croom Helm, 1981), chap. 7.

25. Louis Althusser, "What Must Change in the Party," *New Left Review* 109 (May–June 1978): 39, 43.

26. Membership statistics for the late 1970s indicate that just under 60% of the party members are workers. Another 11% are classified as "clerks and technicians," but almost all come from factories or large public service firms. Another 10% are pensioners who used to work in factories. All 3 categories came to under 55% for the party as a whole in 1973, (the last date for which data on pensioners' previous jobs were published). PCI, *Dati sulla organizzazione del Partito* (Rome, 1975), p. 47.

27. Aris Accornero, "Operaismo e sindacato," in Giorgio Napolitano et al., *Operaismo e centralità operaia* (Rome: Editori Riuniti, 1978), pp. 36–43.

28. For a very useful discussion with reference to several different settings in Italy, see Miriam Golden, "L'austerità e i rapporti base-vertice nel caso dei metalmeccanici," *Laboratorio politico* 5–6 (1982): 62–66.

29. Berta, "Il neocapitalismo." For the Turinese Federation's self-criticism, see the letter to party headquarters now reprinted in Luciano Barca et al., *I comunisti e l'economia italiana 1944–1974* (Bari: De Donato, 1975), pp. 188–99. The "official" position of the PCI and the CGIL can be found in Luca Pavolini, *Inchiesta sui sindacati nel triangolo industriale* (Milan: Feltrinelli, 1957).

30. Romano Alquati, *Sulla Fiat e altri scritti* (Milan: Feltrinelli, 1975), esp. pp. 229–53, 292–302.

31. During the hot autumn, complaints about the long-range effects of this policy were voiced in the largest federations in the Red Belt. See S. Hellman, *Organization and Ideology in Four Italian Communist Federations* (unpublished Ph.D. dissertation, Yale University, 1973), chap. 9.

32. The ratio is 15:1 in the capital and 13.5:1 in the entire province; the national average is 7:1, but 6:1 in the North.

33. On the "normal" organizational behavior of PCI organizations in areas hegemonized by a "white" subculture, see Hellman, *Organization and Ideology*, chaps. 5 and 10. On their *political* behavior, see Alan Stern, "Political Legitimacy in Local Politics: The Communist Party in Northeastern Italy," in Donald L. M. Blackmer and Sidney Tarrow, eds., *Communism in Italy and France* (Princeton, N.J.: Princeton University Press, 1975), chap. 6.

34. It was least successful after 1976 with the Turinese FIOM, however, for reasons that can be deduced from the discussion in this section. For a detailed discussion of the party's mixed success in getting the unions to follow the austerity line in the post-1976 period, see Golden, "L'austerità e i rapporti"; for an exhaustive analysis in English, see Miriam Golden, *Austerity and Its Opposition: Persistent Radicalism in the Italian Labor Movement* (Ithaca, N.Y.: Cornell University Press, 1988).

35. The most extensive study of workers' struggles is the six-volume work edited by Alessandro Pizzorno under the general title *Lotte operaie e sindacato in Italia, 1968–1972*. General conclusions are presented in the final volume, Alessandro Pizzorno et al., *Lotte operaie e sindacato: Il ciclo 1968–1972 in Italia* (Bologna: Il Mulino, 1978). A summary in English of many of the findings and arguments of this research appears in Ida Regalia et al., "Labour Conflicts and Industrial Relations in Italy, 1968–1975," in Colin Crouch and Alessandro Pizzorno, eds., *The Resurgence of Class Conflict in Western Europe since 1968, Vol. I: National Studies* (London: Macmillan, 1978), pp. 101–58. For a general analysis in English which has a focus less restricted to the realm of industrial relations and offers useful comparisons with France, see Michele Salvati, "May 1968 and the Hot Autumn of 1969: The Responses of Two Ruling Classes," in Suzanne Berger, ed., *Organizing Interests in Western Europe* (Cambridge and New York: Cambridge University Press, 1981), pp. 329–63. On the struggles at Fiat, see Gianotti, *Trent'anni di lotte*, pp. 160–204.

36. Gianotti, *Trent'anni di lotte*, pp. 133–44; Alquati, *Sulla Fiat*, chap. 5.

37. An immense amount has been written about the mass worker and the new demands this figure brought onto the scene, both inside and outside the factory. Without the slightest pretext of suggesting a broad range of readings, I would indicate the following as unusually provocative with wildly different emphases: Aris Accornero, *Il lavoro come ideologia* (Bologna: Il Mulino, 1980); Paolo Ceri, "L'Autonomia operaia tra organizzazione del lavoro e sistema politico," *Quaderni di sociologia* 26 (January–March 1977): 28–63; Alquati, *Sulla Fiat*, esp. chaps. 1 and 7.

38. This was candidly admitted by PCI leaders and militants in a series of interviews in Turin in June and July 1973.

39. Renzo Gianotti, "Il movimento operaio in Piemonte: Un bilancio (1960–1980)," in Agosti and Bravo, *Storia del movimento operaio*, pp. 414–16.

40. The phrase is Celso Ghini's; see his *Il terremoto del 15 giugno* (Milan: Feltrinelli, 1976). The idea of an earthquake was challenged by Giacomo Sani in "Le elezioni degli anni settanta: terremoto o evoluzione?" *Rivista italiana di scienza politica* 6 (1976): 261–88.

41. Federazione torinese del PCI, *XVI Congresso provinciale* (Turin: typescript, 1972), p. 319.

42. Ibid., "Mozione politica" (unpaginated), item 3.

43. See Chapter 3, herein, for a complete discussion.

44. The legislation was so called because it had been introduced in Parliament by Oronzo Reale, the (PRI) minister of the Interior.

45. The size of individual *seggi* can vary considerably. The vast majority, however, fall between 400 and 600 eligible voters.

46. For evidence from Bologna, see David I. Kertzer, *Comrades and Christians: Religion and Political Struggle in Communist Italy* (Cambridge and New York: Cambridge University Press, 1980), chaps. 7 and 9. In a place such as Bologna, where immigrants are not so numerous and

the party's home-grown base is immense and well organized, the local PCI is frequently a less than enthusiastic champion of such groups.

47. See Chapter 3, herein, and, for more details, S. Hellman, "A 'New Style of Governing': Italian Communism and the Dilemmas of Transition in Turin, 1975–1979," *Studies in Political Economy* 2 (Autumn 1979): 159–97. A concrete illustration of the dimensions of the problem facing the PCI can be found in a study carried out by the federation which sampled seventy-five hundred families out of a universe of 35,000 in public housing. One-third were found either to pay no rent at all or arbitrarily to pay only a fraction of their required allotment. Federazione di Torino, Commissione casa, *Analisi della politica dell'IACP dal '75 ad oggi* (Turin: mimeograph, 1979), pp. 20–22.

48. Analyzing the 1979 vote in Bologna, Genoa, and Verona, Piergiorgio Corbetta concludes, "the PCI not only lost working-class votes, but it practically lost only working-class votes." "Novità e incertezze nel voto del 3 giugno: Analisi dei flussi elettorali," in Arturo Parisi, ed., *Mobilità senza movimento: Le elezioni del 3 giugno 1979* (Bologna: Il Mulino, 1980), p. 63. My findings for Turin suggest significant losses for the Communists among other strata, but the major point here is that the PCI could not automatically deliver the workers' vote even where it boasts a very large party machine.

49. From 45.9 percent to 45.3 percent. Calculated from the same sources reported in Table 2.3.

50. Arturo Parisi and Gianfranco Pasquino, "Changes in Italian Electoral Behaviour," in Peter Lange and Sidney Tarrow, eds., *Italy in Transition* (London: Frank Cass, 1980), esp. pp. 13–27. For very useful applications of the concepts, see the same authors' individual contributions to Parisi, *Mobilità senza movimento*, pp. 11–40, 103–32.

51. Parisi and Pasquino, "Changes in Italian Electoral Behaviour," pp. 14–18.

52. Aldo Tortorella, "Il partito a Milano," *Critica marxista* 1 (September–December, 1963): 227–45. For a very intelligent analysis of varied organizational performance in diverse environments, see Peter Lange, "The PCI at the Local Level: A Study of Strategic Performance," in Blackmer and Tarrow, *Communism in Italy and France*, pp. 259–304.

53. Technically, 1977 saw the federation lose 115 members and thus might be counted as the beginning of the period of decline. Because a great deal of documentation exists for 1977 (a national congress was held that year), I have counted it as part of the period of expansion.

54. The only exception to this generation was the Federation of Brescia, a medium-sized industrial center in Lombardy.

55. For more details and specific data, see S. Hellman, "Il PCI e l'ambigua eredità dell'autunno caldo a Torino," *Il Mulino* 268 (March–April 1980): 264–65.

56. See, for example, Piero Borghini, " 'Svolte di generazione' e processo rivoluzionario nell'esperienza e nell'elaborazione teorica dei comunisti italiani," *Nuova generazione* Quaderno #2, Supplement to No. 96, (June 16, 1972): 85–86.

57. We should also recall that when the PSIUP was dissolved after failing to win any seats in the 1972 general election, most of its leaders publicly joined the PCI. The Turinese PSIUP had been quite strong and had enjoyed close relations with the PCI, and many of its militants entered the Communist party. See the note in Table 2.4.

58. There is strong evidence that the PCI was initially much less successful in recruiting militants from traditionally unfriendly backgrounds in areas of high social conflict; these differences faded, however, as the 1970s wore on. See Hellman, "Militanti e politica nel Triangolo industriale," in Accornero et al., *L'identità comunista*, pp. 396–97, 428. For an analysis of the party's electoral fortunes over the same period which leads to numerous parallel conclusions, see Marzio Barbagli et al., *Fluidità elettorale e classi sociali in Italia* (Bologna: Il Mulino, 1979) pp. 147–54.

59. For a variety of reactions from within the PCI, see *Rinascita*, (October 24, 1980): 3–10.

60. Barbagli and Corbetta, measuring the PCI's ability to organize an absolute percentage of the working class, have argued that the Turinese party's achievements in this period are less impressive. I have argued that the party's poor showing in absolute terms is by no means

unimportant but that it reflects the PCI's endemic weaknesses in large urban centers and not its performance in recruiting workers since 1968. See Barbagli and Corbetta, "Partito e movimento," *Inchiesta* 8 (January–February 1978); Hellman, "Il Pci e l'ambigua eredità," for my critique; and Marzio Barbagli and Piergiorgio Corbetta, "L'elettorato, l'organizzazione del Pci e i movimenti," *Il Mulino* 29 (May–June 1980): 467–90, for their response.

61. The argument that follows is developed at much greater length and with extensive documentation in Hellman, "Il Pci e l'ambigua eredità."

# Chapter 3

1. For an early example, see the summary of the heated debate in the Central Committee reported in *l'Unità*, October 20, 1976, p. 7; and October 21, pp. 7–8.

2. "Mozione conclusiva Conferenza Cittadina PCI torinese," *I problemi di adeguamento e rafforzamento dell'organizzazione di Partito* (Turin: mimeograph, February 6–8, 1976), pp. 1–2.

3. This dynamic was very effectively described by the regional secretary of the PCI in Umbria, which is one of Italy's "red regions" and therefore much more solidly organized than Turin. See Gino Galli, "I rischi del partito dove governiamo," *Rinascita*, October 22, 1976, pp. 7–8.

4. Relazione del compagno Renzo Gianotti, "Implicazioni strategiche della nostra politica," *Seminario di quadri comunisti* (Turin: mimeograph, September 24–25, 1976), p. 10. See esp. PCI, Federazione torinese, *PCI partito di governo: Il rapporto tra partito e istituzioni, nota congressuale della 1ᵃ commissione del CF e della CFC* (Turin: mimeograph, 1977), pp. 24–27. This document was prepared for discussion at the Sixteenth Congress of the federation.

5. *PCI partito di governo*, p. 27.

6. Ibid.

7. Ibid., p. 25.

8. Miriam Golden, *Austerity and Its Opposition: Persistent Radicalism in the Italian Labor Movement* (Ithaca, N.Y.: Cornell University Press, 1988), chap. 3; Stefano Bevacqua and Giuseppe Turani, *La svolta del '78* (Milan: Feltrinelli, 1978); Michael J. Sodaro, "The Italian Communists and the Politics of Austerity," *Studies in Comparative Communism* 13 (Summer–Autumn 1980): 220–49.

9. Gianni Cervetti, *Partito di governo e di lotta* (Rome: Editori Riuniti, 1977). Cervetti was the head of the Organization Section of the PCI at the time, and this book was his address to the December 1976 Central Committee.

10. This procedure only works when the constituencies in question form part of the Communists' traditional bloc of allies. In the late 1970s, left-wing student mobilizations totally escaped the control of the party in Bologna, with disastrous consequences. For a penetrating analysis of these events, see Gianfranco Pasquino and Angelo Panebianco, "Bologna," *Città & Regione* 10–11 (October–November 1977): 172–92.

11. Marco Cammelli, "Politica istituzionale e modello emiliano: Ipotesi per una ricerca," *Il Mulino* 27 (September–October 1978): 743–67, offers an interesting review and periodization of the Emilian model.

12. Maurizio Marcelloni, "Urban Movements and Political Struggles in Italy," *International Journal of Urban and Regional Research* 3 (June 1979): 251–67. See esp. p. 254 for a good summary of the phases of the struggles and the development of the CdQ nationwide.

13. One source, admittedly biased, estimates that one hundred fifty thousand families in Piedmont practiced *autoriduzione* on their electricity bills late in 1974; that is, they cut their payment by the amount of the most recent increase. Eddy Cherki and Michel Wieviorka, "Luttes sociales en Italie: Les mouvements d'autoreduction à Turin," *Les Temps Modernes* 30 (June 1975): 1794.

14. The term *neighborhood* refers to a very large conglomeration in the lexicon of Italian public

administration. In Turin, the 1977 division of the city created units with an average population of just under fifty thousand; some were as large as eighty thousand.

15. See the comments on the DC in general and on Turin in particular in Claudio Martinelli, "Il ruolo dei partiti nel decentramento a Milano, 1973–74," in Umberto Dragone, ed., *Decentramento urbano e democrazia* (Milan: Feltrinelli, 1975), pp. 167–68.

16. Interview with Renato Valente, in ibid., p. 189.

17. Florence is an exemplary case in point, amply documented by Neri Gori, "Attivismo tradizionale e crisi della partecipazione nel PCI: Il caso di Firenze," *Rassegna italiana di sociologia* 16 (1975): 285–87; Raymond Seidelman, *Neighborhood Communism in Florence* (Ph.D. dissertation, Cornell University, 1978).

18. In his intervention in *XIV Congresso provinciale del PCI Torinese* (Turin: typed transcript, 1972), pp. 264–65.

19. For documented evidence of varying interpretations at the time, see the interventions of Montalenti, ibid., pp. 365–66, as well as those of Gargione, Nebbia, and Dirindin in *XV Congresso provinciale del PCI torinese* (Turin: unpaginated typed transcript, 1975).

20. Interview, July 4, 1978.

21. Novelli consistently made comments to this effect throughout 1978, at a meeting of the Cultural Commission of the federation (February 4); a preparatory seminar for PCI cadres for a conference on "Governing Turin" (July 1); and a meeting of communist militants and administrators from the capital city (July 14).

22. Figures cited at a meeting of the Federal Committee and the Federal Control Commission of the federation, May 15, 1978.

23. Interview, July 4, 1978.

24. *La Stampa*, September 18, 1977, p. 6.

25. For a partial chronicle of events, see *l'Unità*, November 16, 1977, p. 10; and November 27, 1977, p. 8. Also *La Stampa*, November 9, 1977, p. 6. (All references to *l'Unità* refer to the Turinese edition.)

26. *La Stampa*, December 15, 1977, p. 5; December 16, 1977, p. 4.

27. Meeting of the PCI leadership and neighborhood activists, October 10, 1977. The national leader, Armando Cossutta, was called away at the last minute to visit an area close to Turin which had just suffered severe flooding.

28. *La Stampa*, February 16, 1978, p. 4.

29. On DC delaying tactics, see *La Stampa*, July 22, 1978, p. 5. For the status of the councils at the end of 1978, see *La Stampa*, December 14, 1978, p. 4.

30. The PCI actually gained just over a full percentage point in the capital city in 1980, and at 39.1 percent it was remarkably close to its high-water mark of 40 percent achieved in the 1976 general election. In the province, however, it lost 2 percent compared with 1975 but rebounded considerably from the very large drop that had taken place in 1979.

31. For national reactions in the PCI to the defeat of the left in public as well as private schools, see *l'Unità*, December 18, 1977; more extended discussions can be found in Marisa Rodano, "Novità e contraddizioni nel voto per la scuola," *Rinascita*, December 23, 1977, pp. 5–6; and Enrico Meduni, "Perchè la battuta d'arresto nella scuola," *Rinascita*, February 17, 1978, pp. 31–32. Meduni makes some critical comments about the single-list tactic.

32. The Italian constitution only provides for abrogative referenda. A yes vote is therefore always in favor of eliminating the law in question or designated portions of it. A no vote is a vote to retain the contested legislation. See note 36 to Chapter 1, above.

33. The law was known by this name because it was originally introduced by Oronzo Reale, the PRI minister of the Interior in 1975.

34. Official party sources showed, for 1978, an income of twenty-nine billion lire (thirty-six million dollars) from direct fund-raising efforts. PCI, *Dati sulla organizzazione del partito* (1979), pp. 100, 104.

35. A 1979 study showed that the deaths of fifty-three innocent people had taken place at the

hands of the "forces of order" since the adoption of the *Legge Reale*. This is a very high figure for Italy. See *Panorama*, Mach 20, 1979, pp. 146–56.

36. Direzione PCI, Sezione Problemi dello Stato, "Perchè il No dei comunisti all'abrogazione della 'Legge Reale' " (Rome: mimeograph, May 25, 1978), pp. 1–2.

37. As indicated in note 32, above, the referendum is highly specific. Thus, if a law designated in the abrogationist petition is changed, the vote cannot be held. The government attempted to amend the *Legge Reale* by referring it to the Judiciary Committee of the Chamber of Deputies. But voting procedures in committee are very cumbersome (voting on the floor of Parliament is electronic). By presenting hundreds of their own amendments to the law in committee, the Radicals and their allies blocked the governmental maneuver and made it impossible to alter the original law before the referendum deadline.

38. See, for examples, the front page of *l'Unità* for May 24 and May 31, 1978. On June 10, Enrico Berlinguer spoke on national television of "an alliance neither accidental nor temporary" between the PDUP and the MSI. The PDUP's reaction is in *Il Manifesto*, June 11, 1978, p. 1.

39. *Il Manifesto*, June 7, 1978, p. 1.

40. *L'Unità*, June 6, 1978, p. 8.

41. See Berlinguer's speech in *l'Unità*, May 26, 1978, already discussed herein in Chapter 1.

42. *L'Unità*, June 12, 1978, p. 1.

43. Apparatus meeting, May 12, 1978.

44. Apparatus meeting, May 24, 1978.

45. In addition to the apparatus meetings of May 12 and 24, these views were heard repeatedly at a provincewide meeting of activists and leaders on May 29 and at an apparatus meeting on June 5, 1978.

46. Apparatus meeting, May 12, 1978.

47. Zone meeting, June 19, 1978.

48. Meeting of the Culture and School Commission, June 2, 1978.

49. Apparatus meeting, June 5, 1978. For evidence of a similar situation in Milan, see Stefano Bevacqua, "Sindacati divisi sui referendum," *La Repubblica*, May 26, 1978, p. 4.

50. This meeting took place on May 29, 1978.

51. Apparatus meeting, June 5, 1978.

52. Data obtained from *La Stampa*, June 13, 1978, and from material furnished by the federation.

53. All data on *seggi elettorali* are calculated from raw results kindly provided by the federation.

54. PCI torinese, *Il guidizio del PCI sul voto in città* (Turin: printed flyer, n.d. [June 1978]).

55. The precincts with low turnout averaged just under 75 percent of the eligible voters; those with high turnout averaged just over 87 percent. The difference on the party finance referendum was less than 0.5 percent between the two extremes.

56. A good chronicle of postautumn activity and clear evidence of its right-wing origins and connections can be found in Giorgio Galli, *La crisi italiana e la destra internazionale* (Milan: Mondadori, 1974).

57. For details on Bologna, see Pasquino and Panebianco, "Bologna"; and the extensive summary and analyses in *Inchiesta* 7 (September–October 1977): 42–82.

58. A wide-ranging debate in the communist press began late in 1976 and was published as Giorgio Amendola et al., *I giovani e la crisi della società* (Rome: Editori Riuniti, 1977). After the events in Rome and simultaneously with those in Bologna, the Central Committee devoted an entire session to the youth question, and the PCI took the unusual step of publishing the entire debate in PCI, *I comunisti e la questione giovanile* (Rome: Editori Riuniti, 1977).

59. See, in addition to the discussion of the party's model of militancy in Chapter 1 herein, the interesting contribution of Francesca Izzo, "Personale e politico in un impegno di tipo nuovo," in Amendola et al., *I giovani*, pp. 57–65.

60. See Paolo Bufalini's address to the April 1978 Central Committee meeting in *l'Unità*, April 18, 1978. The hard line in the PCI was also consistently expressed by Ugo Pecchioli, the head of the national Section on the Problems of the State.

61. Giorgio Amendola, "Interrogativi sul 'caso' Fiat," *Rinascita*, November 9, 1979, pp. 13–15. A lively debate followed, concluded in the issue of December 7, 1979.

62. See, e.g., Adalberto Minucci (interviewed by Jochen Kreimer), *Terrorismo e crisi italiana* (Rome: Editori Riuniti, 1978), esp. pp. 9–48.

63. In spite of the arguments against emergency legislation, the PCI supported an antiterrorist decree in March 1978 that most jurists claimed was in fact special legislation. See *L'Unità*, April 2, 1978, pp. 1–2, for an initial defense, and compare the issues of April 4, p. 1, and April 5, p. 4, for the party's tortuous retreat.

64. In addition to note 63 above, see also the debate in February and March about the use of exile (*confino*) for suspected terrorists. Here the PCI ended up supporting a law put on the books by the Fascists and often used by Mussolini against Communists. The PCI's position is set out in the unsigned editorial, "Il 'confino' e i 'prigionieri politici,' " *l'Unità*, February 23, 1978, p. 1. For one of the best of numerous responses, see Federico Mancini, "Il confino di polizia," *La Repubblica*, March 7, 1978, p. 6.

65. For a thoughtful discussion of one important case in this period, see Giuseppe Cotturri, "Sta mutando nei fatti il rapporto tra politica e cultura," *Rinascita*, August 8, 1980, pp. 31–32.

66. Recall that the party's long-awaited "Proposal for a Medium-Term Project" was finally produced at the end of the summer of 1977, without effect. In addition to note 47 of Chapter 1 herein, see S. Hellman, "The Italian CP: Stumbling on the Threshold?" *Problems of Communism* 27 (November–December 1978), pp. 35–36.

67. PCI, Report to the Piedmontese Regional Committee of November 21, 1977, reported in *l'Unità*, November 22, 1977, p. 10. Of 109 terrorist acts in the Turin area from the beginning of 1977, 60 were claimed by leftist groups, 10 by rightists, and 30 remained "anonymous"; the others could not be classified.

68. A few earlier targets were killed, but almost always as a result of resisting their attackers. Casalegno was murdered in cold blood.

69. For highly informative, if unsystematic, evidence of Fiat workers' reactions to the Moro kidnapping and murder, see Brunello Mantelli and Marco Revelli, eds., *Operai senza politica* (Rome: Savelli, 1979).

70. The federation called a special meeting of its executive and apparatus on February 27, 1978, to discuss this question. It should be pointed out that jurors in Italy do not play the same role that they do in the United States. They are adjuncts to the judges who preside over the case and therefore are much less central to the deliberations, even though their symbolic presence remains quite important.

71. The points that follow were culled from numerous meetings of the apparatus and federal committees between November 1977 and April 1978. The same points reiterated in these gatherings are found in a document designed to aid middle-level leaders in their preparations for the various public and party assemblies: PCI, Comitato regionale piemontese, *Scaletta per assemblee sul terrorismo* (Turin: mimeograph, n.d. [April 1978]).

72. This "equidistant" position was espoused by most extraparliamentary groups and by a considerable number of left-wing unionists.

73. On p. 6 of PCI, *Scaletta*, the connection is made, but not in a concrete programmatic sense.

74. The Central Committee meeting of October 1976, cited in the first footnote of this chapter, provides many examples.

75. Daylong meeting of party and communist CGIL functionaries, November 24, 1977.

76. Golden, *Austerity and Its Opposition*, chap. 3.

77. Apparatus meeting, April 26, 1978.

78. May 3, 1978.

79. Numerous comments to this effect were expressed in a cell meeting on April 24, 1978 (cellula ENEL–Moncalieri).

80. The incident received wide press coverage. For a thorough but highly critical summary, see *La Repubblica*, March 27, 1979. Information on internal divisions within the federation was obtained in private conversations in May 1979.

81. The highly negative term *qualunquismo* was the one most often employed in discussions of public attitudes. It has its origins in a postwar magazine and movement called *L'Uomo Qualunque* (roughly, "everyman"), which was explicitly antipolitical and argued that all parties, but especially the mass antifascist ones, were corrupt. See Gino Pallotta, *Il qualunquismo* (Milan: Bompiani, 1972).

## Chapter 4

1. See pp. 33–34; the quotations all appeared in Enrico Berlinguer's address to the leaders, printed in *l'Unità*, May 26, 1978.

2. Address to the July Central Committee meeting, *l'Unità*, July 25, 1978.

3. Published in *l'Unità*, September 18, 1978.

4. See especially the political press for the period between September and December 1978. One of the best syntheses at the time was Pasquale Nonno, "Quel diffuso malessere," *Panorama*, October 3, 1978, pp. 36–39, which avoids the gossipy tone of much of the other coverage.

5. Enrico Berlinguer, "Relazione," *XV Congresso del Partito comunista italiano: Atti e risoluzioni* (Rome: Editori Riuniti, 1979), Vol. 1, esp. pp. 69–86.

6. The federation secretary (and he was not alone, as I learned in private conversations and systematic interviews) was on record in his belief that the *compromesso storico* was not a "weak link" strategy for a country like Italy, but in fact the most advanced strategy in the West for radical transformation in a period of crisis. Renzo Gianotti, "Implicazioni strategiche della nostra politica," *Seminario di quadri comunisti 24–25 settembre 1976* (Turin: mimeograph, 1976), pp. 4–5.

7. Zonal assembly, June 19, 1978.

8. Comments of the federation secretary to the Federal Committee and the Federal Control Commission meeting of June 15, 1978.

9. In a zonal meeting on June 29, 1978, and at a meeting of the apparatus, July 19, 1978.

10. This argument was heard at every meeting I attended during this period (of which there were roughly two dozen), and it characterized all general discussions of party policy in 1977 and 1978 in the federation.

11. Meeting of the Federal Committee and Federal Control Commission, June 15, 1978.

12. Apparatus meeting of July 5, 1978. A small march, linked to the *l'Unità* festival of a town in the industrial belt, was eventually held.

13. See the article by the head of the federation's Organization Section which summarizes the postreferendum *autocritica* very much in these terms: Germano Calligaro, "C'è un problema di unità politica," *l'Unità*, July 5, 1978, p. 10.

14. This had been one of the issues to emerge immediately after the 1976 elections. For various reports of similar difficulties from different regions of the country, see Antonio Bassolino, "Che cosa ci insegna la vicenda di Castellammare," *Rinascita*, May 13, 1977, pp. 4–5; Fioravante Pagnin, "Il rapporto governanti-governati," *Rinascita*, December 13, 1976, pp. 14–15; Francesco Mandarini, "Il rifiuto del partito che gestisce tutto," *Rinascita*, August 12, 1977, pp. 13–14.

15. What follows is a summary of arguments heard in a zonal meeting, June 29, 1978; a seminar of activists on "Governing the Turinese Area," July 1; a meeting of PCI administrators and militants, July 14; and an apparatus meeting, July 19.

16. Seminar of activists on "Governing the Turinese area," July 1; and meeting of PCI administrators and militants, July 14.

17. Seminar, July 1, 1978.

18. A more complete picture of Novelli's views emerges in his interview (by Ezio Mauro), *Vivere a Torino* (Rome: Editori Riuniti, 1980), esp. pp. 40–45, 92–98.

19. The comments cited and paraphrased here were made at the seminar of July 1 and at the meeting of administrators and militants on July 14, 1978. A published version of Novelli's criticisms can be found in the roundtable discussion, "La grande città e i comunisti," *Rinascita*, June 29, 1979, pp. 16–19.

20. For an explicit statement, see Giancarlo Quagliotti, "Il partito comunista, la partecipazione, la communicazione politica nelle grandi aree urbane del Nord," in PCI, Dipartimento problemi del partito, *Partito e società nelle grandi aree urbane: Atti del seminario tenuto a Milano il 12, 13, 14 novembre 1982* (Rome: Salemi, 1983), p. 73.

21. Seminar, July 1, 1978.

22. Apparatus meeting, July 5, 1978.

23. Quoted in *L'Espresso*, June 17, 1979, p. 10.

24. A sign of increased disagreement (and anticipated conflict) was the publication of precongressional theses for the first time since 1969. The 1972 and 1975 congresses had used a precongressional "report" authored by Berlinguer; more anonymous theses made it much easier to be critical without appearing to attack the secretary openly.

25. *L'Unità*, July 7, 1979, p. 1. For a discussion of the new leadership, see *La Stampa*, July 7, 1979, p. 2.

26. Gianfranco Pasquino has consistently analyzed this phenomenon with great insight. In English, see "The Italian Socialist Party: Electoral Stagnation and Political Indispensability," in Howard Penniman, ed., *Italy at the Polls 1979* (Washington, D.C.: American Enterprise Institute, 1980), pp. 141–71.

27. Giacomo Sani, "Italian Voters, 1976–1979," in Penniman, *Italy at the Polls 1979*, esp. pp. 56–63. Also Grant Amyot, "Voto giovanile e voto differenziato nelle ultime elezioni italiane: Una confutazione di alcune analisi," *Rivista italiana di scienza politica* 10 (December 1980): 471–83.

28. Giorgio Frasco Polara, "Prime riflessioni sul voto della gioventù," *l'Unità*, June 7, 1979, p. 1; Fabio Mussi, "Che cosa accadde nel '77?" *Rinascita*, June 8, 1979, p. 22.

29. Frasco Polara, "Prime riflessioni"; Walter Vitali, "Che cosa vuole oggi un giovane del PCI?" *l'Unità*, June 15, 1979, p. 3; Leonardo Paggi, "Pr: Crescita lungo le linee di tensione," *Rinascita*, June 8, 1979, pp. 9–10.

30. Massimo Cacciari, "Esame di coscienza di un comunista militante," *La Repubblica*, June 13, 1979, p. 6.

31. Two roundtables hosted by *Rinascita* right after the elections were especially to the point: "La grande città e i comunisti," June 29, 1979; and "Le posizioni perse fra i giovani," June 15, 1979, pp. 11–15.

32. See, for example, Chapter 3, herein, especially notes 57–59.

33. V.P. [Valentino Parlato], "Si riapre il congresso del PCI?" *Il Manifesto*, June 14, 1979, p. 1.

34. See *l'Unità*, July 4 and 6, 1979, for Berlinguer's address and conclusions to the Central Committee. See the issues of July 5 and 6 for a summary of the debate.

35. Meeting of the federation's School Commission, June 28, 1979.

36. See Chapter 8, herein, for a discussion of the functionaries' attitudes on party strategy.

37. Bruno Ferrero (interviewed by Giampaolo Pansa), "Perchè noi del Pci stiamo perdendo l'appoggio della gente," *La Repubblica*, September 23, 1978, p. 3. The practice of providing interviews in nonparty papers had become widespread by the late 1970s for PCI leaders.

38. This was the nearly unanimous opinion voiced at the joint party-union apparatus meeting on the campaign, May 8, 1978.

39. Apparatus meeting, June 5, 1979.

40. Ibid.

41. Federal Committee meeting, May 17, 1978; and apparatus meeting, June 5, 1978.

42. Provincial assembly (*attivo*) of the PCI, June 5, 1979; zonal assembly, June 14 and 18, 1979; meeting of the Schools Commission, June 28, 1979.

43. Reported in *l'Unità*, January 8 and 9, 1981. For the extensive debate leading up to the meeting, see all the issues of *Rinascita* from November 7, 1980, through January 9, 1981. For specific details of the changes that were undertaken, see Chapter 5, herein.

44. Only a few of the PCI's southern strongholds, such as Naples and Taranto, succeeded in containing their losses, while most of the South showed marked declines even compared to 1979.

45. In the 1980s, the PCI was running on joint lists with the PDUP, which had averaged between 1.0 and 1.5 percent in the 1970s, so one could argue that the party's vote had leveled off at around 29 percent before the drop to 26 percent in 1987.

46. On the motives that led to the Socialists' strategic shift, see esp. Antonio Baldassare, "Dall'alternativa alla centralità socialista: il Psi nel sistema dei partiti," in Antonio Baldassare et al., *Partiti sindacato e sistema politico italiano* (Milan: Franco Angeli, 1981), pp. 42–80; and Gianfranco Pasquino, "Centralità non significa governabilità," *Il Mulino* 31 (May–June 1982): 321–38.

47. For details, see Fabrizio Coisson, "La febbre del no," *Panorama*, March 24, 1980, pp. 46–48.

48. In his conclusions to the National Council of the PCI, published in *l'Unità*, April 5, 1980, p. 1.

49. Gerardo Chiaromonte, "Il valore e i problemi della lotta alla Fiat," *Rinascita*, October 24, 1980, p. 3.

50. The events were covered extensively in the Italian press through September and October 1980.

51. I am using the term *layoff* to refer to the Salary Integration Fund (*Cassa Integrazione Quadagni*). The fund supplements a worker's earnings according to the number of hours his regular employment has been reduced; it can run a maximum of two years. In the Fiat case, all the workers affected were reduced to zero hours of regular employment, but this need not have been the case.

52. At a minimum, the unions wanted the layoffs rotated among the work force, rather than having them fall on a single group of workers.

53. There is, of course, a strong relationship between place of birth and job rating at Fiat; hence any "ethnic" issue is also a conflict over status in the workplace. For a sensitive examination of this problem, see Antonio Baldissera, "Alle origini della politica della diseguaglianza nell'Italia degli anni '80: La marcia dei quarantamila," *Quaderni di Sociologia*, 34 (1985). For a view that attributes greater militance to immigrants because of their exclusion from Turinese society, see the interview with Gino Giugni, "La lezione della Fiat," *Mondoperaio* 33 (October 1980): 42.

54. Chiaromonte, "Il valore," pp. 4–5; Renzo Gianotti, "Un rapporto nuovo tra avanguardia e movimento," *Rinascita*, October 24, 1980, p. 5; PCI, Federazione di Torino, *La lotta alla Fiat: Il giudizio del PCI Torinese. Documento approvato dal Comitato Federale, 1 novembre 1980* (Turin: Turingraf, 1980), p. 9.

55. Marcello Fedele sees this as the key to the party's 1983 electoral campaign, in "The PCI in 1983: The Ambiguous 'Alternative,' " in Howard Penniman, ed., *Italy at the Polls 1983* (Washington, D.C.: American Enterprise Institute, 1986).

56. Chiaromonte, "Il valore"; PCI, *La lotta alla Fiat*, pp. 3, 7–9. For the 1983 Congress, see Renzo Gianotti's address, "Il contributo dei comunisti torinesi per l'alternativa, per la pace, per il socialismo," *XVIII Congresso provinciale, federazione torinese* (Turin: printed unpaginated pamphlet, 1983), sec. IV.

57. Giuseppe Bonazzi, "La lotta dei 35 giorni alla Fiat: Un'analisi sociologica," *Politica ed Economia* 15 (November 1984): 33–43.

58. Personal interviews in Turin, November–December 1980. For references to these dis-

agreements in an official party document, see XVIII Congresso provinciale della Federazione torinese del PCI, *Relazione della Commissione Federale di Controllo (approvata nella seduta del 18 gennaio 1983).* (Turin: mimeograph, 1983), p. 3.

59. For a much fuller analysis, see Miriam Golden, *Austerity and Its Opposition: Persistent Radicalism in the Italian Labor Movement* (Ithaca, N.Y.: Cornell University Press, 1988).

60. There were widely publicized meetings and seminars in Turin on these subjects beginning immediately after the events. The most important internal discussion probably was a joint PCI–CGIL apparatus meeting held on November 24, 1980. For reactions in the national party press, see esp. Edoardo Segantini, "Cosa chiedete esattamente al PCI?" *l'Unità,* November 12, 1980, p. 12; and Aris Accornero, "Il capo: Guardiano, tecnico, o qualcos'altro," *Rinascita,* November 14, 1980, p. 9.

61. In addition to the sources cited in note 54, above, see as well Sergio Garavini, "Le contraddizioni del movimento non affrontate a Torino e a Roma," *Rinascita,* October 24, 1980, p. 7. A left-wing unionist himself, Garavini could not simply be written off as one more uncritical supporter of the PCI's more moderate policies "piling on" the FLM.

62. Berlinguer's conclusions to the June Central Committee can be found in *l'Unità,* June 28, 1980.

63. The critical leader is Pietro Ingrao, whose comments are summarized in *l'Unità,* November 5, 1980; for Berlinguer's conclusions, see *l'Unità,* November 6, 1980.

64. *Pace e Guerra* (November–December 1980): 15. The entire discussion of the November Central Committee, on pp. 15–19 of this issue of the journal, is very interesting.

65. Quoted by Sandro Viola, *La Repubblica,* December 23, 1980, p. 5.

66. *L'Unità,* November 28, 1980, p. 1.

67. Aldo Tortorella, "L'alternativa democratica è imposta dalle cose," *Rinascita,* December 12, 1980, pp. 3–5. Emmanuele Macaluso, address to Central Committee, *l'Unità,* December 16, 1980. For the debate, see *l'Unità,* December 16, 1980, pp. 6–7.

68. For similar reactions and reservations from a number of left-wing Catholics highly sympathetic to the PCI, see *Il Manifesto,* December 27, 1980, p. 8.

69. Seminar for the party apparatus, December 19, 1980. For later abundant negative references to the confusion and paralysis of the late 1970s, see the interventions in PCI, Federazione Provinciale di Torino, *XVIII Congresso Provinciale* (Turin: unpaginated typescript, 1983).

70. See, in this regard, Ronald Tiersky, *French Communism 1920–1972* (New York: Columbia University Press, 1972), esp. chaps. 3 and 4; and George Ross, *Communists and Workers in France* (Berkeley and Los Angeles: University of California Press, 1982), chap. 1.

71. Even the strongest supporters of the *compromesso storico* in the federation hierarchy believed in the centrality of the working class, which is one reason why the mobilization during the thirty-five days was so extensive. For a very late explicit statement of the principle, see Gianotti, "Il contributo dei comunisti torinesi," sec. I.

72. For a contemporary illustration, see Riccardo Terzi's contributions to the roundtable on the Communists in the urban centers of Italy published in *Rinascita,* June 29, 1979, pp. 16–19.

73. An exceptionally clear and synthetic statement of this position can be found in Riccardo Terzi, "Trasformazioni sociali e questione delle alleanze," in PCI, Dipartimento problemi del partito, *Partito e società nelle grandi aree urbane: Atti del seminario tenuto a Milano il 12, 13, 14, novembre 1982* (Rome: Salemi, 1983), pp. 52–55.

74. The most crucial phrase in the official statement was that "the propulsive thrust that began with the October Revolution has been exhausted." This was phrased even more bluntly ("the Soviet model" replaced "the October Revolution") in Berlinguer's address to the 1983 National Congress. See *XVI Congresso del Partito comunista italiano: Atti risoluzioni documenti* (Rome: Editori Riuniti, 1983), p. 33.

75. By the 1983 Congress, the precongressional debate no longer involved theses (see note 23, above) but a "document" approved by the Central Committee which included appended minority

motions. These could then be voted on by provincial congresses. One such motion, calling for a broader airing of issues that might divide the party leadership, was narrowly defeated in the Central Committee but then solidly passed in the congress of every federation that debated it.

## Chapter 5

1. See esp. the report of Giorgio Napolitano, head of the Organization Section of the PCI, to the January 1981 Central Committee, published in Giorgio Napolitano and E. Berlinguer, *Partito di massa negli anni ottanta: I problemi del partito al comitato centrale del PCI 7–8 gennaio 1981* (Rome: Editori Riuniti, 1981), esp. pp. 11–17, 20–21. See also Enrico Berlinguer's "Relazione" and the Political Document, *XVI Congresso del Pci: Atti risoluzioni documenti* (Rome: Editori Riuniti, 1983), pp. 63–66, 679–84, respectively.

2. In addition to note 75 in Chapter 4 herein, see the stinging critique of Luigi Berlinguer, "Partito di massa e forme snodate di organizzazione," *Democrazia e diritto* 23 (January–February 1983): esp. 19–22, 30–32.

3. For an interesting discussion, see, in addition to numerous critical analyses cited elsewhere, Franco Cazzola, "Le difficili identità dei partiti di massa," *Laboratorio politico* 2 (September–December 1982): esp. 56–58.

4. Vittorio Rieser, "Sindacato e composizione di classe," *Laboratorio politico* 1 (July–August 1981): 70.

5. Giuseppe Berta, "Il neocapitalismo e la crisi delle organizzazioni di classe," in Aldo Agosti and Gian Mario Bravo, eds., *Storia del movimento operaio*, esp. pp. 155–61. See as well his "Le conferenze operaie," in Ilardi and Accornero, eds., *Il Partito comunista italiano*, pp. 722–30.

6. Some of the best observers point out that the PCI's strength in the largest factories continues to be concentrated among the more skilled workers. On Fiat, see, e.g., Bonazzi, "La lotta dei 35 giorni alla Fiat."

7. Even though the party's focus has tended to dwell excessively on the ideology of young people. For good examples from the period covered by this study, see Giorgo Amendola et al., *I giovani e la crisi della società* (Rome: Editori Riuniti, 1977); and PCI, *I comunisti e la questione giovanile: Atti della sessione del Comitato centrale del PCI, Roma 14–16 marzo 1977* (Rome: Editori Riuniti, 1977).

8. When blame is not assigned to the degradation of society or the contamination of given strata, the tendency is to note that a program and analysis as complex as that of the PCI cannot easily be grasped by the masses. But in this case as well, the remedy remains the same: more effective propaganda stressing the need for a mass party and the value of the PCI's policies.

9. Claudio Petruccioli, "Democrazia statuale e democrazia di partito," *Democrazia e diritto* 19 (January–February 1979): 14–15; and Francesca Izzo, "Personale e politico in un rapporto di tipo nuovo," in Amendola et al., *I giovani*, pp. 63–64.

10. Periods marked by the sharpest drops in recruitment are more clearly related to the PCI's difficulties, however.

11. Enrico Casciani, "Dieci anni di reclutamento nel Pci," *Il Mulino* 30 (March–April 1981): 320–21. The same pattern was found for the entire 1974–76 period; by 1977, recruitment had already dipped.

12. Marcello Flores, "Dibattito interno sul mutamento della struttura organizzativa 1946/1948," in Ilardi and Accornero, *Il Partito comunista italiano*, esp. pp. 43–50. See also the excellent discussion of Orete Massari, "La federazione," in ibid., pp. 135–40.

13. Massari, "La federazione," pp. 146–48. Giordano Sivini, "Struttura organizzativa e partecipazione di base nel Partito comunista italiano," in Sivini, ed., *Partiti e partecipazione politica in Italia* (Milano: Giuffrè, 1968), pp. 143–67.

14. Fausto Anderlini, "La cellula," in Ilardi and Accornero, *Il Partito comunista*, pp. 216–19, contains an exceptionally synthetic statement of this position.

15. Even the most recent (1983) version of the Statute still speaks of it as the basic organizational unit: *Statuto del Partito comunista italiano*, art. 13, in PCI, *XVI Congresso*, p. 698.

16. The then head of the Organization Section put the crucial date at 1972 in his important summary: Ugo Pecchioli, "Politica e organizzazione nel PCI," *Critica marxista* 11 (May–August 1973): 23–38. But the truly transitional period was a full decade earlier; see the contradictory affirmations in the "Document of the V National Conference of the PCI," in PCI, *V Conferenza nazionale del Partito comunista italiano: Atti e risoluzioni* (Rome: Editori Riuniti, 1964), pp. 238–39.

17. The last time workplace cells were reported on a federation-by-federation basis was in 1972, in PCI, *Dati sulla organizzazione del partito* (1972), pp. 65–66. No figures at all were then reported until 1983, and at that time only national totals were presented: PCI, *Organizzazione dati statistiche* (1983), pp. 94–97.

18. Gianni Cervetti, *Partito di governo e di lotta* (Rome: Editori Riuniti, 1977), p. 46. The author was head of the Organization Section of the party in the late 1970s.

19. PCI, *Organizzazione dati statistiche* (1983), p. 81.

20. Ibid., p. 78.

21. This point is made repeatedly in PCI, *Partito e società nelle grandi aree urbane*, passim.

22. See the fascinating analysis in Barbagli and Corbetta, "Partito e movimento: aspetti e rinnovamento del PCI," *Inchiesta* 8 (January–February 1978): 37–38 and esp. tab. 42.

23. The exact figures were 99 in 1967 and 191 in 1978. Except where otherwise indicated, all detailed reporting of the Turinese party's structures is based on data kindly provided from federation archives.

24. PCI, *Dati sulla organizzazione* (1969), p. 77.

25. The major nonfactory workplace sections include railway workers, municipal transport and refuse workers, the Post Office, SIP (the telephone company), the region of Piedmont, RAI-TV, and so on.

26. This proportion remained constant until the early 1980s, when the factory organizations, under the impact of economic crisis, led the general decline in party membership. By 1983, one-fourth of the total membership was enrolled in workplace organizations.

27. For further details on the factories, consult S. Hellman, "Il Pci e l'ambigua eredità," pp. 273–74.

28. *Dual militancy* refers to situations in which activists' time must be divided between two totally different forms of militancy, such as the party and the unions, in this case, or the party and feminist activities, to cite another common example. Where the choice is between party and union, for reasons already noted (see my discussion in Chapter 2, as well as in the next chapter), the party tends to suffer.

29. This is by no means a problem limited to Turin. For evidence of its national implications, see "Documento della commissione per i problemi dell'organizzazione del partito in fabbrica," in PCI, *VII Conferenza operaia del PCI, Napoli 3–5 marzo 1978* (Rome: Editori Riuniti, 1978), pp. 282–83.

30. Intermediate structures proliferated after 1956, but, once again, the official watershed can probably be set at the 1964 Fifth National Conference of the PCI, which focused on organizational matters. See esp. "Document of the V National Conference," pp. 235–36, 242–45. For the contribution that set the tone for the conference, see Enrico Berlinguer, "Lo stato del partito in rapporto alle modificazioni della società italiana," *Critica marxista* 1 (September–December 1963): 186–213.

31. *Statuto del PCI*, art. 36, p. 709.

32. For agreement on the sections' limitations from leaders with radically different perspectives, see the contributions of Quagliotti and Terzi in PCI, *Partito e società nell grandi aree urbane*, pp. 64–84, 151–58. For a comparison of sections' performance in urban, suburban, and

peripheral environments, see Lange, "The PCI at the Local Level," in Blackmer and Tarrow, eds., *Communism in Italy and France*.

33. Again, for evidence, see Lange, "The PCI at the Local Level."

34. Data on electoral results by commune size over time appear in Unione Regionale Province Piemontesi, *Cento anni di voto in Piemonte* (Turin: ILTE, n.d.), p. 115.

35. Cervetti, *Partito di governo*, p. 54.

36. Neri Gori, "Attivismo tradizionale e crisi della partecipazione nel PCI: Il caso di Firenze," *Rassegna italiana de sociologia* 16 (1975): 279–80.

37. Cervetti, *Partito di governo*, p. 54.

38. *Statuto del PCI*, art. 15, p. 699.

39. PCI, *Organizzazione dati statistiche* (1983), pp. 9–11; *Organizzazione dati statistiche* (1986), pp. 9-13. All data on party structure in this study exclude the PCI's thirteen federations and fourteen thousand members (1985 figures, p. 13) outside Italy's national borders.

40. In Rome and in some federations, these commissions are called *sezioni di lavoro*. I have avoided this usage wherever possible because of the potential confusion with the grass-roots *sezione*.

41. Membership fell by forty-five hundred between 1979 and 1982 (see Table 2.4, herein); it has since fallen even further. The 1983 official statistics show that in Turin, each member contributes an average of twenty-five dollars between membership dues and other donations, a total roughly equal to the average for the party in the North and Center of the country. PCI, *Organizzazione dati statistiche* (1983), pp. 127–35.

42. They are mentioned only in art. 27, and then in purely secondary fashion. *Statuto del PCI*, p. 705.

43. For the party as a whole, the most recent figure was 2,200 at a time when the national membership was 1.8 million, and this figure refers to all functionaries, including those in national and regional offices. Chiara Sebastiani, "Il funzionario del Partito comunista: Un profilo," *Bollettino CeSPE, Congiuntura sociale* 1 (January 1980): 1. A study based on 1973 data shows a similar ratio: Fulco Lanchester, "La dirigenza del partito: Il caso del PCI," *Il Politico* 41 (December 1976): 710.

44. *Statuto del PCI*, art. 30, p. 706.

45. The most recent occurrences in Turin took place at the 1969 Thirteenth Provincial Congress and at the 1975 Fifteenth Provincial Congress.

46. *Statuto del PCI*, arts. 39 and 41, pp. 710–11.

47. Massari, "La federazione," p. 151.

48. Giorgio Galli, *Il bipartitismo imperfetto* (Bologna: Il Mulino, 1966), p. 178. For more recent observations, see Gori, "Attivismo tradizionale."

49. An extended debate in the pages of *Rinascita* took place around these themes in the summer of 1977, but letters on the topic continued until well into 1978. In all, more than three dozen contributions were made under the rubric "The Party Today." The tone-setting article was written by Giovanni Berlinguer, the party secretary's brother: "Perchè meno quadri operai e contadini?" *Rinascita*, June 10, 1977, pp. 7–8.

50. Napolitano, in *Partito di massa*, p. 30.

51. See, for example, the concluding comments of Gianni Cervetti, *Formazione dei quadri e sviluppo del partito: Atti del V Convegno nazionale della sezione centrale scuole di partito* (Rome: Editori Riuniti, n.d. [1978]), pp. 179–80.

52. Federazione Torinese del PCI, *XVI Congresso del PCI: Schede statistiche sugli iscritti 1977 della Federazione torinese del PCI* (Turin: mimeograph, 1977), esp. tab. D.

53. By 1983, the mean had risen to thirty-seven years.

54. The relevant interval reported in 1983 was 1969 to 1974, and it accounted for a third of all delegates. By this later date, the next largest group (a fourth of the total) had joined the PCI in the second half of the 1970s.

55. Renzo Gianotti, "Una nuova leva di quadri dalle lotte operaie," *Rinascita*, August 12, 1977, pp. 12–13.

56. *Organizzazione dati statistiche* (1983), pp. 66-67. Unfortunately, these data are only reported by region, rather than by federation.

57. See esp. the first section of Chapter 4, herein.

58. All detailed breakdowns of the 1977 CF are based on 103 cases.

59. The CeSPE data on all provincial delegates in the PCI in 1979 show that 49 percent of the party's cadres had at least a high school diploma; the figure for the Northwest of Italy is 43 percent. Calculations were performed on the raw data kindly provided by CeSPE. For the entire party membership, the 1983 figure for similar levels of education was 13 percent in Piedmont and 10 percent for northern Italy: PCI, *Organizzazione dati statistiche* (1983), p. 70.

60. For an excellent summary of the critique from a perspective sympathetic to the need for an apparatus, see L. Berlinguer, "Partito di massa," pp. 38–39.

61. For official acknowledgment of the problem, see Napolitano, in *Partito di massa*, p. 35. For Turin, the 1983 CF was 55 percent professional: PCI, Federazione provinciale di Torino, *XVIII Congresso Provinciale* (Turin: unpaginated typescript, 1983).

62. Michels's classical analysis of the leadership of the German Social Democrats dates from the turn of the century: Roberto Michels, *Political Parties* (New York: Dover, 1959).

## Chapter 6

1. Bruno Soggia, *La formazione dei militanti e dei quadri del partito comunista: Considerazioni e problemi*, Communicazione alla Conferenza sull'iniziativa culturale dei comunisti in Piemonte (Turin: mimeo, 1977), p. 7. See also Table 2.4 herein.

2. See, e.g., the intervention of Galletto in *XV Congresso provinciale* (1975), or those of Ambrosini and D'Orsi in *XVI Congresso provinciale* (1977).

3. XVII Congresso provinciale, Federazione di Torino, *La Commissione Federale di Controllo e il problema della formazione dei quadri, Torino 7–11 marzo 1979*. (Turin: mimeograph, 1979), p. 3. For an earlier warning by the secretary, see Renzo Gianotti, "Relazione," *Conferenza Cittadina di Organizzazione, 6–8 febbraio 1976* (Turin: mimeograph, 1976), p. 21.

4. For an excellent synthesis, see Soggia, *La formazione dei militanti*, pp. 3–5.

5. Gianni Cervetti, *Partito di governo e di lotta*; see also Chapter 5, herein.

6. Recall that the federation had three hundred fifty sections by the late 1970s and that the total number of factory organizations—cells and sections combined—had reached two hundred eighty.

7. For official acknowledgment of the problem, see Gianotti, "Relazione," p. 15; also PCI, Federazione di Torino, *XVI Congresso provinciale: Indicazioni per il dibattito congressuale* (Turin: mimeograph, n.d. [1977]), pp. 2–3; XVI Congresso della Federazione Torinese del PCI, *Nota congressuale della 3 Commissione del CF e della CFC, "Partito-Organizzazione"* (Turin: mimeograph, 1977), pp. 13, 16–17.

8. The questionnaires were filled out by section representatives (usually secretaries) at the Provincial Festival of *l'Unità* in July 1980. Sixty-four of 105 sections completed the questionnaires.

9. It is reasonable to assume that the most active sections would be more likely to fill in questionnaires of this type.

10. In his report to the apparatus, June 16, 1978.

11. These calculations are based on data from sixty-one sections.

12. Report to a seminar of the apparatus, December 19, 1980. The document circulated before this seminar discusses the problem in blunt and detailed fashion: *Nota di discussione per la giornata del 19-12-1980 sui problemi del Partito* (Turin: mimeograph, 1980), pp. 5–6.

13. Reaffirmations of the policy in the 1970s can be found in Gianotti, "Relazione," pp. 3, 20; and XVI Congresso provinciale, *Nota congressuale della 3 Commissione*, p. 10.

14. Camera di Commercio Industria Artigianato e Agricoltura, *L'Economia torinese nel 1979* (Turin: mimeo, 1980), p. 33. In Chapter 5, we saw that there were 283 factory organizations in the entire federation, but these included multiple units in the same factory or complex.

15. On the "bolshevization" of communist parties in the 1920s, see especially Helmut Gruber, ed., *International Communism in the Era of Lenin* (New York: Collier Books, 1967).

16. Demoralization and demobilization were widely acknowledged in 1978 in local Communist Workers' Conferences held to prepare for the national conference in Naples. I heard such testimony at the following factory conferences: Olivetti Scarmagno-B (February 8); Fiat Mirafiori Meccanica (February 11); and Fiat Mirafiori Carrozzeria (February 18).

17. See, e.g., the intervention of Gargioni in the *XV Congresso provinciale* (1975).

18. I would like to thank Dr. Lino Avigliano, who obtained the raw material on the sections from the federation, for sharing it with me. All calculations and interpretations are my own.

19. That such groups are present at all in workplace organizations is inevitably the result of close friendship or family ties with members signed up in a given work site. The federation permits these anomalies, knowing that otherwise these people would not take out a party card at all.

20. In fact, there was a good deal more turnover of secretaries in the territorial, compared to the workplace, sections in the capital. Between 1975 and 1980, 70 percent of the former and only half the latter had two or more changes of secretary.

21. For evidence that this is a widespread phenomenon, see Angiolo Dionelli and Massimo Baldacci's discussion with reference to Tuscany, "I problemi del partito in fabbrica," *Rinascita*, September 2, 1977, p. 15.

22. The shift in the 1960s in PCI militants' political experience before joining the party is discussed in S. Hellman, "Militanti e politica nel Triangolo industriale," in Accornero et al., eds., *L'identità comunista*.

23. Interview, May 25, 1978. For corroboration, see Vasco Gianotti, "Il 'partito nuovo' potrebbe anche invecchiare," *Rinascita*, June 24, 1977, p. 11.

24. Quotations are from PCI, Comitato regionale e Federazione di Torino, *Seminario su "Classe operaia, politica, partito,"* p. 4.

25. Meeting of a zonal secretariat, June 19, 1978.

26. In fact, a third of all PCI federations in north-central Italy have fewer than seventy-five hundred members according to official statistics. PCI *Organizzazione dati statistiche* (1983), pp. 9–11. See Figure 5.1 for organizational details of Turin's zones.

27. Criticisms of this type were widely expressed at the CF meeting of June 15–16 and the apparatus meeting of June 16, 1978. Both gatherings focused on the party's poor showing in the twin referenda.

28. G. Sivini's analysis of the phenomenon continues to be the best: "Struttura organizzativa e partecipazione di base" in Sivini, ed., *Partiti e partecipazione politica in Italia* (Milan: Giuffrè, 1968).

29. Interview (zone), June 18, 1978. For a nearly identical argument made before the party's worst difficulties, see Manfredo Montagnana, in Comitato regionale piemontese, *Crisi movimento operaio intellettuali* (Turin: Stampatori, 1977) p. 135.

30. This charge emerges in the otherwise well-balanced and intelligent analysis by regional secretary Bruno Ferrero, "Lo stato del partito in Piemonte," *Nuovasocietà*, February 17, 1978, p. 10.

31. Interview, November 28, 1977.

32. Enrico Menduni, "Della quantità e della qualità," *Rinascita*, July 28, 1978, p. 10.

33. Meeting of zone executive, June 29, 1978.

34. The 75 percent figure comes from the 1978 budget cited in Chapter 3, p. 77. By the mid-1980s, the figure had risen to 80 percent, according to the projected budget published in *La Repubblica*, January 27–28, 1985, p. 32.

35. The federation's 1978 budget showed 447 million lire raised through regular membership

fees, with another 400 million collected on other occasions from members and sympathizers. This represents 65 percent of the total operating budget, according to the chief administrator in Turin (interview, July 10, 1978).

36. Seminar of the apparatus on organizational problems, December 19, 1980.

37. The festivals are discussed at greater length in Chapter 7, herein.

38. At the end of 1964, Bonazzi found a third of all functionaries stationed in headquarters: "Problemi politici e condizione umana dei funzionari del Pci," p. 47.

39. Complaints about increasingly hard-to-manage sectoral and corporativistic trends in the Turinese federation were made at both the 1972 and 1975 provincial congresses: *XIV Congresso provinciale* (1972), pp. 209, 225, 263; *XV Congresso provinciale* (1975), interventions of Baroetto, Alasia, and Molineri. See also the "Prima relazione della Commissione elettorale," *XV Congresso provinciale*.

40. Meeting of zone executive, June 29, 1978; apparatus meetings, June 16 and July 19, 1978.

41. ". . .it is above all a political requirement. . .to guarantee in our lists and in our work on the Councils our character as a workers' party. We must therefore insure an adequate working-class presence (1/3 of the candidates) in our lists." Secretariat of the Turinese Federation of the PCI, *Nota organizzativa sulla preparazione delle elezioni dei Consigli di quartiere a Torino* (Turin: mimeo, 1977), p. 3. The minimal desired proportion of workers was reduced to 25 percent three years later. PCI, Commissione Quartieri, *Nota sulla formazione delle liste dei candidati per le elezioni circoscrizionali* (Turin: mimeo, 1980), p. 2.

42. Interview, July 13, 1978.

43. See the discussion concerning the "administrative party" in Chapter 4, herein. See also the intervention of D'Amico, *XV Congresso provinciale*, and the 1977 *Nota congressuale della 3 Commissione*, p. 24. For a serious scholarly effort to analyze PCI organizations in the 1980s in terms of a scheme that includes public officeholders as a distinct elite within the Communist hierarchy, see Fiorenzo Ferrero, "Identità e trasformazione nel Pci: Gruppi egemonici e gruppi funzionali," in Silvano Belligni, ed., *La giraffa e il liocorno: Il Pci dagli anni '70 al nuovo decennio* (Milan: Franco Angeli, 1983), esp. pp. 342–51.

44. "We cannot ignore the development of negative phenomena of 'nobility' which assume various forms (not the least of which is a certain 'annoyance' and 'distance' shown by *assessori* toward section secretaries who ask them for information, for example). " *Nota di discussione*, (1980), pp. 4–5.

45. Interview, May 31, 1978.

46. For details, see Chapter 2, herein.

47. Nearly two-thirds (63 percent) of the public officeholders had been doing full-time party work for ten or more years in 1978; only 23 percent of the active apparatus had equal tenure in the organization. Conversely, just under a fifth of the public officials had become functionaries in 1973 or later, but more than half the active apparatus had done so.

48. In all fairness to the PCI, it should be pointed out that only two Communist public officials were even indicted—as opposed to a host of Socialists.

49. XVII Congresso provinciale, *La Commissione Federale di Controllo e il problema della formazione dei quadri*, p. 4.

50. Democratic centralism remains enshrined in the PCI Statutue (art. 8); it is a constant source of attention from inside and outside the party, and any effort to present a remotely comprehensive set of references would serve little purpose in a discussion that did not analyze the phenomenon in detail.

51. *Nota di discussione*, (1980), pp. 2–3.

52. For example, at the zonal executive meeting of June 29, 1978, and the zonal assembly meeting of June 14, 1979. See also my earlier discussion of the *Comitati di quartiere* in Chapter 3.

53. To cite a simple but important example, the traditional form of democratic centralism forbids all horizontal contact between similar rank-and-file organizations (e.g., sections, cells).

Even the most rudimentary zones would be impossible were these rules enforced in Italy. Such rules appear, however, to be very much alive in the PCF. For evidence, and for a generally fascinating look into the grass-roots operations of the French party, see Jane Jenson and George Ross, *The View from Inside: A French Communist Cell in Crisis* (Los Angeles and Berkeley: University of California Press, 1985).

54. See the previously cited October and December 1976 Central Committee meetings, as well as the one in March 1977 in which the Rome and Bologna "events" were on the agenda.

55. Paolo Franchi interviewed Gianni Cervetti on precisely this point: "Un dibattito di massa sul partito, il movimento, il quadro politico," *Rinascita*, April 15, 1977, pp. 7–8.

56. See Chapter 2 for more details and documentation.

57. See Giorgio Napolitano's address and Enrico Berlinguer's conclusions, *VII Conferenza Operaia del PCI Napoli 3–5 marzo 1978* (Rome: Editori Riuniti, 1978), pp. 30–31, 241.

58. For rank-and-file interpretations of the *compromesso* in Bologna, see Barbagli and Corbetta, "Una tattica e due strategie: inchiesta sulla base del PCI," *Il Mulino* 28 (November–December, 1978): 922–67. For the views of activists—in this instance, a sample of section secretaries from the entire country—see idem., "La svolta del Pci," *Il Mulino* 30 (January–February 1981): 95–130.

59. A panel of section secretaries was reinterviewed in 1980, before the *seconda svolta* but, of course, after the move into the opposition: "La svolta del Pci," tabs. 1, 8, 9.

60. Sidney Tarrow, "Le parti communiste et la societé italienne," in Cahiers de la Fondation nationale des sciences politiques, ed., *Sociologie du communisme en Italie* (Paris: Armand Colin, 1974), pp. 11–12.

61. *Nota di discussione*, (1980), p. 4. See also the earlier (1978) Calligaro, "C'è un problema di unità politica." *L'Unità*, July 5, 1978, p. 10.

62. *Nota di discussione*, (1980), p. 4.

63. Interview, June 13, 1978.

64. Montagnana, in *Crisi movimento operaio intellettuali*, pp. 135–36.

65. A good discussion of proposed educational reforms at the high school and university levels, with emphasis on PCI proposals, can be found in *Inchiesta* 7 (November–December 1977): esp. 11–64.

66. Marco Caneparo, "Ceti medi e alleanze," *l'Unità*, July 12, 1978, p. 10.

67. Except for August 1978 to April 1979.

68. In 1978, the total number of workdays required for the Milanese federation's *Festivali dell'Unità* were estimated at 65,000. Turin's party organization is roughly half the size of Milan's. For the figure, see Giorgio Colorni, *Storie comuniste* (Milan: Feltrinelli, 1979), pp. 8–9.

69. The last such conference was held in 1964. There was, however, a special seminar held in Milan in 1982 to address organizational problems in the major urban centers: see PCI, *Partito e società nelle grandi aree urbane*.

70. Interview, March 8, 1978.

71. For figures and estimates, see Associazione Piemonte Italia, *I comuni del Piemonte 1974* (Turin: Stamperia Artistica Nazionale, 1974), pp. 182–85.

72. S. Hellman, *Ideology and Organization in Four Italian Communist Federations*, chap. 6, discusses the situation in the Bolognese federation of the PCI, where problems of this type arose in the early 1960s.

73. *Mozione conclusiva Conferenza cittadina PCI torinese* (1976), p. 6.

74. Apparatus meeting, July 19, 1978.

75. Report of the organization *responsabile* to the apparatus, June 16, 1978.

76. In the preparatory seminar on the Problem of Governing the Metropolitan Area, July 1; the meeting of Militants and Administrators, July 14; the apparatus meeting, July 19, 1978. Rank-and-file sentiment was expressed at great length, in the presence of three functionaries and the federation secretary, in a June 29 zone executive meeting.

77. Seminar of the apparatus, December 19, 1980.

78. *Nota di discussione*, (1980), p. 3.*

79. Bonazzi, "Problemi politici," pp. 69–70, explored this dimension of apparatus life in Turin in the mid-1960s and found an evolution toward greater comprehension and tolerance among functionaries. In the 1979 CeSPE study of militants' attitudes, only 14 percent of all militants and 19 percent of all functionaries felt that their personal relationship with someone who left the PCI altogether would be negatively affected (31 percent of both groups were not sure how they would react). The reference here is only to those who leave party *employment*.

80. Apparatus seminar, December 19, 1980; and *Nota di discussione*, (1980), esp. pp. 3–4.

81. Information on specific reorganizations plans was primarily obtained in discussions in Turin in May 1984 and, in particular, in an interview with the *responsabile* of organization on May 11, 1984.

82. Seminar of the apparatus, December 19, 1980.

83. Again, for details, see PCI, *Partito e società nelle grandi aree urbane*.


## Chapter 7

1. The reference is, of course, to Roberto Michels's "iron law of oligarchy," made famous in his *Political Parties* (New York: Dover, 1959).

2. Carl E. Schorske, *German Social Democracy 1905–1917: The Development of the Great Schism* (New York: John Wiley, 1955), chap. 5 and esp. p. 127.

3. Sidney Tarrow, "Communism in Italy and France: Adaptation and Change," in Blackmer and Tarrow, *Communism in Italy and France*, pp. 581–86. See also pp. 8–12 of this study.

4. CIRD (Centro Italiano Ricerche e Documentazioni), "Modificazioni strutturali e politiche del Partito Comunista Italiano al suo 9 congresso," *Tempi Moderni* 1 (April–June 1960): 3–42.

5. Donald Blackmer's *Unity in Diversity* remains an excellent source in English for the substance and tone of internal debates into the mid-1960s.

6. Jenson and Ross, *The View from Inside*, part V and esp. chap. 27, describe a similar uneven pattern of evolution for the PCF. The rate of change has been much faster in the PCI, but the lag of the organization is notable in both instances.

7. Chiara Sebastiani, "I funzionari," in Accornero et al., *L'identità comunista*, pp. 125, 139–40, and tab. 19, p. 173.

8. Ibid., tab. 19. It is telling that only those functionaries who had been employed two years or less gave markedly more "satisfied" responses to this question.

9. Federation salaries in Turin are pegged to the take-home pay of an average Fiat worker, which was roughly four hundred fifty thousand lire per month (550 U.S. dollars) in 1978. Functionaries with considerable seniority made upward of 600,000 lire, but the zonal apparatus had, with very few exceptions, the lowest seniority.

10. Calculations based on the CeSPE data show that just under a quarter of all PCI functionaries reported attending, on average, two or more meetings a week in elected assemblies in 1979: Sebastiani, "I funzionari," p. 125 and tab. 19.

11. The CeSPE study reports a near identical 60 percent (ibid., p. 125), but full-time administrators who were recruited out of the apparatus (17 percent of the total) are defined as functionaries. If we used the same criteria in Turin, we would have 28 percent full-time administrators and 74 percent with any significant administrative post at or above the municipal level. See Table 6.4 for reference.

12. Giorgio Amendola, *Una scelta di vita* (Milan: Rizzoli, 1976). See also my discussion in the first section of Chapter 1.

13. My own calculations of the 1979 CeSPE study show that delegates to the 1979 Congress who were not functionaries reported attendance at party meetings as: two or three evenings per week, 40 percent; three or more evenings per week, 20 percent.

14. Early studies were too biased to provide helpful precendents. For classical examples, see Gabriel A. Almond, *The Appeals of Communism* (Princeton, N.J.: Princeton University Press, 1954); and Hadley Cantril, *The Politics of Despair* (New York: Collier, 1962). A later literature, drawing on a different tradition, developed out of Milton Rokeach's pioneering *The Open and Closed Mind* (New York: Basic Books, 1960). For a summary of the generally inconclusive results of a large number of studies, see David J. Hanson, "Political Ideology and Closed-Mindedness," *Il Politico* 43 (March 1978): 139–43.

15. For a good illustration, see Peter Lange, "La teoria delgi incentivi e l'analisi dei partiti politici," *Rassegna italiana di sociologia* 18 (1977): 501–26. A more sweeping effort to survey and apply various insights from organization theory to communist parties is Angelo Panebianco, "Imperativi organizzativi, conflitti interni, e ideologia nei partiti comunisti," *Rivista italiana di scienza politica* 9 (December 1979): 511–36. See also Panebianco's *Modelli di partito* (Bologna: Il Mulino, 1982).

16. See Chapter 2, above, esp. Tables 2.4–2.6 for details.

17. Chapter 5, esp. p. 131.

18. S. Hellman, *Ideology and Organization in Four Italian Communist Federations*, chaps. 8 and 9.

19. Claudio Petruccioli, "Democrazia statuale e democrazia di partito," *Democrazia e diritto* 19 (January–February 1979): 14–15.

20. For two excellent and provocative pieces, see Francesca Izzo, "Personale e politico in un impegno di tipo nuovo," in Giorgio Amendola et al., *I giovani e la crisi della società* (Rome: Editori Riuniti, 1977), esp. pp. 63–64; and Angelo Bolaffi, "Nuovi soggetti e progetto operaio: La 'forma' partito nelle crisi di governabilità," in Pietro Ingrao et al., *Il partito politico* (Bari: De Donato, 1981), esp. pp. 156–62.

21. For some of the best discussions in English of the development of Italian feminism in relation to the left, see Annarita Buttafuoco, "Italy: The Feminist Challenge," in Carl Boggs and David Plotke, eds., *The Politics of Eurocommunism* (Montreal: Black Rose Books, 1980), pp. 197–220; Judith Adler Hellman, "The Italian Communists, the Women's Question, and the Challenge of Feminism," *Studies in Political Economy* 13 (Winter 1984): 57–82; Yasmine Ergas, "1968–1979—Feminism and the Italian Party System: Women's Politics in a Decade of Turmoil," *Comparative Politics* 14 (April 1982): 253–79.

22. These issues and the way they penetrated the Turinese federation are discussed at length in S. Hellman, "Feminism and the Model of Militancy in an Italian Communist Federation: Challenges to the Old Style of Politics," in Mary Fainsod Katzenstein and Carol Mueller, eds., *The Women's Movements of the United States and Western Europe: Feminist Consciousness, Political Opportunity and Public Policy* (Philadelphia: Temple University Press, 1987), pp. 132–52.

23. In 1979, four of five functionaries who joined the party before 1960 had no more than an eighth-grade education; of those who joined in the 1970s, more than half had been to university. The gap was less large with reference to those who had attended a party school (80 percent vs. 59 percent), but the CeSPE study counted courses of a week or more duration: in the past, very lengthy courses were the rule; they are now exceptional (see the next section of this chapter). Calculated from Sebastiani, "I funzionari," tab. 12, p. 167.

24. This meeting was recounted to me by a number of functionaries in 1977 and 1978.

25. As noted earlier, the number of functionaries in Turin during the course of the main field trips for this study fluctuated between forty and forty-five—the number was never absolutely stable. I was able to complete systematic interviews of at least several hours' length with forty-one of these people. Most interviews took place in 1978; a few were held in 1977 and 1979. For convenience, biographical information has been standardized to 1978.

26. In 1964, 78 percent of the apparatus consisted of former factory workers. Bonazzi, "Problemi politici e condizione umana dei funzionari del Pci," *Tempi Moderni* 8 (July–September 1965): 52. Nationally, 40 percent of the functionaries in the 1979 CeSPE survey were former factory workers, a figure that corresponds to that of the general membership, but that also

represents a clear downward trend since the 1960s, when apparatuses were more proletarian than the membership.

27. The figure is almost twice as high for the PCI in general. See Sebastiani, "I funzionari," pp. 85–86, 97–98, and 111–14, for an interesting discussion of the phenomenon, including trends over time.

28. Bonazzi, "Problemi politici," provides the figure for 1964.

29. Sebastiani, "I funzionari," tab. 5, p. 163, shows 49 percent for the Northwest and 55 percent for the entire PCI, but the latter is obviously inflated by the very high percentage (nearly 70 percent) from the red zones.

30. Ibid., pp. 117–18. See also tab. 14, p. 168.

31. Bonazzi, "Problemi politici," pp. 54–55.

32. Panebianco, *Modelli di partito*, pp. 430–31; Luigi Berlinguer, "Partito di massa e forme snodate di organizzazione," *Democrazia e diritto* 23 (January–February 1983): 38–39.

33. Bonazzi, "Problemi politici," p. 52.

34. Twice as many people in the zones were in their twenties (57 percent vs. 28 percent); only a fourth of those in the zones had been functionaries for as long as five years (vs. 78 percent in headquarters); the zones had more ex-workers by a 65-to-44-percent ratio and lagged 33-to-50 in terms of the percentage that went beyond high school.

35. The exception is that one father in eight went beyond high school among the leaders in headquarters, whereas there were no cases of postsecondary parental education in the zones. This is notable but hardly decisive given the figures reported in the previous note.

36. Drawn from my own calculations of the CeSPE data. For a much more extensive discussion, see S. Hellman, "Militanti e politica nel Triangolo industriale," in Accornero, et al., *L'identità comunista*, pp. 399–405, 429–32.

37. Sebastiani, "I funzionari," pp. 104–8.

38. Three of the six had belonged to the PSIUP, which was also represented strongly among volunteers in headquarters and in the regional party apparatus.

39. Because the numbers are small, recall that this is not a sample but the entire apparatus of the federation.

40. Luciano Gruppi, cited in *La Stampa*, "Europe" supplement, (November 9, 1977), p. III.

41. Hellman, "Militanti e politica," pp. 417–20, for details.

42. For the earlier period, see Hellman, *Ideology and Organization*, chap. 7; and Lanchester, "La dirigenza di partito," *Il Politico* 41 (December 1976): 709. Sebastiani, "I funzionari," p. 116 and tab. 11, p. 166, shows a change, but her calculations are aggregated and therefore not very precise.

43. In his report to the seminar of the apparatus, December 19, 1980.


# Chapter 8

1. With much variation among the various offerings, this is nevertheless a striking general finding in Accornero, Mannheimer, and Sebastiani, eds., *L'identità comunista* (Rome: Editori Riuniti, 1983).

2. One small group of four functionaries did not fit any of the four categories. These were veterans of non-working-class origin, equally divided between zones and headquarters. Little unites these people except their uniformly higher education and the fact that most (three) joined the PCI in the early 1960s. The two leaders in headquarters were already spending much more than half their time in their public and semipublic positions at the time of the original field research, and by the end of the 1970s both had effectively left their posts in the apparatus for full-time service in public office. They will only receive fleeting attention in the discussion that follows. The two zonal leaders, however, remained very much a part of the active party organization. For

the sake of convenience and logic, they have been assigned, respectively, to the groups whose main characteristics they most closely share ("veteran workers" and "compromise generation," respectively—the latter because the leader was an inactive member of the PCI until the early 1970s and was moved to become active again by the coup d'état in Chile in 1973.

3. Intellectual or ideological motivations were mentioned as the major reason for joining the PCI by a third (34 percent) of the functionaries; a quarter (24 percent) spoke in terms of the personal influence or example of friends or other third parties. No other response was mentioned by more than 15 percent of the apparatus.

4. The functionaries were asked whether their *formazione* had been essentially linear or whether it had been marked by qualitative leaps. If they indicated that qualitative leaps had taken place, they were asked to describe them. Only three members of the apparatus described their development as basically linear.

5. Many leadership qualities were mentioned in the functionaries' open-ended responses. Those cited most frequently by the entire apparatus were interpersonal skills such as flexibility and human warmth (53 percent); breadth and synthetic abilities (45 percent); expertise or a specialization in some area (30 percent); and the ability to set priorities and achieve concrete results (25 percent).

6. The difference is still greater (3:1) when we compare, within the post-1968 wave of functionaries, workers to all others. Ex-workers who cited family or instinctive motives for joining the PCI represented 38 percent of their group. Nonworkers who cited the same rationales were only 13 percent of theirs.

7. Evidence from PCI militants in general shows the same strong relationship between a Catholic background and the tendency to have militated in a party or formation before joining the PCI. See S. Hellman, "Militanti e politica nel Triangolo Industriale," in *L'identità comunista*, esp. pp. 399–402.

8. In fact, by the very end of the fieldwork for this study, the headquarters-zone distinction was no longer so radically differentiated along this dimension. In the personnel shifts of 1980, two former workers from the generation of 1968 with clustered background experiences were moved into headquarters.

9. For the entire apparatus, stated motivations for joining the PCI were strongly related to the formal education of the respondent. None of those giving idealistic reasons for joining the party had less than a high school diploma; two-thirds had completed at least two years of university. Conversely, of those providing "instinctive" reasons for joining the party, two-thirds did not get beyond junior high school.

10. On the national debate, see the discussion in Chapter 5; and Giovanni Berlinguer, "Perchè meno quadri operai e contadini?" *Rinascita*, June 10, 1977, pp. 7–8. Contributors to the debate from the Turinese Secretariat were Renzo Gianotti, "Una nuova leva di quadri dalle lotte operaie," *Rinascita*, August 12, 1977, pp. 12–13; and Giuliano Ferrara, "Il tema del governo per un partito di classe," *Rinascita*, July 29, 1977, pp. 8–9.

11. See esp. the complaints concerning cadre formation in the first section of Chapter 6, as well as the discussion in Chapter 1 at note 57 and ff.

12. Giacomo Sani, "The Italian Electorate in the Mid-1970s: Beyond Tradition?" in Howard Penniman, ed., *Italy at the Polls: The Parliamentary Elections of 1976* (Washington, D.C.: American Enterprise Institute, 1977), pp. 113–22.

13. For my discussion of the general phenomenon, see Chapter 1.

14. For the interview with Lombardo Radice, see *La Repubblica*, September 11, 1977.

15. For Berlinguer's apparently negative speech at the festival, see *l'Unità*, September 19, 1977. For the open letter, see Antonio Tatò, ed., *Comunisti e mondo cattolico oggi* (Rome: Editori Riuniti, 1977), pp. 27–38.

16. The relevant reference appears in Title III, art. 7(c) of the revised Statute. It says that the militant must ". . .increase his cultural and political knowledge and deepen the study of the history and patrimony of ideas of the Italian Communist Party and the entire workers' revolutionary

movement." The Statute can be found in PCI, *XV Congresso del Partito comunista Italiano: Atti e risoluzioni* (Rome: Editori Riuniti, 1979), Vol. II, p. 759–92. III 7(c) is on p. 764.

17. The PCI did officially sanction much greater openness at its 1983 Sixteenth Congress (i.e., after the completion of the fieldwork on which the above is based), but it did not formally abandon the concept of democratic centralism.

18. That means, in this case, eighteen of thirty-eight respondents (74 percent).

19. Hellman, "Militanti e politica," esp. tab. 8, p. 430.

20. See note 40 in Chapter 7, above.

21. For example, the functionaries were asked to react to the following general assertion: "If there is not the freedom to present many different points of view, there is little chance that the truth can ever be known." An overwhelming 92 percent of the apparatus agreed.

22. Or they at least agreed about public attacks and were unable to choose, in two cases, on the issue of a group's ability to survive too many differences of opinion. Although open to some objections, the decision to classify the undecided as *not* being closed or negative is, in my view, justified in this instance in view of their other response.

23. At the time of the change of policy, it was widely acknowledged within the PCI that the rank and file greeted the change with a collective sigh of relief. In Turin, the federation's report of the change noted that it was received happily at the base but that it led to "perplexity and confusion" among a number of functionaries and top federal leaders. The comment cited above was made in the "Report" to the Federation Seminar for the Apparatus on Organizational Problems, December 19, 1980.

24. The precise figure is 37 percent; a total of thirty-eight functionaries responded to this question.

25. Giuseppe Cotturri, "Il partito di massa tra cultura e politica della metropoli," in PCI, Dipartimento problemi del partito, *Partito e società nelle grandi aree urbane: Atti del seminario tenuto a Milano il 12, 13, 14 novembre 1982* (Rome: Salemi, 1983), pp. 140–41, in a broad-ranging critical discussion, forcefully argues this position.

26. In this instance, the number of interviews with codifiable responses is thirty-six.

27. An astounding 94 percent of the functionaries (N = 36) agreed with the assertion that of all the countries in the West, Italy has the most extensive liberties (*le più estese libertà*).

28. Based on unpublished earlier research; N = 51.

29. From the same data cited in note 28.

30. "Address to the Central Committee Meeting of November 1971," reprinted in Enrico Berlinguer, *La "questione comunista"* (Rome: Editori Riuniti, 1975), Vol. 1, p. 383.

31. See the Secretariat's document, dated December 29, 1981, in PCI, XVI Congresso Nazionale, *Documenti politici dal 15 al 16 Congresso* (Rome: ITER, 1983), Vol. 2, pp. 632–40, esp. 634.

32. Thirty-six functionaries had this question put to them, and of that number thirty-five responses could be classified according to the criteria summarized.

33. The number of respondents for this question is thirty-six.

34. Once again, for documented systematic evidence of grass-roots interpretations of the strategy, see Barbagli and Corbetta, "Una tattica e due strategie: Inchiesta sulla base del PCI," *Il Mulino* 28 (November–December 1978): 922–67. For a compelling argument relating grass-roots resistance to the party's eventual change of course, see the same authors' "La svolta del Pci," *Il Mulino* 30 (January–February 1981): 95-130.

35. Research on PCI militants similarly found a greater emphasis on economic as opposed to political issues among those in the party with working-class origins (and lower educational levels). See Hellman, "Militanti e politica," pp. 416–18, and tab. 10, p. 431.

36. Only federationwide meetings found the entire apparatus in the same place at the same time; for obvious reasons, these meetings were those at which I attempted to be present whenever possible. But, as noted in Chapter 1, each zone was visited, and the largest zones were visited for

approximately a week. The time periods covered by the fieldwork were September 1977 to July 1978; May 1979 to July 1979; and November through December 1980.

## Chapter 9

1. See S. Hellman, "The PCI from Berlinguer to the Seventeenth Congress," in Robert Leonardi and Raffaella Y. Nanetti, eds., *Italian Politics: A Review* (London: Frances Pinter, 1986), Vol. I, pp. 47–68.

2. The reforms begun by Mikhail Gorbachev in the latter part of the decade gave the national leadership the opportunity to argue for the wisdom of their earlier refusal to sever all links or to allow the relationship to degenerate to a point of no return.

3. For these figures and a discussion of overall trends, see Miriam Golden, *Austerity and Its Opposition* (Ithaca, N.Y.: Cornell University Press, 1988), esp. chap. 6.

4. Sergio Ginebri, "Le trasformazioni dell'industria nell'ultimo decennio," in Fondazione CeSPE-Associazione Crs, eds., *Quali risposte alle politiche neoconservatrici?* supplement to *Politica ed Economia* 18 (January 1987): 173.

5. Piero Fassino, intervention in PCI, *Partito e società nelle grandi aree urbane* (Rome: Salemi, 1983), pp. 227–28. For a sharp criticism of the PCI's "culture of crisis," see Vittorio Foa, "Il fascino indiscreto dell'unanimità," *Rinascita*, July 27, 1985, pp. 23–24.

6. The PCI had spearheaded the effort to repeal a governmental decree that denied wage earners the full compensation they were due according to the 1975 agreement on the escalator. For a full account of these events, see Peter Lange, "The End of an Era: The Wage Indexation Referendum of 1985," in Leonardi and Nanetti, *Italian Politics*, pp. 29–46.

7. All data for 1985 were found in Federazione Torinese del PCI, "Il Partito: Dati statistici" (Documento 9), *XIX Congresso provinciale* (Turin: mimeograph, 1986), p. 4.

8. For a succinct statement of the issue in these terms, see Sidney Tarrow, "Introduction," in Leonardi and Nanetti, *Italian Politics*, pp. 1–8.

9. PCI, *Organizzazione dati statistiche* (Rome: ITER, 1986), pp. 43, 44, 46.

10. Ibid., pp. 40–41. Clerical and technical workers increased from 3.5 percent at the beginning of the 1970s to 7.5 percent in 1985.

11. For more details, see Renato Mannheimer and Giacomo Sani, "Electoral Trends and Political Subcultures," in Leonardi and Nanetti, *Italian Politics*, pp. 164–75.

12. These developments are discussed at greater length in S. Hellman, "The PCI from Berlinguer to the Seventeenth Congress," pp. 63–68.

13. Aldo Natoli (interviewed by Massimo Ilardi), "Identità comunista e forme di organizzazione," *Problemi del socialismo* n.s. 6 (September–December 1985): 49–50. Natoli, once a ranking leader in the PCI, was expelled in 1969 for his involvement with *Il Manifesto*.

14. See, e.g., the numerous contributions to the special number dedicated to "The Communist Question" in *Problemi del socialismo* n.s. 6 (September–December 1985).

15. Interviews and private conversations, July 1987.

16. At fifty-one years of age at the time of his selection, Occhetto was a seasoned leader and could hardly be considered youthful. But as someone who joined the PCI in 1953 and was involved in some of the movements and demonstrations of the 1960s, his experience obviously represents a marked departure from that of previous top leaders.

17. *L'Unità*, June 28, 1987. The vote was, of course, front-page news all over Italy for the next several days.

18. For a more extended treatment of the postelectoral debate and developments within the PCI, see S. Hellman, "Italian Communism in Crisis," in Ralph Miliband, Leo Panitch, and John Saville, eds., *The Socialist Register 1988* (London: Merlin Press, 1988), pp. 244–88.

# BIBLIOGRAPHY

Accornero, Aris. "Il capo: Guardiano, tecnico, o qualcos'altro." *Rinascita*, November 14, 1980, p. 9.

Accornero, Aris. *Gli anni '50 in fabbrica*. Bari: De Donato, 1973.

Accornero, Aris. *Il lavoro come ideologia*. Bologna: Il Mulino, 1980.

Accornero, Aris, and Vittorio Reiser. *Il mestiere dell'avanguardia*. Bari: De Donato, 1981.

Accornero, Aris, Renato Mannheimer, and Chiara Sebastiani, eds. *L'identità comunista: I militanti, le strutture, la cultura del PCI*. Rome: Editori Riuniti, 1983.

Agosti, Aldo, ed. *I Muscoli della storia: Militanti e organizzazioni operaie a Torino 1945–1955*. Milan: Franco Angeli, 1987.

Agosti, Aldo, and Gian Mario Bravo, eds. *Storia del movimento operaio, del socialismo, e delle lotte sociali in Piemonte*, Vol. 4. *Dalla Ricostruzione ai giorni nostri*. Bari: De Donato, 1981.

Almond, Gabriel A. *The Appeals of Communism*. Princeton, N.J.: Princeton University Press, 1954.

Alquati, Romano. *Sulla Fiat e altri scritti*. Milan: Feltrinelli, 1975.

Althusser, Louis. "What Must Change in the Party." *New Left Review* 109 (May–June 1978): 19–45.

Amendola, Giorgio. "Interrogativi sul 'caso' Fiat." *Rinascita*, November 9, 1979, pp. 13–15.

Amendola, Giorgio. *Lettere a Milano*, 2nd edition. Rome: Editori Riuniti, 1976.

Amendola, Giorgio. *Una scelta di vita*. Milan: Rizzoli, 1976.

Amendola, Giorgio, et al. *I giovani e la crisi della società*. Rome: Editori Riuniti, 1977.

Amyot, Grant. *The Italian Communist Party: The Crisis of the Popular Front Strategy*. London: Croom Helm, 1981.

Amyot, Grant. "Voto giovanile e voto differenziato nelle ultime elezioni italiane: Una confutazione di alcune analisi." *Rivista italiana di scienza politica* 10 (December 1980): 471–83.

Associazione Piemonte Italia. *I comuni del Piemonte 1974*. Turin: Stamperia Artistica Nazionale, 1974.

Avineri, Shlomo, ed. *Varieties of Marxism*. The Hague: M. Nijhoff, 1977.

Bagnasco, Arnaldo. *Torino*. Turin: Giulio Einaudi, 1987.

Bagnasco, Arnaldo. *Tre Italie: La problematica territoriale dello sviluppo italiano*. Bologna: Il Mulino, 1977.

Balbo, Laura, and Vittorio Foa, eds. *Lettere da vicino*. Turin: Giulio Einaudi, 1986.

Baldassare, Antonio, et al. *Partiti sindacato e sistema politico italiano*. Milan: Franco Angeli, 1981.

Baldissera, Antonio. "Alle origini della politica della diseguaglianza nell'Italia degli anni '80: La marcia dei quarantamila." *Quaderni di Sociologia* 31 (January–March 1985): 1–78.

Barbagli, Marzio, et al. *Fluidità elettorale e classi sociali in Italia: 1968–1976*. Bologna: Il Mulino, 1979.

Barbagli, Marzio, and Piergiorgio Corbetta. "After the Historic Compromise: A Turning Point for the PCI." *European Journal of Political Research* 10 (September 1982): 213–39.

Barbagli, Marzio, and Piergiorgio Corbetta. "L'elettorato, l'organizzazione del Pci e i movimenti." *Il Mulino* 30 (May–June 1980): 467–90.

Barbagli, Marzio, and Piergiorgio Corbetta. "Partito e movimento: Aspetti e rinnovamento del PCI," *Inchiesta* 8 (January–February 1978): 3–46.

Barbagli, Marzio, and Piergiorgio Corbetta. "La svolta del Pci." *Il Mulino* 30 (January–February 1981): 95–130.

Barbano, Filippo, Franco Garelli, Nicola Negri, and Manuela Olagnero. *Strutture della trasformazione: Torino 1945–1975*. Turin: Cassa di Risparmio, 1980.

Barca, Luciano. "L'intreccio politico con l'industria di Stato." *Rinascita*, May 25, 1973, pp. 14–15.

Barca, Luciano. "Per una storia della Fiat dalla Liberazione alla situazione di oggi." *Rinascita* (July–August 1957): 81–82.

Barca, Luciano, et al. *I comunisti e l'economia italiana 1944–1974*. Bari: De Donato, 1975.

Barnes, Samuel H. *Representation in Italy*. Chicago: University of Chicago Press, 1977.

Bassolino, Antonio. "Che cosa ci insegna la vicenda di Castellammare." *Rinascita*, May 13, 1977, pp. 4–5.

Belligni, Silvano, ed. *La giraffa e il liocorno: Il Pci dagli anni '70 al nuovo decennio*. Milan: Franco Angeli, 1983.

Berger, Suzanne, ed. *Organizing Interests in Western Europe*. Cambridge and New York: Cambridge University Press, 1981.

Berlinguer, Enrico. *Austerità occasione per trasformare l'Italia*. Rome: Editori Riuniti, 1977.

Berlinguer, Enrico. *La "questione comunista" 1969–1975*, 2 vols. Rome: Editori Riuniti, 1975.

Berlinguer, Enrico. "Lo stato del partito in rapporto alle modificazioni della società italiana." *Critica marxista* 1 (September–December 1963): 186–213.

Berlinguer, Giovanni. "Perché meno quadri operai e contadini?" *Rinascita*, June 10, 1977, pp. 7–8.

Berlinguer, Luigi. "Partito di massa e forme snodate di organizzazione." *Democrazia e diritto* 23 (January–February 1983): 19-40.

Bevacqua, Stefano, and Giuseppe Turani. *La svolta del '78*. Milan: Feltrinelli, 1978.

Blackmer, Donald L. M. *Unity in Diversity: Italian Communism and the Communist World*. Cambridge, Mass.: MIT Press, 1968.

Blackmer, Donald L. M. , and Sidney Tarrow, eds. *Communism in Italy and France*. Princeton, N.J.: Princeton University Press, 1975.

Bonazzi, Giuseppe. "La lotta dei 35 giorni alla Fiat: Un'analisi sociologica." *Politica ed Economia* 15 (November 1984): 33–43.

Bonazzi, Giuseppe. "Problemi politici e condizione umana dei funzionari del Pci: Una indagine sulla federazione comunista di Torino." *Tempi Moderni* 8 (July–Septermber 1965): 43–77.

Borghini, Piero. " 'Svolte di generazione' e processo rivoluzionario nell'esperienza e nell'elaborazione teorica dei comunisti italiani." *Nuova generazione Quaderno* #2, Supplement to No. 96 (June 16, 1972): 81–88.

Bornstein, Stephen. "States and Unions: From Postwar Settlements to Contemporary Stalemate." In David Held, Bornstein, and Joel Krieger, eds., *The State in Capitalist Europe: A Casebook*. Winchester, Mass.: George Allen & Unwin, 1984, pp. 54–82.

Buttafuoco, Annarita. "Italy: The Feminist Challenge." In Carl Boggs and David Plotke, eds., *The Politics of Eurocommunism*. Montreal: Black Rose Books, 1980, pp. 197–220.

Caciagli, Mario, and Alberto Spreafico, eds. *Un sistema politico alla prova*. Bologna: Il Mulino, 1975.

Cammelli, Marco. "Politica istituzionale e modello emiliano: Ipotesi per una ricerca." *Il Mulino* 27 (September–October 1978): 743–67.

Cantril, Hadley. *The Politics of Despair*. New York: Collier, 1962.

Casciani, Enrico. "Dieci anni di reclutamento nel Pci." *Il Mulino* 30 (March–April 1981): 310–326.

Cazzola, Franco. "Le difficili identità dei partiti di massa." *Laboratorio politico* 2 (September–December 1982): 5–58.

Cella, Gian Primo. "Stabilità e crisi del centralismo nell'organizzazione sindacale." In Fondazione Giangiacomo Feltrinelli, *Annali (1974–75)* 16. Milan: Feltrinelli, 1976.

Ceri, Paolo. "L'autonomia operaia tra organizzazione del lavoro e sistema politico." *Quaderni di sociologia* 26 (January–March 1977): 28–63.

Cervetti, Gianni. *Partito di governo e di lotta*. Rome: Editori Riuniti, 1977.

Cherki, Eddy, and Michel Wieviorka. "Luttes sociales en Italie: Les mouvements d'autoreduction à Turin." *Les Temps Modernes* 30 (June 1975): 1793–1831.

Chiaromonte, Gerardo. "I conti con la DC." *Rinascita*, May 25, 1973, pp. 14–15.

Chiaromonte, Gerardo. "Tre domande sulla strategia della sinistra." *Critica marxista* 18 (July–August 1980): 47-60.

Chiaromonte, Gerardo. "Il valore e i problemi della lotta alla Fiat." *Rinascita*, October 24, 1980, pp. 3-5.

Chubb, Judith. "Naples under the Left: The Limits of Local Change." *Comparative Politics* 13 (October 1980): 53–78.

CIRD (Centro Italiano Ricerche e Documentazioni). "Modificazioni strutturali e politiche del Partito comunista italiano al suo 9 congresso." *Tempi moderni* 1 (April–June 1960): 3–42.

Colorni, Giorgio. *Storie comuniste*. Milan: Feltrinelli, 1979.

Comitato Regionale Piemontese. *Crisi movimento operaio intellettuali*. Turin: Stampatori, 1977.

Cotturri, Giuseppe. "Sta mutando nei fatti il rapporto tra politica e cultura." *Rinascita*, August 8, 1980, pp. 31–32.

Covatta, Luigi. "L'itinerario della sinistra cattolica." *Giovane Critica* (Winter 1973): 17–33.

*Critica marxista 5. Storia politica organizzazione nella lotta dei communisti italiani per un nuovo blocco storico.* Supplement to No. 1, 1972.

Crouch, Colin, and Alessandro Pizzorno, eds. *The Resurgence of Class Conflict in Western Europe since 1968. Vol. I: National Studies*. London: Macmillan, 1978.

D'Agostini, Fabrizio, ed. *Operaismo e centralità operaia*. Rome: Editori Riuniti, 1978.

Dionelli, Angiolo, and Massimo Baldacci. "I problemi del partito in fabbrica." *Rinascita*, September 2, 1977, p. 15.

Direzione del PCI. "Informazioni riassuntive sull'attività delle Commissioni centrali di lavoro per l'anno 1946." *Conferenza Nazionale d'Organizzazione* (January 1947).

Dragone, Umberto, ed. *Decentramento urbano e democrazia*. Milan: Feltrinelli, 1975.

Eckstein, Harry. "Case Study and Theory in Political Science." In Fred I. Greenstein and Nelson W. Polsby, eds., *Handbook of Political Science, Vol. 7: Strategies of Inquiry*. Reading, Mass.: Addison-Wesley, 1975, pp. 79–137.

Ergas, Yasmine. "1968–1979—Feminism and the Italian Party System: Women's Politics in a Decade of Turmoil." *Comparative Politics* 14 (April 1982): 253–79.

Fedele, Marcello. *Classi e partiti negli anni '70*. Rome: Editori Riuniti, 1979.

Fedele, Marcello. "The PCI in 1983: The Ambiguous 'Alternative.'" In Howard Penniman, ed., *Italy at the Polls 1983*. Durham, N.C.: Duke University Press, 1987.

Ferrara, Giuliano. "Il tema del governo per un partito di classe." *Rinascita*, July 29, 1977, pp. 8–9.

Ferrero, Bruno. "Lo stato del partito in Piemonte." *Nuovasocietà*, February 17, 1978.

Franchi, Paolo. "Un dibattito di massa sul partito, il movimento, il quadro politico." *Rinascita*, April 15, 1977, pp. 7–8.

Gabetti, Roberto. *Architettura Industria Piemonte negli ultimi cinquant'anni*. Turin: Cassa di Risparmio, 1977.

Galante, Severino. "Sulle 'condizioni' della democrazia progressiva nella linea politica del PCI (1943–1948)." *Il Politico* 40 (September 1975): 455–74.

Galli, Gino. "I rischi del partito dove governiamo." *Rinascita*, October 22, 1976, pp. 7–8.

Galli, Giorgio. *Il bipartitismo imperfetto*. Bologna: Il Mulino, 1966.

Galli, Giorgio. *La crisi italiana e la destra internazionale*. Milan: Mondadori, 1974.

Galli, Giorgio, and Alessandra Nannei. *Il capitalismo assistenziale*. Milan: SugarCo, 1976.

Galli, Giorgio, and Alfonso Prandi. *Patterns of Political Participation in Italy*. New Haven, Conn.: Yale University Press, 1971.

Galli della Loggia, Ernesto. "La crisi del togliattismo." *Mondoperaio* 31 (June 1978): 53–58.

Garavini, Sergio. "Le contraddizioni del movimento non affrontate a Torino e a Roma." *Rinascita*, October 24, 1980, pp. 6–7.

Ghini, Celso. *Il terremoto del 15 giugno*. Milan: Feltrinelli, 1976.

Gianotti, Renzo. "Il contributo dei comunisti torinesi per l'alternativa, per la pace, per il socialismo." *XVIII Congresso provinciale, federazione torinese*. Turin: printed unpaginated pamphlet, 1983.

Gianotti, Renzo. "Una nuova leva di quadri dalle lotte operaie." *Rinascita*, August 12, 1977, pp. 12–13.

Gianotti, Renzo. "Un rapporto nuovo tra avanguardia e movimento." *Rinascita*, October 24, 1980, p. 5.

Gianotti, Renzo. *Trent'anni di lotte alla Fiat (1948–1978)*. Bari: De Donato, 1979.

Gianotti, Vasco. "Il 'partito nuovo' potrebbe anche invecchiare." *Rinascita*, June 24, 1977, p. 11.

Giugni, Gino. "La lezione della Fiat." *Mondoperaio* 33 (October 1980): 42.

Golden, Miriam. "L'austerità e i rapporti base-vertice nel caso dei metalmeccanici." *Laboratorio politico* 2 (September–December 1982): 59–77.

Golden, Miriam. *Austerity and Its Opposition: Italian Working Class Politics in the 1970s*. Unpublished Ph.D. dissertation. Cornell University, 1983.

Golden, Miriam. *Austerity and Its Opposition: Persistent Radicalism in the Italian Labor Movement*. Ithaca, N.Y.: Cornell University Press, 1988.

Good, Martha H. "The Italian Communist Party and Local Government Coalitions." *Studies in Comparative Communism* 13 (August 1980): 197–219.

Gori, Neri. "Attivismo tradizionale e crisi della partecipazione nel PCI: Il caso di Firenze." *Rassegna italiana di sociologia* 16 (April–June 1975): 243–97.

Gramsci, Antonio. *Selections from the Prison Notebooks*. Quintin Hoare and Geoffrey Nowell-Smith, eds. New York: International Publishers, 1971.

Gruber, Helmut, ed. *International Communism in the Era of Lenin*. New York: Fawcett Publications, 1967.

Gruppi, Luciano. *Togliatti e la via italiana al socialismo*. Rome: Editori Riuniti, 1976.

Hanson, David J. "Political Ideology and Closed-Mindedness." *Il Politico* 43 (March 1978): 139–43.

Hellman, Judith Adler. "The Italian Communists, the Women's Question, and the Challenge of Feminism." *Studies in Political Economy* 13 (Winter 1984): 57–82.

Hellman, Judith Adler. *Journeys among Women: Feminism in Five Italian Cities*. New York: Oxford University Press, 1987.

Hellman, Stephen. "Generational Differences in the Bureaucratic Elite of Italian Communist Party Provincial Federations." *Canadian Journal of Political Science* 8 (March 1975): 82–106.

Hellman, Stephen. "Italian Communism in Crisis." In Ralph Miliband, Leo Panitch and John Saville, eds., *The Socialist Register 1988*. London: Merlin Press, 1988. pp. 244–88.

Hellman, Stephen. "The Italian CP: Stumbling on the Threshold?" *Problems of Communism* 27 (November–December 1978): 31–48.

Hellman, Stephen. "A 'New Style of Governing': Italian Communism and the Dilemmas of Transition in Turin 1975–1979." *Studies in Political Economy* 2 (Autumn 1979): 159–97.

Hellman, Stephen. *Organization and Ideology in Four Italian Communist Federations*. Unpublished Ph.D. dissertation. Yale University, 1973.

Hellman, Stephen. "Il Pci e l'ambigua eredità dell'autunno caldo a Torino." *Il Mulino* 29 (March–April 1980): 246–95.

Ilardi, Massimo, and Aris Accornero, eds. *Il Partito comunista italiano: Struttura e storia dell'organizzazione 1921–1972*. Milan: Feltrinelli, 1982.

Ingrao, Pietro, et al. *Il partito politico*. Bari: De Donato, 1981.

Jenson, Jane, and George Ross, *The View from Inside: A French Communist Cell in Crisis*. Los Angeles and Berkeley: University of California Press, 1985.

Katzenstein, Mary Fainsod, and Carol Mueller, eds. *The Women's Movements of the United States and Western Europe*. Philadelphia: Temple University Press, 1987.

Kertzer, David I. *Comrades and Christians: Religion and Political Struggle in Communist Italy*. Cambridge and New York: Cambridge University Press, 1980.

Kolinsky, Martin, and William Paterson, eds. *Social and Political Movements in Western Europe*. London: Croom Helm, 1976.

Lama, Luciano (interviewed by Massimo Riva). *Intervista sul sindacato*. Bari: Laterza, 1976.

Lanchester, Fulco. "La dirigenza del partito: Il caso del PCI." *Il Politico* 41 (December 1976): 690–718.

Lange, Peter. "La teoria degli incentivi e l'analisi dei partiti politici." *Rassegna italiana di sociologia* 18 (July–September 1977): 501–26.

Lange, Peter, George Ross, and Maurizio Vannicelli. *Unions Change and Crisis: French and Italian Union Strategy and the Political Economy, 1945–1980*. London: Allen & Unwin, 1982.

Ledda, Romano. "Il volto laico dell'Italia." *Rinascita*, July 2, 1976, pp. 1–2.

Lenin, V. I. *Selected Works*, 3 Vols. New York: International Publishers, 1967.

Leonardi, Robert, and Raffaella Y. Nanetti. *Italian Politics: A Review*, Vol. 1. London: Frances Pinter, 1986.

Magri, Lucio. "Problems of the Marxist Theory of the Revolutionary Party." *New Left Review* 60 (March–April 1970): 97–128.

Mammarella, Giuseppe. *Il Partito comunista italiano 1945/1975: Dalla Liberazione al compromesso storico*. Florence: Vallecchi, 1976.

Mandarini, Francesco. "Il rifiuto del partito che gestisce tutto." *Rinascita*, August 12, 1977, pp. 13–14.

Mandel, Ernest. *From Stalinism to Eurocommunism*. London: New Left Books, 1978.

Mannheimer, Renato. "Il voto comunista negli anni '70." *Politica ed Economia* 17 (February 1986): 33-43.

Mantelli, Brunello, and Marco Revelli, eds. *Operai senza politica*. Rome: Savelli, 1979.

Marcelloni, Maurizio. "Urban Movements and Political Struggles in Italy." *International Journal of Urban and Regional Research* 3 (June 1979): 251–67.

Menduni, Enrico. "Della quantità e della qualità." *Rinascita*, July 28, 1978, p. 10.

Meduni, Enrico. "Perché la battuta d'arresto nella scuola." *Rinascita*, February 17, 1978, pp. 31–32.

Michels, Roberto. *Political Parties*. New York: Dover, 1959.

Minucci, Adalberto (interviewed by Jochen Kreimer). *Terrorismo e crisi italiana*. Rome: Editori Riuniti, 1978.

Mussi, Fabio. "Che cosa accadde nel '77?" *Rinascita*, June 8, 1979, p. 22.

Mutti, Antonio, and Paolo Segatti. *La borghesia di Stato*. Milan: Mazotta, 1977.

Napolitano, Giorgio, ed. *Proposta di progetto a medio termine*. Rome: Editori Riuniti, 1977.

Napolitano, Giorgio, and Enrico Berlinguer. *Partito di massa negli anni ottanta: I problemi del partito al Comitato Centrale del PCI 7–8 gennaio 1981*. Rome: Editori Riuniti, 1981.

Novelli, Diego (interviewed by Ezio Mauro). *Vivere a Torino*. Rome: Editori Riuniti, 1980.

Orfei, Ruggero. *L'occupazione di potere*. Milan: Longanesi, 1976.

Paggi, Leonardo. "Pr: Crescita lungo le linee di tensione." *Rinascita*, June 8, 1979, pp. 9–10.

Pagnin, Fioravante. "Il rapporto governanti-governati." *Rinascita*, December 13, 1976, pp. 14–15.

Pallotta, Gino. *Il qualunquismo*. Milan: Bompiani, 1972.

Panebianco, Angelo. "Imperativi organizzativi, conflitti interni, e ideologia nei partiti comunisti." *Rivista italiana di scienza politica.* 9 (December 1979): 511–36.

Panebianco, Angelo. *Modelli di partito.* Bologna: Il Mulino, 1982.

Parisi, Arturo, ed. *Mobilità senza movimento: Le elezioni del 3 giugno 1979.* Bologna: Il Mulino, 1980.

Parisi, Arturo, and Gianfranco Pasquino. "Relazioni partiti-elettori e tipi di voto." In Arturo Parisi and Gianfranco Pasquino, eds., *Continuità e mutamento elettorale in Italia.* Bologna: Il Mulino, 1977, pp. 67–102.

Pasquino, Gianfranco. "Centralità non significa governabilità." *Il Mulino* 31 (May–June 1982): 321–38.

Pasquino, Gianfranco. "Il Pci nel sistema politico italiano degli anni settanta." *Il Mulino* 31 (November–December 1982.): 859–897.

Pasquino, Gianfranco, and Angelo Panebianco. "Bologna." *Città & Regione* 10–11 (October–November 1977): 172–92.

Passerin d'Entreves, Ettore, et al. *Movimento operaio e sviluppo economico in Piemonte negli ultimi cinquant'anni.* Turin: Cassa di Risparmio, 1978.

Paterson, William E. , and Alastair H. Thomas, eds. *The Future of Social Democracy,* Oxford: Oxford University Press, 1986.

Pavolini, Luca. *Inchiesta sui sindacati nel triangolo industriale.* Milan: Feltrinelli, 1957.

PCI. *I comunisti e la questione giovanile: Atti della sessione del Comitato Centrale del PCI, Roma 14–16 marzo 1977.* Rome: Editori Riuniti, 1977.

PCI. *Dati sulla organizzazione del partito.* Rome: ITER, 1975.

PCI. *Dati sulla organizzazione del partito.* Rome: ITER, 1979.

PCI. Dipartimento Problemi del Partito. *Partito e società nelle grandi aree urbane: Atti del seminario tenuto a Milano il 12, 13, 14 novembre 1982.* Rome: Salemi, 1983.

PCI. Federazione di Torino. *Il giudizio del PCI sul voto in città.* Turin: printed flyer, n.d. [June 1978].

PCI. Report to the Piedmontese Regional Committee on November 21, 1977. reported in *l'Unità*, November 22, 1977, p. 10.

PCI. Sezione Scuole di Partito. *Formazione dei quadri e sviluppo del partito: Atti del V Convegno Nazionale della sezione centrale scuole di partito.* Rome: Editori Riuniti, 1978.

PCI. Sezione Statistica, Documentazione e Ricerca. *Organizzazione dati statistiche.* Rome: ITER, 1986.

PCI. *V Conferenza nazionale del PCI: Atti e risoluzioni.* Rome: Editori Riuniti, 1964.

PCI. *VII Conferenza operaia del PCI Napoli 3–5 marzo 1978.* Rome: Editori Riuniti, 1978.

PCI. *XIII Congresso del PCI: Atti e risoluzioni.* Rome: Editori Riuniti, 1972.

PCI. *XIV Congresso del PCI: Atti e risoluzioni.* Rome: Editori Riuniti, 1975.

PCI. *XV Congresso del PCI: Atti e risoluzioni,* 2 Vols. Rome: Editori Riuniti, 1979.

PCI. *XVI Congresso del PCI: Atti risoluzioni documenti.* Rome: Editori Riuniti, 1983.

Pecchioli, Ugo. "Politica e organizzazione nel PCI." *Critica Marxista* 11 (May–August 1973): 23–38.

Penniman, Howard, ed. *Italy at the Polls: The Parliamentary Elections of 1976.* Washington, D.C.: American Enterprise Institute, 1977.

Penniman, Howard, ed. *Italy at the Polls 1979.* Washington, D.C.: American Enterprise Institute, 1980.

Petruccioli, Claudio. "Democrazia statuale e democrazia di partito." *Democrazia e diritto* 19 (January-February 1979): 5–17.

Pizzorno, Alessandro, et al. *Lotte operaie e sindacato: Il ciclo 1968–1972 in Italia.* Bologna: Il Mulino, 1978.

*Problemi del socialismo* n.s. 6 (September–December 1985).

Pugno, Emilio, and Sergio Garavini. *Gli anni duri alla Fiat.* Turin: Einaudi, 1974.

Rieser, Vittorio. "Sindacato e composizione di classe." *Laboratorio politico* 1 (July–August 1981): 56–73.

*Rinascita* Editors. "La grande città e i comunisti." *Rinascita*, June 29, 1979, pp. 16–19.

Rodano, Franco. *Questione democristiana e compromesso storico*. Rome: Editori Riuniti, 1977.

Rodano, Marisa. "Novità e contraddizioni nel voto per la scuola." *Rinascita*, December 23, 1977, pp. 5–6.

Rokeach, Milton. *The Open and Closed Mind*. New York: Basic Books, 1960.

Ross, George. *Workers and Communists in France*. Berkeley: Unversity of California Press, 1982.

Sani, Giacomo. "Le elezioni degli anni settanta: Terremoto o evoluzione?" *Rivista italiana di scienza politica* 6 (March–April 1976): 261–88.

Sassoon, Donald. *The Strategy of the Italian Communist Party*. London: Frances Pinter, 1981.

Scalfari, Eugenio. *L'autunno della Repubblica*. Milan: Etas Kompass, 1969.

Scalfari, Eugenio, and Giuseppe Turani. *Razza padrona*. Milan: Feltrinelli, 1974.

Schorske, Carl E. *German Social Democracy 1905–1917: The Development of the Great Schism*. New York: John Wiley, 1955.

Sebastiani, Chiara. "Il funzionario del Partito comunista: Un profilo."*Bollettino CeSPE, Congiuntura Sociale*. 1 (January 1980): 1–29.

Seidelman, Raymond. *Neighborhood Communism in Florence*. Ph.D. dissertation. Cornell University, 1978.

Sivini, Giordano, ed. *Partiti e partecipazione politica in Italia*. Milan: Giuffrè, 1968.

Sodaro, Michael J. "The Italian Communists and the Politics of Austerity." *Studies in Comparative Communism* 13 (Summer–Autumn 1980): 220–49.

Spriano, Paolo. *Storia del PCI, Vol. 5: La Resistenza, Togliatti e il partito nuovo*. Turin: Einaudi, 1975.

Spriano, Paolo, et al. *Problemi di storia del Partito comunista italiano*. Rome: Editori Riuniti, 1971.

Stame, Federico. *Società civile e critica delle istituzioni*. Milan: Feltrinelli, 1977.

Tarrow, Sidney. "Le parti communiste et la société italienne." In *Cahiers de la Fondation Nationale des Sciences Politiques*, ed. *Sociologie du communisme en Italie*. Paris: Armand Colin, 1974, pp. 1–53.

Tatò, Antonio, ed. *Comunisti e mondo cattolico oggi*. Rome: Editori Riuniti, 1977.

Therborn, Goran. "The Prospects of Labour and the Transformation of Advanced Capitalism." *New Left Review* 145 (May–June 1984): 5–38.

Tiersky, Ronald. *French Communism 1920–1972*. New York: Columbia University Press, 1972.

Togliatti, Palmiro. *On Gramsci and Other Writings*. Donald Sassoon, ed. London: Lawrence and Wishart, 1982.

Togliatti, Palmiro. *Lectures on Fascism*. New York: International Publishers, 1976.

Togliatti, Palmiro. *Nella democrazia e nella pace verso il socialismo*. Rome: Editori Riuniti, 1963.

Togliatti, Palmiro. *La via italiana al socialismo*. Rome: Editori Riuniti, 1964.

Tortorella, Aldo. "L'alternativa democratica è imposta dalle cose." *Rinascita*, December 12, 1980, pp. 3–5.

Tortorella, Aldo. "Il partito a Milano." *Critica Marxista* 1 (September–December 1963): 227–45.

Turin Camera di Commercio Industria Artigianato e Agricoltura. *L'Economia torinese nel 1979*. Turin: mimeo, 1980.

Unione Regionale Province Piemontesi. *Cento anni di voto in Piemonte*. Turin: ILTE, n.d.

Urban, Joan Barth. *Moscow and the Italian Communist Party*. Ithaca, N.Y.: Cornell University Press, 1986.

# UNPUBLISHED PARTY DOCUMENTS

*Note*: Unless otherwise indicated, all meetings and interviews referred to in the notes were attended by the author. Formal minutes for the meetings do not exist. Typed notes from both meetings and interviews are available for scholarly consultation, with the understanding that the anonymity of all individual participants and informants will be protected.

Direzione del PCI, Sezione Problemi dello Stato. "Perché il No dei comunisti all'abrogazione della 'Legge Reale.' " Rome: mimeograph, May 25, 1978.

Federazione di Torino, Commissione Case. *Analisi della politica dell 'IACP dal '75 ad oggi.* Turin: mimeograph, 1979.

Federazione torinese del PCI. *XVI Congresso del PCI: Schede statistiche sugli iscritti 1977 della Federazione torinese del PCI.* Turin: mimeograph, 1977.

Federazione torinese del PCI. *XVI Congresso provinciale.* Turin: typescript, 1972.

Federazione torinese del PCI. "Il Partito: Dati statistici" (Documento 9). *Congresso provinciale.* Turin: mimeograph, 1986.

Gianotti, Renzo. "Implicazioni strategiche della nostra politica." *Seminario di quadri comunisti 24–25 settembre 1976.* Turin: mimeograph, 1976.

Gianotti, Renzo. "Relazione." *Conferenza Cittadina di Organizzazione, 6–8 febbraio 1976.* Turin: mimeograph, 1976.

"Mozione conclusiva Conferenza Cittadina PCI torinese." *I problemi di adeguamento e rafforzamento dell'organizzazione di partito.* Turin: mimeograph, February 6–8, 1976.

*Nota di discussione per la giornata del 19-12-1980 sui problemi del partito.* Turin: mimeograph, 1980.

PCI. Comitato regionale e Federazione di Torino. *Seminario su "Classe operaia, politica, partito."* Turin: mimeograph, 1977.

PCI. Comitato regionale piemontese. *Scaletta per assemblee sul terrorismo.* Turin: mimeograph, n.d. [April 1978].

PCI. Commissione Quartieri. *Nota sulla formazione delle liste dei candidati per le elezioni circoscrizionali.* Turin: mimeograph, 1980.

PCI. Federazione provinciale torinese. *XVII Congresso provinciale: La Commissione Federale di Controllo e il problema della formazione dei quadri, Torino 7–11 marzo 1979.* Turin: mimeograph, 1979.

PCI. Federazione provinciale di Torino. *XVIII Congresso Provinciale.* Turin: unpaginated typescript, 1983.

PCI. Federazione torinese. *PCI partito di governo: Il rapporto tra partito e istituzioni. Nota congressuale della 1ª commissione del CF e della CFC.* Turin: mimeograph, 1977.

PCI. Federazione di Torino. *La lotta alla Fiat: Il giudizio del PCI torinese, Documento approvato dal Comitato Federale, 1 novembre 1980.* Turin: Turingraf, 1980.

PCI. Federazione di Torino. *XIV Congresso provinciale del PCI torinese.* Turin: typed transcript, 1972.

PCI. Federazione di Torino. *XVI Congresso provinciale: Indicazioni per il dibattito congressuale.* Turin: mimeograph, n.d. [1977].

PCI. Federazione di Torino. *XVIII Congresso provinciale della Federazione Torinese del PCI: Relazione della Commissione Federale di Controllo (approvata nella seduta del 18 gennaio 1983).* Turin: mimeograph, 1983.

Relazione del Compagno Renzo Gianotti. "Implicazioni strategiche della nostra politica." *Seminario di quadri comunisti*. Turin: mimeograph, September 24–25, 1976.

Secretariat of the Turinese Federation of the PCI. *Nota organizzativa sulla preparazione delle elezioni dei Consigli di Quartiere a Torino*. Turin: mimeograph, 1977.

Soggia, Bruno. *La formazione dei militanti e dei quadri del Partito Comunista: Considerazioni e problemi. Comunicazione alla Conferenza sull'iniziativa culturale dei comunisti in Piemonte*. Turin: mimeograph, 1977.

# INDEX

267